Media Sport Stars

Media Sport Stars considers how masculinity and male identity are represented through images of sport and sport stars. From the pre-radio era to today's specialist TV channels, newspaper supplements and websites, Garry Whannel traces the growing cultural importance of sport and sportsmen, showing how the very practices of sport are still bound up with the production of masculinities.

Through a series of case studies of British and American sportsmen, Whannel traces the emergence of the sporting 'hero' and 'star', and considers the ways in which the lives of sport stars are narrated through the media. Focusing on figures like Muhammad Ali and David Beckham, whose fame has spread well beyond the world of sport, he shows how growing media coverage has helped produce a sporting star system, and examines how modern celebrity addresses issues of race and nation, performance and identity, morality and violence.

From Babe Ruth to Mike Tyson, *Media Sport Stars* demonstrates that, in an era in which both morality and masculinity are perceived to be 'in crisis', sport holds a central place in contemporary culture, and sport stars become the focal point for discourses of masculinity and morality.

Garry Whannel is Professor of Media Cultures and Director of the Centre for International Media Analysis at the University of Luton. He is the author of *Fields in Vision* (Routledge 1992) and co-editor of *Understanding Television* (Routledge 1990).

San Diego Christian College
2100 Greenfield Drive
El Cajon, CA 92019

796.081
W552m

34.16

Media Sport Stars

Masculinities and moralities

Garry Whannel

London and New York

First published 2002 by Routledge
11 New Fetter Lane, London EC4P 4EE

Simultaneously published in the USA and Canada
by Routledge
29 West 35th Street, New York, NY 10001

Routledge is an imprint of the Taylor & Francis Group

© 2002 Garry Whannel

The right of Garry Whannel to be identified as the Author of this Work has
been asserted by him in accordance with the Copyright, Designs and
Patents Act 1988

Typeset in Galliard by Taylor & Francis Books Ltd
Printed and bound in Great Britain by The University Press, Cambridge,
United Kingdom

All rights reserved. No part of this book may be reprinted or
reproduced or utilised in any form or by any electronic,
mechanical, or other means, now known or hereafter
invented, including photocopying and recording, or in any
information storage or retrieval system, without permission in
writing from the publishers.

British Library Cataloguing in Publication Data
A catalogue record for this book is available from the British Library

Library of Congress Cataloging in Publication Data
A catalog record has been requested for this title

ISBN 0–415–17037–0 (hbk)
ISBN 0–415–17038–9 (pbk)

For Sam and Kate

Contents

Preface

This book has grown out of a lifelong interest in sport, and a considerable period spent analysing media sport, and trying to understand its wider significances. The concern with sport stars developed from my earlier work, in which the central place of stardom in media sport was all too evident. The original research grew out of a bid for Leverhulme funding in the course of which Alan Tomlinson and myself spent considerable time discussing the ways in which it was asserted that sport stars functioned as moral exemplars or as bad examples to the young. We sought a more sophisticated model for understanding the ways in which such stars were represented. In developing research into the representation of sport stars in the early 1990s, the relevance of considering discourses of morality and of masculinity soon became evident. Research began when John Major was still Prime Minister, and as I write these words the 2001 election campaign is underway. During this decade the economic scale of the football industry has been transformed by the growth of satellite television and consequent dramatic escalation in the scale of rights payments. Sport has assumed a greater cultural centrality, with most major newspapers launching dedicated sports supplements, a substantial increase in hours devoted to television sport, and a proliferation of sport related websites. Yet interest in sport is still notably gender specific. It is not simply that interest in sport is far more common among men, and hostility to sport more common among women, but rather that the very practices of sport are still distinctly bound up with the production of masculinities. The relationship between sport, masculinity and the media became the core of the project.

In the context of sport, globalisation presents us with a paradox. On the one hand, sport organisations such as the IOC and FIFA were some of the first globalised institutions, and the Olympic Games and soccer's World Cup have become two of the cultural forms consumed most widely across the planet. On the other hand, there is still a substantial resistance to the media-promoted importation of sport. North America remains largely disinterested in soccer, and almost totally disinterested in cricket, rugby and other British-origin sports. The major sports of North America – American football, baseball, ice hockey and basketball – remain of relatively minor appeal in the rest of the world. Consequently, while there are a few global stars, many sport stars remain within specific cultural contexts. There is also a problem of ephemerality to compound that of localism. Sport stars come and go. When research for this book began Alex Higgins, Ian Botham, and Paul Gascoigne were contemporary figures, whereas in the writing of the book they have, of necessity, been constituted as historical examples.

Publishing is not immune from globalising processes and books are expected to be accessible to audiences around the world. Yet books also explore the specifics of cultural context. While I have endeavoured to explore examples from both Britain and North America, I am aware that my own perceptions of British examples are rendered more elaborate by virtue of my own positioning within the culture – we read the nuances of our own culture with a greater grasp of the historical formation of that culture and its distinctive elements. At the same time, I would hope that the generalisation, the abstraction and the conceptual frame utilised in analysing these situated examples have a pertinence and relevance to other cultural contexts. In short, I have tried to come up with a productive relationship between the particular and the general, the abstract and the concrete.

Acknowledgements

I would like to thank Alan Tomlinson without whom the project would never have started, and while our active collaboration on it ceased at an early stage, I would hope that he can still detect the roots of that work in the end product. Particular thanks are due to Ian Wellard, who, in addition to working as a research assistant for a year, gathering material on sport stars, also collaborated on several conference presentations and acted as a sounding board and discussant for the ideas as they developed. His contribution and ideas were of relevance throughout, but particularly valuable for the chapters on moralities and on identities, where some of our earlier conference presentation work has been incorporated. My thanks also to Carlton Brick, Rachel Cutler, Ellis Badillo, Lee Kattenhorn and Chris Wragg, who all, at various times, worked on research related to this book. My research was sustained by the interest and encouragement of colleagues at Roehampton Institute, particularly Jennifer Hargreaves, but also Eileen Kennedy, Ian McDonald, Steve Wagg, Peter Wesson and Belinda Wheaton. The final phase of writing has been made easier thanks to the supportive interest of my current colleagues in the Department of Media Arts at the University of Luton, especially Luke Hockley, Manuel Alvarado and Geoffrey Nowell-Smith.

I am highly grateful to friends who have discussed the project, or parts of it, with me, and those who nobly agreed to read and comment on draft chapters or, in some cases, the whole manuscript – Manuel Alvarado, David Andrews, Raymond Boyle, Ben Carrington, Christine Geraghty, John Horne, Joe Maguire, Geoffrey Nowell-Smith, Deborah Philips, David Rowe, Alan Tomlinson and Belinda Wheaton. While I didn't accept all their advice, I certainly utilised most of it, and the book benefited greatly from their input. Work on issues related to sport and representation, especially that of David Andrews, Ben Carrington, Joe Maguire and David Rowe, has been a challenging and thought provoking resource. Huge thanks are due to Deborah Philips, not simply for love and support, but also for a sharp intellectual insight and an unerring ability to spot the significances within the ephemera of popular culture that constituted an immense contribution to this project.

Much of the research and background reading for this book has been undertaken in the British Library and made pleasant by the unfailing courtesy and helpfulness of the staff. Occasional tea breaks with Frank Mort and Sean Nixon have provided welcome relief from the slog. The final drafts of this book were written in the British Library, on the Midland Mainline train to Luton, in my office at Luton, and not least, sitting peacefully and undisturbed, in an idyllic country garden amidst the scent of flowers, and the sounds of blackbirds, woodpeckers, cuckoos, sheep and cows, and for this I am very grateful to Ursula Philips.

In the course of researching and writing this book some material has been used in previously published pieces, and I am grateful to the publishers for permission to re-use passages. Oxford University Press for 'The Lads and The Gladiators: traditional masculinities in a post-modern televisual landscape', in *British Television: A Reader* (editor E. Buscombe) (2000); E. & F.N. Spon for 'Sport stars, narrativisation and masculinities', in *Leisure Studies*, vol. 18 no. 3, (1999) the Leisure Studies Association, for 'Sport stars, youth and morality in the print media', in *Leisure Cultures: Values, Genders, Lifestyles* (editors, G. McFee, W. Murphy and G. Whannel) pp. 121–36, (1995); and Routledge for 'Punishment, redemption and celebration in the popular press: the case of David Beckham', in *Sport Stars: The Cultural Politics of Sporting Celebrity*, edited by David Andrews and Steve Jackson (2001).

My children, Sam and Kate, to whom the book is dedicated, grew up during the research and writing of this book, and I am relieved to have finished it while they are still in their teens. Their lively and intelligent responses to the media that surround us have served as a constant reminder to me of the conceptual inadequacy and patronising tone of much 'role-model'-based research on young people and the media. They ask of me only that our fellow television viewer, their pet rat Trotsky, also gets a mention. I owe a thank-you to Mary Warren for excellent sub-editing. Finally, my thanks to Alistair Daniel and Rebecca Barden at Routledge, who never once gave me the impression that they had given up hope of ever seeing a manuscript. They might have got the book earlier, but I stopped to talk to Huckleberry Finn.

1   Introduction

> The increase in the number of children becoming uncontrollable at school is very disconcerting. I think the problem could lie partly in their role models. Many of their heroes, like famous footballers, are loud-mouthed and swaggering. Of course, some people in public life do present a good image, but its a pity that those who don't aren't more aware of the damage they do. Today's heroes should be giving their young fans more to live up to.
>
> (Letter of the week in *Woman's Realm* 6 February 1997)

The image of sport stars, questions of morality, of youth and of masculinity are all bound up together – to consider one is to consider the others. This book offers a study of discourses of masculinities and moralities and the ways in which they are condensed in images of sport stars.[1] It will focus on representation of those male sport stars whose fame spread well beyond the world of sport and its followers – Jack Johnson, Babe Ruth, Stanley Matthews, Muhammad Ali, George Best, Mike Tyson, David Beckham.[2] In particular, it is argued that, as the intensity of media coverage of sport has increased, and as the sporting star system has become central to the media sport industry, the images of sport stars become the point of convergence of social anxieties over morality and masculinity. Analysing representations of sport stars provides a means of examining the processes of social contestation around ideas of morality and concepts of how men should behave. This book is designed to be of interest to those engaged in the study of the media, those interested in sport from a social and historical perspective, and, more broadly, those concerned to understand the political and cultural environment, and how popular culture constitutes a key interface between everyday commonsense and more organised political discourse.

Youth, media, sport

The three terms 'youth', 'media', 'sport' are all associated, in public discussion, with concern, with fears and with discourses of moral decline. The state of youth has, of course, been a cause of perennial anxiety. Traditional authority is always, inevitably, challenged by youth, which represents newness, change, threat and transformation. Socrates, and other Greek philosophers, were apt to pronounce upon the lack of respect young people had for their elders. In Ancient Rome, medieval Europe, Tudor England, eighteenth-century France and in the nineteenth-century English public schools such fears have been present. So, more recent concerns are nothing new, and clearly there is an aspect of the structural relations between young and old that will, persistently, produce such fears.

However, 'youth' is not an eternal trans-historic concept. Indeed the notion that between childhood and adulthood is a distinct significant phase, denoted by such labels as 'teenage' and 'youth', is relatively recent as a social feature. The 'teenager' is very much a construction of the 1950s, that period when, for the first time, a distinct world of cultural consumption associated with youth began to emerge, rock and roll being a central cohesive factor. In recent decades such fears have tended to be crystallised around youth subcultures and the moral panics triggered by them. In the 1950s it was teddy boys and rock and roll; in the 1960s mods and rockers and pills, and then hippies, dope, LSD and free love. In the 1970s it was punks, violence and sexuality, and in the 1980s and 1990s travellers, eco-warriors, raves and ecstasy.

During the 1970s, according to Hall *et al.* (1978), such moral panics increasingly became mapped together within the terms of a generalised discourse about law and order, that in turn provided part of the ideological sub-structure for the emerging discourse that became known as Thatcherism. During the 1980s, the ideological and political successes of Thatcherism fostered a culture of enterprise and consumption, produced a series of political defeats for the left, and gradually defused the 1970s climate of dissent and opposition. Affluent youth became increasingly focused on style, identity and conspicuous consumption (Tomlinson 1990), whilst the poorer strata of youth supposedly became disaffected but apathetic, dubbed by some Generation X – the blank generation, with no ambition, low self-esteem and no self-discipline. It is certainly the case that the alternative and oppositional character of subcultures was much less in evidence in 1980s youth subcultures like the new romantics and the goths, who were far more narcissistic and inward looking. Only with the emergence of the rave scene, the new anarchism and the increasing militancy of the new travellers, towards the end of the 1980s, did this oppositional character begin to resurface. More recently, this oppositional trajectory has taken greater coherence in the activities of eco-warriors and the anti-capitalist movement.

During the 1990s the aspirational character of youth has also been notable. The dress codes of clubbing impose a narcissistic discipline, mobile phones and the internet epitomise a 'plugged-in' and 'wired-up' ethos, and the casualisation of workplaces a heightened emphasis on skills of self-presentation. Two polarisations seem notable. The first is that between the aspirational, socially mobile, employed youth, and the young underclass who lack educational achievement, cultural capital, social skills and life opportunities. The second is that between girls – seen as optimistic and aspirational; and boys – seen as unambitious, pessimistic and under-achieving (see Wilkinson 1994). The fears that adult culture expresses about youth have generally crystallised around boys and their behaviour, but the 1990s have featured a heightened concern about the 'problem with boys'.

The power of the media has always been a source of concern, indeed literacy itself was historically seen as such a threat by dominant groups that for a long time its spread was rigorously controlled. Every new media innovation has served as the focal point of such fears. It always has to be noted then that fears of the power of the media are usually associated with a fear of the loss of power for some other institution, whether it is the ruling class, the state, the church or the family. The power and influence of the media has characteristically been linked to deviance and dissidence, whether political, cultural or sexual. Such fears are usually associated with influence on the young, and these fears usually attach themselves to the latest technology. Thus the spread of printing was seen as a threat to the control of the literate clerisy. Film was seen as dangerous because it reached the less literate lower orders and so needed censorship. Radio entered the home and so required policing. Television has been the focal point of endless debates about the degree of explicit violence and sexuality that should be permitted. Horror comics in the 1950s, pornographic magazines in the 1960s, video in the 1980s, satellite channels and live sex chat lines in the 1990s, have all been the focus of social concerns. Virtual pornography and the distribution of sexually explicit images on the internet are currently causing disquiet. It is noteworthy that one major issue triggered by the growth of the internet is that it enables exchanges between users that are hard for any power to monitor or control. Just as the issue of the power of the media is usually connected to the threat it poses to other possessors of power, it is also the case that the media offers an easy scapegoat that can be blamed for problems whose real causes are more deep-rooted, pervasive and harder to address. The rush to blame the media for violence, copy-cat killings, and moral decay, betrays an unwillingness to face up to the multi-factoral complexity of cause and effect in the social world.

Sport plays a significant role in cultural life. Its major traditional rituals, and broadcasts of them – in England, the Cup Final, the Derby, the Boat Race, the Grand National, Test matches and Wimbledon – are a significant part of the cultural history of the nation, and form part of the fabric of 'Englishness', contributing to a sense of national identity. Similarly, in the USA the Superbowl, World Series Baseball, the Indy 500 and the Kentucky Derby occupy a not dissimilar place in constructions of Americanness. Organised competitive sport has a long history, and has taken diverse forms. It has been part of a culture of self-development, as in Ancient Greece, a form of spectacular entertainment, as in Ancient Rome, part of a pattern of popular festivity, as in Medieval Europe, a form of moral education, as in the nineteenth-century public schools, a symbolic form of ideological contestation, as in the Cold War, and a commodified global spectacle, as in the second half of the twentieth century. As such it has always been subject to contestation and transformation. Historically, sport has been seen as an area of culture rooted in principles of fair play. In the nineteenth century it was seen as a means of teaching moral values (see Mangan 1981). Despite the transformation of sport during the twentieth century (characterised by the growth of professionalism and decline in amateurism) it is still seen as an arena from which cheating should be outlawed; a cultural practice which at its best, still embodies the spirit of fairness (see McIntosh 1979). But now that culture is increasingly media-centred, concepts of sport are rooted more in representation than in any notion of the 'lived' experience of participation.

'Sport', like 'youth' and 'the media', has become the term for a set of troubling conditions. In such public discussion, sport at the elite level is seen as characterised by drug taking, corruption, cheating, and sharp practice. Much of this is attributed to the impact of the commercialisation of sport, corrupting and destroying amateurist Corinthian ideals. Too much money, too intensely nationalistic rivalries, and the collapse of a moral framework, mean that whereas sport has been expected to provide positive role models, it has now also become conceptualised as a fund of bad influences on the young.[3]

The social concerns over youth during the 1980s and 1990s increasingly highlighted fitness, with television and new media such as computer games constituted as a significant element in the threat to fitness.[4] The phrase 'couch potato' served to denote the large number of hours devoted to television watching (ironically it is adults who watch most television). Computer games were believed to be replacing outdoor activities.

Concern over the decline of school sport, and the impact of a diet of junk food, was heightened by the publicising of the research of Neil Armstrong, Professor of Health and Exercise Sciences at the University of Exeter. Briefly, Armstrong showed that children rarely exercised vigorously enough to improve and build adequate cardiovascular fitness.[5] The low level of intense physical activity amongst children was in turn linked to the decline of school sport, both within school, and extra-curricular.[6] The crystallisation of such fears was increasingly linked in public discourse to other concerns – the Americanisation of society, the weakening of marriage and the family, the declining strength of traditional morality. While John Major was Prime Minister, those seeking a regeneration of traditional school sport spoke out with renewed confidence. The then Sports Minister, Iain Sproat, called for the re-establishment of team games as the dominant form of physical education.[7] We are dealing here with a beleaguered cultural condition, with a self-image of a culture at threat, and a discursive structure that links the youth problem, the influence of the media, the moral decline of elite sport, and the need for a return to traditional values.

Crises of morality and masculinity

Crisis may well be an imprecise, subjective and over-used term. It is, however, the contention of this book, that the deployment of the term 'crisis' in discourse is, in itself, significant. It is impossible to determine whether morality and masculinity are 'in crisis', but highly revealing that they should constantly be so described. The theme of a generalised decline in moral standards is neither new nor unfamiliar, but has been more to the fore in the 1990s.[8] During the 1990s, there has been a prominent public discourse about the supposed crisis in morality. For the right, this has been associated with family break-up, the growth in single-parent families, rising crime rates and declining education standards. Moral panics have crystallised around such high profile events as the Jamie Bulger murder, and the Gloucester multiple murders. For the left, the decline of the welfare state and corruption in public life have been central themes.

This sense of 'moral crisis' is associated with two features supposedly characteristic of the contemporary world, relativism and the crisis of authority. From a conservative perspective, relativism has undermined not simply cultural values but the whole notion of cultural value. A once stable system of cultural hierarchisation, in which high culture – Beethoven, Keats, Rembrandt, Shakespeare and Jane Austen – was unproblematically 'better' than popular culture – Elvis Presley, Bob Dylan, Ian Fleming and Jackie Collins; has been disrupted. The rise of modern popular culture, the assault on traditional aesthetic judgements, the development of modes of theorising that question the high culture–popular culture distinction, the supposed process of 'dumbing-down', and the 'postmodern turn' have all combined to dislodge the dominance of a secure set of cultural judgements. The concept of cultural value itself is lost. In such a relativised world, it is no surprise that traditional moral values no longer command respect. From this perspective, then, moral decline is closely linked to the rise of cultural relativism.[9]

The second feature of the contemporary world that has contributed to the sense of moral crisis is the supposed 'collapse of authority'. Moral authority is in the end dependent upon the security of a set of power relations in which the force of pronouncements is consolidated by a set of social institutions and relations that construct positions of authority. The position of the Priest within the Church, the Teacher within the School, and the Father within the Family are all forms in which traditional moral authority is invested in a set of power relations. From a conservative perspective, the decline of religion, the loss of respect for educational authority, and the disintegration of the patriarchal family have all contributed to a weakening of forms of social authority through which moral values are transmitted. From this perspective then, it is logical that in the void created by the absence of such positions of social authority, the concept of role models – symbolic figures that can embody moral principles – should assume a greater importance. In a media-dominated world, the conservative perspective invests its hopes in the emergence of figures who will epitomise moral correctness[10].

Allied to the sense of a crisis of morality is the parallel sense of a crisis in masculinity. Frank Mort has commented that:

> it has become fashionable to talk about a contemporary crisis of masculinity. While such an idea may appear overblown (often erroneously contrasting perceived present-day rapid change among men with past stability) it does pose the sharp end of questions about the shifting nature of gender relations and gendered power.
>
> (Mort 1996: 10)

Mort suggests that this sense of crisis is specific rather than global, and relates particularly to the position and concerns of intellectual men and to the context of the 'Northern European puritan diaspora' (Mort 1994: 126). In recent years, indeed, the concept of a 'crisis' in masculinity has gained extensive public discussion in the affluent West. Whether or not there is a crisis, there is certainly a lot of talk of one. Suzanne Moore in the *Guardian* (29 February 1996) drew attention to the rash of media content relating to male problems, fears and worries, citing as recent television examples *The Men's Ward*, *Bad Time to be a Man*, *Male Survival Guide*, *Women on Men*, Tony Parsons on *Without Walls*, and *Equal But Different*. Dave Hill (1997) speaks of a crisis of male identity in the West. Recent British films *Brassed Off*, *The Full Monty*, and *Billy Elliott* were all rooted in industrial communities hit hard by these changes, in which men were seen as troubled. In all three films the men eventually gain strength and solidarity from their adversity and triumph through a regained self-confidence; but all offer a magical resolution of real conflicts not so readily resolved. Several questions arise. Is masculinity in crisis? Where does this discourse come from? Isn't masculinity always seen as in crisis? Isn't this just a reconstruction of a group in dominance?

The crisis is variously linked to work, education and the family, the media and feminism. For some, the decline of the old manufacturing base, the rise of the service sector, the growth of casualisation, part-time and flexi-time working, have all contributed to both male unemployment and a 'feminisation' of work; whilst, for men in work, greater pressures have exacerbated work–family conflicts. In popular newspaper discussion, boys have been constituted as a problem: they resist schooling, they get involved in crime and there is a breakdown of parental authority, due in part to absent fathers, single mothers and working mothers.

The education of boys is seen as undermined by the growth of an anti-swot culture, new 'lad' culture and dumbing down. Reading is regarded by boys as a feminine activity and studying is 'uncool'. The optimism of girls about the future is contrasted with the pessimism of boys (see, for example, Wilkinson 1994). In the family, it is argued, a breakdown of parental authority, with absent fathers, single mothers or working mothers, has resulted in a failure to instil moral values. Working women neglect the parental function, and absent fathers weaken the disciplinary process.

In the media there is asserted to be a lack of male role models and masculinity is typically defined as a problem, with one of its symptoms being the male inability to display, explore or understand emotions.[11] The effects of two decades of feminism is portrayed as contributing to male uncertainties, producing both responses, such as 'new man', and reactions, such as 'new lad'.[12] The 'new lad', emerging from the late 1980s and given sharper form by the emergence of *Loaded*, and its impact upon the rapidly growing men's magazine market of the 1990s, marked a resurgence of sexism and misogyny, and a new acceptability of sexualised imagery, with the attempted justification of being cloaked in postmodern irony. The concept of a crisis in masculinity is examined in more detail in chapter 2.

Sport, with its ethical structure of fair play, its roots in Corinthian idealism and its separateness from the contestations of the political sphere, appeals to the moral entrepreneurs. Here is a symbolic arena in which heroes can parade, epitomising the finest, most noble values, and providing role models to which boys can aspire. These hopes are doomed to be dashed for three reasons. First, news is negative – and the actions of the good do not make big headlines; second, sport is no more free from the corruptions and temptations of the world than any other sphere; indeed there is some evidence that elite sport performers have less rigid moral principles than the average person; third, there is little convincing evidence that the relation between the young audience and stars in the public eye is as simple as the 'role model' concept implies. Top-level sport has indeed constituted one site on which these 'crises' of morality and masculinity have unfolded. John McEnroe's tantrums and challenges to authority, the widespread use of performance-enhancing drugs epitomised by the Ben Johnson case, the alcohol-fuelled escapades of Paul Gascoigne and others, allegations of bungs and back-handers in football, ball-tampering and match-fixing in cricket, have all been mapped onto the more generalised moral crisis.

In contributing to the growth in popularity of sport, the media have helped produce a sporting star system. (Chapter 3 examines the social construction of sport stardom through a historical account of the development of media coverage of sport.) As a consequence of the development of a sporting-star system, top sport stars, being in the public eye, find themselves under pressure from sport organisations concerned with their public image. Much of this concern is expressed in moral terms. One theme consistently present in such stories is that stars, being in the public eye, are an influence on the young, and that consequently they must be expected to have higher moral standards than people in everyday life. Chapters 7 to 15 offer a series of case study examinations of representations of sport stars.

Sport stars have characteristically been portrayed by the media as role models. Either they are praised as a good example for the young or alternatively they are castigated as being a bad example.[13] Whether they actually do function in this way is in some senses less significant than the fact that they are discussed as if they do, whether as moral exemplars or bad examples. Clearly images of sport stars have, for much of this century, played a role in the construction of masculine identities. However, this process is neither trans-historic nor trans-cultural. The possible significations of sport stars are always determined in part by the social–historic moment and by the particular state of discursive formations. Sport stars are generally assumed to be potentially influential figures. If they are successful and well behaved, they are typically held up as role models and often used in advertising campaigns targeting young people (e.g. campaigns on anti-smoking, anti-drugs and on fitness promotion). Gary Lineker, Tiger Woods, Sebastian Coe and Nick Faldo are examples of the type.[14] If, on the other hand, their behaviour is regarded as inadequate or in some way morally reprehensible, the consequent moral concern frequently focuses on the bad influence this may have on the young. Examples include Mike Tyson, Ben Johnson, John McEnroe, George Best, Ian Botham, Alex Higgins and Vinnie Jones. But to what extent do sport stars provide role models, and what cultural meanings are produced and consumed in the sport star system? By what process are models of correct and incorrect moral behaviour produced and reproduced?[15]

Image and ideology

The central proposition for this study is that in a time when discourses regarding crises of masculinity and of morality have been prominent, forms of popular culture are revealing sites in which to examine the unstable attempts to deal with crisis. Sport stars, in particular, being significantly structured by notions of both masculinity and morality, provide a potentially productive field of study. This book is a study of modes of representation, but it is interested in such representations only in as much as they are also political and ideological, also about power relations. The question then arises of the relation between individual representations, the discourses that they articulate, the ideologies that appropriate these discourses and the relations of power within which particular articulations can form. The modes of analyses developed in this study developed out of Althusser's reformulation of the concept of ideology, Gramsci's concepts of hegemony and common sense, the work of Poulantzas and Laclau, Foucauldian theories of discourse and Bourdieu's concept of cultural capital.

One problem with working with the concept of hegemony is that it tends to encourage an over-politicisation – an assumption that all cultural elements are necessarily part of a political contestation. It is not necessarily useful to declare that 'everything is political', although it may be productive to assert that all cultural elements are potentially political. It then becomes relevant to examine the determinate conditions under which particular cultural elements attain a political effectivity. What is the status of utterances about sport stars? While such utterances may articulate elements of specific discourses, are they in themselves discourses, in the sense of organised, institutionally based and systematised forms of language in which power relations are imbricated?

They are better seen as first level reorganisations of popular common sense, in which the inchoate properties of popular common sense are sifted and organised. In the structured regularities of such organisation one can then detect the elements of sporting discourse. At a more elaborate level, these discursive elements in turn become the raw material for more organised political philosophy – elaborated ideologies.

Poulantzas outlined ways in which ideology performs the work of fragmenting, masking and unifying. It fragments and inhibits the formation of particular coherences (e.g. class or oppositional political identities), masks the inherent and structured inequalities of capitalism and constructs imaginary coherences (e.g. national identities) around which unities can be established (Poulantzas 1973). Laclau argues that ideological elements in themselves have no necessary class belongingness, and it is only in their points of articulation that they acquire a distinct political effectivity (Laclau 1977). Foucault's work suggested both a connection with, and a challenge to, the work of the above writers. It was a link in that it examined the power invested in language and its constructed and contingent nature. It was a challenge in breaking from the Marxist problematic of determination in the last instance by the economic. It is not that Foucault's work is necessarily incompatible with a determinations problematic, not simply that Foucault himself is somewhat agnostic on the issue, but rather that the implications of Foucault's notion of a set of power relations that are dispersed and decentred lead us to examine society in a distinctively different way from both classical and structuralist Marxism (Foucault 1972, 1977). In particular, issues of the decentred self, fractured identities and the constructed self, crossed and figured by a multiplicity of discourses, suddenly become much more pertinent. The primacy of a class subject disappears and class race and gender, while remaining significant forms of subjectivity, also become problematic in that the model for the production of distinctive and unified classed, race-ed and gendered subjectivities is considerably more complex. Indeed the rise of identity politics, in the context both of theoretical work on decentred and multiple subjectivities, and the growing power of a consumption-centred society in which the symbolic power of goods has superseded their use value has posed a crisis for modes of analysis that seek to retain elements of a Marxist concern with the emergence of coherent oppositional forms that have grown out of primary contradictions in economic relations.

Nevertheless, the problems posed by late capitalism will not readily depart and cannot be wished away by the premature rejection of grand narrative, by theorising about symbolic goods that have magically lost their material conditions of production, or by positing the end of history, the end of ideology, a post-industrial society or an information society in which, supposedly, material objects are no longer produced by exploited labour. The commercialisation and globalisation of sport has taken place in the context of wider processes of commodification and consumption (see Bowlby 1985; Shields 1992; Tomlinson 1990). In particular, deregulation of television has enabled the transformation of television from a service to a commodity, with sport as one of the points of appeal driving the process. The circuit of production–consumption–production sketched out by Marx (1973) in the *Grundrisse* in which productive consumption and consumptive production fuel each other has become significantly tighter. The spread of domestic computers, the rapid growth of the internet, and the ability to make consumer decisions and implement them online, shorten the response time between being hailed by commodities and services and choosing to consume them. In such an environment the symbolic appeal of commodities becomes central, and at least in sport stars such as Michael Jordan or Tiger Woods become a key element in marketing strategies. Economic and cultural levels are really not that remote from each other here.

The social construction of sport as a masculine domain and the exclusion of women from it have produced a set of institutions, practices, rituals and discourses that acquire increasing importance precisely as the challenge to patriarchal practices that a feminist politics has been able to mount since 1970 has weakened, to a degree, hegemonic masculine control over some social spheres. Sport, by contrast, has remained a much more entrenched bastion of patriarchy, and hence the ways in which masculinities are produced by its practices are of specific significance. Sport is without question a significant element in the construction of gendered identities. Despite its highly visible presence as an element of popular culture, it is also the element that is most clearly gendered. Men are expected to be interested in sport, women are not.[16] While of course there are exceptions to this rule, women who are keen on sport are seen as somewhat aberrant, just as men who dislike sport are. Sport confers and confirms masculinity; an interest in sport problematises femininity. The social institutions, cultural practices and modes of representation associated with sport are still largely male-dominated. This study focuses on masculinities and images of male stars, in part because masculinities have been insufficiently examined, especially in relation to popular culture. More centrally, it does so as a way of examining a cultural field that is, in part, precisely about notions of maleness. In our pilot study (see note 2) only three of twenty-five sport stars who featured regularly were women. It was no particular surprise that the gender bias should be so skewed (see, for example, Dunne 1982; Gill Lines 1993, 1998; Hargreaves 1994; Bolla 1990), but it did suggest strongly that the study should focus specifically on stars and masculinity. Of course masculinity cannot be understood except in relation to femininity, in relation to that which it is not, and must be examined in relation to the structuring absence of the female. Similarly, the hegemonic heterosexuality of sport cannot be understood apart from the relation of heterosexual to homosexual and associated presence of homophobia. In addition, the relation of the complexities of individual human subjectivities to the rigidities of specific gendered and sexed positionalities must be retained as part of the analytic framework here.

During the 1998 World Cup, there was a British Telecom advertisement that started with an announcement that the World Cup was cancelled. This is followed by a rapid montage of women celebrating, two of whom exultantly say 'YES!'. It ends with a man, watching a football match on television, and saying, with reference to the match he is watching, 'NO!'. This is followed by the caption 'dream on' (BT advertisement, ITV, 1998). Three assumptions are clearly present here – men love sport, women hate it, and men are in control.[17] The persistence of patriarchy in sport means that sexism and homophobia have been central elements in the role of sport in the construction of gendered identities. Knowledge of the esoteric details of sporting cultures functions as a form of alternative cultural capital. Boys acquire a detailed knowledge of facts and information about football (as embodied in the world of *Match* and *Shoot*). Possession of this cultural capital confers status, marks distinctions, and can be stored away, used to advantage, and used as a means to exclude unwanted outsiders (i.e. girls and 'wimpish' boys who don't like sport).

Our initial examination of youth magazines was revealing in highlighting both the very different reading patterns of boys and girls, and also the very different world embodied in that reading. Boys inhabit closed, contained worlds which emphasise performance, consumption and confidence. Girls inhabit far more open worlds, characterised both by possibilities and by problems. Girls' magazines, unlike those read by boys, deal with relations, emotions, problems and advice. It is not simply an issue of difference, however, but of relations and of power. Michele Hanson bemoaned 'This is a dismal time for us. The World Cup is drawing near and already ruining dinner parties. We had one on Saturday and of the four chaps present, three droned relentlessly on about football' (*Guardian*, 4 May 1998). The cultural capital of sporting knowledge serves both as the cement of male bonding, and as a weapon, colonising, holding and controlling social space. It is also founded on an oppressive heterosexist assumption that all men are interested in sport, which many men, both straight and gay, must experience as alienating.

One major impetus of cultural studies, ever since the work of Barthes, has been to notice the unnoticed, and to interrogate the taken-for-granted. The concept of making strange, of defamiliarisation, is an important first step in this process. Analyses of masculinity have, in a sense, made this jump, in starting to render odd the very idea of masculinity in order better to examine it (see Connell 1995; Messner and Sabo 1991; Kirkham and Thumin 1993; Simpson 1994). Sport, as a social practice concerned centrally with the body, has been characterised by its striking repression of sexuality. Yet it has also become one of the central forms of body representation and body practice. Its simultaneous foregrounding of physicality, sexualisation of the body and repression of desire is one of its most distinctive features.

Edward Said said, in *Orientalism* (1978), that 'human societies, at least the more advanced cultures, have rarely offered the individual anything but imperialism, racism and ethno-centricism for dealing with "other" cultures'. It is necessary to do more than understand and analyse the world from one's own perspective. It is necessary also to strive to understand how that world looks from a different position, to attempt to take on board and to apply, the questions about the world that stem from that position, and, in doing so, to confront the racism and the sexism that is etched into one's way of seeing. To do so is to locate and dismantle the tools of power that have been placed, unwittingly, in your hands. The sports hero as constructed in representation is male, implicitly heterosexual and, until the 1920s, largely white. The very processes of construction of sporting heroism have involved exclusion, hierarchisation, marginalisation and symbolic annihilation.[18] The modes of address employed in sporting discourse most characteristically address a male heterosexual and implicitly white audience. Yet there is also always an attempted inclusiveness – an attempt to construct an imaginary coherence of sports fandom and national identity that embraces female as well as male, black as well as white (but not gay as well as straight). Indeed the commercial imperatives of sales and ratings require constant attempts to pull in the marginalised. At the time of the Olympic Games and the World Cup considerable effort is made to win and hold marginal viewers.

Black sport stars are celebrated, but their prominence in such circumstances raises a number of questions. First, does the prominence of positive images of black figures in areas such as sport and show business constitute a form of reproduction of limited expectations, suggesting that blacks succeed here and only here? Second, is there a narrower or more restrictive set of types that will attain celebrityhood among black stars than white ones? Third, are greater constraints placed upon the range of acceptable behaviour of black stars? Significant here is the way in which the dominant element in cultural representations is in certain ways invisible. The class of working-class and aristocratic figures immediately signifies itself; the dominant middle class on the media are more invisible as classed subjects. Women are visible as women, men invisible as men; blacks are visible, whites invisible. So the construction of stardom can never be a neutral or innocent process; it takes place on prestructured ground.

This book is divided into three parts. The first, The tales they tell of men..., explores general issues related to approaching masculinity, the media and sport stars. Chapter 2 explores the ways in which ideas of 'masculinity in crisis' have been articulated. The next three chapters trace the development of media sport, concepts of 'hero' and 'star', and the ways in which the lives of sport stars are narrativised. Chapter 6 returns to the issue of masculinities, surveying the relation between masculinity and sport.

Part II, From sporting print to satellite, examines ways in which sport stars have been represented, through a series of case studies. Commencing with the emergence of a modern media-based star system at the start of the century, the first two chapters discuss examples from before the rise of television. Chapter 9 focuses on two stars, George Best and Muhammad Ali, whose fame was linked to the 1960s and to the triumphant emergence of television. Chapter 10 probes the relation between hedonism and morality in the context of fitness chic and the new competitive individualism of the 1980s.

Part III, The restless vortex of celebrity, assesses the emergence of celebrity at the core of popular culture. The intensity of focus on star individuals has meant that their images have become the point of identification for a multiplicity of discourses about morality and violence, gender and ethnic difference, identity and consumption. Chapter 11 analyses the cyclical process of celebration, transgression, punishment and redemption that structures representation of sport's bad boys. Chapter 12 investigates the ways in which male sport stars have become central figures in consideration of morality, masculinity and male violence. Chapter 13 explores the contradictory and ultimately judgemental modes of representation drawn upon in the portrayal of black sportsmen. Chapter 14 assesses the extent to which identities have to be understood, in postmodern society, in terms of a lack of fixity. Finally, in chapter 15, I examine the phenomenon of celebrity through a case study of English footballer David Beckham. It is suggested that certain peaks of media celebrity are characterised by a temporary intensity of media focus that I have termed vortextuality.

Part I

The tales they tell of men ...

The cultures of sport are characterised by a valorisation of memories (magic moments, great goals, thrilling victories), oral and media-based exchanges by which these memories are recycled, and the consequent generation of an exclusive form of cultural capital, which is part of the currency of hegemonic masculinity. This part of the book establishes the ground for subsequent analyses by introducing and exploring five themes: the supposed 'crisis' of masculinity; the development of media sport; stardom and the heroic; narrativity; and the cultures of sport. Regardless of what is meant in different contexts by a 'crisis' of masculinity, and without passing judgement on whether there is such a crisis, the existence of publicly expressed concerns about men and boys is undeniable. This discourse of crisis provides a framing issue for the subject of this book, and is examined in chapter 2. Concepts of crises in masculinity and morality are articulated in and through images of sport stars, but this would not have been possible without the development of media sport to its present state, a process traced in chapter 3. In chapter 4 I turn my attention to the nature of stardom and to its relation to the heroic; while chapter 5 examines the ways in which the lives of sport stars are narrated. Chapter 6 returns to the issue of masculinities, this time in the specific context of sporting cultures.

2 Discourses of crisis in masculinity

> The identity crises in men and women cannot be solved by one generation for the next: in our rapidly changing society, it must be faced continually, solved only to be faced again in the span of a single lifetime. A life plan must be open to change, as new possibilities open in society and in oneself.
>
> (Friedan 1963: 330)

> Our relationship with the washing machine is similar to our relationship with the clitoris: we may still have trouble understanding how it works, but at least we have discovered where it is.
>
> (Dave Hill, *Guardian*, 29 December 1997)

Betty Friedan's words, written almost forty years ago, remind us that gender relations are always the site of struggle and contestation, whilst Dave Hill's more recent words highlight both change and continuities in the pattern of gender relations. Forms of patriarchal domination have a long history, but gender relations in any particular era are the product of conjunctural factors as well as organic structures. The recent discursive prominence of concepts of 'masculinity in crisis' requires examination. Masculinity cannot be understood separately from its positioning in relation to femininity. In the post-war era a process of denaturalising patriarchal ideology gathered momentum, and masculinity began to lose its unnoticed, taken-for-granted character. One dynamic in the post-war growth of feminism was women's perceived need to escape from definition by masculinity and patriarchy. Simone de Beauvoir (1953) wrote of women as the 'second sex'. Betty Friedan said that it was 'easier to live through someone else than to become complete yourself' (Friedan 1963: 294). Germaine Greer (1970) wrote of femininity in terms of a repressed sexuality; a 'female eunuch'. Sheila Rowbotham (1973a) outlined the location of 'women's consciousness' within 'man's world'. The work of Juliet Mitchell (1971), Ann Oakley (1972) and Sheila Rowbotham (1973b) constituted a launch pad for the rapid growth of feminist scholarship in the 1970s. Although 'getting men to change' was a significant feminist goal, many of these texts were addressed primarily to and through the experience of women, and the need for women to act in order to change their own lives.[1]

The impact and influence of feminism, with its emphasis on the socially constructed nature of gender difference, and its insistence that the personal is political, constituted a challenge both to the naturalisation of gender roles in mainstream male scholarship, and to its characteristic compartmentalisation, that served to marginalise both 'women' and the 'domestic' sphere. Responses to this challenge (Tolson 1977; Hoch 1979; Humphries and Metcalf 1983; Seidler 1989, 1991) which attempted to deconstruct masculinity, paralleled the emergence of men's groups and organisations and publications (such as *Achilles Heel*), that combined, sometimes awkwardly, an anti-sexist intention with a desire to explore maleness from a man's perspective. The privileged power of heterosexual masculinity, and the reluctance of heterosexual men to be self-reflexive, meant that gay men often played a significant role in these early developments of modes of analysing masculinity.

Although, clearly, one of the consequences of the rise of feminism from 1970 was the recognition that getting men to change was an important political priority and so there were implicit and explicit demands on men, this is not written as large in some of the classic texts of feminism as one might expect. These texts are characteristically addressed primarily to, and speak through, the experience of women and to women's needs to act to change their lives. There was, for example, relatively little feminist consideration of men as fathers until the 1983 collection *Fathers*, edited by Ursula Owen (Rowbotham 1989: 16). So, although sexual politics had become more prominent in both the public and the academic sphere, men and masculinity did not undergo extensive theoretical analysis, at least not from a cultural studies perspective, until the late 1980s. In 1984, Rosalind Coward drew attention to the continuing invisibility of men's sexuality:

> Under this sheer weight of attention to women's bodies we seem to have become blind to something. Nobody seems to have noticed that men's bodies have quietly absented themselves. Somewhere along the line, men have managed to keep out of the glare, escaping from the relentless activity of sexual definitions. In spite of the ideology which would have us believe that women's sexuality is an enigma, it is in reality men's bodies, men's sexuality which is the true dark continent of this society.
>
> (Coward 1984: 228)

This avoidance of analysis, Coward argued, was far more than a mere reluctance to be objectified in analysis, but rather was a means of retaining power:

> Men are physical strangers to women and to themselves because in this male-dominated society it is men who have the power to define. Men have absented themselves from the massive work currently being undertaken on sexual definitions. Men's bodies and sexuality are taken for granted, exempted from scrutiny, whereas women's bodies are extensively defined and over-exposed. Sexual and social meanings are imposed on women's

bodies, not men's. Controlling the look, men have left themselves out of the picture because a body defined is a body controlled.

(Coward 1984: 229)

It is interesting to read these words from the perspective of the twenty-first century because it draws attention to some of the shifts that have taken place. Men's bodies are now far more commonly objectified in representation, and there is a greater sexualisation of these bodies, most markedly in movies and in advertising. There is also now a growing amount of work by men that critically interrogates masculinities.

The early political impact of feminism was to lose some of its impetus in the 1980s. The problems of sustaining a unified and coherent perspective that could take on board issues of class, race and sexuality, and challenges by black women, working-class women and lesbians led to a degree of fragmentation, a recognition that there were different versions of feminism that could not readily be fused, and a wry acknowledgement that it is not just men who have problems with co-operative work. Theoretical differences became important, too, as the different trajectories evident in, for example, the writing of Liz Stanley, Sheila Jeffries, Elizabeth Cowie, Sheila Rowbotham and Lynne Segal makes clear. There was not (indeed there never was) a single homogeneous feminist position. The concept of patriarchy, so central to the debates of the 1970s, proved problematic.[2] Rosalind Coward outlined the dangers of essentialism inherent in the problems of understanding the position of women as a sex without presuming that being a sex entails forms of 'natural' behaviour and position (Coward 1983: 3). A more major problem, of course, was the difficulty of attaining social change, given the reluctance of male-defined and controlled institutions to cede power, to change their ways of operating, or to make any significant concessions to feminist demands. Sheila Rowbotham commented that feminists had become increasingly aware of the traps inherent in redefining politics in terms of personal relations without following through the implications by challenging the existing political framework (Rowbotham 1989: 296).

Masculinities

By the 1980s the field of 'masculinity' was being recomposed. There were responses to the challenges of feminism (reduced to the stereotype 'new man'), reactions to it (later crystallised in 'new lad'), the emergence of critiques of traditional masculinity with its heterosexism and homophobia, and the development of a men's movement. All these elements contributed to the more extensive and visible problematising of 'masculinity'. A more self confident gay sub-culture with a more visible public identity, and the development of queer theory, also contributed to these processes. Some analyses of masculinity, by men, implied or advocated the development of a new academic area – 'men's studies' (Kimmel 1987; Brod 1987; Kaufman 1987). Men's studies was attacked by some feminists for me-too-ism, self-indulgence and lack of engagement with feminism or gay politics. It was suggested that men's studies focused on 'men' as opposed to patriarchy, neglected issues of male–female relations, marginalised feminism, or rendered it invisible, lacked a grounding in feminist research, and did not acknowledge its feminist roots (see Griffin in Hearn and Morgan 1990). Chapman and Rutherford (1988: 11) acknowledged that 'masculinity remains the great unsaid ... the cause but still not the site of struggle'. Rutherford wrote of men's silences, the ways in which

> feminism has pushed men into a defensive huddle ... men have used their silence as the best form of retaining the status quo, in the hope that the ideological formations that once sustained the myth of masculine infallibility will resurrect themselves from the fragments and produce a new mythology to hide us in.
>
> (Chapman and Rutherford 1988: 25)

Just as the castle of the 'self' is defended against incursion from criticism (see Jones 1993), so the fortress of masculinity has been defended, until recently, against the fierce gaze of analysis and deconstruction. It is a central argument of this book that the misbehaviour of sport stars has become part of a broader discussion about a supposed 'crisis' in masculinity. In various book titles, masculinity has been discovered, rediscovered, theorised, constructed, deconstructed, dislocated, unwrapped, unmasked, understood, embodied, fashioned, moulded, changed and put in perspective.[3] A sense of crisis is certainly in the air, even if nowhere else. As Lynne Segal has commented:

> Throughout the 1980s, the shifting nature of men's lives, their behaviour, experiences, anxieties, fears and cravings, have been debated with new passion and concern. Books researching fatherhood, men's violence against women, male identities and male mythologies now interrogate men as a sex in a way until recently reserved for women – as a problem.
>
> (Segal 1990: ix–x)

The most interesting issue, in terms of modes of public exchange, is not whether there is, objectively, a crisis of masculinity, but rather what are the circumstances and contexts within which concepts of 'crisis' are uttered. Public discussion, especially, but not exclusively, in broadsheet newspapers, placed the phrase in the public domain. There is, it is suggested a problem with males in which work, education and the family, the media and feminism are all implicated. So how are these elements articulated?

Changes in work

Clearly, there have been profound long-term shifts in the nature of work – for example, the post-war decline in manufacturing and the rise of the service industries, and the increase in the public service sector, the more recent growth of short-term contracts, part-time work, flexi-time, and sub-contraction, and the undermining of union power. Although women now make up around half of the workforce, and according to some there has been a 'feminisation' of the workplace, women's salaries are still only 80 per cent of the male wage, and the small proportion of women in top jobs has been taken as evidence of a glass ceiling in which discrimination against women remains entrenched. Despite this, these changes have expanded opportunity for girls, whilst working-class boys are the group whose historically shaped cultural expectations (job for life in local industry) have been dramatically undermined since the 1960s.[4]

Education

The under-achievement of boys has become a major issue for educational policy and for the broadsheet press. According to OFSTED, boys do worse than girls at GCSE, are more likely to be expelled, whilst failing schools suffer from a higher-than-average concentration of boys as well as weak leadership (*Guardian*, 6 March 1997)[5]. Nearly 60 per cent of girls achieved a pass grade in GCSE English in 1997, compared with only 40 per cent of boys. Chris Woodhead, former Chief Inspector of Schools, said 'the failure of boys and in particular white working-class boys is one of the most disturbing problems we face within the whole education system'. A high proportion of crime is carried out by children in school hours and the majority of truants are boys (*Observer*, 4 January 1998). Greg Brookes, National Foundation for Educational Research, said 'boys tended to catch up in secondary schools but increasingly over the last 10 to 15 years the girls have been staying ahead and the boys have not been catching up at the later stages' (*Guardian*, 6 January 1998). At present only 47 per cent of boys reach the expected standard in English at 14 compared with 66 per cent of girls (*Observer*, 11 January 1998).

The Government regarded the problem as having reached crisis proportions and called on local education authorities to remedy the growing gender gap. Only one of more than 130 education authorities in England had more boys than girls getting five good GCSE grades. In the worst areas 15 per cent more girls than boys reach that standard; 28,500 boys, compared to 21,500 girls leave school each year with no qualification. School Standards Minister Stephen Byers said there was a need to 'challenge the laddish anti-learning culture' (*Guardian*, 5 January 1998). The problem is by no means specific to Britain, and the Government planned to make the issue of disaffected boys a central issue during its European presidency (*Observer*, 4 January 1998). Changes in the nature of work are seen as a factor, but so is the growth of an anti-swot culture. A junior school headmaster in Nottingham was quoted as saying 'a lot of it is down to peer pressure being put on boys not to be seen as swots. It has a tremendous impact. A worrying subculture has emerged that is almost anti-education' (*Guardian*, 6 January 1998). Linda Grant referred to 'the toxic effects of lad culture, which teaches boys to despise activities such as reading, sitting still and paying attention, as unmasculine'. She quoted a boy who regarded high-achieving boys as geeks, and says that he instantly identified with the low-achieving boys in his class because they were the ones with the coolest clothes and music; they were the ones smoking cigarettes and rolling joints on the school playing fields at break. She blames the lack of competitive incentives in the comprehensive school (Linda Grant *Guardian*, 6 January 1998).

Reading is regarded as a feminine activity, studying is 'uncool'. Schools have been urged to concentrate on choosing reading material (adventure stories, sport, non-fiction) which is more likely to interest boys; a notion that embeds assumptions about masculinity. The increasing emphasis on course work is believed to favour girls (*Observer*, 4 January 1998). Alan Smithers, director of the Centre for Education and Employment Research, said 'girls are more conscientious and better able to prepare for course work. Boys have been found to be better at exams and multiple choice questions' (*Guardian*, 6 January 1998). There are dangers in exaggerating these problems because, as the *Observer* (4 January 1998) pointed out, the gender gap is nowhere near as severe as the class gap.

For some the problem is in part due to lack of role models. The head of St George's Community School, Ray Priest, found that most children in their year 7 intake were two or more years below their chronological reading age. They found girls progressed much faster than boys. 'It is still often seen as un-macho for boys to be keen on schoolwork' said Priest. 'Partly this is because many boys have so few male academic role models' (*Guardian*, 13 January 1998). The solution they pursued drew upon the links between masculinity and sport. They brought in local sportsmen like Bristol City striker Sean Goater to stress the importance of learning. They 'made sure the school library has enough football books and suchlike to appeal to boys' (*Guardian*, 13 January 1998). For some, such as Angela Phillips, author of *The Trouble with Boys*, there is no longer a good case for single-sex schools:

> when I was at school, it was a well known fact that boys did not fancy clever girls. So it was necessary to act stupid whenever boys were around and wise parents sent their girls to girls-only schools. Today girls can have sex and brains too, so they have stopped pretending to be dumb. Now it is boys who are under-achieving.
>
> (*Guardian*, 6 January 1998)

She argues that poor self-esteem is behind the drop in male attainment and asserts that parents do not like boys-only schools. She argues that girls no longer need the protection of single-sex schools and says that feminism has been a massive exercise in raising the self-esteem of a generation. She concludes that:

> There is no argument for privileging girls at the expense of boys. We have served our daughters well and they are a credit to us; now it is time to turn our sights on their brothers. It is really not good enough to put a wall

around the girls and then leave the boys outside to fight amongst themselves.

(Phillips, *Guardian*, 6 January 1998)

Betty Friedan (1963) wrote of women in the 1950s that 'they felt that their
lives were empty. They did not know who they were or what they wanted to
become.' The phrase is strangely similar to recent representations of the feelings
of boys in school.

Parental authority

The perceived crisis of masculinity is also an element in the debate over the
nature of the family and the supposed decline in parental responsibility. For the
moral and authoritarian right, parents no longer exercise sufficient authority, fail
to instil moral values in their children, working women neglect the parental
function and absent fathers weaken the disciplinary process. In more progres-
sivist discourses, the pressures of work, the failure of men to be adequate fathers
and the culture of laddism all contribute to the problem. A *Daily Express* (13
May 1998) series on 'The Secret World of Boys' quoted survey findings that
when looking for emotional support 25 per cent of girls but only 7 per cent of
boys looked to their fathers. Mother and friends topped both lists. Fifty-seven
per cent of boys were sometimes depressed and 24 per cent had contemplated
suicide. The article asserted that 'Teenage boys are caught up in a world where
traditional role models of manliness are upset or changing. Ideas about
masculinity have narrowed down to lads or wimps.' In fact, it is questionable
whether this represents a significant change in that boys' masculinity may have
been defined by this opposition in which schoolboys are either 'lads' or 'ear-
holes', for a long time (see Willis 1978). Indeed there would seem arguably to
be a slightly larger set of options now.

Many fathers, the survey reveals, avoid chats about anything meaningful –
rarely talking about their sons' fears and worries, and nor do they take time to
share their life experiences. Boys learn quickly that 'real men' don't talk about
relationships. Boys are increasingly likely to be in an environment without a
strong male role model – reared by lone mothers and frequently taught by
female teachers. Although three-quarters of the sample did in fact have a father
(or father figure) at home, 'he often fails to be a source of advice and comfort'.
In scores of interviews, not one boy mentioned his father when asked to identify a role model. The boys feel they have to 'protect their already exhausted
parents from more stress' (*Express*, 13 May 1998). More than 10 per cent of
boys say their fathers spend no time with them. Fifteen per cent say he shows
no interest in their school work. More than a third say that they can't talk to
their fathers about their worries and more than half say they never talk to their
fathers about relationships. More than half say that he never hugs them.
Commenting on the findings, Neil Lyndon argued that:

We need to stop making boys feel stupid at school. We need to start making boys feel good about themselves in the way that we have been making girls feel good for the last thirty years. We need a generation of teachers who will see it as their social responsibility to raise the status and respect of boys, as we have had a generation of teachers who took this attitude towards girls ... instead of growing up in a culture that denigrates masculinity, boys need to be encouraged to be proud of being male and they need to learn to like and trust other boys, as women and girls have learned to like and trust each other in the last thirty years.

(*Express*, 14 May 1998)

Susie Orbach suggests that we lack an effective process of redefining masculinity (*Guardian*, 1 March 1997). Dave Hill suggests that maybe men can 'mother' as effectively as women; he suggests that the best fathers are often those who discover they can do the things mothers usually do, and asserts that when families fall apart the best interests of the mother and those of her children are not automatically the same (*Guardian*, 29 April 1998). Leaving aside the contradictory mixture of insight, generalisation, prejudice and banality of public discussion concerning parenting and the relation between boys and fathers, what is striking is the general prevalence of the view that male parenting constitutes part of the 'problem with boys'.

Gender relations

A number of different factors associated with gender relations are articulated in public discourse. The rise of feminism, followed by its fragmentation, the emergence of a post-feminist sensibility, and the new populist geneticist discourse of gender differences as biological combine to produce a particularly contradictory field. Men's magazines agonise about the problems of men's responses to women, and sometimes indicate a striking confusion about 'women' and how to relate to them. Listed among 'Man's top 10 Stresses' in *Maxim* (July 95) was:

3. Do they really hate me?

The gender world has been turned upside down and while nowadays you can eat quiche and still retain your manhood, you're definitely in deeper water with women. Do you hold open the door or leave it to swing in her face? Would a compliment on her new suit be greeted with a smile or a kick in the goolies? The new PC world is like a sexual minefield. One step wrong and you'll end up in court accused of sexual harassment. Two steps wrong and you and your penis could part company on a permanent basis. 'I think it's terrible for men at the moment', says Markham [Ursula Markham, author of Managing Stress] 'men who were brought up simply to be polite are called sexist pigs. It's the not knowing how to play it that's so hard. If there were set rules it would be much easier'.

(*Maxim*, July 1995: 39)

Gender relations are unsettled by male confusions and by diverse and conflicting characterisations from both men and women. Carol Sarler wrote (*Observer*, 11 January 1998) that the qualities of a man who will win success are the same qualities that will win him a woman: 'ruthlessness, single-mindedness, selfishness, ambition, and a happy willingness to brawl in the gutter if necessary' and described new man in impatient and dismissive terms:

A question for the ladies: do you remember when New Man appeared in a puff of baby powder, eager and ready to share nappy duty and his inner emotions? Do you remember how pleased we were to see him – until we discovered how damn tiring he was? Do you remember those tender but long hours as he re-learnt to shed the tears he had not felt on his cheeks since childhood? And do you remember that first flicker of irritation when you realised that every time a man cries it's a woman who gets to hold the Kleenex?

(*Observer*, 11 January 1998)

Hester Lacey (*Independent on Sunday*, 11 January 1998) cited the range of books on parenting as evidence for a crisis of confidence among parents and asserted that the old Cosmo notion of 'having it all' was taking a battering among women writers.[6] The culture of narcissism, the growing focus on the body and body image, and the more prominent sexualisation of male bodies, especially in advertising, may also contribute to male doubt, insecurity and anxiety. A *Daily Express* article (15 May 1998) commented, 'Page after page of lithe muscular models can be a real downer if you've got a beer belly and bandy legs'. Concurrently with this sexualisation of male bodies, their possible redundancy is evoked through discussion of surrogacy, lesbian couples with children, cloning and implantation.[7]

The most worrying and reactionary development has been the way in which relatively sophisticated findings in genetic research are being appropriated in popular discourse as evidence for the naturalness and inevitability of stereotypical assumptions of gender difference. In this move, science, pseudo-science, superstition and convention are blended in a new insidious common sense, as in the Channel 4 series *Why Men Don't Iron*.[8] Explaining human behaviour and gender difference by reference to biology and genetics has returned with a vengeance. The *Evening Standard* (16 June 1998) announced that after a key football match, the English supporters' testosterone levels rose by 10 per cent.[9] Under the influence of the new geneticism, gender differences are translated back from the cultural to the natural, with men and women at the mercy of their genes and their biology.

So, in the confused and contested ground of masculinity and morality, there is a constant process of condensation and displacement in which the micro and the macro get mapped onto each other, culture is collapsed back into nature, science gets re-presented in the terms of popular common sense, and sport stars are both scapegoat and potential salvation. In writing on masculinity in crisis, both journalistic and academic, three inflections of this theme can be detected:

1   There *is* a specific crisis of masculinity, with specifiable social determinants, unfolding, according to various accounts, from the 1970s onwards/1980s onwards/1990s onwards.
2   Masculinity has *always* been in crisis, or has since a specific point, which could be the industrial revolution, World War I, World War II, or the 1960s, and it is just the forms through which the crisis is manifest that change.
3   Masculinity is *not* in crisis, and is actually quite secure, but colludes in representations of itself as in crisis, precisely as an ideological mask for the continued reproduction of patriarchal relations.

There is some rationality in all three propositions. I would suggest that there is a specific crisis, but masculinity has never been especially stable or fixed, so it is possible to exaggerate the degree to which current circumstances constitute a crisis. There is not really a crisis in male power, but rather a crisis in the cultural modes through which masculinity presents itself – a peculiarly Goffmanesque crisis in a way, in that it concerns modes of self-presentation. This constant reshaping of masculinity can indeed be seen as a set of practices which constitute a mask behind which the dominance of patriarchy seeks to reproduce itself. However, the imaginative representational forms through which culture, in contradictory ways, constantly remakes itself, also help to reveal where the points of tension and struggle lie. In public discourse, then, there has been a generalised, ill-defined and internally contradictory expression that 'maleness' is unsettled, but masculinity has always been subject to unease and internal tensions. Its boundaries have always been policed and its parameters reinscribed (take, as an example, guides to gentlemanly etiquette throughout the eighteenth and nineteenth centuries). Current masculinity is relatively secure in its dominance, but such hegemony always has to be fought for and is constantly subject to renegotiation. Roper and Tosh argued that

> Masculinity is always bound up with negotiations about power and is therefore often experienced as tenuous. It is clear that there are periods when changed social conditions frustrate on a large scale the individual achievement of masculinity, and at such times the social and political fall out may be considerable.
>
> (Roper and Tosh 1991: 18–19)

There is no single essential trans-historical masculinity. Investigation of such 'moments' as the Roman circus (Wiedemann 1992; Crowther 1996), the chivalric conventions of the sixteenth century (Brailsford 1969), gentlemanly behaviour in the eighteenth century (Cohen 1996), nineteenth-century muscular Christianity (Mangan 1981), or the Empire adventurers of the late nineteenth century (Dawson 1994) illustrate that masculinity is shaped in ways that have a social and historical specificity. It is necessary to consider discontinuities as well as continuities (see the introduction to Roper and Tosh 1991). We need to be cautious of over-simplified accounts of a single unified and homogeneous masculinity. Given the prevalence of naturalised and essentialist portrayals of gender in the popular media, there is a pressing need to understand masculinities in the round – as dominant but also contradictory; contradictory, but also dominant. Clearly, masculinity must be understood in relation to femininity; we need to think in terms not just of masculinity but of masculinit*ies*; recognise that masculinities change over time, and consequently there are, always, dominant residual and emergent masculinities.

Bob Connell (1995: 71) has argued that masculinity cannot be understood outside of its relation to femininity, and is simultaneously 'a place in gender relations, the practices through which men and women engage that place in gender, and the effects of these practices in bodily experience, personality and culture'. Masculinity is a relational construct, incomprehensible apart from the totality of gender relations (Roper and Tosh 1991: 2). Recent figures such as 'new man', 'new lad' and 'soft lad' cannot be fully understood apart from their location in a pattern of gender and sexual relations.

The impact of the Thatcher era spawned a less optimistic analysis of the possibility of socialist–feminist transformation (Rowbotham 1989; and see also Butler and Scott 1992). Indeed a reaction against feminism could be charted (Faludi 1991) and a new revisionist post-feminist feminism was being elaborated (Walter 1998). Rosalind Coward argued that 'men's outlook, priorities and contribution to the home have remained largely unchanged. The main difference is that men are now thought to be doing more than in previous generations. But the reality in most families is that the man's work still takes precedence'. Coward argued that the absence of confrontation was surprising because 'whatever the disagreements among feminists, there had been one point of consensus: nothing would improve the lot of women unless men themselves changed' (Coward 1992: 6–7). The backlash against feminism, the revisions of it, and the political pessimism, all suggest a masculinity structured in dominance and resistant to change. Yet there is a difference between resistance to change and immunity from it, and examination of the tensions within masculinity can be revealing.

In academic analyses in the 1990s there was a growing emphasis on masculinit*ies* and on the discontinuities, contradictions and tensions within masculinity.[10] Lynne Segal argued that 'looking not at "masculinity" as such, but at certain specific masculinities', and 'understanding of the differences between men' was central to the struggle for change (Segal 1990: x). The growth of identity politics has produced a heightened visibility, not just of gay masculinities but also the complexities and instabilities of sexual identities (Weeks and Holland 1996; Garber 1992; Simpson 1994; Ekins and King 1995). As Connell argues, dominant masculinities also oppress some other masculinities, and some masculinities consequently occupy a subordinate position in relation to masculinity as a whole. Hegemonic masculinity oppresses women, but at any given historical moment there are competing masculinities – some hegemonic, some marginalised and some stigmatised (Connell 1995). Examples of marginalisation or stigmatisation might include gay masculinities, black and Asian masculinities, Jewish masculinities, anti-sexist masculinities, men who don't like sport, pacifist masculinities.

Sport for boys has, since the mid-nineteenth century, had a close association with the inculcation of the values of dominant masculinity, and those left marginalised, those who were oppositional, those who sought alternatives, have been relatively voiceless within dominant masculine culture. Sabo and Jansen (1992) draw attention to the socially structured silences that marginalise the physically unfit, gays and lesbians, the disabled and the old. Sport has the appearance of being a cultural practice which unites men; yet it is also a practice that divides men. Eve Sedgewick (1985) has compared the greater sense of a communality amongst women through sisterhood to the 'opposition between the homosocial and the homosexual amongst men'. Sporting practices marginalise and stigmatise gayness. Brian Pronger, in his discussion of sport and homosexuality, comments that despite the growth of a gay gym culture, sport for many homosexual men is still a place of estrangement (1990: 39).

Black men, too, are in a particular position in relation to the white heterosexual male sporting culture. The cultural construction of 'blackness' in the European context has roots, according to Paul Hoch, in story-telling and a myth of the 'white hero' who achieves his manhood by winning victory over the 'dark beast' (Hoch 1979: 10). In sport, this struggle is dramatised in diverse forms, such as the search of the boxing establishment, in the early twentieth century, for a 'great white hope' – a white man who could win the world heavyweight title. The common mobilisation of stereotypical representations of Latin footballers and African athletes draws on a similar opposition between white (European) and dark (Latin–African) modes of sporting behaviour. English manager Alf Ramsey's castigation of the Argentinians as 'animals' was still being recalled as recently as the England–Argentina match in the 1998 World Cup. Black prowess in sport has also been the focus of a culture of celebration, validation and approval, but one which largely takes place within the frame of reference that Cashmore (1982) referred to as 'the myth of natural ability' – the notion that black sporting prowess is rooted in racial biological difference. In representations of sport, and especially football, non-European worlds are interpreted through contrasts between black tactical naivety and European sophistication, and by the linking of genius and flair to the myth of 'natural' ability. Carrington (1998) has analysed the operation of marginalisation and incorporation in images of black male athletes.[11]

Masculinity is not an eternal and static object; masculinities change over time and the boundaries of masculinity are almost always the subject of redrawing, policing and contestation, as was the case in such diverse moments as Ancient Greece and Rome, the Renaissance, the Enlightenment and the Industrial Revolution. The mid-nineteenth-century public schools promoted muscular Christianity on the sporting field, and this became a central mechanism for the production of manliness, playing a significant role in the shaping of the dominant masculinity of the late Victorian male bourgeoisie. Yet other versions of manliness also emerged in the second half of the nineteenth century, in part in opposition to the conformity of team games. The notion of 'rugged individual self reliance' can be detected in a lineage that has roots in the 'hunting, shooting and fishing' tradition that the word 'sport' denoted before the rise to dominance of organised team games in the 1840s, and resurfaces in the late nineteenth century in such forms as the Boy Scout Movement and, after World War II, in the Duke of Edinburgh's Award Scheme. A more ascetic variant of masculinity is foregrounded in *Eric, or Little by Little* published in 1858, which featured a 'portrayal of pious Christianity and moral fervour' that was in 'stark contrast to the muscular Christianity and rugged chivalry of *Tom Brown's Schooldays*' (Kirkpatrick 1990: 1). If this rugged individualism constituted an alternative masculinity to that of the team game ethos, both grew out of muscular Christianity, which dealt with the feminine by processes of exclusion and marginalisation. A more distinctive alternative, that of the non-sporting aestheticism epitomised by the bohemian culture of Beardsley and Wilde, was not only defined in opposition to dominant sporting masculinity, but was typically stigmatised by it as effete and foppish.[12]

If there is not one essential masculinity, but rather a dominant masculinity and a range of subordinate masculinities, and if the pattern of social relations and gender relations is subject to historical shifts and transformations, then at any one time there are, in Raymond Williams' (1977) use of the terms, residual and emergent cultures of masculinity. That is to say, the process of transformation necessarily requires that some forms of masculinity (devout piety, Victorian 'heavy' patriarchs) are of declining significance, whilst others (new laddism) are of emergent importance. Lynne Segal suggests that 'heterosexual institutions and relations, from marriage and coupledom to adolescent romance, have always been more contradictory than our dominant conception of them in terms of men's power and women's subordination would suggest' (Segal 1994: xii). If there are overlapping and competing 'masculinities', then the cultural forms through which our understandings are produced and consumed requires attention. The next three chapters examine the emergence of a star-based media system, concepts of heroism and stardom, and modes of narrativising the careers of stars. After this, chapter 6 returns to the issue of masculinity, this time with specific reference to sporting cultures and to the construction of representations of sport.

3 The development of media sport

You couldn't see your heroes on television in those days, but we knew what a great player he was from the clips we saw on Pathé News at the cinema, reading *Charles Buchan's Football Monthly* and from information on the back of cigarette cards.

(Bobby Robson, on the death of Stanley Matthews, *Sunday Mirror*, 27 February 2000)

The BBC [radio] commentary teams came to be as much a part of the English summer as the BBC itself became part of English life, defining and shaping sporting values from the 1930s through to the 1960s, after which the increasingly sensational tabloid coverage of sport changed the terms of the debate.

(Richard Holt, in Holt and Mangan 1996: 63)

We British still lead the world in something. Unfortunately it's tabloid journalism.

(Adam Sweeting, *Guardian*, 26 April 1994)

The current dominance of the media by television tends to blind us to two facts. First, television broadcasting was only established in 1936 and before the mid-1950s it was at best marginal. Representation of sport has been at various times dominated by literature, magazines, cinema newsreel, newspapers and radio. Second, even now, despite the apparent dominance of the television screen, there are many other significant forms of media representation of sport, such as men's and boys' magazines, advertising, computer games, radio, cinema and the internet.

In examining the process of the social production of sport stardom, individual media cannot be seen in isolation. The media feed off each other and audience readings of representation in one medium are always already shaped and structured by representations in other media. The late nineteenth-century magazines and the early sport coverage in newspapers both addressed and fed an audience interest in sport, but cigarette cards offered also a cultural sifting, a form of selective tradition, in which a pantheon of top stars – and their names, faces and biographical details – were made more familiar to the audience. By the 1920s, the brief glimpses of great stars and sporting moments available through cinema newsreel helped make newspaper stories more vivid, by building audience familiarity with star performance. Radio provided the ingredient of immediacy, whilst by the 1960s television combined immediacy and realism – the sense of being there as it happened. During the 1970s, the gossip and sensation of the tabloid press augmented the more sober conventions of television's star-focused presentations. The growing cultural centrality of representations of sport during the 1990s rested partly on an expansion in the range of cultural forms through which sport was provided – the dedicated sport channels of satellite and cable television, the pull-out sport supplements of newspapers, sport magazines, websites. Even the magazines *Hello* and *OK*, that have a largely female readership, included, during the 1990s, a significant number of cover spreads and features on sport stars.

By the end of the nineteenth century, several factors were in place to enable the rapid emergence of modern mass media. The development of the technologies of mass reproduction, the spread of literacy, the growth of education and creation of a mass reading public, and developments in transportation together produced the conditions for those techno-cultural forms that became known as the mass media to emerge and flourish.

Print media

The gradual emergence and development of organised spectator sport during the late eighteenth and early nineteenth centuries was accompanied by interest from literary figures and social commentators.[1] As long as spectator sport has existed, stars have played a role in the process of audience building, and much sports writing focused upon charismatic performers (see Holt *et al.* 1996: 50). New sport magazines and guides began to appear in the mid-nineteenth century.[2] In the 1870s and 1880s there were a range of technological innovations associated with the making, preserving, transmission and dissemination of images that Boorstin (1961) has referred to as 'the graphic revolution'.[3]

In the USA, Pulitzer established the first newspaper sports department in 1883 at the *New York World*, and Hearst introduced the first sports section in a paper in the *New York Journal* in 1895 (McChesney 1989: 53). Then came 1896, the launch of the *Daily Mail*, and the transformation of newspaper production by the establishment of a mass circulation popular press in a process that became known as the Northcliffe revolution. From the first issue, the new *Daily Mail* devoted at least 10 per cent of its space to sport (Mason 1988: 49). In the 1920s, the Associated Press established a sports department with a staff of twelve (McChesney 1989: 56). In Britain, sports reporting has since this time been dominated by national newspapers, and multi-sport magazines have found it hard to survive for long (see Horne 1992). On the Continent, and in the USA, however, specialist sporting newspapers have thrived.[4] The emergence of sports sections, and the growing use of photography helped to establish the beginnings of an individualisation of sport in which star individuals began to inhabit the public imagination.

Cigarette cards

The first cards were probably issued in France around the 1840s. The Paris shop Bon Marche began issuing cards in 1853, and by 1912 had issued over 400 sets. The practice spread to America, and it is probably in America that tobacco companies first became involved. Cigarettes were then sold loose or in paper packs that required a cardboard stiffener. It was realised that printing a picture and brand name on the stiffener would be a good form of promotion. This may first have been done around 1879. By 1890 almost every American tobacco firm had issued at least one series. Often they featured actresses or female 'glamour' shots, but the first sports series appeared towards the end of the nineteenth century (Murray 1987: 18–22).[5] According to Murray, 'Before the First World War smokers were nearly all men and the earlier subjects that appeared on cards tended towards the three things that most interested them – sport, women and militaria' (Murray 1987: 24). Cigarette cards ceased production in 1917 during World War I due to paper shortages, and did not resume until 1922. Ogden issued a large number of racing cards during the 1920s including jockeys, owners, trainers and other turf personalities. In the early 1920s, almost all boys' and girls' papers, and in particular those issued by Amalgamated Press and D.C. Thompson, contained cards. Often these were photographic and, in the case of the boys' books, featured sportsmen – for example, *Boys' Friend* with 'Rising Boxing Stars', *Pal's* 'Football Teams' and *Boys Realm* 'Famous Cricketers'. Marking a distinct gender difference, the *Schoolgirl* contained 'Wild Animals' and *Girls Mirror* had 'Actors and Actresses' (Murray 1987: 56). Here, as elsewhere, sport is one of the most distinctive ways in which gender difference is culturally constructed.

Cinema newsreel

Cinema brought movement and hence sporting action to the audience for the first time (Aldgate 1979: 17). The first public cinema performance in Britain was in 1896, and there were between 4,000 and 5,000 cinemas by 1914. The first regular topical coverage was by the Biograph Company, a US firm with a base in the UK. Among other events, they covered the Derby and the Boat Race (*ibid.*: 17). The Pathé organisation was set up in 1908 and their first newsreel featured a sculling contest, as well as a factory strike and a Royal trip (*ibid.*: 19). In 1911, cameras filmed Billy Wells (the great British boxing hope) being knocked out by Gunner Moir in the third round (Shipley 1989: 95). For the first time, a mass audience was able to see sport stars in moving action.

By 1919, 50 per cent of the British population went to the cinema once or twice a week. During the 1920s and 1930s there was a substantial increase in investment in cinemas, with around one thousand being built between 1924–31. The introduction of sound at the end of the twenties provided a boost to industry and encouraged investment in new cinemas, with three hundred being built between 1932–34. In Britain there were by 1934, 4,300 cinemas with 4.5 million seats showing newsreels to an average weekly audience of 18.5 million. By 1940 the average weekly audience was 21 million. (Aldgate 1979: x). Smaller cinemas were being replaced by larger ones. In this period cinema was the most important form of mass entertainment and in particular a major source of working class entertainment with 23 million tickets sold a week in 1939. Annual admissions grew until reaching a peak in the late 1940s.

Radio

If cinema brought action and movement, radio provided immediacy and it brought sport into the domestic sphere for the first time. In both Britain and the USA early radio broadcast experiments were underway by the start of the 1920s. In Britain, a radio service was launched in 1922 when six radio and electrical companies combined to form the British Broadcasting Company Ltd, which four years later was transformed into a public corporation. The Newspaper Proprietors Association successfully lobbied Parliament to ensure that the new company would not be allowed to cover news and sport and so threaten their sales, but after the establishment of the British Broadcasting Corporation (BBC) in 1927, this stricture was removed and sport broadcasts became a well-established element in the schedules (see Whannel 1992).

The percentage of households with radio rose rapidly in the inter-war period, from 10 per cent in 1924 to 71 per cent in 1938. In the USA, too, radio rose to prominence and sport broadcasts played a significant role in its popularity. By 1929 one-third of American households had radio. The radio broadcast of the Dempsey–Tunney fight in 1927 was reported to have generated $90,000 of radio sales in one New York store alone (McChesney 1989: 59). As the first domestic medium, radio enabled the establishment of new shared national rituals – the Christmas message, Cup Final Day, the Boat Race, and the Last Night of the Proms. In the USA, baseball, boxing and American football were broadcast to large audiences. Just as cinema brought moving images of sport to the mass audience, radio brought the excitement and drama of the immediacy and uncertainty of sport into the home. Television was subsequently to combine the spectacle of the moving image with the immediacy and domestic reach of radio and in the process would transform sport. [6]

The television era

Television as a broadcasting technology was established in the 1930s, although it did not start to catch on with the public until the 1950s and did not reach a plateau of technical accomplishment until the 1970s. Television was launched in Britain in 1936 and relayed a range of sport events before 1939 when the television experiment was suspended with the outbreak of war. But in this period reception was restricted to the London area and the high price of receivers meant the audience never rose above 20,000. In the USA, by 1939, NBC was televising baseball and American football. In Germany in the late 1930s television technology was used to relay live pictures of sporting events to cinema screens. The relaunch of television in Britain in 1946, seen as an element of post-war reconstruction and designed to boost the electronics industry, was slow to gather momentum. Major sporting events included the televising of the Boat Race and the 1948 Olympic Games. In 1950 there were only five million television sets in the world, and only Great Britain, the USA and the USSR had established television systems. Television was launched in Australia in 1956, the year of the Melbourne Olympics. By 1970 there were 250 million sets in 130 countries, and television spread rapidly in Africa, Asia and Latin America (Green 1972). Television combined the moving pictures of the newsreel with the immediacy and domestic delivery of radio, and took over from both as a primary means of consuming images of sport. The long-term impact on the press was that newspapers ceased to be the medium of first resort for sport news, and turned increasingly to gossip, rumour and scandal, a process accelerated by the tabloid revolution.

It wasn't until the 1953 Coronation and the launch of ITV in 1955 that television began to catch the popular imagination and set sales began to rise dramatically. By 1966, 81 per cent of British households and 93 per cent of American households had televisions (Chandler 1988: 175). The Television Act of 1954, which provided for the inclusion of advertising, ended the BBC monopoly of broadcasting, although it wasn't until the 1960s that sport began to assume an established place on television; it took a series of transformative technological innovations during the 1960s (video recording and editing, replay and slow motion, colour pictures and satellite relays) to fully establish sport broadcasting in the form we now recognise.

By 1965, the BBC had established *Sportsview* (1954), *Grandstand* (1958) and *Match of the Day* (1962) as regular programmes, ITV had launched *World of Sport*; in the USA, ABC Sport had launched *Wide World of Sport* with its subtitle 'the thrill of victory, the agony of defeat', and adopted its slogan 'up close and personal'. In the 1960s, the youthful theme of ABC echoed the Kennedy idealism of the new frontier, the sporting emphasis echoed the Kennedy's image of muscular athleticism, and, as Ron Powers put it, 'shrugging off the darker morbidities of the Cold War and McCarthyism', the country was in a mood for newness and regeneration (Powers 1984: 118–21). In 1970, ABC launched *Monday Night Football*, which was such a huge success that bars and restaurants saw a significant drop in trade. ABC were in the forefront of the attempt to make sport more dramatic and spectacular – they put microphones inside golf cups, on basketball hoops, on referees – and even inside the Olympic Flame to catch the sound of it being lit. These developments transformed the nature of sport stardom as stars, their actions, their words, and their appearances attained a more generalised familiarity, beyond the more narrow world of sports fandom. In particular, television shifted focus onto the face.

The media sport industry, dubbed by Aris the 'sportsbiz', began to emerge (Aris 1990). The banning of cigarette advertising on television in Britain (1965) and the USA (1970) triggered a growth in sport sponsorship led by the tobacco companies. New associations formed in often unsuccessful attempts to get airtime. (Examples include the American Basketball Association (1967), the World Hockey Association (1972), World Team Tennis (1973) and the US Football League 1983). New quasi sports events such as *Superstars*, called by their critics trash-sports, and their proponents, synthetic sports, grew out of the desire to exploit the fame of sport celebrities. This sub-genre went into decline in the 1980s to be replaced by more aggressive attempts to extend the global reach of established major sports. American Football, Australian Rules, basketball, cricket, baseball, and even sumo, sought to broaden their audience. The staging of soccer's World Cup in the USA in 1994 was the most dramatic example to date. These developments have meant that the fame of major stars such as Michael Jordan or Ronaldo has a global dimension which, thanks to merchandising and advertising, reaches even those who do not follow the sports which they play.

The newsreels, robbed of their relevance by television news, withered on the vine, while cinema itself was plunged into a long decline by the growth of television. The slump seemed to bottom out in the mid-1980s since when, boosted by new investment in multiplex cinemas and a renewed enthusiasm for 'going out', cinema attendances have been growing. Sport films were still regarded with suspicion by the studios, and films about 'British' sports (rugby, soccer, cricket) had little chance of finance from, or success in, North America.

The tabloid revolution

The national newspaper industry became increasingly beleaguered in the three decades that followed the Second World War. It was a period in which the *News Chronicle* and the *Daily Herald* came to an end, and there was a consolidation of ownership. Three key events reconstructed the British newspaper industry – the tabloid revolution, the crushing of the print unions, and the introduction of new computer-based layout techniques. Together these developments also contributed to the blurring of the division between the public and private spheres.

First, the purchase of the *Sun* by Rupert Murdoch, and its relaunch as a tabloid in 1969 triggered off a tabloid revolution in which the *Daily Mirror* and the *Sun* competed for the working-class reader with more explicit pin-ups, sport and scandal (Murdock and Golding 1978). Second, the destruction of the power of the print unions in 1986, when Murdoch moved his four titles to Wapping, opened the way to a technological revolution (Goodhart and Wintour 1986). Full computerisation and colour printing accelerated the drift away from traditional page layout and towards a collage style in which headlines and photo displays came to dominate. This, in turn, heightened the force and impact of stories about easily recognised star figures. Through a process of pushing the boundaries back, and aided by the eccentric, unpredictable and expensive nature of English libel laws that discourage risky litigation, the clear division between public and private spheres has been blurred, and areas of life once resolutely private are now in the public domain. Much of the new sensation, scandal and gossip that has become a staple of tabloid content has featured sport stars, and has contributed both to a public fascination with the personality and private life of sporting celebrities, and to the construction of discourses of moral censure.

New men's magazines

Comics for children were declining in the 1980s and 1990s, but men's magazines were commencing a boom period. Since the 1960s, Britain has had a thriving magazine sector, with women's magazines providing many of the biggest sellers. Titles typically purchased by men were either soft-core pornography (*Playboy, Penthouse*, etc.) or related to motoring, hi-fi, DIY, gardening and sport. During the 1980s, the potential for male magazines associated with style, fashion and appearance began to become evident (see Nixon 1996, Mort 1996, Edwards 1997). The first wave of the men's-style press centred on *The Face, GQ, Arena* and *FHM. Arena* was launched in 1986. The launch and runaway success of *Loaded* in 1994 transformed the field of men's magazines. *Loaded* was of particular significance in its laddish discourse of 'beer, birds and football', uniting 'sport' and 'men behaving badly'. All titles retargeted themselves down-market, and soft-core pornographic imagery re-entered the mainstream of front covers. *Loaded* increased its circulation by 85 per cent during 1996, but the revamped *FHM*'s circulation went up 271 per cent to achieve monthly sales of 365,000. By 1997 it sometimes sold over half a million, giving it an estimated readership of over 2 million. This compared to a circulation of less than 50,000 in 1994, when it was acquired by EMAP and redesigned. EMAP spotted the middle ground between the laddishness of *Loaded* and the aspirational advertising-driven content of *GQ* (Guardian, 17 February 1997). The successful launch of *Men's Health* in the mid-nineties offered a more middle-class aspirational discourse of body maintenance, but also contributed to the growing cultural centrality of sport, and increasing body-image awareness amongst men.

Advertising

Advertising is the hidden hand in the story of the media. While its role is often marginalised in accounts, it is perilous to underestimate its significance. As a dynamic force for change, in which capital seeks to reproduce through new forms of sales promotion, it has been significant in the battles between rival newspapers, the cigarette card phenomenon, the formation of commercial broadcasting, the launch and development of satellite and cable television and the growth in men's magazines. While it did not invent the World Wide Web, it is rapidly colonising it. In the form of sponsorship, product endorsement and corporate hospitality, it has also played a role in the transformation and commodification of sport through its influence on the presentation both of events and of individual stars. Indeed, the need of television for sports with audience appeal, combined with the needs of the advertising industry to find figures with market appeal and dynamic images with positive connotations, have combined to make top sport stars extremely wealthy and highly visible.

Advertising has a long prehistory, but began to adopt its contemporary forms during the second half of the nineteenth century. In particular, the retailing boom and the emergence of the modern mass media at the end of the nineteenth century together produced the modern advertising industry. In the late nineteenth century there was a significant increase in the volume of commerce, and a rapid growth in chain-store retailing, with stores such as Lipton's, Home and Colonial, Freeman, Hardy and Willis, Hepworth's, and W.H. Smith becoming established.[7] During the same period, a growth in sport participation boosted the development of the sport goods and clothes industry. Lipton's were one of the first firms to invest significant sums in sport sponsorship. Trade associations were formed in the emergent advertising industry.[8] Sport stars began to be involved in a more systematic exploitation of their images during the inter-war period – tennis players Fred Perry and Rene Lacoste both established successful sports clothing companies, for example. During the 1950s, sport stars began to appear more often in billboard and display advertising. Cricketer Dennis Compton and footballer Johnny Haynes both endorsed Brylcreem. Sports agents, such as Bagenal Harvey in Britain and Mark McCormack in the USA established lucrative businesses exploiting the celebrity of their clients.

However, it took television and the globalisation of sport to turn sport stars into hot properties from a marketing point of view. The growing global visibility of major sport was of considerable appeal to advertisers. In the staging of the 1982 World Cup and the 1984 Olympic Games it was demonstrated that selling sponsorship for global television events on a global basis in limited products categories with exclusive rights within each category was to become a major new source of revenue for sport. The technique forced major competitors (for example, Coca Cola and Pepsi, Kodak and Fuji) into an auction for sponsorship rights. The 1984 Olympic Games made over $100 million from sponsorship, ten times that made in previous games. In the USA, only the McDonald's logo, (recognised by 100 per cent of respondents) is more recognisable than the five rings of the Olympics (recognised by 99 per cent). Almost half of the people interviewed in the USA, Singapore, Portugal and West Germany thought the Olympic rings indicated that a product was of good quality (Wilson 1988: 28).

Merchandising became a key part of sports promotion. Replica shirts, sports clothes, shoes, wallets, belts, luggage, bone china, preserves, sheets, blankets, towels, stationery and calendars are among the branded goods associated with the name and livery of top sporting clubs and events. Corporate hospitality accounts for an ever greater portion of seats at major events – almost 25 per cent of seats for the 1998 World Cup went to sponsors and corporate entertainment. In the USA, sport programmes were seen as a good way of targeting affluent young men between 25 and 45. In 1984, Apple used the television coverage of the Superbowl to launch Macintosh with one 30-second slot that cost $500,000 to make and almost as much to screen. Superbowl advertising now costs around $2 million a minute. One significant feature of the media sport industry is the convergence of interests between sports promotion, television, advertising, sponsorship and merchandising. The exploitation of the fame of Michael Jordan across a range of cultural forms and products, turning him in the process into a globally recognised figure, is an instructive example. In 1992, Nike paid Michael Jordan £10 million to promote their shoes in 1992 which, according to a London-based radical newspaper, was more than the entire Indonesian workforce of 7,500 people were paid to make them in one year.[9]

The processes of consolidation and integration, characteristic of developed capitalist societies, developed at a slower pace in sport than in much of the rest of the entertainment business. In the last twenty years, though, driven by the growth of television and now by the internet, and by the digital revolution, the pace has speeded considerably. The transformation of football clubs into public limited companies, the links being forged between media corporations and sporting organisations, the consolidation of sports marketing companies within broader corporations, and, in particular, the links being established by major media barons such as Ted Turner and Rupert Murdoch with sport organisations, illustrate a growing integration of sport into the mainstream of capitalism and of sport stars into the system of image production. ABC's sport subsidiary, ESPN, reaches over 127 million households in 150 countries. The Capital Cities/ABC group is now owned by Disney. Through its satellite companies like BSkyB and Star in South-east Asia Murdoch's News Corporation now reaches two-thirds of the world's television households (Bellamy 1998: 77).

Satellites, digitalisation and the electronic media

At the start of the 1990s, Sky Television was losing around £1 million a week, and English football was only just recovering from two decades of problems with crowd behaviour, the Bradford fire, the Heysel Stadium incident and the Hillsborough stadium disaster. By the end of the decade, football was earning hundreds of millions in rights payments from television, its new chic appeal had impelled almost all papers to launch massive football-dominated sport supplements, and a highly profitable Sky was making more and more inroads into BBC's diminishing sport portfolio.

The deregulation of rights negotiation allowed television channels to acquire the rights to the European games of specific clubs and competition between the five terrestrial channels and Sky meant that there was more live football on television than ever before. The establishment of the Premier League and revamping of the European Cup as the Champions League, the introduction of all-seat stadia and the importation of glamorous foreign stars increased the spectacularisation of football. New, more affluent, customers were attracted, admission prices rose dramatically and grounds filled up. The cost, and the need at many clubs to purchase season tickets to ensure access, inevitably excluded poorer supporters. The new more affluent football following attracted a new range of sport magazines. The rapid growth in pubs and bars featuring football fostered a whole new communal culture of television sport spectatorship. Major matches in the European Champions League attracted considerable attention, culminating in the victory of Manchester United in the 1999 final – the first British team to win the event since 1984.

The imminent digital revolution is set to accentuate these trends further. More money will flood into football and more games will be available; and although some will be pay-per-view, others will be on the internet. The combination of the growth of satellite television, sport in pubs and bars, sport supplements in papers, the launch of new sport magazines and the extension of the fame of top sport stars beyond the confines of the sport pages has placed sport in a more central position than ever before in the cultural life of the nation.

The new electronic media of the late twentieth century – video games, electronic arcade games and computer games – contributed to the secondary circulation of images of sport and sport stars, although secondary circulation in the media-saturated environment has become an ambiguous concept. It is no longer always straightforward to distinguish between the primary activity and the spin-off. The popular computer game *PGA Tour Golf* – set up to capitalise on the players' tour – incorporates images of and comments from star golfers. Lara Croft is the world's first virtual star, but may be only paving the way for the emergence of a computerised sports performer who, through digital magic, can be pitted against 'real' performers. Yet, given the apparent public fascination with erratic behaviour, with misbehaviour and with the unpredictable, the virtualisation of sport may be an impossible task. For it is the ways in which, despite the increasing discipline and sophistication of modern scientific coaching, things still do not always go according to plan that is part of the enduring, and very human, fascination of sport. Despite the commodification of sport, there is always some element of unpredictable spontaneous uncertainty that eludes the marketeers (Whannel 1994). Sport stars have undoubtedly acquired a high level of audience appeal and sport plays a significant part in the range of content of most media. The next chapter explores the ways in which concepts of the heroic and of the star serve to organise the representation of sport.

4   Heroes and stars

Almost every one of these heroes of sport taught me something, gave me some insight into how to live and added to my philosophy of life. And I think these champions and the way that they lived have something to say to all of us especially in these uncertain times, which the editorial writers call 'The Age of Anxiety'.

(Rice 1956: xvi)

Hopes are still invested in the ability of sport to produce heroic role models, and the frustration of these hopes feeds into a critique of sport as having become corrupted. In these constructions, what sport produces is not heroes, but stars. Yet in popular discourse the concepts of hero and star, celebrity and personality are often confused and any notional boundaries between them blurred. The very concept of the hero is troubling and ambiguous. Statements about heroism, the heroic and heroes are frequently statements not just about the society in which we live, but statements that carry a marked positionality, inscribing both the perspective from which they are made and the frame through which we should perceive society.

Heroes, heroism and the heroic are related but distinct notions. Some feel, pace the Stranglers, that there are 'no more heroes any more', yet heroic acts (e.g. of rescue) still take place. Tom Wolfe regarded the astronauts as 'the Last American heroes'. Yet there seems to be evidence of a cultural need for heroics in which some are 'holding on for a hero'. Heroes, for some, belong to a more naive, less cynical and less morally ambiguous time when you had 'to be a football hero to get along with a beautiful girl'.[1] Comic super-heroes, such as Superman, developed as if to fill the void left by the rise of moral ambiguities. American writer Ken Kesey felt, in somewhat Nietzschian fashion, that people had it within them to be super-heroes. Bowie sung that 'We can be heroes ... just for one day'. The term reoccurs in a wide range of popular cultural forms regardless of the presence or absence of specific identifiable 'heroes'.

A hero is, of course, the central character in narrative fiction, and the heroic is a place constructed in representation of one form or another. The heroic role can be taken to imply exceptional courage and self-sacrifice and involves the idealisation of a man of superior qualities or virtues.[2] The heroic life,

Featherstone (1995: 59) suggests, is the sphere of danger, violence and risk in which the hero departs from the realm of everyday life only to return to its acclaim when a task or quest is complete. The genealogy of the term gives it density and complexity, including as it does elements of Greek mythology, Arthurian legend, Chivalric romance, eighteenth-century romantic art, and nineteenth-century imperialist adventure. The tragic Aristotelian hero, the great man with a fatal flaw, the concept of quest and adventure, or trial by ordeal, of initiation, of peril and rescue and of triumphant return all contribute to our sense of the heroic.[3]

Some analyses of the heroic conceptualise the hero in terms of Jungian archetypicality, leading to a tendency to be trans-cultural and ahistorical.[4] Heroes are indeed different from heroines, and the place of the hero typically constructs a notional relationship with a feminine other. Narratives constructed within patriarchal cultures have this in common. But storytelling and ideology always have to deal with the difficult, the troubling and the unresolved and repressed, even if they resolve these matters, symbolically, on the terrain of a dominant ideology. Heroic tales do provide a fund of metaphoric allusion – think of the resonances of the tales of Theseus killing the Minotaur, Ulysses and the sirens, Jonah and the whale, David and Goliath, Samson and the lion, Perseus and the head of Medusa. Representations of sport draw upon the connections to the traditional and the legendary that such allusions facilitate.

By contrast with the trans-cultural tendencies in Jungian analyses, Ebbutt (1995) recognises both that conceptions of the heroic change over time and that different readings of 'the heroic' are possible. He also acknowledges the multiple cultural sources of heroic tales that have fed into British concepts of heroism. He discusses the complex mix of Frank and Norman and Saxon and Dane and Roman and Celt and Iberian that make up the British heritage of myth and legend and says 'With all these nations, all these natures amalgamated in our own, it is no wonder that the literature of our isles contains many different ideals of heroism, changing according to nationality and epoch' (*ibid.*: 16). The term 'hero', then, arrives with a complex history – a compositthat of cultural allusions.

The heroic problematised

Analyses characteristically place the heroic in the past and many of them regard the concept as problematic in the context of modernity. Campbell pinpoints the problem of the heroic in the modern era as to do with the rise of science, the decline of religion and the triumph of rationality and modernity.[5] Jenny Calder suggests that the romantic movement of the early nineteenth century existed in the context of a feeling that the 'heroic idea' was threatened by commerce, industrialisation and the inevitable fragmentation of society. However, she also argues that 'heroism is a vital aspect of human behaviour and human endeavour and that the idea of the hero is at the centre of our cultural thinking. Heroes are not only enjoyable, they are necessary' (Calder 1977: ix). Since the rise of the bourgeoisie in the nineteenth century, the concept of hero has become increasingly problematised. A nostalgia for a purer, less compromised past was evident for much of the twentieth century. The rise of bourgeois democracy has been accompanied by a decline of the heroic. In visual art the aristocratic patronage that used to sustain representations of the heroic has been eroded.

In the modernist sensibility, man, rather than being heroic, is more characteristically portrayed as victim, or as anti-hero. Consider writers as diverse as Franz Kafka, Tennessee Williams, Arthur Miller and Jack Kerouac. Klapp describes the anti-hero as having a style of 'tired apathetic, cool and beat rejection of lofty goals' (Klapp 1962: 157). On the pages of novels, and in the movies, the rebellious, the disaffected and the confused rambled everywhere. Neither Yossarian (*Catch 22*), Dean Moriarty (*On The Road*), nor Holden Caulfield (*Catcher in the Rye*) were remotely heroic. The leading characters of late 1950s and early 1960s English social realism were young men who railed against the barriers and taboos of what was portrayed as an archaic society that had failed to modernise – had not shed the trappings of class, nor loosened the corsets of Victorian morality. But Billy Fisher (*Billy Liar*), Jimmy Porter (*Look Back in Anger*), Joe Lampton (*Room at the Top*) and Arthur Seaton (*Saturday Night and Sunday Morning*) were no more heroic than the American examples cited above. Indeed, all were self-centred and self-pitying figurers who wished merely to escape the disciplines of class and feminised domesticity.

One response was for storytelling to become more concerned with moral ambiguity and with amorality – the spaghetti westerns of Serge Leone constituted an elaborate, dark and morally ambiguous joke at the expense of the more rigid moral certainties of the classic western. In a different response to the threat of technology, science and the Cold War, and as a counter-trend to the moral ambiguities of the anti-heroic, the comic super-heroes – Batman, Superman, Spiderman, Wonder Woman, etc. (see Reynolds 1992) – grew in popularity from the 1940s.[6] Boorstin's influential study, *The Image* (1961), argues that culture has become saturated with pseudo-events, that the hero, has been replaced by the celebrity and that travellers have been replaced by tourists. For Boorstin, celebrities are reflexively constructed by their own fame – 'well known for being well known'. He distinguishes between the hero and the celebrity, saying that 'We can make a celebrity but we can't make a hero'. Boorstin charts a shift in which, whereas before 1914, 74 per cent of the biographical articles in the *Saturday Evening Post* and *Colliers* came from politics, business and the professions, in the 1920s, well over 50 per cent came from the world of entertainment. He also argues that there was also a shift from high art to popular culture with a decreasing proportion of profiles of figures from the serious arts – literature, fine arts, music, dance and theatre, and an ever-increasing proportion from the fields of light entertainment, sports and the night club circuit (Boorstin 1961: 68). Boorstin argues for the essential emptiness of celebrity:

> In the democracy of pseudo-events, anyone can become a celebrity, if only he can get into the news and stay there ... What is remarkable is not only that we manage to fill experience with so much emptiness, but that we manage to give the emptiness such appealing variety.
>
> (Boorstin 1961: 69)

Yet it is clear that the image of celebrity, far from being content-less, is a rich and resonant cut into the structure of popular common sense as re-trod on the ground of popular journalism. Boorstin sketches the temporary nature of celebrity, when he asserts:

> The very agency which first makes the celebrity in the long run inevitably destroys him. He will be destroyed, as he was made, by publicity. The newspapers make him and they un-make him – not by murder, but by suffocation or starvation.
>
> (Boorstin 1961: 72)

However, in the wake of tabloidisation and the erosion of old assumed divisions between public and private, indeed death from over exposure seems more of a threat than starvation. Figures do, it is true, disappear from the limelight, but major stars tend to remain fairly newsworthy, as the continuing coverage of the lives of George Best and Muhammad Ali suggests.

John Berger argued that bourgeois culture was no longer capable of producing heroes, only idols, stars, television personalities and pin-ups (quoted in Inglis 1977: 85). Edelstein (1996) is another subscriber to the notion that there are no heroes any more. Political correctness and revision of history has led to a degree of debunking of past heroes. There is still a desire for heroes but not a production of them. He cites the large number of books and articles, fiction and non-fiction, that are subtitled 'the last hero'. Klapp (1969: 214) said that celebrities are a new type of hero – typically individual rather than collective – we all have our own heroes, and many celebrities do not support tribal or other collective identities. Raymond Williams refers to his efforts to locate the moment of romanticised nostalgia for a recently destroyed organic community as being like stepping on an escalator – every age seems to have produced such a discourse (Williams 1973: 9–12). Nonetheless, there are still specificities about particular moments. So it is with the place of the heroic. The concept of 'no more heroes anymore' can probably be detected at many points in history, but it may well be that the rise of the modern mass media have produced a distinct sense of the lack of the heroic. Williams writes of the constructions of a 'golden age', the idea of an ordered and happy past, that involves 'an idealisation based on a temporary situation and on a deep desire for stability, served to cover and to evade the actual and bitter contradiction of the time'. In this context, the nostalgic longing for heroes and the regret at the decline of heroes involves a searching for a magical resolution of the contradictions of the present. From this perspective, the expressed desire for heroes is as meaningful a social indicator as their imagined presence or absence.

From the perspective of this book, one notable development in the twentieth century has been the gradual incorporation of sporting exploits into the pantheons of the heroic. Indeed, as concepts of the heroic have been destabilised by the rise of anti-hero and moral ambiguity, sport performers have become more central to attempts to reconstruct unproblematic heroism. A book called *Heroes and Heroines* published in 1981 had on its back cover the blurb:

> Feats of courage, bravery and endurance both in peace time and in war. Read about the fearless fighter pilot, Douglas Bader; Lindbergh, first to fly the Atlantic and Amy Johnson who flew around the world. Hilary and Tenzing, first men on Everest's summit; Armstrong, first man on the moon. Graham Hill, race track wizard; Mary Peters and Virginia Wade who fought their way to championships in their chosen sport.
>
> (Kenyon 1981)

Travel and exploration has become less fascinating as much of the world is now accessible to tourists. Mechanisation and speed have passed beyond the realm of individual heroics and are now thoroughly in the hands of science and technology, with the driver just a disciplined and controlled cog. War heroism has been undercut by the dominance of technology. Sport has filled the gap. In this sense, the exceptionalism of boxing becomes clearer too. Calder argues that

> Some sports have clearly evolved as a means of legitimising aggression, and the hero of the boxing ring, for instance, is a conqueror in much the same sense as the military hero. In fact, he is bigger and better and more exaggerated than the military hero, because his victory is entirely his own. Thus the immense status that has been accorded to heavyweight champions.
>
> (Calder 1977: 183)

Calder writes of Ali with an interesting blend of fascination with, and racist fear of, the black other: 'With every fight and every threat, with every ringing assertion of his superiority, he is reminding us of what he could do to the white population' (Calder 1977: 183–4). She talks of the anarchist element in sport stars, suggesting that the most popular are those who appear to defy the rules and conventions. The public like the fast bowlers who seem to contradict the gentlemanly ethos, the assertion of individuality, the difficult and rebellious personalities. However, she recognises the limited and bounded nature of this rebellion:

> The sporting hero retains the characteristic duality, i.e. aggressive, and officially supported, anarchist and institutionalised, testing himself privately for the benefit of thousands who want to reward him with adoration and imita-

tion. He is both representative and elite, collective and individual. In many respects he is a very satisfactory hero for he can be controlled; the world in which he operates and in which he can succeed is limited.

(Calder 1977: 184)

The concept of heroism requires a degree of homogenisation in audience response. Such consensuality doesn't just exist, it has to be produced. A view of audiences as fragmented must lead us to ask, 'heroes for whom?' Black and white audience attitudes to figures such as Carl Lewis, Mike Tyson, Tiger Woods, Chris Eubank, Frank Bruno, O.J. Simpson may be strikingly distinct. The 'great white hope', as the play of the same title makes clear, was a figure intended to put blacks in their place. Given the overwhelmingly masculine focus of media sport – whom are sporting heroics for? Indeed, in considering heroes in relation to heroines and to the female, it appears that sport characteristically provides a space for the eradication, marginalisation and symbolic annihilation of the feminine. Sport heroes are often self-sufficient heroes – heroes without a need for women – male egos resplendent and narcissistic, confirmed in their victory by admiring (male) team-mates and (male) fans, with no fear of symbolic castration by unsatisfactory encounter with the other. Heroes, in a sense, transcend sexuality – they become immortal – their memory lives on. The cult of youth embedded in fitness chic fosters a desire for immortality – note the lyric of the theme song of Fame: 'I want to Live Forever'. Efforts to preserve memories of great sporting moments are precisely because sport is a performance and not a product and hence transitory: thus the growing fascination with 'Halls of Fame' and programme formats such as '100 Sporting Memories'. Memorable in this context was the cry of one BBC Wimbledon commentator at the record sixth championship victory of Bjorn Borg, 'Borg has become immortal'.

Janet Harris's work on sport heroes commenced with a consideration of the literature on the heroic, which she characterises as a debate between the pessimists and the optimists as to whether we have heroes any more. She goes on to pursue this through survey evidence as to the sort of people young people have as heroes. Her study does not fully unravel the problems of the concept – she seems to assume a consistency as to the meaning of the term. But of course 'hero' is a construction within discourse which will signify differently in different discourses, at different moments and in different contexts. So the issue for us is how the 'sporting hero' is constructed. Harris does touch on these points, but doesn't really fully escape from essentialism. She contrasts idealistic and archetypal views of heroes, typically likely to be pessimistic, with relativistic views more likely to be optimistic. Pessimists often link deterioration of heroes with 'broader defects in modern life' and to a sense of disillusionment with modern America, and she comments that 'It is worth noting that neither the pessimists nor the optimists have much to say about power inequities among members of dominant and subordinate groups in American society' (Harris 1994: 4–5).

Ingham, Loy and Swetman (1979) argue that sport does not produce heroes because sport is a cultural phenomenon heavily determined by more basic political and economic processes. They maintain that heroes must be active in the empowerment of subordinate groups and that this cannot be achieved simply within sport. The characteristic opposition between hero and celebrity posits a celebrity that is cheap and tawdry but above all content-less. Ingham *et al.* (1993) developed the theme further by utilising Gramsci's distinction between the organic and the conjunctural, proposing modes of analysis that seek to understand the relation between biography, structure and history, and in so doing determine the relation of stars to social change. Segrave (1993: 183), by contrast, argues that the cultural hero-system of sport is regressive and that sport culture is rooted in social moral and emotional simplicity which infantilises those within it.

Celebrity, for many of these writers, is intrinsically vacuous and banal. I contend the opposite – that the type of figures who accomplish celebrity status provides important and revealing evidence about the cultural formation they exist within, and it is relevant and important to pay close attention to the ways in which they are celebrated, examining the themes, values and discourses that are in play. The cultures of sport still depend in part upon a constant re-enacting of the heroic. From the early days of the sporting press, through cigarette cards, cinema newsreels, radio, television and video, tales of the heroic have played a key role. This frame constitutes a structuring device for the past – videos reconstruct the past of sport in terms of heroic deeds – and the present. Footballers Paul Gascoigne and Ryan Giggs have had to carry the burden of figures expected to provide the heroic. Such figures are supposed to provide genius and flair, yet unlike 'Roy of the Rovers', are also, especially since the 1970s, expected to submit to the disciplines of teamwork, dedication and system. In addition, they have to carry the added burden of embodying and representing national hopes and aspirations.[7] The stardom of such figures can be seen as constituting an intersecting point of contradiction and tension. Far from being less interesting, or less significant, or more empty of content, the images of stars in contemporary society constitute rich tools for cultural analysis, providing thermometers and barometers that may be utilised to take the social temperature and to assess the pressures generated by tensions and contradictions.

Stars and the media

James Thurber, the American humourist, once wrote a story called 'The Greatest Man in the World'. It imagined a hero ill-equipped to be a celebrity – a man with 'insufficient intelligence, background, and character successfully to endure the mounting orgies of glory prepared for aviators who stayed up for a long time or flew a great distance'. Jack ('Pal') Smurch is a charmless and arrogant aviator (in contrast to the real-life gentlemen-aviators Lindbergh and Byrd), who sets out to be the first to circumnavigate the globe by air, solo.

While the flight was underway, 'the accounts of the epoch-making flight touched rather lightly upon the aviator himself. This was not because facts about the hero as a man were too meagre but because they were too complete'. Reporters discovered his mother to be rude, his father in jail, his younger brother on the run from the reformatory: 'It was of course impossible to reveal the facts, for a tremendous popular feeling in favour of the young hero had sprung up, like a grass fire, when he was halfway across Europe'. Smurch, it is discovered, once knifed his head teacher and, when caught stealing an altar cloth, bashed the sacristan over the head with a pot of Easter lilies. When Smurch returns he is rushed, after a rapturous reception, into seclusion so that a committee of dignitaries can 'instruct him in the ethics and behaviour of heroism'. Smurch does not acquiesce:

> 'Youse guys' he said – and the *Times* man winced – 'Youse guys can tell the cock-eyed world dat I put it over on Lindbergh, see? Yeh – an made an ass o' them two frogs'. The 'two frogs' was a reference to a pair of gallant French fliers who, in attempting a flight only halfway around the world, had, two weeks before, unhappily been lost at sea. The *Times* man was bold enough, at this point, to sketch out for Smurch the accepted formula for interviews in cases of this kind; he explained that there should be no arrogant statements belittling the achievements of other heroes, particularly heroes of foreign nations. 'Ah, the hell with that,' said Smurch. 'I did it, see? I did it an' I'm talkin' about it.' And he did talk about it.
>
> (Thurber 1963)

But the newspapers conspire to produce a sanitised version. 'My achievement has been, I fear, slightly exaggerated,' the *Times* man's article had him protest with a modest smile. Eventually they resolve the dilemma of the unmarketable hero by pushing him out of the window, passing the event off as a tragic accident.[8]

Thurber draws our attention to the distinction between the deed and the celebration and thus to a difference between hero and star – the heroic deed has an existence separate and distinct from its circulation, stardom depends on circulation, on representation, on telling, on narrativisation. Nowadays, of course, the publicists would have sought a way to market Smurch successfully, whilst the tabloids would have given merciless exposure to the scurrilous aspects of Smurch, his past and his family. Arrogance is now a well-tried marketing technique from Gorgeous George the wrestler, who inspired Muhammad Ali's 'I am the Greatest' show-boating, through to 'Prince' Naseem. Yet the tensions between the expectations of those wanting a role model (sport administrators, sponsors, some journalists, and maybe some parents) and those for whom sport is an entertaining soap opera produce conflicting pulls in which controversy and respectability are the poles. The careers of Ian Botham, Alex Higgins, Mike Tyson, Darryl Strawberry, Paul Gascoigne and Dennis Rodman provide examples of the ways in which controversy fascinates the public and panics the sporting establishment. Indeed, the public fascination with the combative, dramatic, exciting and unpredictable elements of sport is an important part of the dynamic, as Jean Rafferty identifies in her discussion of the media presentation of sport stars:

> The post match press conference is a sadistic invention anyway. We're such hypocrites about modern sport, demanding sportsmanship, civilised manners, conformity to rules, when all the time what we like best are the glimpses of more primitive emotions, the Bothams and Conors of the world going berserk and winning matches on a great surge of animal aggression, the adrenalin-lifted performances of losers struggling to survive. We'd be disturbed in real life to be confronted by such raw emotions but they excite us when they're caged behind an eighteen inch television screen. The post match interview is just another part of the fiction that sport is for gentlemen. It implies that competitors, after going through a prolonged ordeal of emotional stress, should be prepared to come in and explain themselves afterwards.
>
> (Rafferty 1983: 128)

Rafferty's book portrays the world of snooker, and no television sport has illustrated so clearly how much of the appeal of sport is down not simply to the struggle to win and lose, but also to the contrasting nature of the characters involved, as ex-*Observer* editor Donald Trelford suggests:

> Snooker could have been designed for the TV screen, down to the rounded corners on the table. The camera not only captures the colours of the balls and the subtle texture of the play in its entirety, unlike the larger arenas of soccer or cricket; it also catches the moods and personalities of the players, the telltale twitches or swagger as the game develops, building up their characters in a national soap opera. And the cast is suitably colourful too. No scriptwriter could have invented the wild Irish gun-slinger or the Tooting tearaway, both with kamikaze tendencies; the huge Canadian bear with an epic thirst for lager; his compatriot with the cool air of a riverboat gambler, settling down for the heat of the night; the tall tense Englishman with the Samurai's self-discipline and dedication; the Welsh Dracula, the Prince of Darkness, the man of many masks.
>
> (Trelford 1986: 12)

Despite the denial above, of course these characters in a way did have scriptwriters. The Welsh Dracula and the riverboat gambler are products of the media's ability in vision to confront us with their giant faces in moments of tension whilst, verbally, aspects of their appearance and character are highlighted. It was this characterisation that made snooker. After Higgins won the World Championship in 1972, according to commentator Clive Everton, snooker was never the same again. Trelford relates that:

The image so carefully fostered by Joe Davis was transformed utterly. This thin, pale, hollow-cheeked ex-jockey was something new to the professional game, cutting through its genteel pretensions like a swordsman. Apart from George Best, Higgins's idols were Muhammad Ali and Lester Piggott, men who went their own way and in the fashionable argot of the time, did their own thing. 'Suddenly' as one paper put it, 'snooker is trendy'. Higgins styled himself 'the people's champion', wisely abandoning an earlier promotional idea that he be billed as Alexander the Great. He had Che Guevara posters on his walls. He carried around with him the air of the pool-room shark, the hustler (a world made familiar to people at the time by the Paul Newman film), the matador or the lone silent gunslinger of the Old Wild West.

(Trelford 1986: 90)

The contrived intertextuality and self-consciousness about stardom, and the production of a discourse about star as lone genius are clear here both in the description and in the marketing strategies described. Stardom is a form of social production in which the professional ideologies and production practices of the media aim to win and hold our attention by linking sporting achievement and personality in ways which have resonances in popular common sense. The heightened drama of major sport events often involves three features associated with the structure of heroic narrative – separation or departure; trials and victories of initiation; return and reintegration within society. Stars and teams competing in events like the Olympic Games, the World Cup, Test Cricket Series, or Boxing title fights go into a period of training away from society, they travel to the event, they endure testing against the world's best, and then return triumphant (the hero's welcome) to be absorbed back into society.

Star image is a social product, the result of a set of institutional structures, production practices, representational conventions and the relations of production and consumption. This process has a historical formation and the current discursive formation at any moment is always a complex amalgam of dominant, residual and emergent cultural elements. Richard Dyer writes that 'Star biographies are devoted to the notion of showing us the star as he or she really is. Blurbs, introductions, every page assures us that we are being taken 'behind the scenes', 'beneath the surface', 'beyond the image', 'there where the truth resides' Dyer 1979: 11). But of course stars are radically unknowable – we have virtually no unmediated contact with them. Representations of them are heavily conventionalised. Those who construct profiles of them do so according to well-established professional practices. Indeed, the more heavily represented the star, the more any possibility of access to a 'real' seems to recede.

Berger famously commented that 'men act, women appear' (1972), and it is striking that men in representation are very often doing something. They are rarely just there for our gaze, objectified. In order to legitimate the gaze, they are going about their business and they just happen to have been apprehended. This 'business' often involves sport – carrying a tennis racket, a sports bag, or casually bouncing a basketball. Dyer comments that in the portrayals of many male stars – Clark Gable, Humphrey Bogart, Paul Newman, Steve McQueen – sporting activity is a major, perhaps the major, element in their image; they are defined above all as people for whom having uncomplicated fun is paramount, and this is explicitly carried over into their reported attitude to work. But equally, 'work isn't important, it's just something you do so as to have the wherewithal to play polo, sail yachts, race cars' (Dyer 1987: 7). A process of mutual reinforcement is at work here in which two discursive systems – masculinity and sport – do not simply feed each other, but support each other. Dyer notes that with recent stars (Clint Eastwood, Harrison Ford) there is a tendency to either adopt a send-up tongue-in-cheek quality, or a hard desolate, alienated quality 'as if the values of masculine physicality are harder to maintain straight-facedly and unproblematically in an age of microchips and a large scale growth (in the USA) of women in traditionally male occupations' (*ibid.*: 12).

Dyer's work on stars suggests that we need to understand star images both as textual and as social. Stars signify, but the forms that that signification can take are socially shaped. Transformations of the media industry, which provides the dynamic in the shaping process, in turn transform the nature of stardom. Charles Critcher (1979) analysed the processes of change working to transform football in the post-war era. He sketched out a periodised model of cultural identity which divided football stars into four types:

1   traditional/located;
2   transitional/mobile;
3   incorporated/embourgeoised;
4   superstars/dislocated.

1 Traditional/located were those players (such as Stanley Matthews, Tom Finney, Tommy Lawton) who remained embedded in the working-class communities from which they came and both represented/drew upon values of traditional respectable working-class culture.

2 Transitional/mobile was the new affluence that footballers could attain following the abolition of the maximum wage rule in 1961 that enabled a greater degree of social mobility, but many players retained a cultural working-classness. Bobby Charlton, for example, was a 'working class gentleman who could live like one. Arthur Hopcraft called him "the classic working class hero who has made it to glamour and nob hill"' (Hopcraft, quoted in Critcher 1979).

3 Incorporated/embourgeoised represented the new opportunities that came with greater affluence and social mobility that made some footballers 'self-conscious participants in the process of their own embourgeoisement' (Critcher 1979). Critcher's examples included Alan Ball, Bobby Moore, Kevin Keegan and Trevor Francis.

4 Superstars/dislocated   were players of great talent who were unable to negotiate and manage the dislocation produced by these transformations. Remaining
an ordinary working-class bloke was no longer an option (as the career of
Gascoigne indicated all too sadly), while incorporation and embourgeoisement
was resisted, or could not be attained. Examples of this type included were
George Best, Alan Hudson, Charlie George, Peter Osgood, Rodney Marsh and
Stan Bowles.

George Best is the archetypal dislocated football hero whose talent, personality
and background were insufficient to withstand the pressures, both on and off
the field (Critcher 1979). Critcher thought that the crisis of superstar would be
short-lived; as expectations became clearer and more rationalised, players would
learn to tread the path of incorporation. While many present-day footballers do
indeed embrace embourgeoisement, there are still plenty who occupy the dislocated category. Indeed, while Critcher's types are based around a model of
transition, they still work well as a typology for examining sport stardom.[9] The
model draws our attention to the relation between the social position of the
performer, processes of social change at work transforming that place, the new
economic power of the media sport industry and the symbolic power of representation. However, as the media sports industry grew in power and as
representations of sport assumed a greater cultural centrality from the 1970s
onwards, media representations of stars acquired a greater power to shape
perceptions. The comparison of image and reality, of represented star and real
person, becomes problematic when all we are dealing with is layer upon layer of
mediation. It is in this sense that the work of the media in selecting, in framing,
in focusing, and, above all, in narrativising the lives of sport stars, is a work of
construction and production. Meanings emerge precisely from the productive
representational practices of the media, and not simply from the inherent characteristics of the star represented. The next chapter examines this process of
narrativisation in greater detail.

5 Narrativity and biography

> In this book, Joe Louis tells his own story. From the share-croppers cabin to the top of the world. The fights. The money. The women. All the triumphs, all the tragedy.
>
> (Louis 1978)

> World Cup Woe; One of the lads, briefly; Cardiff Catastrophe; The Ecstasy; And the Agony; Guilty ... Until proved Guilty; Guilty Again; Final Rehearsal; The Greatest Game; World Cup Knockout; Wine Women and Song; Ooh La La!; Mr Arrogant; The Best Lost Weekend; Captain Again briefly; Back to the Future.
>
> (Selection of chapter titles from biography of Will Carling (Norrie 1993))

If stars are the central figures of sport representation, it is only through transforming their doings into the form of stories that they come to signify. The image of sport star is part of the domain of the mythic, in the Barthesian sense of the word. As Silverstone suggests, the mythic dimension of culture contains traditional stories and actions

> whose source is the persistent need to deny chaos and create order. It contributes to the security of social and cultural existence. The mythic is a world apart, but it is also close at hand. It acts as a bridge between the everyday, and the transcendent, the known and the unknown, the sacred and the profane.
>
> (Silverstone 1981: 70)

Sport is an organised and ritualised activity, that clearly contributes to the domain of the mythic. How, though, is the mythic constructed? We need to examine the time and space of sport, and the time and space of media sport. What is the nature of the pleasures of spectator sport and how is the time and space of performance organised?

Time can be understood here as 'moment', as 'period', as 'memory', as 'scarce commodity', and as 'era'. Time can be the moment when the golden memory was created – the winning goal in the Matthews' final, England's winning goal in the 1966 World Cup, Sebastian Coe winning gold in Moscow,

Ali knocking out Foreman in 1974. Such moments are instantaneous at the time of happening and immortal in the space of memory – constantly retold, reprinted and rescreened. Time can also be the period of performance; much sport is reduced to statistical time – in Brohm's memorable phrase, sport is a 'prison of measured time' (Brohm 1978). Bannister's 'four-minute mile' was the staging of the breaking of a barrier, a barrier both arbitrary and imaginary, yet laden with great mythic force. Time is also constituted as memory – as the past, the 'time when ...'. It is the material of anecdote, bar chat and reminiscence – 'do you remember the time ... ?' As such it also provides the material of sporting cultural capital, so effortlessly acquired, distributed and used by men. Indeed, men often react with considerable suspicion to women who have acquired this capital. Time can be a scarce commodity, about to run out altogether – time is limited, short, running out, there are minutes to go, seconds to go. We are in overtime, extra time, injury time. Indeed, the very scarceness of time can greatly add to the dramatic value of incidents that occur when time is at its shortest – for instance, Manchester United's two goals in the last minute of the 1999 European Champions Cup Final to win the game 2–1. Time can also refer to an era, usually a 'golden era' – the time of the great heavyweights, the Edwardian summer of cricket. The instantaneous magic moments and the golden memories of eras each enhance the other. The moment fixes the star in memory – his/her performance and our memory of it.

The space of the sport performance is important too. Usually this means the place of the arena – demarcated otherness. Arenas are closed and separate (see Daney 1978; Bale 1982, 1992). They constitute a special space, outside and separate from the normal flow of existence. The space of the arena is other, it is somewhere else, exotic, far removed from ordinary life. The space of the event – the track, the pitch, the course – is a demarcated space within the arena, in which the star can perform. Mythic power attaches itself to particular places; there is a sense of place that gives particular venues – Wembley and the 'twin towers', Hampden Park and the Hampden roar, the Santiago Bernabeu stadium of Real Madrid, Yankee Stadium, 'the house that Ruth built' – their specific resonance and aura. Mythic power is to be found in more focused form at the junction of time and place – Botham's Headingley Test in 1981, Ali's 'rumble in the jungle' in Zaire in 1974, George Best's performance in Lisbon in 1966, the Dempsey–Carpentier fight in Boyle's Acres in 1921.

However, time and space are, crucially, mediated through media representation, and it is in the media that the crucial interface between the space and time of the sporting event, popular memory, the reproduction of sporting capital and audience pleasure takes place. Media sport is organised around time – the time of the results, the previews, the live transmissions and the highlights. There is a routinised segmentation of schedule in which the week is punctuated by its regular moments – *Grandstand*, *Match of the Day*, and *Sportsnight*. The theme music of the Radio 5 show *Sports Report* is an evocative symbol of the importance of time, heralding in this case the classified football results (with, the timeless James Alexander Gordon).[1] Evening papers arrive, in provincial towns, if no longer in London, with results and reports.

Sport has its distinct spaces – the sports pages, sports news on television and radio, and the mushrooming trade in pull-out sport sections. Sports news still has an other-worldly character – to consume it is to move into an alternative parallel universe with its own values, its own institutions, structures and practices. Indeed, this is part of its pleasure – it is a time out of ordinary life – a gateway to the mythic. If this gateway is given a structure by media representation it is the structure of narrative form. The sporting contest itself, while not a narrative, has a structure homologous to that of narrative form. Specifically, all sport contests, like narratives, pose an enigma (who will win) and offer a resolution.

Stories are one of the means by which a society provides structured maps of meaning of its past, its traditions, its image of itself, and the nature of social relations within it. Narratives have characters and a set of codes for setting in place the deeds of leading characters. Narrative, though, is not limited to the fictional sphere. The media, in order to make events meaningful, characteristically turn them into narratives. This process of narrativisation is particularly striking in the coverage of the events of sport, already prestructured with their own hermeneutic code.[2] Sport coverage is dominated by stars, who, as the bearers of this process of narrativisation, play a central role in the strategies employed by media organisations to win and hold audiences. The work the media performs on sport in turning it into representational form is essentially that of narrativisation – it works upon the materials of the sporting contest and organises them into narrative form. Narrativisation involves the recomposition of space, place and time (see Whannel 1992). This work takes diverse forms – the structuring effect of commentary, the addition of preview and post-mortem material, the individualisation, personalisation, sensationalisation and caricature of the tabloid press, the career narration of sporting biography and the long running soap-opera form through which the sagas of characters like Mike Tyson or Paul Gascoigne are narrated.[3]

Some of the principles of narrative analysis as outlined by Propp (1984), Barthes (1974) and Genette (1980) are of value in the analysis of the narrativisation of sport.[4] Propp reduces all folk tales to seven spheres of action and thirty-one fixed elements or 'functions'. The range of narrative functions in the narrativisation of careers in the biography of sport stars might include:

the emergence of a striking talent
the accomplishing of extraordinary feats
public celebration
secondary circulation of star image
displays of arrogance
a failure to deliver
public doubts
erratic behaviour

public scandal
failure
the hero redeemed by extraordinary performance
forgiveness
the power wanes

and then these last four have a tendency to repeat in the form of a loop until the extraordinary performances dry up, as they inevitably must. Indeed, precisely one of the reasons that the rise-and-fall hermeneutic structure tends to dominate in this field must be associated with inevitability of the loss of sporting powers. Such stories have no necessary resolution, apart from the inevitability of decline. One of the things that made the Cantona tale exceptional was his sudden unpredicted retirement while still at the height of his powers.[5] The structure of public reaction is interestingly formulaic – the media turn to the accredited primary definers – to old players, to managers, to celebrity fans, to celebrities in other fields, to the fans, to 'people in the street'. Hence, when Paul Gascoigne was dropped from the squad for the 1998 World Cup, Ian Botham was interviewed on television commenting on the pressures of stardom. These stories rapidly become pegs on which to hang other stories – for example, a Lynda Lee Potter homily about family life speculated about the possibility of Gascoigne in despair begging wife Sheryl for help, and her welcoming him back into her mothering arms. Others used it as a moral text on the dangers of drinking and indiscipline, whilst others again (Chris Evans, Danny Baker) rejected any notion of the responsibility of friends like themselves for Gascoigne's decline.

Genette (1980) distinguishes between narration (the act and process of telling a story) and narrative (what it is that is actually recounted). This permits us to distinguish, for example, between the narrative sequence of events that led to England winning the World Cup and the narration of those events in the film *Goal* (1966). There is a difference, in other words between 'recit' – the actual order of events in the text – and 'histoire' – the sequence in which those events actually occurred (Genette 1980; see also Eagleton 1983). The media narration of the events – the recit – leading up to Gascoigne's omission from the 1998 squad, was, like a detective story, partly a matter of uncovering. For example, on 4 June it was revealed in retrospect that three senior players had been unhappy about his appearance and had expressed these doubts to Hoddle. There is also a distinction between the tale, the telling, and the manner of telling – the narrative 'voice' can be personal or impersonal, present or absent, in the events of the story.[6] Sport stars are both producer and product; they are the providers of the magic moments and golden memories that allow their elevation into the heroic and mythic, and transformation from performer to product. The back-cover blurb for Joe Louis's book *My Life* proclaims:

> In the bright ring, the beautiful brown-skinned human fighting machine stalked his opponent. In the stadium darkness, the crowd screamed. Across

the nation, millions leaned towards their radios. Boxing had its king. America had its hero.

(Louis 1978)

Through the media, sport stars are turned into familiar figures, household names, but also into heroes, mythologised icons, producing an immense public desire to know the 'real' person. Yet, of course, they are radically unknowable – all we have is layers of discourse – and stars can only be 'known' through media representation. Two rather contrary processes can be detected in these processes of narrativisation: mythologisation and reinscription. Part of the mythologising process involves the attribution of magical powers or superhuman qualities, and a mystification of the 'presence' of the celebrity. Davis Miller recently wrote of Muhammad Ali:

> Even through the walls, his was the most elemental voice I'd heard; it was huge, melodic and sounded somehow eternal. Listening to it made me so nervous that I shook a little and felt that I needed to pee … no-one else on the planet looks quite like him. His skin is unmarked and without wrinkles and he glows in a way that cannot be seen in photographs or on television.
>
> (*Arena*, March 1997)

By reinscription, I mean the process whereby star biographies are constantly rewritten in the 'continuous present' – their lives are interpreted according to dominant concerns at the time of writing. Iconic status is always conferred in retrospect, and constantly reinscribed in accordance with dominant discursive patterns of specific moments. The image of figures such as George Best or Muhammad Ali is the result of the accumulation of these inscriptions in which some earlier traces have been obscured or erased, whilst others are etched in more deeply (see chapter 9). Best, celebrated at the height of his career, has had his fame overwritten, but not obscured by, his decline; Ali, vilified in the 1960s, has advanced through celebrity to sanctification. The past, far from being fixed, is constantly being reinvented. This process of reinscription – the constant rewriting of star biographies involves three related processes: the mobilisation of popular memory, selective tradition, and a process of writing history in the present. Representations of sport's past are constructed largely around magic moments in which popular memory is evoked. The oral transmission of mythologised moments and the media representational process operate in parallel here, each feeding off the other. In the process, some moments are gradually dropped from circulation, whilst others (Bannister's four-minute mile, Gazza's tears at the 1990 World Cup, Ali's defeat of Foreman in Zaire) remain in the pantheon of golden moments. There are four distinct cultural forms in which narrativisations of the lives of sports stars are produced:

1   Newspaper news stories. Where major news stories feature stars, they are often accompanied by brief resumés of the career so far. Such features,

often utilising photomontage, are characteristically framed in terms of the ups and downs of their careers to date.

2   Magazine profiles. Celebrity profiles, often seeking to reveal the domestic, the personal and the private, while situated in the present, frequently also include a short biographical resume. Profiles now appear in a wide variety of magazine contexts: newspaper magazine supplements, celebrity magazines, men's magazines and women's magazines.

3   Television previews of major sporting events. As stars and narrativisation are the two key elements in the way television sport hails its audience, the preview material preceding major events serves to suture these two elements – the narrative of the event to come, with its key hermeneutic question, Who will win?, and the narrative of the stars who may play a key role. In the process, elements of biographical narration of major figures are frequently included.

4   Biographies, autobiographies and biopics. Unlike the previous three forms, which typically occur in the middle of the career of a star, biographies, autobiographies and biopics present themselves as a summing up, a conclusion. Often, in fact, they appear after a moment of major success, which can be quite early in a star's career, but in many cases their appearance marks the climax of a career, although not necessarily the end.

In order to pursue the issue of narration I am going to focus on the example of sporting biographies. The 'recit' of sporting biographies tends to be predominantly chronological, except for the very common device of commencing with a peak moment, a moment of triumphant success. In the case of the brief resumés offered by newspaper, magazine and television journalism, major moments are typically chronological, and occasionally divided into categories such as 'highs' and 'lows'.

Most sporting autobiographies are written with the assistance of a professional writer, often a journalist, whose anonymity or low profile gives rise to the term 'ghost writer'. The ghost writer is producing, through collaboration, an auto-diagetic voice, in which writer poses as subject. In some instances, both subject and writer speak within the text. Mel Stein appears as a third-person character within his own biography of Paul Gascoigne (Stein 1996). Alex Higgins and his ghost writer Tony Francis both have passages in the first person in *Alex Through the Looking Glass* (Higgins 1986). Footballer Paul Merson's wife Lorraine contributes a chapter to his autobiography (Merson 1995), as does the wife of Ian Rush to *My Italian Diary* (Rush 1989). Some sporting 'autobiographies' contain first-person experiential accounts from the star and third-person descriptive passages from his ghost. In some cases a star has been used as the subject by someone of less prominent stature in order to enhance sales. Snooker player Jim Meadowcroft's *Higgins, Taylor and Me* (Meadowcroft 1986), football manager Peter Taylor's *With Clough by Taylor* (Taylor 1980) and coach of athlete Steve Ovett, Harry Wilson's *Running Dialogue* (Wilson

1982) are all instances in which a first-person narrative voice is the vehicle through which the life of a third-person subject is created.

As readers or as analysts, we can make few assumptions about who actually wrote the various passages in the above examples. Of greater significance is the structuring of voices in the text, and the consequent positioning of a reader as the recipient of an insider viewpoint. We can, however, make some deductions about the nature of collaborations in different examples. Sometimes the collaboration between subject and writer can be close, intense and prolonged, and this interaction is sometimes alluded to in the text; sometimes, by contrast, the ghost writer has detectably worked up a book from press cuttings and a few quick interviews. It is one of the jokes of the trade (cf. the parodic figure of Darren Tackle in *The Guardian*) that the sport star sees his autobiography for the first time at the press launch. However, this authorial sleight of hand, although possessing low cultural status, should not be condemned lightly, nor can its products be regarded as trivia. There is no necessary or absolute reason why this relation between sport star and writer should result in 'bad' writing. Some ghost-written books are rich in revelatory detail, but structured with the care of a competent and insightful 'professional' writer. As a young footballer, Terry Venables was urged by his ghost, Gordon Williams (scriptwriter for *Straw Dogs*, among other credits), to take up writing himself and as a result they collaborated on four novels, inventing the London-based detective, James Hazell (see Williams and Venables 1971; Yuill 1974, 1975, 1976; and Alvarado and Buscombe 1978).

However, several factors combine to produce a conventionalised and formulaic approach to the production of the sporting biography. The demands of the book trade for a product to be delivered quickly, to coincide with a major promotional opportunity, and the need of a journalist to produce the work rapidly, often while other commitments are fulfilled, tends to produce an over-reliance on the quick interview and the press-cutting archive. A cynical attitude to the exercise on the part of star, writer and publisher mitigates against analysis and insight. Some examples of the form are vacuous, banal and cliché-ridden. In such examples the chronological structure frequently peters out about halfway through the book, which is then typically padded out with chapters on 'favourite stars', 'managers I have known', and selections of 'my greatest world team' (to play, presumably in true schoolboy fantasy fashion, Mars). Such books may achieve initial sales, boosted by the prominence, visibility and success of the subject, but soon reappear in remainder shops, supermarket dump bins, second-hand book shops, charity shops and car boot sales.

It may be that the public expectation of the form is not high. Rowe (1992), has commented on the low status of sports writers amongst other journalists and, within the professional practices of sports journalism, low self-esteem and a tendency to accept the label 'hack' are not uncommon. Nevertheless, set against this, is the apparent substantial public appetite to 'know' more about the stars of the world of sporting celebrity. The cover of the autobiography of sports journalist Peter Wilson, *The Man They Couldn't Gag* (Wilson 1977) contains a still-life photograph which shows a battered Underwood typewriter, a glass of whisky on a box of cigars, a soda syphon and, strewn on top, photos showing the journalist with famous people. The cover links the elements of a stereotype journalist and the notion of inside knowledge, in which 'the man they couldn't gag' is seen as having privileged access to the stars.

Sport stars have a much greater visibility in the 1990s than was the case up to the 1950s. The growth of television has made the faces of stars recognisable to a much larger audience. The tabloidisation of the print media has eroded the old division between public and private spheres. Sport has always been presented in the media as a world apart – with its own sub-sections within newspapers and television news broadcasts. A great deal of sports journalism is self-reflexive and rooted in gossip – Eco has called it 'sports chatter' (Eco 1986). The prominence of 'celebrity' in both print and visual media has contributed to the familiarity of sport stars, even to non-sport fans. The speed of communication exchange has produced a tendency for single stories to dominate the media for brief periods (for example, stories on various occasions featuring stars like Mike Tyson, Paul Gascoigne). This greater visibility, along with the 'mystery' posed by celebrities – 'what are they really like' – in turn fuels a public 'desire to know' that can be addressed by the media as a point of appeal in celebrity profiles. The back cover of one biography of Paul Gascoigne promises

> here for the first time, is the *truth* behind the headlines, the *truth* behind the tears and tantrums – and the *truth* behind the struggles and successes, both on and off the field, for this remarkable footballing legend.
>
> (Stein 1996)

In fact the author Mel Stein (a lawyer), together with accountant Len Lazarus (who handles Gascoigne's business affairs), are not best placed to offer a disinterested discourse of 'truth'; nevertheless – and not surprisingly, given the fertile material available – they produce an engrossing narrative that contributes to the layers of discourse out of which our 'knowledge' of 'Gazza' is composed. Broadly, there seems to be two main formal approaches to the production of sporting biography. The 'golden success story' is most characteristic of narratives produced soon after an early triumphal achievement, whilst the account of 'ups and downs' is most characteristic of narratives produced at or near the end of a long career.

Golden success story

Biographies and autobiographies of this type are frequently tied to 'the big moment', a culminating triumph, setting the seal on a career, or on a rapid rise to the top. Many biographies, for commercial reasons, are written at the moment of triumph, so the final triumph tends to be the culmination of the book. In some cases, the big moment remains the central emblem for the fame of the subject, as in Roger Bannister's autobiography *First Four Minutes*, which relates his progression from taking up athletics to his becoming the first man to run a mile in less than four minutes (Bannister 1955). In other cases, it is the summary of achievements over a career that signifies golden success. For example, a biography of ice skater Gordie Howe lists his 732nd goal, his six NHL scoring records, six Hart Trophies and ten elections to the NHL All-Stars first team (Fischler 1967). A typical structure of this type of account starts with a taster of the 'major triumph' and then proceeds to a chronological account of the career, culminating in a triumphant moment, in this pattern:

> Major triumph – childhood – early prowess – being discovered – helpers – first successes – advancement – major triumph

Set-backs and failures tend to be marginalised, written about as the source of new determination, new challenges, and the provider of a forward impetus. 'Rags to riches' is a typical theme – Wayne Gretzky's autobiography is subtitled 'From the backyard rink to the Stanley Cup' (Gretzky and Taylor 1984). As with all non-fictional tales of success, as we know in advance that success is achieved, so our interests are engaged with other questions – How was it achieved? What went on behind the scenes? Has success made him happy? The autobiography of Enzo Ferrari makes this hermeneutic question explicit:

> So it is true that there have been changes. Have these been brought about, I sometimes ask myself, because I have at last realised my boyhood dreams? Have I done anything really worthwhile – or enough to make me satisfied? In order to find the answer to questions like these I have decided to write my memoirs.
>
> (Ferrari 1963)

More typically, though, the sporting biography focuses on the issues of how success was achieved and what went on behind the scenes, and anecdotes play a significant role in the construction of the story. A common variant of this narrative of 'golden success' features the 'rapid rise': the new kids on the block who leap rapidly from rags to riches. The celebration of youthful success and attention to newness is part of the neophiliac character of culture; the tendency to venerate the new, the trendy, the hip and the cool. In the 1998 World Cup, the established stardom of England striker Alan Shearer and the tabloid misadventures of Gascoigne and Sheringham became overwritten by the 'meteoric rise to stardom' of Michael Owen. In the 'rapid rise' narrative, a typical pattern of the narrative is:

> triumph – childhood – early prowess – first successes – advancement – successes – triumph

Problems and set-backs are typically marginalised, and there is a focus on a rapid – indeed, almost magical – rise, with the role of helpers often marginalised.

The ups and downs

In contrast, the 'ups-and-downs' narrative has, as a typical pattern, an oscillation between good times and bad:

> successes – failures – successes – set-backs – successes – problems – successes

This form is more commonly used in accounts of those who didn't quite achieve the heights, and in those who did but who were also the subject of scandals, or in those whose 'genius' is balanced against their 'indiscipline'. Narration typically oscillates between highs and lows, often with no major triumph as conclusion. Rugby player Will Carling's biography was described in a review, reproduced on the paperback edition book jacket as a 'warts and all account'. The sample from the forty-one chapter titles at the start of this chapter suggests the character of this typical oscillation between highs and lows (see Norrie 1993). The need to keep sport stars in the public eye, to sustain their marketability, is often a factor in the generation of ups-and-downs narratives, although few are built around such a long cycle as that of George Foreman, whose recent book *By George* recounts the story of a man, still boxing, twenty years after the Zaire fight with Ali (Foreman 1995). One variant of the ups-and-downs form is the 'rise-and-fall' narrative, which contrasts the promise of the first half of a career with the decline of the second half:

> Childhood – early prowess – being discovered – first successes – advancement – successes – failures – set-backs – problems

Decline is inevitable in all sporting careers. Sporting prowess inevitably fades, often at a fairly young age and, typically, stars tend to go on past their prime, retiring only when the evidence of decline is there for all to see. Not surprisingly, the rise-and-fall structure is more common in biography than in autobiography, most stars being reluctant to confront the details of their waning years, although when the decline is part of the tale the public wants to hear, commercial pressure may prevail. The rise-and-fall rhetoric is well represented on the back cover of Joe Louis's autobiography with its various motifs – log cabin to White House, the fame, money and sex, the decline, and the golden memories:

> In this book, Joe Louis tells his own story. From the share-croppers cabin to the top of the world. The fights. The money. The women. All the triumphs, all the tragedy. Now he is gone. They say champions never come back. But Joe Louis comes back in this book. And helps us remember what greatness is all about.
>
> (Louis 1978)

Sporting biographies always mobilise a nostalgia for the past, when sporting performance acquires an aura of greatness severed from its time. The film biography of Ali, for example, built around his fight with Foreman in Zaire, was entitled *When We Were Kings*. *The Babe Ruth Story* (Ruth 1992) is a tale of golden success followed by decline into illness. The rise-and-fall structure is also a well-established fictional format. Sports journalist, Brian Glanville's novel, *The Rise of Gerry Logan*, mimics the form of the rise-and-fall biography (Glanville 1963). *Fallen Hero*, adapted from a Granada TV series by Peter May (May 1979), charts the post-injury life of a rugby league player and bears on the cover the caption 'All his life he had been a star: now he was nothing'. The uncertainties of sport sometimes mean that this form of writing can result in premature obituaries. In retrospect, the defeat of Ali by Joe Frazier in 1971 was merely one more chapter in the long story, but at the time it was seen as a possible full stop and one that signified the end of the 1960s. *Sports Illustrated*'s cover proclaimed it 'The End of the Ali Legend', and Hunter S. Thompson described the fight as 'A very painful experience in every way, a proper end to the sixties' (Thompson 1972: 27); even though some of Ali's glory moments were in the 1970s, his eventual defeat by Leon Spinks in 1978 was still constructed by Hunter Thompson as linked to the ageing of the sixties generation as 'the last great prince of the sixties went out in a blizzard of pain, shock and angry confusion' (Thompson 1980: 581). The rise-and-fall biography reveals the frailty of stardom and, as with Botham, Higgins and Gascoigne, sooner or later the wayward star is bound to fall off the tightrope – indeed, this vulnerability is part of the voyeuristic appeal. As Parkinson wrote of George Best, 'he was finding it more and more difficult to define the line between his social activities and his career as an athlete' (Parkinson 1975: 75). One of the more remarkable examples of the form is Frank Deford's biography of tennis player Bill Tilden, in which, after telling the story of Tilden's success in the 1920s, he goes on to narrate a story in which

> in retrospect, Tilden is one of the most tragic of the immortals. Urbane, proud and haughty, he could not make real friends of his contemporaries of either sex. Instead, he sought the company of small boys, always striving to find in one the son and successor he could never have. Finally snubbed and barred as a result of his criminal convictions for homosexuality, Tilden was reduced sometimes to pleading 'Does anyone – *anyone* – want a game?'.
>
> (Deford 1977)

Another variant of the ups and downs format is the 'critical biography' produced by those with a cynical, negative or jaundiced view of the subject. In this variant, a typical pattern tends to foreground the problems and weaknesses of the star:

successes – failures – set-backs – successes – problems

The accounts usually acknowledge the success but identify the failures and problems as the key to the subject. Don Mosey's biography of Ian Botham tips its hand clearly as early as the contents page – which lists chapters entitled 'The Flaws', 'The Recluse', 'The Misguided Loyalist' and 'The Waster' (Mosey 1986).

The 'diary' format is a strictly chronological variant of the 'ups-and-downs' form, invariably with a limited time frame – a week, a year, a season. It is characteristically episodic – dealing with a distinct career phase. Football manager Lawrie McMenemy produced *The Diary of A Season* (McMenemy 1979), footballer Ian Rush wrote *My Italian Diary* about his less than happy stay in Italy (Rush 1989), American Football coach Vince Lombardi wrote the diary of a week in *Run to Daylight* (Lombardi 1963). The point of appeal of such texts is the offer of privileged access to the 'private' thoughts of a participant as events develop. An exemplar of this form was the book by the then Millwall footballer Eamon Dunphy, *Only a Game*, in which the collapse of Dunphy's own initial pre-season optimism, Millwall's promotion chances and Dunphy's career prospects, within four months of the start of the season provided a very different view of a footballer's life than that available through the more anodyne clichés of back-page journalism and post-match television interview (Dunphy 1976).

In all these formats, the narrativised careers of sport stars are told and retold, constantly reinscribed into popular memory, so that even those who never saw them compete are familiar with the tales of a Muhammad Ali or a George Best.[7] The power of media narrativisation of events in the 'real' world lies precisely in the ways in which it makes them meaningful, makes them signify and enables the linking of individual, biography and structure. The stories of sport stars and social concerns expressed through discourses of masculinity and morality are brought together in the process of narrativisation.

In order to situate these formal practices of media representation in the wider context, it is necessary in the next chapter to return to a consideration of discourses of masculinity, this time with specific reference to sporting cultures.

6 Sporting masculinities

There is no normal boy in the world who doesn't thrill at the call of outdoor life;
who doesn't like to play football or baseball, golf or tennis, who doesn't like to
camp out, fly kites, have a camera, go fishing and swimming, shoot a rifle, jump,
run or sail a boat, or dream of riding in an aeroplane that will take him far above
the trees he climbs and the birds that have eluded his reach.

(*The Boys Book of Sports*, Rice 1917: vii)

The 'normal boy' here is represented as active, outdoor and sporting, and
although these are still central elements in that formation that Connell called
hegemonic masculinity (Connell 1995), it is hard to imagine nowadays that a
concept like 'the normal boy' could be taken totally straight. The widespread
awareness of the concept of the social construction of reality, the rise of a feminist critique of masculinity and postmodern self-referentiality combine to make
everyone far more sensitive to the artificiality of the 'natural' and the 'normal'.
Yet part of the ideological work that is performed through the representation of
sport stars is precisely to do with the normalisation of hegemonic masculinity
and the marginalisation of alternative masculinities. Images and representations
of sport characteristically involve contestation and categorisation, marginalisation and incorporation of elements of masculinity.

One strand of British individualism was constructed precisely in opposition
to team games. The three main characters in Kipling's school story, *Stalky &
Co.*, are individualists who despise the dull conformity and submission to discipline of the team game ethos. Their world is one of self-reliance,
resourcefulness and a degree of the dare-devil. These notions can be seen as
linking such diverse elements as the schoolboy fiction of Kipling, Baden-Powell
and the scout movement, the writing and career of T.E. Lawrence, Kurt Hahn
and the spartan Gordonstoun school, the Duke of Edinburgh's Award Scheme,
the Outward Bound movement, and the 'individual' heroics of figures like
Edmund Hilary and Francis Chichester. Such individualised concepts of physical
self-reliance frame an alternative form of physical culture that saw its embodiment in the post-war era in the Outward Bound movement and the Duke of
Edinburgh's award scheme. In fictional form, this individual self-reliance finds
expression in characters as diverse as Dick Barton, Sexton Blake, Biggles, Dan

Dare and James Bond. It links exploration, colonialism, imperialist adventure and romanticist notions of the individual against society (see Dawson 1994; Rutherford 1997). Kipling's Stalky and his friends have a contempt for the games players in their school, preferring individual self-reliance and initiative. Kipling was sceptical about the supposed 'civilising influence' of cricket on native populations.[1]

The athleticism and muscular Christianity of the nineteenth-century English public schools was originally built around a reappropriation and reconstruction of Greek idealism, and proposed the construction of rounded and harmonious development of mind and body. However, the cult of athleticism rapidly became an end in itself. In turn the emergence of an athleticism sufficient unto itself sharpened the division between the sporting Philistine and the non-sporting aesthete that has continued to mark the peculiar development of English cultural life. The schoolboy fiction of writers, such as Frank Richards, constantly counterposes the hearty sporting type with the more aberrant and slightly foppish character. Archetypal fat boy Billy Bunter, too, serves to show-case the muscular normality of a Harry Wharton. Orwell's famous summary of the world of Greyfriars portrays it as a cosy world:

> sitting down to tea after an exciting game of football which was won by the odd goal in the last half minute … After tea we shall sit round the study fire having a good laugh at Billy Bunter and discussing the team for next week's match against Rookwood. Everything is safe, solid and unquestionable. Everything will be the same for ever and ever.
>
> (Orwell 1961)

But it is also a world that constantly and brutally marks distinctions between insiders and outsiders. Turner highlights the contradiction between sporting and non-sporting modes of behaviour highlighted in schoolboy fiction:

> Any historian of the remote future relying exclusively on old volumes of boys' magazines for his knowledge of the British way of life in the early twentieth century – notably the nineteen-twenties and nineteen-thirties – will record that the country was the battleground of an unending civil war between a small vigorous race known as Sportsmen and a large, sluggish and corrupt race known as Slackers.
>
> (Turner 1976: 273)

However, the hearty sportsmen, far from being a vigorous minority, constituted in English masculine culture a hegemonic group who contributed to the consti-tution of an anti-intellectual philistinism that has served to oppress generations of boys not drawn to the sporting field. Noel Coward, a non-sporting aesthete par excellence, described the repressed sexuality in the world of schoolboy fiction, as represented by Frank Richards, with customary arch insight:

They were awfully manly, decent fellows, Harry Wharton and Co. and no suggestion of sex, even in its lighter forms, ever sullied their conversation. Considering their ages, their healthy-mindedness was almost frightening.

(quoted in Turner 1976: 232)

The dissenters from this world of hearty and muscular heterosexual camaraderie are not simply outsiders, but typically loners, portrayed as eccentric, aberrant, inadequate, decadent or dangerous. Recent analyses of masculinity have highlighted the oppressive nature of this hearty hegemony, but a critical perspective on sporting masculinity is, of course, nothing new. Writing in the 1930s, Robert Benchley deplored the effects of 'The Boys Camp Business':

When your boy comes home from camp he is what is known in the circular as 'manly and independent'. This means that when you go swimming with him he pushes you off the raft and jumps on your shoulders until you are good as drowned – better in fact.

Benchley offers a different notion of maleness in proposing opening his own camp for 'manly' boys:

and by the word 'manly', I will mean 'like men'. In other words, everyone shall sleep just as long as he wants, and when he does get up there will be no depleting 'setting-up' exercises. The day will be spent just as the individual camper gosh-darned pleases. No organised 'hikes' – I'd like a word on the 'hike' problem some day too – no camp spirit, no talk about Tomorrows Manhood and *no pushing people off rafts.*

(Benchley 1970)

Benchley proposed here a distinction between 'sporty' boys and more sensible 'men'. Other male eyes also took a jaundiced view of public school athleticism. In Waugh's *Decline and Fall*, 'the hero athletes of the school are all confirmed cheaters' (Watson 1992: 156). The account of the night of the Bollinger Club dinner at the start of *Decline and Fall*, as seen through the eyes of two dons, offers a stark view of the philistinism of public school life, in which those students interested in art or music are portrayed as targets for the hearty oafs of the Bollinger Club (Waugh 1992: 11). Evelyn Waugh also highlights the sexual repression involved in public school athleticism in the episode in *Brideshead Revisited* in which a bunch of hearties approach the foppish and exotic Anthony Blanche with the intention of throwing him in the fountain (Waugh 1949: 36–8). *The Loom of Youth* (Waugh 1917), a novel by Evelyn Waugh's brother, Alec, contained 'the first public representation of homosexual acts between schoolboys, as opposed to the ardent but chastely romantic friendships of earlier fiction' (Watson 1992: 154). Watson writes that 'Athletic skills gradually win Caruthers rewards and esteem on the public school battleground. He prudently conceals an interest in literature'. As a result of *The Loom of Youth*, the names of

Alec Waugh and his father were removed from the roll of old boys at Sherborne, and younger brother Evelyn was refused admittance (Watson 1992: 154). More recently, in the 1970s, Viv Stanshall of the Bonzo Dog Band wrote of the repressive effects of public school sporting masculinity in his song 'The Odd Boy', in which he comments sardonically that 'its an odd boy who doesn't like sport' (Stanshall, 'The Odd Boy', on the album *Keynsham*).

There have, of course, been many casualties of the homophobia of sporting masculinity, not least Oscar Wilde, who eventually came to grief as a result of a disastrous court case against the sporting peer Lord Queensberry. If this culture stigmatised non-sporting men and gay men, it also marginalised women. Sport was for the boys, with the role of women decorative and limited to the roles of admirer and provider of cricket teas. This late nineteenth-century image was being recycled in Lillywhite's advertising during the 1980s, featuring groups of young white men with sports equipment, with, as centre point, an attractive woman in clothing that proclaimed her non-involvement in sport. As John Berger commented on the representation of the genders – men act, women appear.

In the developing field of sport sociology during the 1970s, masculinity was occasionally marked as a concern, but usually only as a minor one. Three of the earliest book-length critiques of the social practices of sport all showed a concern with sport and sexual repression, and the influence of Freud via Frankfurt School Marxism can be detected in the work of Brohm (1978), Hoch (1972) and Vinnai (1973). The impact of feminism helped to generate a growing field of analysis of sport that challenged the cosy masculine hegemony within sport sociology, and the expansion of sport-related feminist scholarship prompted some more critical examinations of masculinity and sport.[2] By the second half of the 1980s, sporting masculinities were the focus of greater attention.[3] An emphasis in analysis on the constructed nature of masculinities required attention to the various modes of representing men (see Easthope 1990; Kirkham and Thumin 1993, 1995; Craig 1992). Recent work on sporting masculinities has focused on portrayals of male bodies and descriptions of male exploits (see Sabo and Jansen 1992; White and Gillett 1994).

For many men, sport provides a bounded universe, part real, part fantasy, in which fantasies of the perfection of performance can be exercised. George Plimpton recalls that James Thurber once wrote that the majority of American males put themselves to sleep by striking out the batting order of the New York Yankees. Plimpton records his own conversation with *Sports Illustrated* editor Sid James in which he expanded on the fantasy, imagining such a dreamer suddenly called upon to pitch in a major league game (Plimpton 1962: 17).[4] Here, sport memory and sport fantasy come together, providing a magical arena for masculine performance in which the fantasist can be both performer and audience. Sport, in this sense, is a form of magical performance in which, despite its manifest physicality, sexuality has been masked and marginalised. Encounter with female sexuality can be erased and encounter with homoerotic desire can be repressed. But, to preserve these fragile barriers and to police heterosexual masculinity, cultures of hardness develop.

Hardness

Roger Bannister, writing of adolescence, portrayed physical stress and challenge as character building, advocating 'demanding activity that tests to the limit our bodies as well as our mind' (Bannister 1955: 187). Of his own world record mile run, he wrote 'My body had long since exhausted all its energy but it went on running just the same. The physical overdraft came only from greater will power' (*ibid.*: 164). Grantland Rice (1956: 162) bemoaned the fact that 'there aren't any iron men in sport today' and devoted a chapter to celebrating those stars who were big and strong and had stamina. An emphasis on hardness is not a new element in discourses of sport, but one striking consequence of the shifting forms of gender relations during the 1970s and 1980s appeared to be a reassertion of hardness.

Relations between men and women in representation have gone through a series of transitions. Hollywood romance began to appear old fashioned in the context of the women's movement of the 1970s. Mainstream Hollywood cinema turned to buddy movies in which women were marginalised. By the 1980s, new male characters typically lacked even buddies and were powerful, isolated and invulnerable. The machoisation of masculine culture in the 1980s constitutes an example of an emergent form of masculinity. Whilst aggression is identified as an element of masculinity in many social and historical contexts, the forms it takes, the degree of approval it gains and the extent to which it is constrained by social convention are socially and historically specific. Hearn and Morgan argue that 'many of the central concerns of men and masculinities are directly to do with bodies – war and sport are two obvious examples' (1990: 10). Gerhard Vinnai wrote, of the socialisation of boys, that

> toughness, as an expression of virility, is drummed into them on the football field. The importance of rock-hard muscles, absence of sentimentality in harsh duels, acceptance of frequently painful injuries and ability to consume vast quantities of beer after the game ... characterises the moral atmosphere among the sportsmen.
>
> (Vinnai 1973: 74)

Some of the key ingredients of a particular form of sporting masculinity are specified here – being a rock-hard, unsentimental heavy drinker. Lasch (1980) argues that, rather than a form of escapism, this is a form of intensity. As Barthel (1992) points out, sport provides a separate sphere for the acting of this intensity, a form of masculine proving ground.

Writing in 1983, Humphries and Metcalf highlighted the way in which the male audience was increasingly 'bombarded with extreme images of the sexual male'. They cited movie stars like Clint Eastwood, and male rock vocalists, but by the 1980s such images were augmented by those in films such as *Terminator, Top Gun* and *Blade-Runner.* Humphries and Metcalf's analysis, written at the start of the 1980s, was prescient. The 1980s were very much the decade of ultra hard macho and the rise of the cyborg. Five film series (*Die Hard, Lethal Weapon, Predator, Rambo* and *Robocop*) accounted for fourteen popular films in the genre, with *Rocky* providing another five films. The fusion of machine and flesh, or flesh made invincible, represents in almost parodic form the desire to transform the male body into a muscular invulnerability. Rutherford makes a distinction between 'new man' and 'retributive man'. Retributive man represents the struggle to reassert a traditional masculinity, a tough independent authority, as in the *Rambo* films. Retributive man – John Wayne with the gloves off – confronts a world gone soft, pacified by traitors and cowards, dishonourable feminised men (Chapman and Rutherford 1988: 28). The professionalisation of sport and the rapid increase in the earning power of winners combined, during the 1980s, with a new competitive individualism in which retributive man strutted his stuff on the sporting field. In American football, in world soccer, in rugby, and increasingly in cricket, vulnerability was equated with weakness, competitiveness with toughness. Single-mindedness was seen as a key quality for winners.

English footballer Vinnie Jones was the presenter on a video collection of brutal and vicious tackles. The video, *Soccer's Hard Men,* posed the question 'What makes hard-men a breed apart?'. Jones asserts that being hard means confrontation, 'not flinching in a tackle … if you're going to dish it out you've got to be prepared to take it back, and you've got to have tough character to be a winner'. He comments of the 'hard men' that 'They're not just aggressive on the field, they're aggressive in all walks of life, whether it is an argument with the baker or an argument with the manager.' Jones himself was subsequently convicted of assault on a neighbour, and went on to play hard men in the critically acclaimed *Lock, Stock and Two Smoking Barrels,* and its sequel, *Snatch.* The hard retributive masculinity of recent years took on a more beleaguered quality in the 1990s in an attempt to defend the castle of masculinity against the imagined threat of emasculisation. The wave of vicious condemnation of David Beckham, for being sent off in England's 1998 World Cup Match with Argentina, targeted a stylish player already derided in male terrace subculture for being a male model, a partner of Posh Spice and for being pictured wearing a sarong. Hard man David Batty, who missed the crucial penalty (like the rest of the squad, he hadn't practised them) escaped without such censure. Popular press articles and cartoons questioned the 'manliness' of Beckham. Stan Collymore, in the same period, was heavily condemned in the press for his assault on Ulrika Jonsson, but few labelled the act 'unmanly'.

The work of Richard Dyer suggests we examine masculine modes of self-presentation more carefully. Dyer, drawing on the work of psychologist Nancy Henley, points out the way in which, in male pin-ups, staring is used to assert dominance – men stare at women from a distance, women look away; whereas close up, men look away. Men are presented as though unaware of viewer.

Lynne Segal suggests that 'As Dyer's graphics confirm, when focusing on the viewer the male gaze appears to stare straight back, through and beyond him or her, whereas the female looks invitingly at the viewer ... Disavowing passivity, images of men are often images of men in action – playing sport, at work – or at least tightening the muscles ready for action' (Segal 1990: 88). Dyer suggests there is a hysterical quality in much male imagery – he refers to the clenched fist, the bulging muscles, the hardened jaw, all straining after what can hardly ever be achieved – the embodiment of the phallic mystique.

So how are we to make sense of the interaction of sport and masculinity within the discursive ground on which representations of sport stars are now constructed? One of the striking cultural developments of the last two decades has been the repositioning of cultures of fitness at the heart of adult life. In the process, the sharp division in which sport is for boys has been somewhat blurred in the gym cultures of contemporary lifestyles. Sport has always been one of the social practices that most clearly serves to demarcate gender. The two biggest selling sport magazines, *Shoot* and *Match*, are read largely by boys between 8 and 14. In them any trace of femaleness is almost entirely absent. Even in a 'Home Alone' feature about footballers at home, wives, girlfriends, sisters and mothers may be alluded to, usually as invisible carers, but never appear visually. In contrast, the stories in the only significant girls' sport magazine, *Horse and Pony*, whilst superficially about pony maintenance, in fact offer a discourse about the responsibilities of the caring and nurturing role and the need to acquire social skills for interacting with others. In general, in magazines read mostly by girls, such as *My Guy* and *Just Seventeen*, sport is largely absent but much of the content deals with emotions, problems and relationships – themes generally absent in boys magazines.

Body culture

The growing popularity of jogging, weight training, working-out and aerobics from the 1970s onwards produced fitness chic.[5] A significant element in the growth of weight training was its strength within the gay subculture. The transformation of Freddie Mercury from the thin, long-haired androgyne of the 1970s to the cropped bare-shouldered muscularity of the 1980s was a visible indicator of this shift. Committed weight training and body-building produced an intense, inward-looking and narcissistic culture in which appearance, rather than performance, was the key element. The photographic codes in weight training and body building publications focus on and highlight muscularity, as does promotion for the television series *Gladiators*. Muscular man operates at the shifting boundaries of the normal–abnormal. A Charles Atlas body-type was portrayed as enviable in the 1950s but, by the 1960s, had become a joke as attention turned to face and clothing and the seven-stone weakling rose to prominence as desirable.[6] By the 1990s, the Charles Atlas look has returned with a vengeance, with pop stars often looking as hunky as sport stars, although in the mid-1990s the wispy waif look, wasted chic, emerged in a reaction against hearty muscularity.

During the 1980s and 1990s, the men's magazine sector (as discussed in chapter 3) grew rapidly, with such titles as *GQ,*, *Arena* and *FHM* in the fore-front. These magazines were part of a reconstruction of masculinity in which fitness began to play a more central role. A concern with grooming, appearance and fashion is typically articulated through the concept of performance. Men in these magazines perform, whether they are playing sport, looking sharp or dating. The commodities are marketed in the same terms – performance shoes, performance watches. The men are typically clean cut, sharp and stylish, predominantly white, with a carefully cultivated appearance. The individualism of fitness chic, the competitiveness of Thatcherism and the health consciousness of new man are articulated together in the new growth sector – men's health magazines, such as *Men's Health*. The 'new man' of these publications is also clean and sharp, but is aware of health issues and has taken to body mainte-nance with the same enthusiasm that the 1950s men showed for motorcycle maintenance.

The growth of body culture, the popularising of personal grooming and the changing forms through which gender relations are lived have placed the focus upon the appearance of men in new ways. Jennifer Hargreaves (1994) argues that during the 1980s images of women sport stars became increasingly sexu-alised. During the 1990s, male images have also been subject to this process. The introduction of tight body-hugging Lycra, the portrayal of attractive male bodies through the photographic codes of the pin-up, the spread of body-centered cultural products like the television programme *Gladiators* and cabaret acts such as the Chippendales have all contributed to this trend.

But just as the iron-willed dogma of Thatcher required some ideological adjustment to retain its adherents, so the punishing regimes of self-transforma-tion required modification. The *Observer* quoted Dan Collins, of Canons Sports Club, reminiscing about the 1980s: 'and our remit was "go out and kill 'em, make 'em crawl out of the gym" '. A little ruefully, he adds 'two thirds of the class couldn't really do what we were asking them to do' (*Observer*, 4 January 1998). By the 1990s self-punishment was appropriated into corporate ratio-nality as companies capitalised on the merits of fit, healthy employees.[7] Male health-oriented magazines and girls' magazines alike foreground the lean muscular stomach (the six pack). The launching of *Men's Health* and *GQ Active* was followed by the appearance of 'the first diet book aimed at men' – *No More Mister Fat Guy*. Phil Hilton, editor of Men's Health, argues that 'Men have to try harder these days. They have to keep in shape, dress better and pay more attention to personal grooming because if they don't, then women will leave them, pure and simple'. Sales of men's toiletries have risen from £370 million a year in 1991 to an estimated £550 million in 1997 (*Observer*, 8 March 1998). According to one recent report men's interest in their bodies now mirrors tradi-tional female anxieties.[8] A growing number of young men think their stomachs are too large, their muscles too weak, their weight too great and their chests too puny. As men lose power appearance will become ever more important. Says Rachael Duckett, who wrote the report, if they can't be defined by status they will seek identity in appearance (*Observer*, 8 March 1998). Lucy Bannister, associate director at advertising agency Davies Riley-Smith Mackay, says that men feel that the beautiful and scantily clad muscle men that they have noticed more and more often in TV ads these days offer them an ideal shape that they find impossible to achieve. Male anorexia is on the increase (*Independent on Sunday*, 11 January 1998).

Sociologists, too, have identified significant shifts in attitudes to male physicality. Susan Bordo argues that where once losing weight was enough, now it is the appearance of the body that matters. Unsightly bulges must be eroded and bodies must be taut (Bordo 1990). Sabo and Jansen (1992) talk of those 'socially structured silences' through which certain types, the physically unfit (i.e. those who do not fit into the 'ideal' body type), gay people, the disabled and the unsuccessful are also marginalised. Clearly, though, there are more complex cultural shifts going on in body culture. Gay men were significant in the growth of a weight-training-centred gym culture during the 1980s. The shifts within gay subcultural options away from styles with a fey, camp or androgynous character and towards a super-muscular, macho look (seen in extremis in the cartoons of Tom of Finland), a shift traceable in the image of Queen singer Freddy Mercury, marked out gay male bodies as somehow fitter, more muscular, more masculine, than heterosexual male bodies, especially those working-class male paunches associated with beer, football and laddism.

During the early 1990s, John Major embarked on a project of, in effect, masking the hard economic disciplines of Thatcherism with the (almost) human face of one-nation Toryism. In the process he grafted on his own form of nostalgic longing for an organic Englishness in which the moral force of nineteenth-century athleticism could be resurrected. In his policy document on sport, *Raising the Game* (DoE 1995), Prime Minister John Major referred to sport as a binding force between generations and across borders, and linked it specifically to moral education:

> Sport is open to all ages – but it is most open to those who learn to love it when they are young. Competitive sport teaches valuable lessons which last for life. Every game delivers both a winner and a loser. Sportsmen must learn to be both. Sport only thrives if both parties play by the rules and accept the results with good grace. It is one of the best means of learning how to live alongside others and make a contribution as part of a team. It improves health and it opens the door to new friendships.
>
> (DoE 1995: 2)

Having utilised sport as a cultural form which enables the ideological handling of defeat and masks the brutal impact of win-at-all-costs competitiveness, he then claims the whole package for the nation. Competitive team sport, the document claims, is a distinctly English legacy:

We invented the majority of the world's great sports. And most of those we did not invent, we codified and helped to popularise throughout the world. It could be argued that nineteenth century Britain was the cradle of a leisure revolution every bit as significant as the agricultural and industrial revolutions we launched in the century before.

(DoE 1995: 2)

The document makes explicit the connections between sport and social order, between tradition and modernity, between heritage and citizenship, in which respect for authority and self-regulation are key elements in a new discourse of responsible citizenship:

sport can provide lessons for life which young people are unlikely to learn so well in any other way. Lessons like team spirit, good sportsmanship, playing within rules, self-discipline and dedication will stand them in good stead whatever their future holds.

(DoE 1995: 6)

In the social context of the 1990s, with the egalitarian aspirations of the Welfare State being dismantled, the Government sought here to translate its political project into moral terms:

The Government believes that such concepts as fair play, self-discipline, respect for others, learning to live by laws and understanding one's obligation to others in a team are all matters which can be learnt from team games properly taught.

(DoE 1995: 7)

The muscular Christianity of Hughes and Kingsley, over one hundred years on, is inscribed into Government doctrine in sentiments they would have applauded, and in a form of expression that John Major devised but that another Christian, Tony Blair, would be happy to endorse:

If sport is to play a proper role in building a healthy society in general and in the personal, moral and physical development of young people in particular, we must ensure that young people are introduced to it early in life.

(DoE 1995: 40)

Faith, however groundless it may be, is still placed in the ability of team sport to transform the young into acting moral subjects in the same manner as that celebrated in the narrative structure of *Tom Brown's Schooldays* (see Whannel 1999). Yet this image of organic community and moral enrichment through team sport remained marginal as against the continuing dominance of competitive narcissistic individualism.

By the late 1990s there were also signs of a reaction against body culture. A

'Head to Head' article in the *Guardian* (10 January 1998) featured an exchange of letters between television fitness trainer Mr Motivator and Richard Klein about health, fitness and 'health nazis'. Klein pointed out that 'Nazis used health as a way of imparting moral imperatives and disciplining the population'. In reaction to the muscle-bound hunk, recent years have seen the re-emergence of the male waif – thin, awkward and odd, often featured posing in nylon trousers in seedy settings. This figure, often associated with drugs, as in *Trainspotting*, marks a re-emergence of a more self-destructive hedonism, which, like the sex, drugs and rock and roll moment of the early 1970s, is in opposition to sport and body cultures. *Billy Elliott* features a young boy who rejects boxing in favour of ballet. Yet the strongly forged configuration between sport and masculinity is still firmly in dominance and football occupies more space than ever on prime time schedules.

New men, new lads, new labour

The contradictory field of masculinity can best be understood as a struggle in process between competing elements – the discursive figures of new man and new lad, the first a response to feminism, the second a reaction against it. The dynamism of this struggle – the constant need to shore up the castle of masculinity – should not be underestimated. If feminism problematises hegemonic heterosexual masculinity, then so does queer theory. Growing out of struggles over language – how shall gayness be labelled – and a fightback against homophobia, queer theory also problematises a uniform homosexual identity. Seidman argued that queer theory constituted a challenge to 'the dominant foundational concept of both homophobic and affirmative homosexual theory: the assumption of a unified homosexual identity' (Seidman 1996: 11). Queer theory typically sees personal life and society as both sexualised and heterosexualised. Michael Warner (1991) argues that queer theory has a goal to make research theory queer and not merely have a theory about the queer.

However, despite the ways in which postmodern-oriented theories posit a 'pic-n-mix' society in which identities are one more commodity that can be purchased in the form of the outward signifiers of identity, such as clothing and accessories, hairstyles, and personal possessions, it is important to reassert that we do not simply choose, in unconstrained and unmediated ways, our identities. Nor are we able to shift identities with the facility of the quick-change artist. The psychological and social processes of identity formation, our entry into language, into subjectivity, and into a structured and hierarchised social world are significant determinants on identity, exerting pressures and setting limits. Identities are neither fixed and unitary, nor are they infinitely mutable. Indeed, this combination of lack of fixity and limited mutability would seem precisely to account for the tensions, contradictions and struggles around differences of gender and sexual orientation.

One prominent site for the working through of these tensions during the last twenty years has been around those two discursive figures 'New Man' and 'New

Lad'. 'New Men', as a label, denoted men who had responded to and taken on board aspects of the critique of masculinity offered by feminism. Such men endeavoured to become more involved with domestic labour and childcare. They got in touch with their emotions and tried to combat their own sexism. Responses to these developments involved derision of such behaviour, castigated as wimpish (by women as well as men), and denial that such figures existed outside the fantasies of advertising. Clearly there have not been dramatic changes in the allocation of domestic labour but, at the same time, it seems foolish to deny that there have been no changes in practices and attitudes. It is no longer exceptional (although still not typical) to see men pushing prams and buggies or doing the family shopping. Baby-changing facilities now appear in men's toilets as well as in women's. Paternity leave has been introduced. More people of both sexes believe that domestic chores and childcare should be shared.

In the 1970s, desires amongst men for change were largely limited to the politically engaged and active, manifest in such organisations as Achilles Heel, the Gay Liberation Front and the various informal organisations that sought to respond to the challenge of feminism with support for activities organised by women. More recently it is possible to point to a range of instances in which reconstructions of masculinity have been manifest. The self-reflexive aspect of the writing of figures like Dave Hill, Nick Hornby and Tony Parsons constitute examples. Blake Morrison's *And when did you last see your father* (1993) explores the complex relations men have with their fathers. Mick Cooper and Peter Baker's *The MANual: the complete man's guide to life* (1996) argues that 'Men can be just as good parents as women'; not a new argument, but less common from a man. The emergence of 'New Man' as a label carried, for some, connotations of a metropolitan elitist movement from the soft south; the unsettling of established dominant masculinity, was, by the 1990s a somewhat wider theme. A men's group on a North Tyneside estate, named the 'Canny lads', was set up to challenge the macho image of spend-thrift brown ale swilling and domestic violence. Some of them had themselves been witnesses to or victims of domestic violence in their own childhoods (*Guardian*, 8 March 1997). So, the 'new man' is arguably something more than a media label but certainly less than a major new social movement or a transformative social force, yet does signify forms of unsettling of some mainstream assumptions about gender relations.

If 'new man' was a response to feminism and a reaction against the constraints and limits of mainstream hegemonic masculinity, the 'new lad' was a reaction against feminism and a magical recovery of aspects of hegemonic masculinity seen as threatened. Specifically, it sought to recuperate unabashed pub-and-porn hedonism without any of the constraining elements of self-restraint, public decency or respectability that in other contexts have acted as breaks on undisciplined hedonism. This form of laddish masculinity that most distinctly reacts against, rather than responds to, feminism, has taken place around what have been termed by the media the 'new lads'. New laddism, though, is only a convenient label for a rather diverse set of media phenomena –

the rise of men's magazines like *Loaded*, the success of Nick Hornby's *Football Fever*, the television programmes *Fantasy League Football* and *They Think It's All Over* and *Never Mind the Buzzcocks*, and the radio football show *606*. This magical recovery of some traditional young working-class masculine values – 'booze birds and falling off the dance floor', as Terry Collier once expressed it (*Whatever Happened to the Likely Lads*, BBC 1975) still has football at its heart, although 'new lad' culture has increasingly begun to seep into cricket.

Together these elements constitute an odd cultural formation containing both an adjustment to, but also a reaction against, feminism, and both a reconstruction, yet a reaffirmation, of elements of traditional masculinity. At its crudest, in *Loaded*, this constitutes old-fashioned lecherous sexism that tries to avoid complicity by attempting to hint that everything is in postmodern 'irony' quotes; whilst at its more subtle and nuanced, in some of Hornby's writing, for example, it constitutes a search for a new masculine identity – aware of, yet not defined by, feminism. To take a critical perspective on the cultural context of sport requires that men recognise the sexism and misogyny of new laddism as represented by titles such as *Loaded* and *FHM*, and television programmes such as *Fantasy League Football*. This culture has been heralded in some quarters as post-feminist, self-confident and a form of postmodern irony. In fact it is none of these things, although it does represent a reaction to the rise of feminism. It also represents a reconstruction of a pre-feminist objectification of women, rendered more explicit in the post-tabloidisation world, in which the soft-core imagery restricted during the 1980s to the top-shelf adult magazines has been reintegrated into the more visible mainstream via the front covers of the new men's magazines. Ian Botham, and Paul Gascoigne in his early years, were emblematic new lad figures, although George Best (before his recent liver failure) is probably the ideal new lad identification figure. *Loaded* had as its masthead strapline, 'For men who should know better', and reasserted a lecherous and boozy masculinity. The new lad culture celebrated bad boys with ability and a couldn't-care-less attitude:

> If football was ever the new rock'n'roll, then Diego Maradona was its Led Zeppelin and Black Sabbath rolled into one. On the one hand: guns, coke, bans and aggro by the truckload; on the other inspiration, guile and the quickest thinking feet on the planet.
>
> (Andy Winter, editor of *Shoot* in '20 Icons', a promotional pamphlet for Macintosh computers)

The formative moment could be located with the launch of *Loaded* in 1993, the success of which forced *FHM* downmarket by 1994. Lad television also fuelled this form of masculinity with programmes like *Fantasy League Football, They think It's All Over, Men Behaving Badly*. Chris Evans – first on *Breakfast Television* and then on *Don't Forget Your Toothbrush* and *TFI Friday* also contributed to the ethos. Emily Barr's column, 'The Other Half', satirised the type. The female protagonist has given her partner ('Bloke') a black eye, accidentally:

'How's your eye', I call, 'did you tell your mates it was me?'

'Yeah, right', he shouts with a mouthful of toothpaste. 'Beaten up by a girl? I don't think so.' He has, it transpires, invented a story about a Fulham Road ambush by drunken Spurs fans, and has received plaudits for his heroism. 'You should have seen the other guys', he says excitedly, before remembering that I know the truth.

(*Guardian*, 24 April 1998)

New lad culture has also been part of the inspiration for laddettes, women who adopt the same hedonistic behavioural style, and for some this makes it 'all right', although more astute commentators are not taken in by the complicity of some women in new laddism. Charlotte Raven (*Guardian*, 10 October 1994) commented on the return of 'unreconstructed man' and noted the tendency in some publications for a competitive edge, with women and men daring each other to be more sexually brazen, although 'men, spurred on to greater extremes, are better than women at naked sexism'. Referring to the ironic masthead 'For men who should know better', she asks, 'if they should, why don't they?'

Nick Hornby, in his writing, is not simply a new man or a new lad. The discourse of the book is situated in the tension between the two, a factor that probably enabled its success. It is 'new man' in the sense that it is aware of feminism and self-reflexive about masculinity. But it asserts a dogged resistance to changing behaviour that is, from a female perspective, odd. In this sense it has aspects of a new lad sensibility. But it is not reactive in the new lad sense – it does not imply, as does *Loaded*, that 'you may think this is a pig-headed reassertion of traditional masculinity, and in fact I can see that it is, but actually I don't give a toss, I'm going to do it anyway'. Neither, however, does it attempt, as new man might, to deconstruct masculinity to reconstruct a new feminist-friendly man. Nor does it triumphantly reassert traditional laddish masculinity under the cloak of postmodern irony. In fact, the rather pragmatic compromising synthesis of the two poles of masculinity echoes the 'third way' of new Labour, in which capitalism is neither celebrated or vanquished but rather re-branded. Hornby's huge success with *Fever Pitch* (1992) is in part due to the chord his self-reflexivity has struck with women – it is constantly being touted as the first, or the only, book about sport that has been widely read by women. Hornby has subsequently become the paradigm case for new fiction about men and emotions. His success has also triggered a huge sport publishing boom. The rise of new lad and the post-Hornby sport publishing boom have together contributed to a reassertion of the close relationship of masculinity and sport. It reproduces again a discursive formation in which sport both confers and confirms masculinity.

In Part II of this book, I turn my attention to examining the ways in which the relation between sport and masculinity became an underpinning element in the representation of sport stars as the development of the technology, institutions and cultural practices of the media industry enabled the media to assume a cultural centrality, producing in the process a sporting star system.

Part II

From sporting print to satellite …

Popular memory is a key element in the cultures of sport, and the discourses of masculinity and morality that this book examines characteristically construct a comparison between present day stars and stars of the past, usually in order to reinforce a negative view of the present. Part II of the book examines the process of sport star construction in its historical context. The intention is not to offer a historical or chronological account of sport stars, but rather to use a series of examples to illustrate both the continuities (themes of masculinity and morality being nothing new) and the specificities of the forms of representation of sport stars. Chapter 7 covers the period up to 1939. Sport stars emerged as a central pull factor in the growing popularity of spectator sport and media sport, but in this pre-televisual era, in which public–private boundaries were still relatively clear, they were less frequently the focal point of public concerns about morality. However, this does not mean that such cases were absent, as the example of Babe Ruth suggests. Chapter 8 focuses on the 1950s as a moment on the threshold of the television age. The sporting feats of Joe DiMaggio, Roger Bannister and Stanley Matthews were all televised, yet their fame was largely constructed in the print media. It was a time when national sport was becoming a more prominent element in international political contestation, and the decade subsequently constituted a fund of nostalgic imagery to set against the supposed corruption of the sporting present by excessive monetary rewards. Chapter 9 examines sport stardom in the era of pop culture, the generation gap and television through the examples of Muhammad Ali and George Best. Both caught the public eye through a combination of extraordinary ability, a degree of arrogance and striking good looks. Both have had their stories constantly reinscribed ever since. Chapter 10 explores the tensions between hedonism and competitive individualism during the 1970s and 1980s – a period, following the growing tabloidisation of the media, when the indiscretions of sport stars were more likely to hit the headlines.

7 The birth of the sport star
Pre-war fame

Football in itself is a grand game for developing a lad physically and morally, for he learns to play with good temper and unselfishness, to play in his place and play the game, and these are the best of training for any game of life. But it is a vicious game when it draws crowds of lads away from playing the game themselves to be merely onlookers at a few paid performers ... Thousands of boys and young men, pale, narrow chested, hunched up, miserable specimens, smoking endless cigarettes, numbers of them betting, all of them learning to be hysterical as they groan and cheer in panic in unison with their neighbours.

(Baden-Powell, quoted in Birley 1995: 230)

There are likely to be many more brave men in the future, men as brave as those I have mentioned, who have dared in every walk of life, and I hope that you will honour them as they deserve, and try to live up to the standard they set.

Honour the brave! Salute the gallant!

(*Boys' Book of Heroes* 1938: 188)

Baden-Powell contrasts the 'healthy' cultures of participating with the newly emergent 'unhealthy' cultures of spectating at the moment that modern elite spectator sport was emerging. The *Boys' Book of Heroes*, itself couched rather in the Boy Scout spirit, was nevertheless dependent upon a media-based process of mythologising heroism, and indeed many of their 'brave men' were sporting figures. One of the tensions at work in images of masculinities in sport is suggested here – the nineteenth-century public school ethos of fair play and moral development, the ideology of empire adventure and the professionalisation of sport do not fit easily together. In ideological terms sporting masculinity was one of the sites on which the tensions between these elements were worked through. Representations of the sport stars of the pre-war period both embody and reveal some of these tensions.

Just as the period between 1880 and 1914 saw the emergence of the modern mass media, so it also was the period in which modern spectator sport was established and consolidated its position. During the 1890s, the present grounds of Everton, Celtic, Blackburn Rovers, Bolton, Wolves, Aston Villa, Sunderland, Sheffield Wednesday and Portsmouth were all established. Almost sixty of the present grounds of the English Football League clubs were opened between 1890 and 1910 (Inglis 1983). Spectator sport, in turn, provided the economic basis on which professional sport could develop. By 1910 there were over 200 first-class professional cricketers, 6,800 footballers and 400 jockeys and apprentices. By 1907 there were 20,000 full-time employees in golf clubs, and 80,000 part-time caddies.

It was in this period that the process of globalisation began to develop, and the emergence of international sport produced some of the first social institutions with global aspirations. The International Olympic Committee was formed in 1894 and the first Olympic Games of the modern era were staged in 1896. FIFA (Fédération internationale de football association), the world governing body of football, was established in 1904, although the first World Cup was not staged until 1930. Tennis's Davis Cup was launched in 1900 and World Series Baseball began in 1903. The International Amateur Athletic Federation (IAAF) was formed in 1912, and many other sports formed international governing bodies in the opening two decades of the twentieth century. The groundwork was established, although it took the emergence of jet travel and television following World War II for global sport to become a reality. The alliance of the media and spectator sport produced the sport star.

The career of W.G. Grace bridged the transition from pre-industrial cricket to the Edwardian age and occupied the ground of the emergence of modern sport and the modern media system. Grace also embodied the tensions between individual and collective notions of sport and was the first sport star of the media age. He began playing when the institutions of modern cricket were barely in place, and finished his career with the Test Match and the County Championship well established. His image continues to be eminently marketable in the UK and amongst cricket fans worldwide – indeed, he is probably the only pre-World War I sport performer who might be readily recognised by twenty-first-century readers.

During his career the sporting press, the sports page and the mass circulation popular press all emerged. Grace was a heroic figure in terms of his cricketing exploits, but, in terms of competitiveness and commercial sensibility, he also personified some of the forces at work producing the new professionalised elite spectator sport. The later part of his career was during the period many now regard as the golden era of cricket. In the contradiction between his amateur status and professionalised manner he embodied the contradictions between tradition and modernity, fair play and ruthless competitiveness, authority and rebellion, technique and flair that continue to be the discursive sub-structure of so much sporting representation.

Jack Johnson

If in Grace, the media produced their first star, in boxer Jack Johnson they produced their first significant controversy. As a black boxer, Johnson had to struggle for years to get a shot at the title, despite his manifest pre-eminence as a heavyweight. The emergence of a supreme black champion exposed the ethics of fair play to the ideology of racism in a particularly public manner. Johnson became world champion in 1908 after eventually getting a fight with Tommy Burns. His triumph, and his unwillingness to play the humble 'Uncle Tom' role, led to a frenzied search for a 'great white hope' to defeat him, and in 1910 James J. Jeffries fought him. Guttmann reports that, as Johnson approached the ring, the band struck up 'All Coons Look Alike to Me'. He recounts that after Johnson pummelled James Jeffries into a bloody mess, 'the entire nation was swept by a wave of violence in which mobs of blacks and whites murdered whites and blacks' (Guttmann 1988: 123).

Films of the fight were banned throughout the South and two Southern senators got Congress to outlaw the interstate transportation of fight films (Guttmann 1988: 123). Significant here is the first strong evidence of the power of the media in relaying a star image and, along with it, the attempt to suppress circulation of images of blackness as powerful, gifted, successful, and acting rather than acted upon. The power of images showing a black fighter beating white fighters produced attempts to prevent the images reaching audiences:

> Johnson was used by white film-makers as a symbol of black masculinity that 'flaunted white values as he battered a train of white opponents'. Johnson's defeat of white fighter James Jeffries on July 4 1910 resulted in fight pictures being banned within the motion picture industry because whites both resented and feared witnessing a black physically assault, and thereby exert control over, a white. Black men could not be seen to dominate whites, and despite the fact that Johnson was a marketable commodity, the picture was banned. Racism was thus a more powerful force than profitability in the Hollywood motion picture industry in the early 1900s. Black masculinity had to be clearly non-threatening to whites in order for it to be portrayed on the screen or on stage.
>
> (Regester, in Kirkham and Thumin 1993: 171)

In 1911, in England, cinematograph cameras filmed Billy Wells (the British great white hope) being knocked out by Gunner Moir in the third round (Shipley 1989: 95). According to Shipley:

> The popularity of Bombardier Billy Wells, the fame and success of Jack Johnson, and the colour of his skin all contributed to a desire to see a Wells Johnson fight ... Johnson trained at Walthamstow and a local paper reported that 'the huge black's exhibition bouts ... have been rapturously applauded and his genial way of either making a speech or singing a song ... considerably enhances the popularity of the smiling giant.
>
> (Shipley 1989: 96)

However, the Free Church Council launched a campaign against the fight on the grounds that the contest would be 'repulsive' and the film of it even more so (Shipley 1989: 96). Racist fears of blackness associated with power were here again linked to fears of the power of a new medium. The promoter was forced to cancel the fight, although, Shipley says, 'there is no evidence whatsoever to suggest that the general public, without access to the press and the law, wanted the match to be suppressed' (*ibid.*: 96).

Back in the USA, persecuted for his success, Johnson was sentenced for a violation of the Mann Act in 1913 (it outlaws the transportation of women in interstate sexual commerce) and then spent seven years in exile before being beaten in Cuba by Jess Willard, subsequently suggesting that his defeat was part of a deal with the FBI. The fight is still a matter of controversy, with many boxing experts agreeing that the fight was 'thrown' by Johnson. Writer Damon Runyon, who regarded his article on Johnson's defeat as the best sports writing of his career (Weiner 1948: 108), believed it was not a fixed fight and argued so in another piece thirty years later, but many retrospective accounts have viewed the fight with considerable suspicion. Johnson, his image and his style, constituted a challenge to the racism of the white establishment in his refusal to act out the role of a humble and respectful black man. As was to be the case with Ali, the Johnson myth was subject to a process of reinscription, where the racism he suffered was decentred in favour, of a retrospective recognition. For example, Weiner wrote in 1948 that 'there was almost unanimous agreement among fight fans that Jack Johnson was the greatest heavyweight of his time' (Weiner 1948: 106). Weiner goes on to portray the racism as both inevitable (and therefore 'natural'), and also as the fault of Johnson himself:

> It was inevitable that Johnson's continued mastery over white men in the ring would disturb and anger many Americans but the fighter didn't trouble himself to aid the cause of racial intolerance by his personal conduct. He had been jailed several times on various charges ranging from breaking the peace to bigamy, and had a propensity for marrying white women, one of whom committed suicide.
>
> (Weiner 1948: 107)

The racist tone of this account makes for an interesting comparison with the understanding, tolerance, license and outright celebration accorded to white sporting heroes like Babe Ruth and Ian Botham. White commentary on sport has typically distinguished between the 'respectful' (Joe Louis, Jesse Owens, Carl Lewis, Tiger Woods) and the 'upstart' (Jack Johnson, Muhammad Ali, Mike Tyson). Grantland Rice (1956) acknowledged the racism evident in his earliest contacts with sport around 1900 when there was 'a vast discrimination' in which, with the exception of boxing, 'big time sport was almost entirely a white man's playground' (Rice 1956: 155). However, he then proceeds to contrast Johnson – 'a poor representative for his race. He certainly didn't help the cause of the negro' with Joe Louis – 'In this respect, no one in the sporting world has helped his people to advance with as much speed as Joe Louis'. He goes on to call him a clean fair sportsman, completely honest and a 'glowing example also for the white race to follow' (*ibid.*: 156). Successful black men were all right as long as they knew their place. Black sporting masculinity was under pressure to conform to a respectful subordination to the white world. A chapter in Kieran (1941), described in the contents as 'Boxing – With Notes on Bare-Knuckle Bruisers, Modern Masters of the Sweet Science and High Lights of Heavyweight History from John L. Sullivan to Shufflin Joe Louis', manages to go through from the mid-nineteenth century to Jack Dempsey without mention of Jack Johnson, and mentions Joe Louis only in passing. The chapter is forty-nine pages long!

By the 1920s, sport was reaching the mass audience in dramatically new ways – cinema brought moving images of sport to the mass audience, whilst radio added immediacy and domesticity. These two media brought the exploits of inter-war sport heroes – Jack Dempsey, Fred Perry, Jesse Owens, Don Bradman, Babe Ruth – to the audience in a new direct and immediate manner. Sport was a site of struggles in representation, as when the success of black athlete Jesse Owens in the 1936 Olympics stood in contrast to the celebration of Aryan power by the Nazis and in the famous Leni Riefenstahl film *Olympia*. The inter-war era was a period in which the discourse of sporting heroism was firmly established. It was also a period when the contradictions produced by the commercialisation of sport, the heightened pressures to win, the appropriation of sport as a symbolic element in political contestation and its particular version of hegemonic heterosexual masculinity can all be traced in the representation of sport stars. Fred Perry's move from tennis player to brand name for sport clothing, Don Bradman's pivotal role as target of the bodyline strategy in the 1932 cricket tour of Australia, Jesse Owens dramatic triumph in the Nazi heartland in 1936, Big Bill Tilden's repressed homosexual desires, and the contrast between Babe Ruth's wild adult self-indulgence and the use of his image to promote values of respect for the rules are all testament to the contradictions at work within the world of sport.

Jack Dempsey

With the establishment of modern mass media, promotion and celebrity became significant features in elite sport. Boxing manager Doc Kearns developed a strategy for promoting the career of Jack Dempsey which involved getting the boxer in the sports page headlines. He proclaimed that he would bet $10,000 that Dempsey could beat any two heavyweights anyone could come up with on the same evening (Schoor 1956: 78). He dubbed Dempsey 'Jack the Giant Killer, and despite the fact that Dempsey already had a very strong left, announced that he had Dempsey training in the ring with his right hand tied up 'to develop that left hand of his' (*ibid.*: 79). The world heavyweight title fight between Dempsey and Jess Willard, on 4 July 1919, promoted by Tex Rickard, was the last major sport event before the rise of radio, and then television. It was in Toledo and gate receipts were \$452,522 (*ibid.*:109). Once Dempsey was world champion, he sought to exploit his fame with lucrative personal appearances:

> Jack would appear on the stage for a few minutes, do a little shadowboxing, skip rope, answer a couple of questions. That brought in a lot of money. Everyone wanted to see the new heavyweight champion of the world and they paid plenty to see him.
>
> There were dinners too, and banquets and all sorts of state functions. 'You're a celebrity, Jack! People want your autograph! They want to say that they saw you, said hello to you. You're the man of the hour!' [said manager Doc Kearns].
>
> (Schoor 1956: 117)

The Dempsey v. Carpentier fight on 2 July 1921 in Boyle's Acres, Jersey City was watched by 80,000, and grossed \$1,600,000. Dempsey earned \$300,000 and Carpentier \$200,000 (Schoor 1956: 125). Dempsey could be promoted as the perpetrator of aggression in ways that would not have been so acceptable had he been black. According to Schoor, though, Dempsey was at first not popular with the punters, who disliked his ruthless style, publicised as the 'mauler from Manassa'. Later, after his fight against Firpo, they began to acknowledge that he was a great champion. He eventually lost the championship to Gene Tunney in front of 120,000 people in 1926. When he returned to the dressing room, battered, his wife asked :

> 'What happened to you, Jack?'
> She looked at his battered face.
> Jack smiled painfully through his swolled lips.
> 'I just forgot to duck, honey' he said.
>
> That little speech made every sports page in the country. The Manassa Mauler had been a super-human fighter. That little speech made him a human being and won him the admiration and affection of the whole sports world. Thus, in defeat, he achieved what he had never had in all his years of triumph.
>
> (Schoor 1956: 157)

The line was so well established in popular mythology it was later used by Ronald Reagan, to his wife Nancy, after he was shot in a failed assassination attempt. The rematch, in 1927, was watched by 140,000 and grossed around \$3m. Schoor says that Dempsey was the most widely publicised sports hero of his times and he certainly was one of the first in which publicity was a central factor. Dempsey was written into boxing's mythology with more unambiguous praise than Johnson would ever get.

For a black boxer like Joe Louis, success in the ring was only part of the battle. Constant vigilance was necessary to guard against bad publicity. Consequently, Joe Louis was forced into a restricted mould. His backers, mindful of the racist public pillorying of Jack Johnson, laid down ground rules: no photographs with white women, no solitary nightclub visits, no fixed fights, no dirt fights, no gloating over defeated opponents, no politically radical statements (Guttmann 1988: 124).

The way to court acceptance from, if not popularity with, the white audience seemed to be to minimise blackness, not to draw attention to cultural differences and to remain apolitical. According to Guttmann, athlete Jesse Owens' popularity with white Americans was 'partly attributable to his undeniable athletic ability and his far from militant approach to civil rights' (Guttmann 1988: 125). He also represented the USA in what became a symbolic battle with fascism. Owens won four gold medals (100m, 200m, 400m relay and long jump, in what became seen as a blow against the supposed racial superiority of the Herrenvolk. Hitler's supposed refusal to shake hands with him was a journalistic fabrication, but became part of the myth. The Leni Riefenstahl film *Olympia* contributed to the solidifying of the Owens's myth (Guttmann 1988: 125). Hitler referred to the black American athletes as America's 'African Auxiliaries' (Rice 1956: 158). Owens' own autobiography (1978) is a rather strange interior monologue, of spiritual focus, and not of much relevance for this research, but his post-Olympic career was ruined when the white and patrician athletics authorities used spurious evidence of 'professionalism' to outlaw him from the sport. Re-evaluations of his career in the 1990s have suggested that racism in the USA was a far more significant factor in his career than the heavily mythologised 'embarrassing' of Hitler in the 1936 Olympics.

Fred Perry

The new earning power of top sport stars began to heighten the contradictions and tensions between amateur and professional models of sport. Fred Perry was in a Davis Cup winning side in 1933, won three Wimbledons, three US championships, won the French Open and the Australian Open before turning professional in 1936. No Englishman has won any of these titles since (Perry 1984: 9). So, he was the last Englishman (as of 2001) to win Wimbledon; but rather than representing the end of the era of the gentleman amateur, he represented, in turning professional and in establishing his name as a brand, the beginning of the era of commercialisation.

Perry was an open advocate of change – his 1934 autobiography contained a chapter advocating that the amateur authorities recognise professional tennis, and that open tournaments be staged (Perry 1934: 147–53). When Perry turned professional, Wimbledon took away his honorary membership and the tie that went with it (!) (Perry 1984: 110). He was reinstated 12 years later. Perry commented that:

I deeply resented not having been accepted by the officialdom at home. I was from the North Country rather than old-school tie country, and I didn't get on with Sir Samuel Hoare, the president of the Lawn Tennis Association. Most of my confrontations were with him and certain other members of the LTA hierarchy, or with a couple of committee members at the All-England LTC. It was a question of a lack of understanding with the establishment and I always had the feeling that I was tolerated but not really wanted – I had forced my way in. Maybe I was wrong, but I never really bothered with people who didn't want to bother with me. I was simply never part of the Establishment end of British tennis.

(Perry 1984: 108)

He was the son of a Labour MP and suggests that former Wimbledon members would be turning in their graves on the occasion of the establishment of a statue to Perry, 'the man they regarded as a rebel from the wrong side of the tennis tramlines' (Perry 1984: 10). Class and professionalism were closely allied here – it was not just that Perry was in favour of commerce, or that he was, for the English establishment, the wrong kind of chap. Rather, it was that the two elements were seen as intimately related.

Babe Ruth

The emergence of stars was a significant factor in the commercialisation of sport. In 1920 the first season that Babe Ruth played for the New York Yankees after his transfer from Boston, 1,200,000 people watched the Yankees, more than double the previous season's attendances (Durso 1995). The new Yankee Stadium, paid for by these revenues, became nicknamed 'The House that Ruth built'. In 1922, Ruth was earning $52,000 a year just on his baseball contract, and another $15,000 from ghosted columns. By 1927 he was being paid $70,000. One index of his stature is the stanza of an Ogden Nash A-Z of baseball, that reads:

> R is for Ruth
> to tell you the truth
> there's no more to be said
> just R is for Ruth.
> Ogden Nash

Following the Black Sox scandal in which eight baseball players were found to have accepted money to lose the World Series, baseball had been badly in need of a new charismatic hero (Rice 1956: 81). The emergence of radio, bringing actuality into the domestic sphere produced a wider audience, expanding the fame of top sport stars dramatically. The 1922 World Series was broadcast, and newspaper advertisements proclaimed that

Grantland Rice, famous sports editor of the New York Tribune, will describe every game personally, play by play, direct from the Polo Grounds. His story, word by word, as each exciting play is made by the Yankees or Giants, will be broadcasted from famous Radio Corporation-Westinghouse Station WJZ.

(Durso 1995: 54)

Babe Ruth was well placed to become a populist hero – perceived by the audience as 'one of us', not a company man, something of a rebel, but able to produce magic moments. His wife commented:

I thought I was the only one who loved him. Now I know I wasn't. A nation loved him. Not just because he hit 714 home runs and did all sorts of wonderful things on a baseball field, but because the people sensed that he was one of them. He had their faith and their weaknesses. They loved him because he was above all else, a great human being. And they were … and are … so right.

(Ruth 1959: 208)

Like Ali, Botham and, for a while, Alex Higgins and Paul Gascoigne, he was more than just a sport hero, he was 'the people's champion', someone who fitted the popular sensibility. Eleanor Twitchell described him as

the 18 carat center of the golden age. He was a huge good natured lummox who called everybody kid or Joe because he couldn't remember their real names. He had an incredible flamboyance with the talent to back it up.

(Durso 1995: 81)

Audiences appear to respond more to popular heroes who have their weaknesses. Ruth liked booze and women, but above all fast food and fizzy drinks. He was no great intellectual:

On a scripted radio programme, once, Babe Ruth was supposed to refer to the Duke of Wellington's remark that the Battle of Waterloo was won on the playing fields of Eton. Instead, he managed to come out with 'As Duke Ellington once said, the Battle of Waterloo was won on the playing fields of Elkton.'

(Rice 1956: 87)

As the most famous and charismatic figure of the inter-war years in baseball, Babe Ruth's name and image had commercial value, and in a coaching book for young aspiring players, his name is attached to an idealised eulogising of the virtue of fair play. The final chapter on 'General Advice' highlights five points:

1. Play hard all the time, no matter what the score may be
2. Follow the orders of your captain or manager, whether or not you agree with his judgement
3. Observe all the rules of fair play by playing cleanly
4. Don't abuse the umpire, or umpires
5. Be a good loser if you have to lose.

Babe Ruth's Baseball Advice (Ruth 1936)

And some of the advice includes:

work with your team leader, play as he wants you to play, and though he may be incorrect in his judgement, if you have given him your best efforts, he will not blame you. Team play is needed for success and the way to be a real help to your team is to co-operate with your fellow players. Play cleanly all the time. Never try to cause injury to an opponent. A player who attempts such things is not worthy of playing the game ...

Be a good sport when you don't agree with the umpire's ruling. When you are greatly interested in a close play you are likely to see it differently from the fellow who is doing his best to be fair to both sides. If you were satisfied to let him be the judge when the game started, you should be willing to accept his decisions until the last man is out. Remember that the umpire has a harder job than any of the players. No game was ever won by both teams. One of them must lose. If you play hard and clean baseball, and are fair to yourself, your team, your opponents and the umpire, you need not be down-hearted over defeat. If the other team wins be a good loser, and give it the credit you expect for your team when it wins.

(Ruth 1936: 32)

Ruth himself was a product of a professionalised pragmatism in which such values may not have been quite as much to the fore. His own life, rich in publicised escapades and scandals does not seem to have been a monument to the principles of following orders and observing principles of fair play. The mode of address throughout the book is specifically to boys, and Ruth does seem to have been sincere in his feelings about the sport and youth. His wife recounts that even when he was dying, speaking to the crowd at a Yankee Stadium at Babe Ruth Day, 'he spoke huskily and briefly, of what baseball meant to boys and the rewards baseball offered boys who worked to learn the game' (Ruth 1959: 201). Ruth found it ironic that when he stood alongside doctors, engineers and statesmen, it was he who was cheered by the crowd (Klapp 1962: 143).

The construction of the fame of sport stars involved the systematic exclusion of black sportsmen. Baseball was segregated until after the war, and the black league teams struggled in mediocre stadia, in poor areas, to media disinterest. Allen Guttmann points out that while white Americans 'thrilled to the antics and exploits of Babe Ruth', black Americans had 'a wholly justified sense of injustice when they alone applauded Julie Johnson, Cool Papa Bell and Satchel Paige' (Guttmann 1988: 60).

Babe Ruth's past has the classic structure of immature behaviour – the cycle of self-indulgent binge and misbehaviour followed by remorse (Gascoigne comes to mind here). He was, in short, a 'lad', and as a white lad, allowed a degree of license. Indeed the ability to be hedonistic and successful at sport was a badge of his masculinity. Even his wife writes in indulgent terms that

> there are facts, there are legends, there are escapades of record and escapades only whispered about. There are reports of detectives, pictures of wild revelry in breweries, stories of heavy disciplinary fines. Stories of weeping apologies made to 'the dirty-faced kids in the street' followed by collapses in a railroad station in Asheville and auto wrecks galore.
>
> (Ruth 1959: 57)

The Yankees are described as wild men off the field. 'They fought among themselves and then went out and painted the town' (Ruth 1959: 80). Mrs Ruth did occupy the classic feminine role of wife and carer in attempting to civilise and control her partner and found it necessary to 'cut down on his eating, his drinking, his late hours, and his friends' (*ibid.*: 104). Her biography is richly revealing about conventions of sporting masculinity. She states

> I was no jailkeeper. The Babe could be tamed perhaps but he couldn't be caged. He surely couldn't be henpecked into staying in shape. I knew only too well that the country was filled with understanding females who would be more than enchanted to lighten the woes of a famous, wealthy, exciting and misunderstood husband.
>
> So if Babe straightened himself out, and the world knows he did, it was because he was man enough to fight off his wilder impulses towards wine, women and song. And the reason those impulses were so unbelievably strong within him is terribly simple – he was a pauper and caged in his early youth. And he was rich and free as a bird in his earliest twenties.
>
> (Ruth 1959: 15)

The domestic is seen here through the metaphors of prison and entrapment, in which masculinity should not be caged or locked up. It may be tamed but not henpecked. The 'real' man triumphs over desire only if allowed to grapple with it. But Mrs Ruth did see it as her role to combat the incautious over-indulgences of masculinity:

> Now that I was Mrs Ruth I felt Mrs Ruth had a job to do. It's the job every wife does in one form or another, I imagine, no matter how many of them insist on denying it. I had a few reforms to institute ... the Babe ate too much, and he was prone to indigestion. Whether this was cause or effect, I know not. In addition to eating too much food, he ate too much

junk. He sometimes drank too much. Whiskey, perhaps. Or beer. Or, as often as either, too much soda pop. He would no more go anywhere without a box of bicarbonate of soda than I would without lipstick. He didn't like to go to bed. And there were always plenty of people around to help him keep out of bed.

(Ruth 1959: 96)

Masculinity is a bounded system, with the bounds policed by women as well as other men. Any sign of 'effeminacy' is ruthlessly derided in locker room culture, and the homophobic character of this culture is so strong that very few male sport stars have been known to be homosexual. In describing the first baseball game she watched after marrying Ruth, Mrs Ruth recounts that he hit a home run and as he trotted around, he blew her a kiss. She subsequently told him 'You better stop that kiss-throwing, Babe. You looked like a big sissy out there, the players will be telling you about it next time' (Ruth 1959: 36).

In the policing of sporting masculinity, no feminisation, no public sentimentality, and, of course, as tennis player Bill Tilden found out to his cost, not the slightest hint of camp or male desire for other men can be tolerated if the castle of heterosexual masculinity is to remain powerful and impregnable. In sporting terms this masculinity was still about being heroic and admirable. In 1938, a boys' annual, *Sporting Heroes*, singled out a mixture of figures, including W.G. Grace, Jack Hobbs, Big Bill Tilden, Austin and Perry, Sir Henry Segrave, Sir Malcolm Campbell, Carpentier and Dempsey, Jack Lovelock, Captain Webb and T.W. Burgess. The blend includes stars of sports covered by the new media – Alex James, Jack Hobbs, Bill Tilden, Jack Dempsey and Fred Perry; those who were pioneers of the new mechanisation – Sir Henry Segrave and Malcolm Campbell; and those who battled against the elements – Captain Webb and T.W. Burgess. The book signs off with

we have reached the end of this book of heroic men, but do not think that we have reached the end of the list of heroes who have done great things in the face of terrific odds since the dawn of time. Do not think, again, that we have reached the end of heroism. There are likely to be many more brave men in the future, men as brave as those I have mentioned, who have dared in every walk of life, and I hope that you will honour them as they deserve, and try to live up to the standard they set.

Honour the brave! Salute the gallant!

(*Boys' Book of Heroes* 1938: 188)

Sport then was, in ideological terms, one of the models for correct and appropriate masculine behaviour. The author could not have fully anticipated the horrors of the imminent war, nor could he have registered the coming significance of a new medium – television – then just two years old. Yet, within a decade of the publication of the *Boys' Book of Heroes*, the 1948 Olympics, the first to be televised, marked the opening of an era in which television would not simply become the dominant medium, but would also exert a transformative influence on sport stardom. The related commercialisation of sport would serve to heighten the tensions between a media-driven stardom and the romantic and innocent expectations of heroism embodied in the *Boys' Book of Heroes*

8 Good boys

Stars, nations and respectability in the 1950s

I had become a symbol in athletics of British sport against American and for the sake of national prestige I felt I had to win.

(Roger Bannister 1955: 125–6)

As a child, soccer-mad Stan would buy a pig's bladder from the butcher and use it as a makeshift ball. He said 'We couldn't afford the real thing. I never saw a proper ball until I became a schoolboy international'.

(Obituary for Stanley Matthews in the *Sun*, 24 February 2000)

Where have you gone, Joe DiMaggio?
A nation turns its lonely eyes to you.

(Paul Simon, 'Mrs Robinson')

The new world that was being made in the wake of World War II was to be characterised by the consolidated economic dominance of the USA, the emergence of the Eastern bloc, the 'iron curtain' and the 'cold war', the development in the West of an affluent society and, above all, by the rise of television. It was a moment of transition in which the traditional structures and values of sport were about to be reshaped by new commercial forces associated with the rise of television, the growing importance of advertising and sponsorship, the emergence of a media-based celebrity system and the development of 'sport business'. Figures like Roger Bannister, Stanley Matthews and Joe DiMaggio were products of this transitional moment, and the subsequent mythologising of all three marks the beginning of a period in which nations would indeed turn their lonely eyes in the direction of sporting heroes.

During the period 1945–63, Britain moved from wartime austerity towards a degree of affluence and relatively full employment, although the gap between rich and poor was not narrowed. Post-war hegemony was rooted in an economic and political stability buttressed by the external threat posed by the cold war, the Iron Curtain and nuclear weapons. The moment of the Welfare State – no return to the 1930s, wartime popular radicalism, the popular appeal of the Beveridge Report – all fed into the Labour landslide and the subsequent establishment of the conditions for a degree of political consensus, later dubbed

'Bustkellism', around principles of welfare provision, an expanded state and a mixed economy, universal state education, a commitment to the Western Bloc in the cold war, and a containment of working-class aspirations within the logic of capitalism.

During the late forties, fuelled by the return of the troops and the celebratory mood engendered by the end of the war, there was an unprecedented boom in public entertainment. In Britain, and in North America, cinemas, dance halls, sports stadia and bars were packed. The boom was short-lived. Throughout the fifties, the old public communal entertainments declined as television spread. The growth of television, car ownership and the record business were indicators of a leisure culture that centred on home and family. In the USA, major league baseball attendances dropped by one-third between 1948 and 1956, while in minor league baseball attendances slumped from over 40 million to 13 million. Madison Square Gardens' crowds for boxing dropped from an average of 12,000 in 1950 to 1,200 in 1957. In 1950, Stillman's gym had 300 fighters in training, while in 1958 this figure had dropped to 90. There were 300 fight clubs in the country in 1952, and in 1960 less than 50 (Rader 1984: 45). In the USA, fears of a crowd decline caused by television, to some extent justified, prompted the widespread introduction of local television blackouts, preventing fans within reach of the stadium choosing the television option. Unlike some sectors of the leisure industry, such as the record business which began to expand rapidly in this period, the organisations of sport, still shaped by their formative moment as institutions of upper-middle-class patriarchal benevolence, and fundamentally redistributive rather than accumulative in character, were chronically resistant to the concept of entrepreneurship. Yet it was in this moment that the forces that were to transform sport, internationalisation, spectacularisation and professionalisation, all in turn driven by television, were taking shape.

Joe DiMaggio and Marilyn Monroe

In the USA, the growing importance of television persuaded two major sporting institutions to move cities in search of more lucrative deals. The Brooklyn Dodgers and the New York Giants moved to California in 1958. The Dodgers were already the most profitable baseball franchise in the league, but the owner wanted to be in an uncontested media market (with no other teams). Brooklyn residents felt a deep sense of betrayal at the loss of this unifying force in the area, and in 1983 the American sport magazine *Sports Illustrated* commented 'When the Dodgers left Brooklyn, we lost our innocence forever' (Rader 1984: 62).

In the mid-fifties, baseball star Joe DiMaggio, despite an extraordinarily successful career, was about to be elevated to a new dimension of eminence by marrying film star Marilyn Monroe. DiMaggio's baseball career, interrupted by the war, ended with his retirement in 1951 after 13 years with the Yankees. In 1941 he set a new record, going 56 games without striking out.[1] He was mythologised as a gentleman, with a 'reputation as one of the greatest gentlemen ever to play the game' (Oakley 1986: 252). He married Marilyn Monroe in 1956, becoming her second husband, after her marriage to an aircraft worker, which lasted two years, and before her marriage to playwright Arthur Miller, which lasted four years. The DiMaggio marriage lasted nine months, but DiMaggio apparently never stopped loving her and put flowers on her grave until his own death in the late 1990s. In representation, they appeared to epitomise the perfect 1950s couple – she glamorous and pretty, he big, strong, rugged and sporty – they could have constituted models of traditional heterosexual masculinity and femininity. In keeping with his appearance as an emblem of traditional masculinity, DiMaggio would have preferred his wife to drop her acting and become a housewife. He found it hard to handle the attention and limelight that her fame brought her. The resulting stresses and tensions led to their break-up. DiMaggio's public reputation survived the break-up, which featured a clumsy surveillance attempt during which DiMaggio and a group of cronies, including Frank Sinatra, burst into the wrong apartment, apparently in an attempt to catch Marilyn, whom DiMaggio had begun to suspect of being a lesbian, with a woman. DiMaggio's retreat from the media limelight contributed to the aura surrounding him with over thirty books about him appearing, and it became possible to represent him as a figure from an earlier, more golden, yet more innocent, age:

> The public also seemed to have a divided awareness of him, seeing and hearing and speaking no evil and excusing any suggestion of it. Heroes were getting harder to come by as the century spiralled into its final violent decades and there weren't many heroes with the enduring grace of this one.
>
> (Durso 1995: 244)

DiMaggio had been offered two million dollars to co-operate with Durso's book, but eventually decided that he was not prepared to speak publicly about Marilyn Monroe (Durso 1995: xi). Like Roger Bannister and Stanley Matthews, DiMaggio disliked the glare of publicity and, like them, he was one of the last pre-television stars. The technology of television was emerging and sport was on the dawn of a profound transformation. The governing bodies of sport were slow to grasp their emergent commercial potential, but they, and the state, were quick to see the new enhanced propaganda dimension of sport in the context of the cold war.

Sport and national prowess

For the first time, sport emerged as a major signifier of national prowess on the international stage. The Olympic Games became a symbolic battle between capitalism and communism to demonstrate supremacy. The entry of the Soviet Union into the Olympic Games in 1952, followed by East Germany in 1956, made the Games a major symbolic site for East–West contestation. National sporting success was seen as a symbol of national virility and well-being. The Eastern Bloc countries devoted extensive resources towards the identification and training of a sporting elite, a policy that was to produce extraordinary Olympic successes, especially for relatively small countries such as the German Democratic Republic (GDR) and Cuba (see Riordan 1977, 1978). The USA responded to the challenge posed, by striving to remain top of the (unofficial) Olympic medals table. In the UK, The Butler Education Act established a clear role for sport and physical education, and the Central Council for Physical Recreation established a series of National Recreation Centres as part of a drive to produce excellence.[2]

These investments were fuelled by the growing public concern over elite performance, particularly the trauma of England's football defeat by Hungary in 1953, and its Olympic disappointments in 1952 and 1956. The rise of USA and Eastern Europe meant that the United Kingdom was being eclipsed as a major sporting power. In football, England's assumed superiority was demolished, freakishly, 1–0, by the USA in 1950, and, decisively, by the Hungarians, 6–3, in 1953. The press reacted with bewilderment at the USA defeat, which was written off as an aberration. The defeat by Hungary was greeted with an embarrassing admittance of the superior skills of the Hungarians and initiated an inferiority complex that has still to be fully dispelled (partly because it is based on a fairly realistic view of the inadequate skill development of English football). The sense of a national decline was reinforced by the growing prominence of foreign football stars such as Pele and Puskas.

Against this background, national identity became a much more significant element in the portrayal of sport stars, both in Britain and in the USA and Eastern Europe. Leo Lowenthal, in his 1943 essay 'The Triumph of Mass Idols' (Lowenthal 1961), had already drawn attention to the growing prominence of sport stars in popular magazines. In the post-war period, top sport stars were increasingly articulated in terms of national prowess. It is from this period that the symbolic importance of sport as part of national identity begins to be a significant element in sport coverage in the popular press, although it was still somewhat muted by today's standards. The population of the early 1950s are portrayed as wanting, indeed needing, national successes:

> In the Coronation Year of 1953, the public hoped to see success crown finally three unfulfilled endeavours. Gordon Richards, winner of every other classic in the racing calendar, had still to win a Derby, despite twenty-seven attempts. Mount Everest had yet to be climbed. And Stanley Matthews had yet to get his Cup winners' medal.
>
> (Davis 1962 :83)

All three goals were achieved, and England won the Ashes,[3] causing some to regard 1953 as a vintage year for sport. The linking of sport and national virility continued to grow throughout the next three decades, and by 1990 England manager Bobby Robson would be quoted as saying, after England's semi-final defeat in the World Cup, 'I'm just so sorry for the 50 million people back home crying like us', while the *Sun* referred to the 'bulldog spirit that has carried this England team through so much' and in the editorial called on the nation to 'Salute our brave lads' (*Sun*, 5 July 1990). In the context of national decline, British sporting successes, such as those of Roger Bannister, assumed a greater symbolic importance. Bannister's four-minute mile became a potent national symbol against the grain of a perceived loss of national prowess. Boys' comics contributed superhumanly heroic characters – Roy of the Rovers, the Incredible Wilson, Tupper of the Track. Such feats echoed the real-world achievements of Stanley Matthews, who finally won his Cup Winners' medal in 1953, inspiring his team to come from behind to win the FA Cup Final in the dying seconds of the match.

As a consequence of the developments outlined above, the period between 1945 and 1965 was a period of transition in sport stardom. It began in post war austerity in a pre-television era, when the principle means of secondary circulation of star image was by newsreel and cigarette card. Cultural forms that have become somewhat residual, at least as far as the secondary circulation of star image is concerned, such as the Blackpool Illuminations, were still in their heyday. In the autumn of 1951, Stanley Matthews switched on the 300,000 lights for Blackpool's Festival Year illuminations.

> Eight thousand people jammed against the Town Hall steps to watch as he pulled the switch. He had a surprise. Above his head an illuminated set-piece came to life. Picked out in lights, it showed Stanley scoring a goal, the goalkeeper sprawling beaten as the ball entered the net. The winking lights repeated the scene again and again.
>
> (Davis 1962: 79)

A book on sports of the period began 'When the original *Sports Book* was published in 1946, it was felt that the public needed a chance to catch up with events in their favourite sports and pastimes after six years of war, and some guidance from knowledgeable sports writers on the future' (Rivers 1946:1). The introduction mentions the star writers, but it is striking that there is no highlighting of star sports people, although the frontispiece is a picture of Dennis Compton. Less that twenty years later, by the mid-1960s, television was well established, the sponsorship boom was imminent, and stars like George Best and Muhammad Ali were familiar domestic faces to those with little close interest in boxing or football. Many of the dramatic events of the period – Bannister's four-minute mile in 1954, Matthews' FA Cup Final of 1953, England winning the Ashes in 1953, Real Madrid's 7–3 European Cup Final victory in 1960 – were captured by the television cameras yet still seem part of a pre-televisual world. Bannister's four-minute mile was caught on film by *Sportsview*'s cameras, but in a very inadequate form – the camera position was inside the track oval, at ground level, rather than outside it and raised, and the view was largely blocked by excited fans and officials. England winning the Ashes in 1953, Matthews' Cup Final triumph and the Real Madrid game survive only in very grainy tele-recordings.[4]

Bannister and the four-minute mile

Bannister's breaking of the four-minute mile barrier was announced to the Oxford crowd with a well-judged piece of theatre by Norris McWhirter, who teased the crowd by listing the various records broken before revealing the extent of the feat by saving the announcement of the time until last. He concluded with the phrase 'in a time of THREE minutes ... ' and huge cheers meant that the rest of the sentence was inaudible on the recording. Otherwise, the event was striking for the lack of any stage management for the media. A camera was there for the new television sport magazine *Sportsview*, but it had such a rotten position that it gave a poor view of the race, and the extensive crowds on the in-field meant that even still photographers did not capture the event very clearly.[5]

It is in this period, though, that the pressures from the media and the weight of public expectation becomes a more common element in constructions of sport stars, and indeed becomes part of the growing pressure for professionalisation. National prestige is portrayed as boosted by sporting success. Commenting on his thoughts before running the Benjamin Franklin Mile in Philadelphia in 1951, Bannister reflected:

> Though I had barely dared to admit it, I know that in England the publicity about the race had been enormous, and the result had great significance for the British public. On this occasion, rightly or wrongly, I had become a symbol in athletics of British spirit against American and for the sake of national prestige I felt I had to win.
>
> (Crump 1989: 58)

Media attention is also identified for the first time as a pressure on performers. Bannister writes of the press focus on his attempts to break the record:

> The press technique had become something like this. If Smith has entered for a race they can get two headlines out of it; first, 'Smith to attack World Record', even though Smith disclaims any such intention. If the record is not broken, their second headline is all ready, 'Smith fails in world record bid'. The feelings of Smith about this would be interesting but perhaps unprintable. It does no harm, I suppose, so long as the public and Smith do not take it too seriously.
>
> (Bannister 1955: 148)

And when he finally beat the record, he recalls that, 'The press were on my trail everywhere all next day' with no mention of television, although *Sportsview* screened a film of the race (Bannister 1955: 166). Bannister's mythologised achievement has particular resonance in the British context in that it represented both a sporting milestone and a British success. It came in the context of a broadcasting environment that was notably marked by class – the Oxbridge world of the BBC still devoted a striking amount of time to Oxford v. Cambridge events (not just the Boat Race, but rugby, cricket and athletics, too). There was a striking class difference in athletics during the 1950s between the Oxbridge athletes, such as Bannister and Chataway, and the northern and/or working-class athletes such as Ibbotson and Pirie, who seemed, by contrast with the Oxbridge set, outsiders.

Stanley Matthews

Roger Bannister and Stanley Matthews were both portrayed as hard working and dedicated, but while Bannister was the middle-class professional, Matthews was the working-class artisan. Matthews, like Bannister, was also aware of, and exposed to, media pressure. In *The Stanley Matthews Story* he complains that in the build up to the 1951 Cup Final his telephone never stopped ringing, with calls both from sports writers and from people asking if he was considering retirement. Matthews commented that, 'I was hopping mad. What right had these people to invade the privacy of my own home, to make my life almost unbearable?' (Matthews 1960).

In this period, the distinction between public and private spheres was more firmly marked in the media. Coverage of sport stars before the tabloidisation of the 1970s was characteristically respectful and full of praise. In *Sport Stars of Today: Stanley Matthews* (Matthews 1963), he is described as 'the best known and best-loved footballer of them all'. His characteristics are enumerated in a manner that highlights their noble qualities. He 'looks like a wise old eagle ... strong lines from thin cheeks lead past a mouth notable for a dominant top lip and teeth free from dentistry, to a slightly pointed chin' (Matthews 1963: 3). Anthony Davis's biography of Matthews (1962) refers to him inspiring young people the world over and 'his modesty, simplicity and sportsmanship have won him the inalienable affection of millions' (Davis 1962: 3). His life is narrated as a moral homily in which embedded traditional values are emphasised. The role of his father in instilling 'a rough and ready code of honour and physical fitness' is emphasised. The father ensured that Stanley 'kept his body right and his thoughts straight' (Matthews 1963: 3). Anthony Davis recounts that 'Stanley went in awe of his father, a strict disciplinarian, a stand-no-nonsense man – but a good man and a man who tried always to do what he believed was best for his family' (Davis 1962: 6). The discipline was part of the process of constructing masculinity, of turning boys into men. Matthews himself describes a revealing conversation with his father after his first game for Stoke reserves at the age of fifteen:

Boy-like, I couldn't wait to get home quick enough to hear what my father thought. He was reading a paper when I got in the house and looked at me over the top of it. He said, 'Son, you'll play a lot better and you'll play a lot worse'. He paused, then went on 'Forget about the good things you did; remember the mistakes you made, study them, and correct them, then forget them completely. You'll never keep repeating them if you do that. Remember a man who never makes a mistake never gets anywhere. Have you got that, son?' I nodded and said, 'Yes Father'. 'Well, sit down and have your tea', he said, and together we discussed the rest of the game.

(Matthews 1960: 26)

Matthews was brought up in the respectable working-class virtue of thrift. On making a first team debut at seventeen, his father insists that he puts half his earnings in a savings bank, and gives the other half to his mother for his keep. As for pocket money for himself, his father says he will have to earn that by securing his win bonus. Matthews comments 'We won and my pocket money was safe. I didn't play for the first team again for the rest of the season, so I couldn't have had a good game. But I had gone on that field a youth and come off a man' (Matthews 1960: 31). If Stanley's father is portrayed as moulding Stanley according to the conventions of respectable working-class masculinity, it is his mother who orchestrates his relationships. Emotions and sexuality were part of the domestic sphere and the domain of women. When Stanley is nineteen, his mother suggests it is time he settled down and that there are other things in life beside football, and proceeds to orchestrate his courtship of his future wife, Betty:

My mother called out, 'where are you going?'. I turned and said 'To pack a bag. You are right, I do love her. I'm going right up to Scotland to ask her to marry me, and shan't leave Scotland until she does so.' My mother said, 'Don't bother about packing a bag, son, I've already done it; it's behind the door.' I gave her a hug, picked up the bag, and I caught up with Betty in Scotland. We were married in the clubhouse of the Bonnyton Golf Club near Glasgow.

(Matthews 1960: 35)

There is a notable contrast between the masculine world of work and the feminine domain of domesticity in these narrativisations of Matthews's life, in which the civilising and rounding impact of women are associated with the transition from carefree youth to family responsibility. If fathers turn boys into men, mothers turn youths into husbands. The remarkable talent of Matthews, and his commitment to personal fitness, resulted in a career of unprecedented longevity in which he played top level football until he was fifty. The highlight, mythologised as 'Matthews' Final' came in 1953, when, after several near misses, he finally won an FA Cup Winners' Medal. The potency of this mythology in media narrativising of the world of sport was clearly revealed at the time of his death in 2000.

The death of Matthews: reinscription of a mythology

Stanley Matthews had not been a major news figure for thirty years at the time of his death, but his story was reinscribed in obituaries as part of a contrast between past and present that served to highlight the supposed inadequacies of the present. Three themes were ubiquitous in constructions of the image of Matthews at the point of his death in early 2000. First, he was a gentleman – in some accounts 'the last gentleman of soccer'. He was a model sportsman – quiet, reflective, modest, reserved and courteous, and from humble origins. Second, he was a genius, an artist. Third, he had rigorous self-discipline. Never booked, he was totally dedicated. The picture that is drawn of Matthews as the working-class gentleman who embodied the classic Corinthian virtues is more idealist than archaic, although, in implying a contrast with the present, Matthews is inevitably cast in a nostalgic glow:

> He was the last gentleman of soccer; a player with artistry in his feet and integrity in his soul. He played in the days when love of the game was enough and the most he could earn was £20 a week … But he was quiet with it, a reflective man who was never boastful and never gloated in victory. He was never temperamental. He did not argue with referees. He said it all with his feet. The son of a barber-cum-smalltime featherweight boxer, Matthews was brought up with an old-fashioned work ethic in the Potteries. His first club was Stoke and he would run to the ground, weaving between people on the pavement, rather than take the bus.
>
> (*Daily Mail*, 24 February 2000)

His talented artistry – 'the wizard of the dribble' – was everywhere highlighted. The *Daily Mail* headlined: 'A Genius and a Gentleman: The Magical mixture of Matthews' (*Daily Mail*, 24 February 2000). The *Daily Telegraph* proclaimed that he not only 'tormented and destroyed full-backs', but did it with 'a sportsmanship that emphasised the brilliance he tried to shrug off' (*Daily Telegraph*, 24 February 2000). His dedication was portrayed in terms of hard menial work, tough journeys and privations:[6]

> He was taken on as an apprentice by Stoke, where every day he had to clean 46 pairs of the senior boots and sweep out the dressing room after training. 'Then I had to walk home' he recalled. 'It was eight miles a day unless it snowed. Then my father would give me my bus fare. It was cold enough in those days without central heating and hot water but I used to pray for snow.' … And what did Matthews do when he got home? He went

straight out into the street to practise his legendary dribbling skills with a pig's bladder under the light of a gas lamp.

(*Daily Mail*, 24 February 2000)

His preparation is constructed as one of monkish asceticism and self-denial – '*strict* dieting', '*total* fasting' (*Daily Mail*, 24 February 2000, my emphasis). All the papers drew attention to his disciplined approach:

It required rigorous self discipline to sustain his speed for so many years; every day, during his professional career, his diet was the same: carrot juice at lunchtime, steak with salad for dinner, a fast on Mondays. And every morning there would be a training run.

(*Daily Telegraph*, 24 February 2000)

He was totally and utterly dedicated to the game in a way that you just don't see nowadays. He was a self trained dietitian long before that science came into the game. He ate raw carrots and drank blackcurrant juice. Stan never drank alcohol, didn't smoke, and used to get up early every morning at Blackpool to exercise on the beach before training. And despite his huge fame he was always modest, courteous and the epitome of the perfect gentleman.

(*Sunday Mirror*, 27 February 2000)

Characteristically, descriptions sought to combine the elements of 'gentleman', 'artist' and 'dedicated professional':

He was a true hero, whose dedication, professionalism and lifestyle shame the overpaid, over-rated players of today. … And though hard men tried to kick lumps out of him every week, he was never booked in a 33 year career.

(*Sun*, 24 February 2000)

In his own case that mental superiority was never arrogant or vain. On or off the field he was a modest, reserved and courteous man. He was a scrupulously clean player who avoided physical contact; he never sought it, and his deceptive movements ensured that he rarely suffered it.

(*The Times*, 24 February 2000)

[H]e was an icon revered as much for his quiet dignity and modesty as for his footballing skills.

(*Daily Mirror*, 24 February 2000)

In most accounts there is a taken-for-granted naturalised character which ignores the process of image construction that produces stardom. One quote, however, which gave a rich insight into this process of construction, should remind us of the importance of historical specificity:

> You couldn't see your heroes on television in those days, but we knew what
> a great player he was from the clips we saw on Pathé news, at the cinema,
> reading *Charles Buchan's Football Monthly* and from information on the
> back of cigarette cards.
>
> (Bobby Robson, ex-England manager, in *Sunday Mirror*, 27 February 2000)

Not surprisingly, it was the *Guardian* that, in the spirit of post-modern self-
reflexiveness, sought to situate Matthews in relation to fictional heroics:

> Matthews was a hero of 1940s and 1950s children's cigarette cards and
> comic books as well as newsreels. He was the real life counterpart of Wilson
> the Wonder Man [*sic*], who – long before Roger Bannister – once ran a
> mile in a still unbeaten 3 min 43 sec wearing a black, long-sleeved
> Victorian bathing costume. Matthews' wizard dribbles were viewed as
> almost as remarkable.
>
> (*Guardian*, 4 March 2000)

The establishment of this image of the dedicated gentleman genius in turn
enabled the insertion of the narrating of Matthews into a discursive structure
that compared the past of sport with its present in order to produce a critical
account of the present. The past was a time when footballers had a maximum
wage of £20 a week, and 'the love of the game was enough'. Played by men in
baggy shorts, watched by men in cloth caps, football was a 'tough but honest
sporting contest between men who took their knocks without complaint'.
England then was 'a country in which modesty was respected or worshipped
almost as much as popular virtuosity'. In the present day, by contrast, players
are overpaid, overrated, flamboyant, flashy and pampered, with their showbiz
lifestyles and million-pound homes, Ferraris and celebrity wives.[7] Football has
become a 'money driven circus fuelled by dissent and deceit' full of 'bad-
tempered stars who regularly drag the game into the mire'. Although it is not
always mentioned explicitly, the abolishing of the maximum wage in 1961 functions as a pivotal moment between past and present, separating thrift and greed,
respectability and hedonism, the discipline and stability of tradition and the
instability and indiscipline of professionalised spectacle. In the modern game, in
these accounts, sportsmanship has gone. The *Daily Mail* recalls Matthews' FA
Cup Final victory, when there was a 'spirit of manly sportsmanship in the
mutual congratulations that is so wretchedly missing from the game today'. The
modern game, by contrast, is characterised by cynicism and cheating: 'In his
own 33 year career Matthews was never booked. He found intensely distasteful
the way some players hurled themselves to the ground in the hope of getting a
player sent off' (*Daily Mail*, 24 February 2000). According to these assess-
ments, money has corrupted football:

> Matthews never resented the wealth of the modern footballer. What he did
> resent was the way the game itself changed from a tough but honest

sporting contest between men who took their knocks without complaint, to a money driven circus fuelled by dissent and deceit.

(Daily Mail, 24 February 2000)

The material rewards nowadays, it is suggested, are too great, as opposed to Matthews' era, when honour and glory were to the fore:

> Whether flying down the wing, hair immaculately in place, or smiling gently, presenting an award, he represented his profession with grace, charm, honour and integrity. In an age when many players are pampered millionaires criticised for being cut off from reality, Sir Stan – on £20 a week – represented another era when footballers were heroes.
>
> *(Daily Mirror,* 24 February 2000)

It is profligacy and extravagance, it is constantly suggested, that have brought about the conspicuous consumption and show business glamour that have corrupted sport:

> How different he was from the flamboyant, flashy, highly paid stars of today, with their Ferraris and celebrity wives. Nor did he ever miss a single day's training, which is why he was able to go on playing league football until he was 50, by which time he was back again with Stoke.
>
> *(Daily Mail,* 24 February 2000)

By contrast with the modern era, there were 'No Ferraris for Stanley, he trudged 16 miles a day to go training' (*Sun,* 24 February 2000). Poverty here is transformed into a character-building virtue. Matthews is portrayed as an embedded figure, true to his roots, who got his boots courtesy of the Co-op and, 'while modern idols like David Beckham rake in fortunes from lucrative sponsorship, the wing wizard was just grateful to get his football boots provided free by the Co-op' (*Sun,* 24 February 2000). A romantic nostalgia for the egalitarian comradeship of shared origins, rarely to be detected elsewhere in the popular press treatment of football fans, surfaces here:

> A gent on and off the pitch, he gave so much to soccer and took so little back – in stark contrast to today's overpaid bad-tempered stars who regularly drag the game into the mire. In his baggy shorts and heavy boots, he was a true hero to legions of flat-capped fans – and earned little more than they did.
>
> *(Sun,* 24 February 2000)

Reasserted here is the concept of star as hero, deserving the adulation, and having a responsibility to be a good role model, along with a cultural pessimism that suggests that moral decline means that such figures are situated only in the past:

It is only right that his passing knocks the loutish antics of the likes of Collymore and Gazza out of the headlines. They may get paid more in a week than he earned in a soccer lifetime. They may be more feted in an age of easy celebrity. But they are not fit to lace Sir Stanley's boots. He was an idol who truly deserved the fan worship that placed him on a pedestal. We shall never see his like again.

(*Sun*, 24 February 2000)

The discursive structure into which all this is fitted, is one that sutures together themes associated with the decline of morality, the crisis of masculinity, the decline of Britain and the threat to family values. The declining power of authoritarian morality, associated with the supposed declining influence of the church, the school and the family, provides the structure of a traditional conservative cultural pessimism in which television and conspicuous consumption are threatening stability. One way of understanding this is as a crisis of adaptation, marking the long historical decline of thrift and the work ethic. Matthews' death 'marked the passing of a different kind of England, one which was thought to have been almost forgotten long before he died, a country in which modesty was respected or worshipped almost as much as popular virtuosity' (*Guardian*, 4 March 2000). Such qualities are not merely lost and mourned, there is a desire to resurrect them, for they are seen as a necessary element in the battle against moral crisis. The Rector of Stoke, Canon Edgar Ruddock, described Matthews as a genius and added, 'We thank God for Sir Stanley's skill, courage, energy, and example. We must reflect on how much we need those characteristics in our personal community and national lives today' (*Sun*, 4 March 2000). As another figure whose discourse draws on religion,[8] the Prime Minister Tony Blair commented, 'Sir Stanley was and will always remain one of the all time sporting greats. He was not only one of the finest players this country has ever seen, he was also a model sportsman' (*Daily Express*, 24 February 2000).

The coverage reveals the extent to which, in the context of the declining significance of Priest, Father and Teacher in moral education, sport stars are constantly looked to fill the void, constituting moral exemplars. The death of Bobby Moore, captain of the England football team that won the World Cup in 1966, resulted in press coverage that made very similar comparisons between a golden age of sportsmanship and rectitude situated in the past, and a present day characterised by corruption and venality (see Williams and Taylor 1994). The regularity with which this pious hope is not fulfilled, with so many sport stars constituting 'bad examples', has yet to make a dent in such unrealistic expectations.

There is one other curious feature of the obituaries of Matthews and it lies in the lacunae – in particular, his divorce, which is (as is, admittedly, conventional within the form of obituary) glossed over. After retiring in 1965, at age fifty, (a career of unsurpassed longevity) Matthews was for a short period the manager of Port Vale, a club with a long but undistinguished history. His first marriage to Betty ended in divorce in 1975 and he married a younger woman. Given that this divorce happened when he was 60, and that it potentially contradicts the image of honest, sincere integrity, and therefore, does not fit the dominant frame at all, it is not too surprising that most accounts ignored the events, or reduced the events to a bland uninformative sentence. At age 52 he commenced an affair with a Czech interpreter, concealing the fact from his wife for over a year before eventually going through a divorce in 1975. He and his new wife, Mila, eventually went public with their story in 1981 in the book *Back in Touch* (Matthews and Mila 1981). The tale of Stanley Matthews' love affair with Mila is pretty dramatic – it involves romance, adventure, danger, a life on the run and, in the context of Matthews' public image, it is rather shocking. It has evident news value, which makes the erasure of the episode from the obituaries all the more striking.

They first met in August 1967 when Matthews took Port Vale to tour Czechoslovakia, and also spent some time negotiating a football boot deal. Walking around the grounds of a grand house during a party, they became so engrossed in each other that they walked into the swimming pool. Matthews returned to Czechoslovakia soon after this initial meeting and they spent more time together. When he returned they corresponded regularly and he sent her flowers every week. Before the end of the year, she had confessed to her husband that she was in love with Stanley, and she had paid a visit to England in which they travelled around the Peak District, only a short distance from Matthews' home. On New Year's Eve, Matthews spent an hour on the phone to her, and early in the new year, in receipt of invitations to South Africa and Canada, he had decided to invite Mila to join him.

By the standards of conventional morality, they also behaved pretty badly – Matthews couldn't face telling Betty about Mila for long after he and Mila had agreed that they wanted to divorce their partners and get married. Mila's husband George refused a divorce, so she tried to arrange for an actress to seduce him so that she could accuse him of adultery. On a subsequent visit to Mila in the summer of 1968, Matthews was stranded in Prague when the Russians moved in. Soon after, Mila fled Prague for the West. In turn, Matthews abandoned England, leaving his wife, his home, his friends, and, in his words, 'everything I considered important', and commenced a life of hiding and concealment with his lover. During their time on Malta, an elaborate system of precautions and warnings provided by friends and neighbours helped them to dodge the press. A supporters' history of Port Vale recounts that Matthews described the 1967 pre-season tour of Czechoslovakia as 'the best tour I have been on' (Kent 1990: 220). After reading *Back in Touch*, the reasons for Stanley Matthews' enthusiasm for the tour are, of course, all too easy to understand.[9]

Nowadays, had the press got hold of the story, it would have been a front-page feature in the tabloids. The lack of space given to it at the time of Matthews' death stems partly from the culture of respect and reticence within which the conventions of obituary writing are framed, but it is also the case that it did not fit neatly within the very well-established frame of reference within which Matthews was cast as the ultimate working-class sporting gentleman.

Postscript: a tale of two Stanleys

As with Bobby Moore, the mythologised Matthews has, even since his death, continued to be a figure in a discursive structure that offers a comparison of past and present to underpin a discourse of moral decay. As this book was being completed, the following appeared:

> Two of Staffordshire's most famous footballing sons were in the news this week. Stanley Collymore for scrapping with a fellow Leicester City player. And Sir Stanley Matthews, as one of the boots he wore in the 1953 FA Cup Final was auctioned. Collymore, a petulant disgrace throughout his career, is in a raging sulk because he wants his salary raised to £40,000 a week. Stanley Matthews' famous boot raised £640. A small but priceless snap-shot of how our beloved national sport is hurtling towards moral and financial bankruptcy.
>
> (Brian Reade in *Daily Mirror*, 19 October 2000)

That sport stars should nowadays constantly be appropriated for popular discourse regarding the moral state of the nation serves to remind us of some significant developments since the 1950s. The rise of television, with its ability to bring the faces of the famous into the domestic sphere and make them familiar, enabled the stars of sport to acquire a greater degree of celebrity, becoming known to non-sport fans. The cheapness (on average) of sport-based content, along with the audience-winning powers of major sport events, gave sport a significant place on the television screens of the world. Sport has been the main beneficiary of the massive growth in the numbers of television channels. In Britain, for example, the five terrestrial channels, in 1999, screened around 4,000 hours of sport.[10] This figure, though, is dwarfed by the massive 22,000 hours of sport broadcast by the satellite television broadcaster BSkyB in 1998 (*Observer*, 3 January 1999).

The next chapter focuses on two stars, boxer Muhammad Ali and footballer George Best, whose fame was given a significant boost by their good looks and charisma, which, through television, reached a larger public. Their fame marks the beginning of a new era in which a celebrity becomes a more central component of popular culture, a process that reaches a crescendo in the 1990s in the period of *Hello*- and *OK*-style journalism.

9 Pretty boys, the 1960s and pop culture

A whole new generation coming of age in the early sixties thought of the preceding generation as slower, dumber, less musical, less honest, more hung up, less where-its-at.

(Schulberg 1971: 44)

Along came George Best; he was young, he was handsome and he had great hair. There hadn't been anyone like him before: he was the vision of maleness I wanted to be.

(Terry Hall, ex-member of 'The Specials', in *Men's Health*, December 1997)

'Take a look at my face', said Ali, thrusting it forward for the lights and the cameras. 'Can you see a mark on it? Can you believe that this is the face of a 32 year old man who has just fought Joe Frazier twelve rounds?' No we couldn't.

(Frank McGhee, in the *Daily Mirror* 30 January 1974)

George Best and Muhammad Ali were regarded by many as pretty, and to have real style. The rise of television, as a medium, changed the nature of stardom, and the nature of sport, and these changes can be examined through representations of Best and Ali. There are two key aspects – mythologisation and reinscription. By reinscription, I refer here to the process whereby star biographies are constantly rewritten in the 'continuous present' – their lives being reinterpreted according to the dominant concerns of the present.

The 1960s commenced with a significant shift from cultural patterns of the fifties and the inter-war era. The collapse of the Macmillan Government in 1963 amidst scandal, and the satire boom, the emergence of the Beatles and the swinging London era were followed by a series of social reforms under the 1964–70 Labour Government. In the USA, the election of John F. Kennedy, the first major world leader to have been born in the twentieth century, in succession to the ageing Republican, Eisenhower, also signalled a new youthful tone. An increase in youth spending power combined with new cultural forms such as rock and roll to produce a distinctive, youth-based market for fashion and style.

The roots of 'the Sixties' lay in 1956. The Suez fiasco destroyed the last remnants of British imperial pretensions, whilst Stalin's crushing of the Hungarian uprising constituted a crisis for the Communist Party and led to the emergence of the new Left. The cultural impact of rock and roll and the greater visibility of youth culture, described dourly by Richard Hoggart (1958) as 'juke box boys with drape-suits, picture ties and an American slouch', was the marker for a growing cultural distinction between generations. Indeed, politics in the early 1960s were characteristically articulated around the relation of age, class and technology. The inept handling of the Profumo affair made the Tories seem aristocratic and out of touch. The new Labour government under Wilson tried to sell itself as modernising through 'the white heat of the technological revolution', just as Kennedy's rhetoric talked of 'the new frontier'. In Britain, a changing social climate was marked through a series of liberal reforms involving censorship, divorce law, homosexuality, abortion, licensing and Sunday Observance.

The old public entertainments (the pub, dance halls, cinema and football) all continued to decline, as they had done throughout the 1950s, whilst ownership of consumer durables (electric irons, vacuum cleaners, washing machines, fridges, televisions, cars) grew rapidly. The home and the family became more central to leisure. Traditional communities, with their extended kinship networks, mutual interdependence and local economy, were broken up by slum clearances and housing developments. New estates, high-rise flats and rehousing disrupted kinship networks and the integrative function of the street (Cohen 1972). There was a greater youth mobility linked to the expansion of university education and the growth of large-scale protest movements, such as CND and the anti-Vietnam war movement.

In England this was the start of a period of greater cultural self-confidence, in which English products in music, fashion, and even film, challenged foreign imports. Masculine dress codes underwent a series of changes with a more feminised styling – the male peacocks of 'mods', 'dedicated followers of fashion', and the long flowing asexual and androgynous hippie styles. A greater stylistic emphasis fell on the face – in mod slang, a sharp looking character was 'the ace face'. The 'British invasion' of America, spearheaded by the Beatles, popularised mod fashions, as well as British beat music. In the USA, the election of Kennedy ushered in a period in which the young were acquiring greater cultural power, while the conventions and values of the older generation were coming under pressure; the rise of the civil rights movement, folk song as political protest with Bob Dylan's own move into electric rock music, the emergence of black power, the growth of the anti-Vietnam war movement and the emergence of a new militant feminism were to combine in a counter-cultural hegemonic challenge. The rise of television as a technology and as a cultural form transformed the nature of celebrity and of sport stardom. Television produced a greater transformation in the relation between sport and its audience in two respects – domestication and globalisation. It brought live colour pictures from around the world into the home.[1] The importance of close-ups in the new medium foregrounded faces and personalities.

Best and Ali in the 1960s

Best and Ali were the first sport stars whose fame was fuelled primarily by television. They were celebrated for their looks at a time when concepts of beauty centred more on the face and clothes than the body in the culture of the beautiful people. They have come to be regarded as sixties icons. But iconic status is always conferred in retrospect and constantly reinscribed in accordance with dominant discursive patterns of specific moments. The Best and Ali that representation offers us now are the accumulation of these inscriptions, in which some earlier traces have been obscured or erased, whilst others are etched in more deeply. Best, celebrated then, has had his fame overwritten, but not obscured, by his decline. Ali, vilified then, has advanced through celebrity to sanctification. The past, far from being fixed, is constantly reinvented.

George Best emerged as the most extravagantly gifted performer in a talent-rich team – the Manchester United of the 1960s. At a time when the image of a professional footballer was still rooted in baggy shorts and Brylcreem, Best was young, cool and pretty. His image was associated with discos, boutiques, 'dolly birds' and pop music. In America, the emergence of Cassius Clay, later Muhammad Ali, marked a similar moment.[2] Ali was fast, smart and pretty, breaking with both the deferential and the monosyllabic traditions of black boxers confronting the white world. Like Best, he rapidly became a familiar face even to non-sport fans. The process of mythologising these two figures was well underway by the mid-1960s and, revealingly, both are linked to those iconic figures of the 1960s – the Beatles – each being dubbed 'the fifth Beatle'. George Plimpton quotes a conversation with columnist Jimmy Cannon during Ali's training for the first Liston fight in 1964:

> 'He's the fifth Beatle', said Cannon. 'Except that's not right. The Beatles have no hokum to them.'
> 'Its a good name', I said. 'The fifth Beatle.'
> 'Not accurate', said Cannon. 'He's all pretence and gas, that fellow ....' He went on nodding up at Clay. 'No honesty.'
> I looked in his columns later to see if 'the fifth Beatle' designation turned up. It seemed too good to use – even if it was inaccurate. I never could find it. Cannon was a man of his word.
>
> (Plimpton 1978: 86)

But Ali did of course get dubbed the fifth Beatle, as did George Best, and also disc-jockey 'Murray the K', and doubtless others. (After his star performance in Lisbon, Best was also dubbed 'El Beatle'.) Indeed it is a token of how much the Beatles were the paradigmatic celebrities of the period, that so many were thus linked. While training for the Liston fight, Clay met the Beatles shortly after their appearance on the Ed Sullivan show, and there is a picture of them in the ring with him (Hauser 1996). Best's haircut was frequently dubbed 'a Beatles cut'. Part of the appeal of these figures is ascribed to a combination of *Zeitgeist* and generational specificity – they 'captured the spirit of the times', but the spirit of the times is conjured up in terms of a youthful culture sweeping away the old fashioned, the traditional and the archaic. Budd Schulberg wrote that his sons 'find in his [Ali's] uninhibited ego-tripping nonsense that indescribable pleasure of being different from us, yes and better than us' (Schulberg 1971: 43).

George Best

George Best emerged as the first modern sport star – adopting a 'Beatle haircut' and smart mod-style clothes, frequenting discos and investing in boutiques. Best was a long distance from the ruggedly working-class baggy-shorted stars of the fifties. For the first time, a sport star had a significantly cool appeal, bringing together the very different worlds of sport, fashion and music. Best was wiry rather than beefy, and the rise of the mods and later the hippies marked the triumph of the seven-stone weakling, with the muscle-bound Charles Atlas figure becoming an archaic figure of mockery. An early profile spots the newness of the Best style: 'a sober and discreet blue tailored suit, maroon hand-kerchief peeping from the pocket, maroon knitted tie. There are signs of exuberance – the cuffed sleeves of his jacket, the sheepdog abundance of his hair style' but paints a picture of him as 'remarkably balanced, modest and self-contained' and, like Stanley Matthews before him, 'a model of thrift who puts most of his money in the building society, lives in digs, and goes to the pictures twice a week' (Brian Glanville, in the *Sunday Times*, 3 January 1965). Descriptions drew attention to the combination of frailty and poise that he exhibited. He was 'that wispy waif on the left wing', portrayed as 'maintaining an incredible icy calm' (*Daily Mirror*, 27 April 1965).

From the mid-1960s onwards Best built his reputation with a series of devas-tating performances, most notably his role in Manchester United's 5–1 win away to Portuguese champions Benfica in 1965, one of the key elements in the Best mythology. He is the 'wilful, skilful waif' and 'the young pretender to the King of European football title' (*Daily Mirror*, 10 March 1966). The 1968 European Cup Final, in which Best has subsequently been written up as the hero, gained him only moderate praise on the night. The *Daily Mirror* said 'Best had a mixed-up match, displaying great skill, but robbing others of oppor-tunities because of his greed on the ball' (*Daily Mirror*, 20 May 1968). By this point, however, Best was firmly established as one of the greatest footballers in the world and, along with Law and Charlton, part of the most exciting forward line British club football had ever had.

Best reveals much about his own attitude to football in his comments about other players in his book *On The Ball*. The description 'a natural footballer and a showman, Rodney Marsh believes his job is to entertain the crowd' is also clearly how Best sees himself (Best 1970: 18). The myth of the superbly talented sportsman with a desire to show off and a hedonistic and undisciplined streak is an enduring one that has provided the framework for stars such as Best, Alex Higgins, Ian Botham and Paul Gascoigne. In that all four stars had well-

publicised private lives involving drink and partying, the apparent magical resolution of the attraction of hedonism and the demands of the work ethic gives
their image considerable appeal for laddish masculinity. Michael Parkinson's
biography was part of the mythologising of Best, and both documented and
celebrated his Jack-the-lad insouciance. The highly publicised champagne
lifestyle that George Best took to leading featured an acquisitive promiscuity, in
which virility was publicly marked by status. In this objectification of women,
bedding Miss World advertised that you had 'made it'. After the retirement of
Manchester United's gently patriarchal manager, Matt Busby, who had tried to
'father' Best through the seductive pleasures of fame, none of the managers
who followed could handle the errant child. Wilf McGuiness was appointed
chief coach in April 1969 and sacked from the job in December 1970. Michael
Parkinson wrote that 'In those twenty months United went from crisis to crisis.
Invariably George Best was at the eye of the storm, and not Wilf McGuiness,
nor Matt Busby, nor all the heavenly hosts could have done a thing about it'
(Parkinson 1975). While the image of Best now revolved around champagne
and affairs with Miss World winners, the magical resolution of hedonism and
work ethic is a frail one – sooner or later, the star is bound to fall off the
tightrope – indeed this, too, is part of the voyeuristic appeal:

> He was already a confirmed sybarite, a considerable drinker, a successful
> womaniser and a stop-out. He still trained hard, still pulled out the stops
> most Saturdays but he was finding it more and more difficult to define the
> line between his social activities and his career as an athlete.
>
> (Parkinson 1975: 75)

Even as early as the 1970s, unbridled hedonism, with its inevitable trail of
tabloid headlines, conflicted with public image requirements of sponsors and
advertisers. The chairman of Bellair, who paid Best to promote their after-shave
said, 'We are trying to promote a clean-cut image, and Mr Best is not helping.
He will have to keep his nose clean in future, a lot of our dealers have a puritan-
ical outlook on life' (quoted in Parkinson 1975: 77). In the autumn of 1970
The Times devoted half a page to a description of Best's new house, but, by
January 1971, Best was back in the headlines for more negative reasons. First,
he missed a disciplinary commission hearing and was fined £250, and then, four
days later, he missed a game but spent three days in actress Sinead Cusack's flat,
besieged by the press. *The Times* ran a leader shortly after, called 'THE PRICE
OF INDISCIPLINE'. By May, Best had announced his retirement, triggering off a
period of alternation between retirement and comeback that was to continue
for the next few years. The cycle was characterised (as also with Gascoigne later)
by the sequence: misdemeanour–contrition–warning–forgiveness. In 1973, the
Daily Mirror quoted what it described as a bearded overweight Best as saying

> I know I've said before that I've come back to stay but this time I'm
> sincere. I'll prove it in the only way I know how and for United, the only

club I want to be with ... Sir Matt Busby came to see me and said 'when are you coming back, son?' From that moment I decided to try once more. I realised what a fool I'd been and just how much I'd missed it all.

(*Daily Mirror*, 7 September 1973)

The pressure for self-discipline, later to become a prominent part of press writing about the misdemeanours of sport stars is apparent here. Harry Miller wrote:

I welcome Best's return because the Irishman is the one British player in an era utterly devoid of genuine personalities who can attract a 'Full House' wherever he plays. But Best must know no club, not even United, can tolerate a repeat of his many indiscretions. Best has proved that an individual can be bigger than the game. He still has to convince us he is worthy of such an accolade.

(*Daily Mirror*, 7 September 1973)

The misdemeanour–forgiveness cycle collapsed in on itself amidst the growing chaos which Best's increasingly alcohol-fuelled lifestyle seemed to engender:

THE CASE OF GEORGE BEST AND MISS WORLD'S FUR COAT

Soccer star George Best stood pale and dazed in a London courtroom yesterday, accused of stealing property from Miss World. Best was given £6,000 bail and warned to keep away from Miss World, 19 year old Marjorie Wallace. Last month, Best, who has been transfer listed by Manchester United, announced that he planned to retire from football.

(*Daily Mirror*, 22 February 1974)

Manchester United finally lost patience in 1974 and Best became a carpet-bagging footballer, on hire to whoever wanted to meet the price per game. A long sad decline had begun. To this day Best is fond of telling the story of the hotel employee who, having delivered room service to the suite in which Best was ensconced with Miss World, champagne and a large sum in banknotes, enquired of him, 'Mr Best, where did it all go wrong?'. The sadness is that Best himself understands the superficial irony of the question, but not the deeper substance. He has never really come to terms with the fact that many football fans did mourn the lost years, the talents squandered and the glories never fulfilled.

Muhammad Ali

While Best's rise to fame was accompanied by acclaim, and controversy only came later with his slide into boozy indiscipline, Ali's career was controversial from the start. His outspoken style, and habit of predicting the rounds his opponents would fall in, provoked a racist reaction that he was 'an uppity nigger'. Jack Olsen's biography, which constitutes an example of the degree of hostility that white journalists had for Clay, refers to him as 'insulated and isolated in his cocoon of yes-men and hero worshippers' (Olsen 1967: 26). In the British press, Clay did sometimes get a more sympathetic portrayal, as in a review in the *Daily Mirror* (12 May 1963) of a BBC 1 programme on Clay – *I Cassius* – which commented, 'to become world champion at 22 after only twenty professional fights, you need more than comments which pack a punch'. Despite his defeat of Britain's Henry Cooper, though, most British journalists didn't give him much chance against Liston, the *Daily Mirror* (19 June 1963) writing that the idea of matching Clay with world champion Sonny Liston was laughable. Even George Plimpton, who subsequently became a friend and supporter of Ali, started out with a degree of hostility. In his book *Shadow Box*, Plimpton reveals a fondness for Archie Moore, with whom he fought an exhibition bout and, as a consequence, resentment against Clay, who beat Moore in his 16th pro fight, just four fights before his defeat of Liston to win the World Championship. Plimpton reports that Clay 'did a strutting prance over him, stomping up and down in his white ring boots like a Masai warrior' (Plimpton 1978: 82). However, in the build-up to the Liston fight, Plimpton, already warming to him, comments on the stiffness of the journalists in the training camp press conferences in 1964:

> The press sat in their rows at the Miami Auditorium staring balefully up at him. It seemed incredible that a smile or two wouldn't show up on a writer's face. It was so wonderfully preposterous. But I didn't see any.
>
> (Plimpton 1978: 87)

There followed two weeks of dramatic events that had a shaping influence on the construction of Ali as image. On 25 February 1964, he defeated Sonny Liston to become heavyweight champion of the world. On 27 February, he announced that he had joined the Nation of Islam and, on 6 March, he changed his name to Muhammad Ali (Hauser 1996: 11). Hunter Thompson links the unexpected victory over Liston to the hostility of sport journalists to Clay, arguing that he:

> made a permanent enemy of every 'boxing expert' in the Western world by beating World Heavyweight Champion Sonny Liston, the meanest of the mean, so badly that Liston refused to come out of his corner for the seventh round.
>
> (Thompson 1980: 582)

The name change, the espousal of the so-called 'Black Muslims' and the refusal to be drafted into the services produced massive hostility in the white media. Olsen cites newspaper criticism of Ali, which includes phrases like:

a self-centered spoiled brat of a child

a sad apology for a man

the all time jerk of the boxing world

the most disgusting character in memory to appear on the sports scene

bum of the month, bum of the year, bum of all time

Governor of Illinois called him disgusting

Governor of Maine said he should 'be held in contempt by every patriotic American'

Chicago Tribune launched a campaign to prevent him fighting in Chicago
(Olsen 1967: 31)

In England, Peter Wilson wrote that Clay was 'possibly the greatest embarrassment to the USA as a whole that sport has ever produced'. He referred to the Black Muslims as 'a stench in the nostrils of most white Americans', but conceding Clay's sincerity, he was generously prepared to allow Clay one more fight before following the example of Joe Louis and joining the forces, saying that 'this foolish, brash, rather cruel young man should be given the opportunity of making yet another million before he goes out to take his chance like any other fit young American of his age' (*Daily Mirror*, 2 March 1966). Olsen's portrait of Clay is of a man grown too big for his boots who 'seemed to skate right to the edge of mania in his pre-fight scenes. He lost track of the difference between buffoonery and nastiness and the public began to sour on him' (Olsen 1967: 43).

Racist hostility to Ali crystallised around his involvement with the Black Muslims (see Marqusee 1999). In George Plimpton's interview with Malcolm X, Malcolm attributes white hostility to Ali's foregrounding of his blackness, saying that 'he wouldn't eliminate the colour factor. But the press and the white people saw it another way. They saw him suddenly as a threat. Which is why he has become the villain – why he is booed, the outcast' (Plimpton 1978: 97). Ali himself also links white racism to his willingness to make a stand. Of the ten Louisville businessmen who each subscribed a thousand dollars to back him, Ali said:

They made it seem as if they were doing me a one-sided favour, and whenever I refused to carry out their commands – as later I did, especially when they ordered me to drop my religion, or have my championship fight with Sonny Liston cancelled – I was pictured as insolent, ungrateful, an unmanageable racist who hated all whites.

(Ali 1977: 72–3)

There are of course various types of celebrity biography: the exposé/hatchet job, the hagiography, the 'real' person revealed, the chronological account, the 'meaning' of the subject as capturing the *Zeitgeist* or reflecting his or her time, and the subject as creative genius (i.e. not like the rest of us).[3] Most celebrity profiles, in the very act of purporting to shed light on the 'real' person, characteristically contrive to contribute to the webs of mystification that precisely contribute to celebrity:

> Clay's personality is like a jig saw puzzle whose pieces were cut by a drunken carpenter, a jumbled collection of moods and attitudes that do not seem to interlock. Sometimes he sounds like a religious fanatic, his voice sing-song and chanting and all at once he will turn into a calm, reasoning, if confused, student of the scriptures. He is a loudmouth windbag and at the same time a remarkably sincere and dedicated athlete. He can be a kindly benefactor of the neighbourhood children and a vicious bully in the ring, a prissy Puritan totally intolerant of drinkers and smokers, and a teller of dirty jokes.
>
> (Olsen 1967: 107)

After the refusal to be drafted, Ali is increasingly a figure in a discursive battle between hawks and doves. For the conservatives, his refusal of the draft was a provocative and unpatriotic act, for the liberals he was being persecuted for his principled stand, for the counter culture his stand was both a vindication and a personification of the anti-war movement:

> Ali began to taste the bitter fruit of ostracism. When his draft status was changed abruptly from 1-Y to 1-A without re-examination, he made the statement that would send shock waves through hawks and hard-hats while winning 'right ons!' from young blacks and white doves, 'I don't have nothing against them Viet Congs. They never called me nigger.'
>
> (Schulberg 1971: 56)

Budd Schulberg (1971: 52–3) claims that Ali was the first black champion to proclaim his blackness and also that he did not merely reflect the times, but helped shape them:

> having learned that we cannot separate a champion from his times, now we had a champion who not merely reflected his time, like Louis and Schmeling, but, as a superb athlete-black activist, was beginning to shape his times.
>
> (Schulberg 1971: 55)

He counterposes Ali to the hero of right wing hawkish conservatism, Lieutenant Calley:

So we had Lieutenant Calley weighing in against Muhammad Ali. Not man to man, but symbol to symbol. Calley the unimaginative trigger finger of an atrocious war. Ali, who struggles to make his way through a book but who can read the history of our brutalisation in Indo-China as if the words were electrodes on his skin flashing the message to a brain non-intellectually but intuitively anti: 'I don't have nothin' against them Viet Congs'.

(Schulberg 1971: 59)

Like other sportsmen and women since the 1960s, Ali discovered that those who insist that politics be kept out of sport, really want simply to keep the politics of sport as they are. Once challenged, the liberal veneer chips away to reveal a reactionary conservatism. The discourses of fair play and of patriotism were in conflict:

Peter Wilson Says: Take your Choice, – Clay or Country

How does one stand on the question of Muhammad Ali – Cassius Clay? On one side is the revulsion felt by most people for a man who will not answer the call of his country when it needs him – reinforced by the thousands of American families who have already lost sons, brothers, lovers and friends in the Vietnam conflict ... On the other hand, Clay has beaten the only other two men still boxing who have held the world heavyweight title: Sony Liston in six and one round, Floyd Patterson in twelve. He has stopped the European champion Karl Mildenburger in twelve and the Empire champion Henry Cooper in five rounds before he was world champion, and in six in a title fight. He has beaten any and every legitimate challenger out of sight. So ... how can any other fighter be proclaimed champion while Clay is still around? Yet ... how can he be allowed to fight when he won't serve his country? The irresistible force meets the immovable object.

(*Daily Mirror*, 1 May 1967)

One perverse feature of celebrity is that the more a person is in the news, the more their lives are obscured by layers of discourse and mythologising. In a 1994 television industry supplement celebrating 30 years of the ABC series *Wide World of Sport* there is a profile of Howard Cosell that makes much of his relation with Ali and also an article about Muhammad Ali:

Howard Cosell helped break down some of America's fears about race. He would show up on racing broadcasts or *Wide World of Sports*, matched with a young phenomenon who had been baptised Cassius Marcellus Clay. Talk about odd couples. They became Frick and Frack, Mutt and Jeff, Abbott and Costello. The obnoxious and intelligent New York lawyer ... was matched with the brash and humorous black man from Louisville who had all the good lines because he came up with his own stuff.

When Ali dropped his slave name, to become Muhammad Ali, young sportswriters tended to make the change whilst some of the older ones, defiantly, persisted with 'Clay'. According to this *Wide World of Sport* supplement, their commentator, Howard Cosell, in opting for Ali, helped tip the balance:

> 'Moo-HOMM-ad Ah-LEE!' Cosell barked. The name stuck. There was also a war going on in Vietnam. Cosell, early and often, gave Ali a forum for explaining why he, in his classic word, 'ain't got no quarrel with them Viet Congs'. Ali was deprived of his heavyweight championship, and Cosell criticised that move, while the nation listened.

Plimpton, on the other hand, does not portray Cosell as quite the crusading liberal of this account. After Ali's refusal of induction into the forces, Plimpton is part of a group lobbying for his reinstatement. He goes to see broadcaster Howard Cosell, 'later a keen supporter of Ali', to ask if he can support Ali publicly. Plimpton reports Cosell as saying:

> 'Let me articulate my position, Georgie-Boy, I'd be shot, sitting right here in this armchair, by some crazed red-neck sharpshooter over there in that building' – he motioned over his shoulder – 'if I deigned to say over the airwaves that Muhammad Ali should be completely absolved and allowed to return to the ring. I'd be shot – right through that window!' he said, his voice rising as if he were broadcasting the event. 'My sympathies are obviously with Muhammad.' His voice became mellow. 'He has no greater friend among the whites, but the time, at this stage, in this country's popular feeling' – the voice rising and emphatic – 'is not correct for such an act on my part'.

Plimpton comments:

> Later on, of course, Howard Cosell became a leading and vocal proponent of Ali's reinstatement to boxing: but at the time, he appeared to reflect a universal disinclination toward the Ali case.
>
> (Plimpton 1978 : 137)

However, the rapid growth of the anti-war movement, the impact of the war on white middle-class children and its exposure on nightly news produced a sea change. By 1971, in the build up to the Frazier fight, 'almost 75 per cent of America was now agreeing with Ali that we had no moral justification for fighting in Vietnam' (Schulberg 1971: 131). In retrospect the defeat of Ali by Frazier in 1971 was merely one more chapter in the long story, but at the time it was seen as a possible full stop, and one that signified the end of the 1960s.

Sports Illustrated's cover proclaimed it 'The End of the Ali Legend', and Hunter S. Thompson wrote:

> A very painful experience in every way, a proper end to the sixties: Tim Leary a prisoner of Eldridge Cleaver in Algeria, Bob Dylan clipping coupons in Greenwich Village, both Kennedys murdered by mutants, Owsley folding napkins on Terminal Island and finally Cassius/Ali belted incredibly off his pedestal by a human hamburger, a man on the verge of death. Joe Frazier, like Nixon, had finally prevailed for reasons that people like me refused to understand – at least not out loud.
>
> (Thompson 1972: 27)

Yet the obituaries were very premature. Ali returned from defeats by both Frazier and Norton, to challenge for the world title again. The press coverage in this period occasionally had a tone of perplexity, as if not quite sure how to take Ali. The *Daily Mirror* (21 January 1974) reported that his voice 'ranged between a whisper and a shout. He postured and ranted and acted a host of different Muhammad Ali's.' To a large degree, though, the coverage remained hostile:

> By the time Muhammad Ali had been in this city for just an afternoon he had ... Promised to quit boxing if he loses to Ken Norton next Monday. Insulted his opponent by walking out of a lunch reception at the start of Norton's speech ... Threatened to fly back home across the continent because his new training headquarters were unsuitable. Staged a snarling angry unpleasantly racial scene with the fight promoter. Conducted a dozen TV radio and press interviews ... and also boxed eight dazzling dancing rounds with three sparring partners.
>
> (*Daily Mirror* 7 September 1973)

However, by the time of the second fight against Joe Frazier in 1974, his ability was at last beginning to win recognition from the press:

> The Astonishing Ali

> Ali the magnificent and Frazier the brave [McGhee's judgement on the second Frazier–Ali fight, which surpassed the pre-fight build up].

> 'Take a look at my face', said Ali, thrusting it forward for the lights and the cameras. 'Can you see a mark on it? Can you believe that this is the face of a 32 year old man who has just fought Joe Frazier twelve rounds?' No we couldn't.
>
> (*Daily Mirror*, 30 January 1974)

The presence of stars, whose image and charisma can be successfully communicated to a global audience was of course a crucial element in the development of globalising processes in sport. One key moment in this process, the Ali–Foreman fight illustrates both the dynamic processes involved in the construction of myth, and also the tensions within them. Muhammad Ali was of course already established as the biggest boxing star ever and perhaps the biggest sport star ever. However, he was not world champion, having lost it to Joe Frazier, who in turn lost to George Foreman. American sports commentator Howard Cosell talked of the potential bonanza of an Ali–Foreman fight, and said the main concern of the Foreman team in 1973 was keeping Foreman alive and unbeaten until a match with Ali could be arranged. He reported Ali's confidence that he could beat Foreman, and acknowledged that you could never rule Ali out (Cosell 1973: 252–4). However, most boxing experts expected Foreman to win.

The fight took place in Zaire, the first major world sport event to take place in Africa. The event was shaped by the interaction between the needs of American television, international capital in the entertainment and leisure sector, the political aspirations of Ali, the desire of Zaire to establish a presence on the world stage and the ambition of black ex-convict turned boxing promoter, Don King. Early in 1974, the Zairean Minister of Publicity, Tshimpumpu realised he needed something to put the country on the map. Meanwhile Don King was busy trying to become a big time boxing promoter. Access to Foreman had led to access to Ali. King said he could make them $5 million each (*Total Sport*, December/January 1995–6). Zaire and Risnailia, a Swiss Corporation believed to be linked to Mobutu, the Zairian president, put up much of the money on condition the fight was staged in Zaire (Mailer 1976: 104). President Mobutu felt that the publicity would show how his country, formerly the Congo, was freeing itself from the legacy of Belgian domination (Plimpton 1978: 225). Don King regarded it as the biggest event in the history of sports, declaring 'The Italian government want to stage it in the old Colosseum in Rome where the gladiators fought.' (Ali 1977: 453). For the Zaireans, Ali was a major part of the appeal. Mandungu Bulu, the Foreign Minister of Zaire, said 'Zaire is mainly interested in bringing Muhammad Ali to Africa for a title fight. We are only interested in Ali fighting whoever has the title' (Ali 1977: 456).

The African site with 'two black champions returning to their ancestral homeland' also had clear appeal for Islamic convert Ali (Ali 1977: 453). Ali's advisors were also well aware of the future possibilities and the ways in which they would boost Ali's intention to become a world statesman for Islam. Herbert Muhammad, Ali's manager said 'Zaire's the first country in history to sponsor a World Heavyweight title fight … if it comes off, other countries will follow' (Ali 1977: 458). Herbert Muhammad went on to arrange fights for Ali in Malaysia and the Philippines, with at least six other countries making offers. Alert to the symbolic dimension of the fight, King set about marketing it with an aggressive hyperbole, declaring 'Julius Caesar never paid his best gladiators half that much. Jesse James never performed for that much. No actor, dancer or singer in the history of the planet Earth ever got that much for a single performance' (Ali 1977: 450). He also claimed that it would draw 'a trillion fans' (*Total Sport*, December/January 1995–6). Joining in the hype, Ali had to be persuaded that his favoured promotional phrase, 'The rumble in the jungle', was not in the best interests of a country on the move and he was asked to drop it (Plimpton 1978: 236). Ali, by 1977, was already aware of the ways in which remarks earlier in his career had revealed a lack of grasp in this area, saying that

> later, when I did travel many times to Africa, I was even more ashamed that I had grown up so brainwashed about the history and life of the people I descended from.
>
> (Ali 1977: 75)

Ali's victory over Foreman, probably the most dramatic and certainly one of the most discussed moments in boxing history, set the seal on his reputation. A third destructive fight with Frazier was his last great performance, and possibly the beginning of his declining health. The victory over Foreman also heralded an escalation of the mythologising process, culminating in his near sanctification in the 1996 Olympic Games in Atlanta. Part of the mythologising process involves the attribution of magical powers or superhuman qualities and a mystification of the 'presence' of the celebrity:

> Even through the walls, his was the most elemental voice I'd heard; it was huge, melodic and sounded somehow eternal. Listening to it made me so nervous that I shook a little and felt that I needed to pee ... no-one else on the planet looks quite like him. His skin is unmarked and without wrinkles and he glows in a way that cannot be seen in photographs or on television.
>
> (Extracts from *The Tao of Muhammad Ali*, Davis Miller, in *Arena*, March 1997)

Mailer writes of Ali as, in effect, disrupting the power of the male gaze:

> There is always a shock in seeing him again. Not *live* as in television but standing before you, looking his best. Then the World's Greatest Athlete is in danger of being our most beautiful man, and the vocabulary of camp is doomed to appear. Women draw an *audible* breath. Men look *down*. They are reminded again of their lack of worth.
>
> (Mailer 1976: 1)

Plimpton casts the experience of Ali's presence rather differently, but still as 'special':

> Norman Mailer once told me that he felt men didn't like to look at Clay – he emphasised just about everything they were not and it cranked up all sorts of antagonisms they were ashamed to admit to – much as one avoided

looking at a beautiful girl at a cocktail bar for fear of a disruption of equanimity. I never could quite understand Mailer's notion. In Clay's presence, such as at those press conferences I always found myself staring at him, my jaw slightly agape, and always a smile in the works somewhere there, because so much of him came out in little digs and flourishes that we had to be on our toes to catch.

(Plimpton 1978: 87)

Ali's inevitable decline took a different form to that of George Best. Where Best was perceived to have dropped out of top level football too early in his career, Ali, like so many boxers, went on too long, suffering the indignity of defeat by boxers with only a fraction of his own talent. But his continued high profile, his involvement with black Africa, his combination of humour and dignity, recognition of his place in boxing history and public sympathy for his suffering the impact of a wasting disease all contributed to a process of reinscription in which his current sanctification has served to erase the traces of his earlier vilification.

Reinscriptions

If Ali moved from controversy to acclaim during the course of his career, Best took the opposite journey; yet twenty years after his retirement, he is still evoked in some contexts as the spirit of masculine hedonism. In the process of reinscription, star biographies are constantly rewritten from the point of view of popular memory, within the context of a selective tradition by which a canon is reproduced. Representations of the past of sport are constructed largely around magic moments and golden memories, in which popular memory is evoked; indeed the oral transmission of mythologised moments and the media representational process operate in parallel here, each feeding off the other. In the process, some moments are gradually dropped from circulation, whilst others (Bannister's 4-minute mile, Gazza's tears, Ali's defeat of Foreman) remain in the pantheon of golden moments. The process is analogous to the selective tradition, identified by Raymond Williams (1961) whereby certain works and authors become reified, others marginalised.[4] The images of Best and Ali have, of course, been subject to a great deal of secondary circulation – in newspapers, magazines, boys' annuals, video, cinema and advertising. *Men's Health* (December 1997) described the process of star identification this way: 'true heroes are people you feel you know better than anyone else, people who have a positive direct influence on your life'. They asked six men to write about their role models, and one of the six, Terry Hall (ex-member of the band 'The Specials'), recalled that 'it is hard to look at Bobby Charlton and say "I want to be like him". He looked about 60 or something. But along came George Best; he was young, he was handsome and he had great hair. There hadn't been anyone like him before: he was the vision of maleness I wanted to be' (*Men's Health*, December 1997).

Best was one of those stars, along with Botham and Gascoigne, that the 'lad' cultural world of *Loaded* was happy to appropriate. The slogan on the Philosophy Football T-shirt celebrating Best encapsulates a laddish perspective on life: ' "I spent a lot of money on booze, birds and fast cars. The rest I just squandered": George Best'. The slogan summarises the 'two fingers up to the world' hedonism measured in the consumption of objects, the male culture of drinking and the objectification of women. Dave Hill recycles the notion of George Best as the fifth Beatle:

> [After Bests display in Lisbon] England was perceived from abroad as the home not only of John, Paul, George and Ringo but also of Georgie Best, a star footballer whose style made him the first to belong naturally in the same swinging firmament as the Fab Four.
>
> (*Guardian*, 27 February 1998)

And he goes on to refer to the unutterable squareness of all the others from that era, contrasting Best to other ex-footballers who became celebrities on the 'panel of Experts' that first became a feature of television football in the 1970s:

> They may have all grown sideburns, invested in kipper ties and had sports cars on their drives, but these were men who'd been formed by the deferential puritanical disciplines which still pervaded football and were personified by manager Alf Ramsey – a son of Dagenham who'd learned the game while doing National Service and had taught himself to talk posh.
>
> (*Guardian*, 27 February 1998)

So Best is linked here firmly to concepts that the 1960s changed things and that figures like Best, were, in some ill-defined way, in the vanguard. While the process of hanging on to the golden moments provided by Best on the pitch in his prime is still intact, and his image has been mythologised, more recent representations of Best as an alcoholic who has resisted all treatments and ignored all warnings inscribes a rather different image – that of the sad drinker who has frittered his talent away. Indeed, from the perspective of the twenty-first century, Best's talents must seem to much of the audience rather remote. Only those over 40 can have seen him play at his peak, and these moments, captured on black and white telerecordings and videos of considerable graininess, are probably not totally persuasive to the young. Yet his iconic status is continually rewritten. Any British montage of the sixties is likely to include brief images of him. Similarly, even though some of Ali's glory moments were in the 1970s, his image is characteristically tied to the 'sixties generation'. His defeat by Leon Spinks in 1978 is constructed by Hunter Thompson as linked to the ageing of this generation:

> Dundee was not the only person who was feeling old with Muhammad Ali on that cold Wednesday night in Las Vegas. Somewhere around the middle of the fifteenth round a whole generation went over the hump as the last

great prince of the sixties went out in a blizzard of pain, shock and angry confusion so total that it was hard to even know how to feel, much less what to say when the thing was finally over.

(Thompson 1980: 581)

If Best's present is being written over the exploits of Best past, with Ali it is a rather different process. The eclipse of the man, through his sad decline with Parkinson's disease, has been accompanied by a purification of the myth, in which Ali stands for utter goodness. Celebrated by America at the 1996 Olympic Games, it was if all the earlier controversy of his career had been magically washed away. This gradual incorporation of, and depoliticisation of, Ali in representation, aided by the way the onset of the disease has slowed and limited Ali's own speech, has achieved what the white establishment could not do – it has silenced him. Consequently, stripped of both his physical power and the power of his voice, he is no longer a threat and is a symbol available to be appropriated and celebrated by others. Much is made of the poignancy of the contrast between then and now. An article headed 'Big Fight Over £1m Ali auction' (*Guardian*, 21 October 1997) is illustrated with three pictures: Ali with dark glasses, looking pudgy and captioned 'Muhammad Ali: Suffering from Parkinson's disease'; a picture of a memorabilia collector with the robe Ali wore for the Foreman fight; and Ali standing over Foreman at the end of the fight. As so often with controversial figures, once they are past their peak, retired, have lost their powers and are symbolically impotent, the very people who condemned them in the past feel able to praise them – as has happened with tennis player John McEnroe and cricketer Ian Botham. In the case of Ali, it is noteworthy that it is now, when, through disease the mouthy black has been silenced, the uppity nigger humbled, that he has won most universal acclaim. George Foreman was quoted as saying, 'He may not have been the greatest fighter, that may have been Joe Louis, but he was the greatest man who was ever a fighter' (*Guardian*, 23 May 1998). Ali's own words are quoted to reinforce the 'great man' image:

There is the moment after the first fight, in 1971, when Ali, beaten for the first time, shunned the uniform of the braggart to say quietly, 'we're all going to have various defeats in life, whether we lose loved ones or we lose our titles. Many people just can't stand those pressures and they crack up under them. But when a man can come through this after so many years of victory and being so supreme in his field and be able to handle defeat also victoriously, this makes him a bigger man'.

(*Guardian*, 23 May 1998)

Ali here is constructed as exemplary of a masculinity consisting of standing up to adversity and taking what comes. Yet Ali in the 1960s and 1970s was precisely a man who refused to accept the given and challenged it, whether it was the Vietnam war, the treatment of black Americans, or the neo-colonial exploitation of the Third World. Along with the reification of the man of courage in the face of adversity, goes an unwillingness to confront the realities of the disease, which, in being almost certainly boxing-related, challenges the very core of Ali's endeavour. Many writers, even the most insightful, have seemed to want to convince themselves and us that he's all right really. An *Observer Review* profile (15 June 1997) talks of Ali staging a levitation trick and doing conjuring tricks, lifting props from his bag with 'the delicacy of a surgeon selecting the correct instrument':

> In part it is just Ali amusing himself with magic tricks that he has been doing over and over for many years for anyone who comes to see him. But he is also, as always, making a more profound point. He has transferred his old boxing skills and his poetry and his homespun philosophy to another realm, from word to magic. The world sees him now, lurching a bit, slurring some, getting old, trembling, and recalls the unspeakably great and gorgeous and garrulous young man that he once was. He understands the contrast. But, he is saying, nothing is as it appears. Life is always a matter of perception and deception. And of course, this is what Ali has always been about.
>
> (*Observer Review*, 15 June 1997)

Ali's appearance at the Atlanta Games, frail and brave, and complicit in the curious combination of internationalism, nationalism and global television spectacle that the Olympic Games has become, was taken as a symbol of his full absorption into the mainstream of America, with Nation of Islam separatism now forgotten. It completed his sanctification:

> It wasn't easy doing what Ali did in Atlanta. But this is a man who, all his life, has come up with one gutsy performance after another. There was no way he could beat Sonny Liston. So he went out and beat Sonny Liston. There was no way he'd give up his title. So as an act of principle, he gave up the heavyweight championship of the world. He beat George Foreman when everyone knew he couldn't. He won the heavyweight crown for a third time, against Leon Spinks, when he was too old to win. Each time the world thought Ali was out of miracles, he performed another miracle. That's Muhammad Ali in Perspective. And what you had in Atlanta was a wonderful reaffirmation of just how much Muhammad Ali means to the world. Three billion people were in love with one man. Three billion people, even if it was just for a moment, had all the hate and petty prejudices removed from their hearts, and felt noting but love. That's a miracle.
>
> (Hauser 1996: back cover)

Hauser's summing up of Ali is certainly not simply celebratory, and assesses his 'flaws', but concludes with a eulogistic positiveness:

Ali was far from perfect and it would do him a disservice not to acknowledge the flaws. Its hard to imagine a person so powerful yet at times so naive – almost on the order of Forrest Gump. On occasion Ali has acted irrationally. He cherishes honor and is an honorable person but too often excuses dishonorable behaviour in others. His accommodation with dictators like Mobutu Sese Seko and Ferdinand Marcos and his willingness to fight in their countries stands in stark contrast with his love of freedom. There is nothing redeeming in one black person calling another black person a gorilla, which was the label that Ali affixed to Joe Frazier. Nor should one gloss over Ali's past belief in racial separatism and the profligate womanising of his younger days. But the things that Ali has done right in his life far outweigh the mistakes of his past. And the rough edges of his earlier years have been long since forgiven or forgotten.

What remains is a legacy of monumental proportions and a living reminder of just how good people can be. Muhammad Ali's influence on an entire nation, black and white, and a whole world of nations has been incalculable. He's not just a champion. A champion is someone who wins an athletic competition. Ali goes beyond that.

(Hauser 1996: 20)

The life of George Best, on the other hand, has been transformed into a moral homily – a warning, like a nineteenth-century moral tract, concerning the dangers of giving way to emotion, desire, hedonism and alcohol. His career is re-read through his supposed 'indiscipline', which no one talked much about in the 1960s and only became significant in the early 1970s, after eight years at the top. Football manager Lawrie McMenemy compared the exemplary Bobby Charlton with the wayward Best:

Bobby maintained a wonderful self-discipline throughout his career, keeping himself in perfect condition; and his behaviour on the pitch was exemplary – you would never find him retaliating, despite frequent harsh treatment, and he never once showed dissent with a referees decision.

George, on the other hand, allowed himself to be provoked on the field, with the result that he eventually retaliated – And he was usually the one to be sent off and suspended ... Off the field too, he got into the wrong company and did many things that a sportsman should not do.

(McMenemy 1981: 22)

It is ironic that two such intensely mythologised figures should have ended up at opposite ends of the moral–religious spectrum – Ali as a sanctified figure, Best as the object lesson of a Victorian moral tract about the evils of drink. Indeed, it neatly illustrates the ways in which major sport stars become the condensing point of broader social discourses about the way in which we should live, about how to be a man – in short, about morality and masculinity.

From the 1970 onwards, the long-term structural weaknesses of the British economy began to undermine the stability of the post-war political consensus around the welfare state. The rapid rise in world oil prices, high and rising levels of unemployment and inflation and the threat of recession contributed to the emerging political power of that combination of neo-liberalism, economic monetarism and competitive individualism that became manifest as Reaganomics and Thatcherism. On the ideological level, this produced in sport a growing tension around flamboyant hedonism. Flamboyant stars attracted public enthusiasm by swaggering and swashbuckling approaches to their sport, but the combination of the greater restructuring of sport organisation by the needs of capital, the resultant professionalisation, the rise of a new competitive individualism, the enterprise culture, and an attempt to regenerate 'Victorian values', introduced a new moralism that was to place the bad boys of sport under greater scrutiny and pressure. In addition, the restructuring of the conventions of tabloid journalism after Murdoch's acquisition of and redesign of the *Sun* contributed to a redrawing of divisions between public and private spheres that enabled scandal to acquire a much higher profile. The privacy accorded to a Bannister or a Matthews in the 1960s, and the relative licence granted to Best in the 1960s, was to be replaced by a surveillance of greater intensity. The next chapter examines the ways in which this political and ideological restructuring was to impact upon the ways top sport stars were represented.

10 Bad boys and the work ethic

Botham represents the bridge between the relatively deferential treatment meted out to Best in the 1960s and the vilification of Gazza in the 1990s.

(Bowler 1997: 4)

Bourgeois culture is no longer capable of producing heroes. On the highbrow level it only produces characters who are embodied consolations for defeat and on the lowbrow level it produces idols – stars, TV personalities, pin-ups. The function of the idol is the exact opposite to that of the hero. The idol is self suffi-cient; the hero never is.

(John Berger, quoted in Inglis 1977: 85)

While there are problems with this over-simple distinction between heroes and idols, it is certainly the case that sport stars in the age of media spectacularisa-tion and tabloidisation do not typically serve as exemplars of moral worth. More typically, it is the indiscretions and misdemeanours of their private lives that become the focus of headlines. Indeed, with a few exceptions, it is more typi-cally the stars of the past (e.g. Bobby Moore, Stanley Matthews, Joe DiMaggio), who are constructed as embodying moral principles and contrasted with the supposed egotism and amorality of present-day stars.

Three things made the period from 1970–90 distinct. First, by the mid-1970s, television technology had reached maturity and communication satellites had made television a global medium with sport playing a significant role. Second, the rise of a new political philosophy in the Western world placed an emphasis on economic monetarism, enterprise culture and competitive individu-alism. Third, an exercise boom developed, producing the establishment of 'fitness chic' and a convergence of the worlds of sport and fashion.

Advances in television technology during the 1970s meant that by the 1980s the trade in television sport had become global. Attempts were made to market American football, baseball and basketball around the world. Australian Rules Football appeared on the screens in Europe. Efforts were made to market soccer in the USA and Japan. The technological perfection of television and the establishment of a network of communication satellites, resulting in a conse-quent growth of television sport during the 1970s placed the traditional paternal, benevolent and redistributive structure of the governance of sport under considerable strain. In athletics the massive ideological investment in amateurism, reinforced by the place of athletics as central to the ideology of Olympism, meant that the growth of a television-, sponsorship- and advertising-driven elite level of competition sharpened the contradictions between amateurism and professionalism considerably. The need of television for star personalities, and the conventions of television, particularly narrativisation, had a transformative impact on athletics. I have written elsewhere about the narrativisation of the careers of Sebastian Coe and Steve Ovett, and the restaging of a race featuring Mary Decker and Zola Budd (Whannel 1982, 1986, 1992). Sport stars became television personalities in new ways through the growing popularity of programmes like *Superstars* and *A Question of Sport.* The growing power of top sport stars and their agents boosted the celebrity-centred secondary circulation of star image.

In England the post-war watershed between Bustkellite Welfare Statism and Thatcherism could be placed at 1976, with the IMF loan bailing out the British economy and signalling Labour's capitulation to monetarist control of the economy. One of the features of a crisis in hegemony is a disturbance in relations between social classes and political parties. Symptoms of such a disturbance could be seen in many political arenas: the polarisation of the Tories between wet and dry; the split in the Labour Party during the constitutional reforms; the deputy leadership contest between Benn and Healey in 1981 and the resultant formation of the SDP; the growth in electoral support for the extreme right National Front, and consequent emergence of the Anti-Nazi League; and the rise of nationalist politics in the Celtic nations. In America, during the 1970s, the anti-Vietnam war movement, the Watergate affair and the rise of issue-based politics was similarly suggestive of a disturbance in relation between electorate and political parties. The election of Ronald Reagan enabled the establishment of a new economic philosophy, dubbed in the press, 'Reaganomics', characterised by strict control of the money supply, cuts in direct taxation and attempts to reduce the role of the state.

Thatcher's rise to power in the United Kingdom ushered in the further imposition of monetarist economics, 'squeezing inflation out' and producing a massive rise in unemployment and a recession. The Falklands War helped counteract the unpopularity of Thatcher in the early 1980s, and curbs on union power helped the Government defeat the miners in 1984, paving the way for more destruction of workers' rights. North Sea oil revenue and wholesale privatisation enabled reductions in income tax, producing a mid-eighties boom in which 'enterprise culture' and 'popular capitalism' were the key terms in the culture of yuppies, filofaxes and mobile phones. For sport, the new entrepreneurship meant that policy emphasis shifted to privatisation, entrepreneurial partnerships, sponsorship brokerage and compulsory competitive tendering. Ironically, the Thatcher government was to be far more interventionist in areas where sport and politics were articulated together – such as the boycott of the Moscow Olympics and the attempted imposition of a National Identity Card Scheme for football supporters.

In the seventies, during the formative years of Thatcherism, the emergence of a new aggressive competitiveness in sport was epitomised by the rise of stars such as the tennis players Borg, Connors and McEnroe. Work-rate became a key term in football culture, epitomised by Kevin Keegan's Liverpool, and by Keegan himself, a player seen as compensating in his application for lack of real flair. The film *Rocky* (1976) also celebrated the ability of an ordinary figure, through hard work in training, to overcome the odds. The rise of competitive individualism and the work ethic paralleled the rise of Thatcher, Reagan and monetarism.

The rise of a 'sex, drugs and rock and roll' hedonism at the end of the sixties had been followed by a spate of rock casualties through death or heroin addiction. Progressive rock collapsed into self-parody with glam-rock, and eventually produced in reaction, punk rock, with its hostility to musical over-elaboration and the ostentatious trappings of stardom. By the eighties, major rock acts tended to opt for more finely honed and heavily rehearsed modes of self-presentation with a higher degree of professionalisation of lighting, sound, performance and presentation. While rock remained a domain in which excess retained its symbolic purchase, undisciplined over-indulgence was no longer simply celebrated – a moral climate favouring the work ethic and career advancement had made significant inroads into the world of rock. Fitness chic developed in distinct contrast to, and almost as a reaction against, the hedonistic excesses of the sixties and early seventies.

The growth of an exercise culture during the 1980s had its seedbed in three separate cultural contexts, which only later began to converge. A jogging boom during the 1970s and 1980s led to thousands of new recruits, mostly male and middle class, to exercise, a moment marked by the phenomenal success of Jim Fixx's *The Complete Book of Running* (1979). Aerobic exercise and working-out grew rapidly in popularity amongst women, with Jane Fonda's 'Work-Out' video a key moment. Weight training was taken up with enthusiasm within gay sub-cultures, and weight-training gradually attained a broader popularity with straight men, and with women. These three developments came together in the fitness chic of the eighties.

Looking fit – 'fitness chic' – became fashionable, with a boom in designer sportswear, and foregrounding of the importance of looking fit, regardless of actual state of fitness. The stress on work – work-outs, 'feel the burn', 'no pain, no gain' – became central. The themes of Thatcherism – individual self-reliance, hard work, enterprise and self-promotion were echoed in fitness chic. The activities of the new competitive individualism placed an emphasis on the work ethic. The slogans of the gym 'no pain, no gain', 'if it ain't hurting, it ain't working' and 'feel that burn' paralleled the political rhetoric of Thatcherism. The narcissistic focus on appearance and 'self' emergent in the 1970s (note in *Fame*, the song's refrain 'I want to live forever' along with the line 'Fame costs, and here's where you start paying') moved centre stage.

Sport-related enterprise was boosted by the new competitive individualism of the 1980s. There was a convergence of sport and fashion in which hitherto functional garments (the leotard, the tracksuit, etc.) became stylised fashion items, while mainstream fashion borrowed from the repertoire of styles more familiar from the sporting context. The leisure industry grew fast. Rivalry between leading makers of sport shoes and the booming market for trainers saw Nike and Reebok rise to challenge Adidas. Private health and fitness clubs grew in popularity. The new technologists of the body, personal fitness consultants, found lucrative employment. High tech sports like hang-gliding, jet-skiing and microlite flying emerged as new forms of conspicuous consumption.

During the late 1970s and early 1980s tennis was dominated by three figures, Bjorn Borg, Jimmy Connors and John McEnroe. Bjorn Borg epitomised the new professionalism – dedicated, focused and unemotional – it seemed that nothing could disrupt his game plan as he remorselessly drove the ball back from the base line. It was very effective but low in entertainment value. Jimmy Connors epitomised the new competitive individualism in that his desire to win was all too evident in his body language, the directness and muscularity of his playing style, his grunting and groaning and his passionate intensity. His emotions were always close to the surface and his fans suffered along with him. His manner of playing marked a distinct break with the gentlemanly amateurism that pervaded and dominated Wimbledon. John McEnroe combined the professionalism of Borg and the intensity of Connors and added a cavalier flair all his own. His genius for the game was matched by an intense perfectionism which led him to punish himself, his opponents and the officials with argument, abuse and emotional outburst. It was in and through such outbursts that the conflicts between the codes of gentlemanly amateurism and the new professionalism and competitive individualism were dramatised. Although plenty of other players had been regarded as misbehaving, it was around the clashes between McEnroe and the officials of Wimbledon that a whole code of conduct for punishing players was formulated.

The problem for the sporting authorities was twofold. First, in the new television era, the wider audience was able to consume such episodes in extensive repetition, until, like McEnroe's 'You cannot be serious' cry, they became mythologised. Second, such mythologised moments enhanced the celebrity appeal of the star and heightened public fascination with them. Borg was every bit as good a player, but McEnroe and Connors were more interesting and more exciting to watch. Coaches, managers and officials demanded dedication, concentration and application; whilst television producers and the public sought drama and excitement. Sport stardom continued to be structured by the opposition between flair and work-rate. Ian Botham and Alex Higgins became heroes of lad culture by offering a magical resolution of the hedonism–work ethic opposition in performing extraordinary feats against the background of hedonistic lifestyles. Yet, by the end of the decade, they and others were increasingly likely to be punished, whether by sports' governing bodies or by tabloid scandal; they had to pay the price of excess. As if to symbolise the shift, ex-athlete and aspiring conservative MP Seb Coe finally eclipsed the more working-class and rebellious Steve Ovett after a long rivalry. It is not entirely surprising that given the growing pressures and stresses of this work-oriented environment, stars whose lives appeared to be a magical resolution of the conflict between hedonism and work should have had a particular resonance.

The interesting thing about many of the bad boys, in the context of the eighties, is that they were operating against the grain of the times. In a period that demanded the work ethic, they clung on to sixties' hedonism. 'Individualism' is a significant element in the portrayal of stars of exceptional ability, often articulated in terms of the myth of the lone creative genius – brilliant but erratic and often misunderstood. Flamboyance and aggression, individualism, idiosyncrasy and unpredictability, the loss and recovery of magical powers, and vulnerability, all play a role in the construction of star-narratives in the popular press, in magazine profiles, and in biographies. Flamboyance is frequently represented as complemented by certain visible idiosyncrasies of style which contribute to the development of celebrity:

on Ian Botham:

twirled his arms and stretched his muscles to warm them up. The familiar buzz was felt round the ground.

(Ward 1993: 42)

on Alex Higgins:

Restless, on edge, twitching with temperament, he leaps to his feet every time he thinks his opponent might miss.

(Meadowcroft 1986)

Often the very exceptionalism of a star is portrayed as isolating, in a version of the myth of the romantic artist – the lone creative individual, such as Alex Higgins, who 'has never ceased to carry the air of the loner, the gambler and the harum scarum teenager' (Hale 1983). Frequently, this flamboyance, and 'individual genius' is also seen as at odds with authority (e.g. George Best, Paul Gascoigne) and this opposition to authority provides a populist appeal. Along with rebelliousness, strengths of character are highlighted. At Botham's first county game in 1974, he was 'Bristling with aggression and showing no sign of nerves' (Langley 1983: 18). Higgins had ' tremendous grit'. Muhammad Ali is described as having the character to cope with defeat as well as victory. These same qualities of individual flamboyant aggression are also singled out in more recent media discourses about the supposed crisis in masculinity as part of a problematisation of masculinity.

Alex Higgins

Janice Hale describes Alex Higgins as straddling the 'bygone and the modern eras' of snooker (Hale 1983: 30). In 1972 he earned £480 for winning the World Snooker Championship, and in 1982 winning it earned him £25,000. His image, at the start of the 1980s, was cast in romanticism, evoking a mythic history of hustlers. Indeed accounts of snooker ever since have tended to portray the period from the mid-seventies to the mid-eighties as one in which there were 'characters' – Ray Reardon, John Spencer, Doug Mountjoy, Willie Thorne, Eddie Charlton – who somehow connoted the seedy yet glamorous *demi-monde* of the pre-television era. Cliff Thorburn was described more than once as being like a Mississippi river boat gambler. It was Alex Higgins, with his pale face, chain smoking, nervous mannerisms and air of total intensity, who most caught the public imagination. Accounts of his early career are cast in terms of the romanticism of the tormented genius. He was portrayed as the 'loner … Brought up in the hard school of the Jampot'. His arrival – 'He came to England, his worldly possessions, apart from his cue, in a small suitcase' (Hale 1983: 30) – has become an element of the Higgins mythology. A passage in a book by fellow snooker player Jim Meadowcroft describes the moment:

> He stood there surrounded by all his worldly possessions; the clothes that he wore, a plastic carrier bag with a few personal effects, and a battered cue case that he had to hold on to at one end to stop the cue falling out.
>
> (Meadowcroft 1986: 25)

Meadowcroft's book is ghosted by John Hennessy, then snooker correspondent of the *Daily Mail*. In the context of sport journalism, the swapping of anecdotes in bars, the casting of events in clichéd fashion, the assembly line literary production of the ghost writer, all feeds in to the cut-and-paste mode of journalism, which helps ensure that such tales become the material for the narrativising structuring and restructuring process by which sport performers become stars and become mythologised. The *TV Times Snooker Special* reported that in 1972 Higgins:

> was every punter's dream, the rank outsider, first past the post, winning the world title at his first attempt, proving overnight that professional snooker players need not be sober, well dressed, conservative figures. He had found a new route from the back-streets to the big time.
>
> (Hale 1983: 30)

Charisma and controversy are highlighted as elements in his appeal:

> He had the charisma that commanded the attention not only of snooker devotees but the public at large. Some were outraged by public displays of

bad temper and lack of respect for convention, others dreamt of changing him. His appeal became universal.

(Hale 1983: 30)

He won the Benson and Hedges Masters in 1978 and 1981, the British Gold Cup in 1980, was a losing finalist in the Coral UK Championships in 1980 and 1982, the Masters in 1979 and 1980, and in the World championships in 1976 and 1980. But star quality is always about more than talent and accomplishment, and other qualities are necessary. In the case of Higgins, it was his compulsive involvement with the process of playing that was highlighted:

> He remained snooker's biggest attraction and most talked of figure. His audience is always breathless with anticipation, with dread, with disbelief. It is never relaxing to watch Higgins because he never relaxes ... Impatient for the last roll of the ball so that he can play his next shot, he is in a doomed hurry to conquer a game whose variables are infinite. It is a quest which fascinates, cajoles and haunts him ... The signs were in the 1981–82 season, that it was beginning to destroy him.
>
> (Hale 1983: 31)

The recovery of the hero from a position of peril is a well-established narrative device and one characteristic of the narrativised careers of stars like Higgins, Botham and Gascoigne has been the return to the top just at the point that the press and the public are about to start writing obituaries. As Janice Hale reported it,

> after the most disappointing season of his professional career, punctuated by rows born of frustration, fate suddenly dealt him the winning hand and, opportunist that he is, he played it to the full.
>
> (Hale 1983: 31)

Stardom has to be constructed in terms of a tension between knowledge and mystery. The utterly familiar is combined with the mysterious and enigmatic. Public desire to know the 'real' man and the full truth, is constantly invoked and can never be fully satisfied:

> Invariably true to himself, Higgins is no one's man. Moody, capable of great charm and equally great aggression, he is neither the perfect husband and father nor the uncontrollable wild man which the press paints him with equal enthusiasm. He is a complex, mercurial man, with a touch of genius for Snooker.
>
> (Hale 1983: 31)

Fellow snooker player Cliff Thorburn says:

He had a knack and a gift for the game and he was the best natural potter I
had seen until I saw Jimmy White ... He also had tremendous grit ... But
he's run his life like a guy driving with one wheel in the sand.

(Thorburn 1987: 45)

Thorburn tries to avoid controversy in the book, and describes two or three
incidents involving him and Higgins in a cool and detached way. One involved
the referee calling a foul because he had not heard Thorburn nominate, and
Higgins said he hadn't either. One involved Higgins missing a blue, but
holding up play to go to the TV scanner to see the replay; and following this,
Higgins made public insinuations to Thorburn regarding his alleged drugs use.
But this composure seems to crack after Thorburn's sponsorships are jeopar-
dised by talk of drug use:

Robert put in a complaint on my behalf about Higgins's conduct. A couple
of months later, Higgins head-butted Paul Hatherell at the Tennants at
Preston and grabbed and abused a couple of referees at the Dulux quali-
fying. Because of all these incidents and I guess his previous record, he
ended up being fined £12,000 and suspended from five tournaments. I
thought he got off easy if anything. Can you imagine what would happen if
a top golfer head-butted a golf official? He'd be barred for at least a year,
life maybe, if he had any kind of bad record.

(Thorburn 1987: 130)

Higgins went into a long decline in which his drinking habits appeared to esca-
late, culminating in a depressing and embarrassing TV appearance when, after
his elimination from the World Championships, he remained slumped in his
chair in the arena for some time, subsequently appearing semi-coherent in a
television interview. As was the case with George Best, while he continued to be
a newsworthy celebrity after his disappearance from the elite level, that news-
worthiness declined considerably. Public fascination requires both the elite
performance and the misbehaviour – the combination between the two and the
tension between them is precisely what generates the public interest. Once the
elite performance is no longer occurring, the misbehaviour, as Paul Gascoigne
has discovered, may occasionally hit the headlines, but never for very long.[1]
Alex Higgins, currently seriously ill, was most recently featured in a television
portrait, in which the contrast between the cocky flamboyant 'Hurricane'
Higgins of his finest days, and the shrunken, haggard figure sitting in a pub
counting the coins for small horse-racing bets was all too vivid, and the implicit
moral homily readily detectable.

Ian Botham

Ian Botham presents a different figure. Where Higgins, in popular imagination,
can be pictured emerging from the nicotine and alcohol *demi-monde* of the

backstreets snooker hall, Botham can be imagined, clad in pristine white, striding across green grass in the sunlight with a swashbuckling charisma. A biography of Botham establishes and emphasises his exceptional and flamboyant talent:

> Ian Botham is the sort of cricketer every schoolboy dreams of becoming. He hits huge sixes into the crowd when he is batting, sends the stumps flying when he is bowling, and picks up brilliant catches when he is fielding. He never seems to be worried by failure or defeat and inspires his team-mates with his endless confidence in himself. Out on the cricket field he is always on the attack.
>
> (Langley 1983: 5)

and the book ends with the assertion that 'you can be sure that there are plenty more heroic performances to come from him yet' (Langley 1983: 62). Descriptions of his early years offer him as the proud and patriotic youngster, wearing 'clothing that made him proud: a cap, a tie, a blazer, and sleeveless and long sleeved sweaters with the three lions of England on the front' (Ward 1993: 15). So, he is represented as every schoolboy's hero, but he is also a 'man' – the hardness of masculinity is portrayed as forged partly through adversity – and real men work hard and play hard – one account commenting that 'Botham went on hitting the ball hard and during his two years in London he lived hard too' (Langley 1983: 13). Aggression, too, is both highlighted and celebrated in the language utilised to describe his performances:

> a stunning spell of swing bowling at Lord's to unhinge the Pakistanis in 1978; an explosive acceleration towards the Test match double in 1979; ... a murderous double hundred against the overwhelmed Indians in 1982; bludgeoning the punch drunk Aussies into submission in 1985 with a fusillade of boundaries and bouncers.
>
> (Bowler 1997: 1)

And being a real man also means inhabiting a male-defined world in which, for much of the time, women are marginalised or excluded. Bowler describes Botham as:

> one of the lads, a 'new lad' before the term meant anything. He loved a few beers and a yarn in the pub. He loved to hunt, shoot, fish, play football and go out with the boys. That was the root of much of his popularity for it struck a chord with the general public.
>
> (Bowler 1997: 160)

Indeed, Bowler produces here a capsule description of laddish masculinity and the way that, despite the swaggering tone of its tales of sexual conquest, it is embedded largely in masculine exclusivity; in male groups.[2] One characteristic feature of heroic tales is the ability of the heroic figure to recover from adversity. Mythologised figures have, as with the cartoon character *Roy of The Rovers*, magical powers (see Tomlinson and Young 1998). In 1979 'there now seemed to be no limit to what Ian Botham could do on a cricket field' (Langley 1983: 45). This is the language of golden days, and fairy tale endings. But as in folk tales, magical powers can be lost. When Botham became England captain for the 1981 Test Series, 'he was a young captain, too young perhaps' (Ward 1993). Poor performances and Botham's own dismissal for nought in both innings in the Second Test culminated in his humiliating resignation of the captaincy. It was one of the lowest points of his career. His heroic status seemed diminished:

> He had lost some of his happy confidence too, and with it the good luck that seemed his by right … He was a shadow of his former world-conquering self and there was a worried look on his face instead of the devil may care smile.
>
> (Langley 1983: 50–1)

The hero thus loses his magical powers and needs to regain them through some agency, such as the intervention of a friend (in Botham's case the wise captaincy of Mike Brierley), a paternal authority (Venables and Hoddle in relation to Gascoigne) or by the love of a good woman (Kathy Botham, Sheryl Gascoigne, Angie Best). A major element in the appeal of major stars (such as Ali, Best, Botham or Gascoigne) is their apparent indestructibility, their ability to return to their best after a period of adversity – to make a come-back. At one stage in the famous Third Test of 1981, England were 174 all out and 135 for 7 against Australia's first innings total of 401 for 9 declared. Then Botham came in to bat and turned almost certain defeat into a near unbelievable victory, and 'his heroic effort had suddenly brought the series alive again, and the whole England team was inspired by it' (Langley 1983: 55). Such heroic exploits, inspiring a team, were also linked into the morale of the nation. As Ward described it, 'What started as a happy-go lucky slog had turned into a great innings. More than that, the mood of the whole nation had been lifted by Ian Botham's bravado in the face of defeat' (Ward 1993: 27).

The moment, and its subsequent inscription into cricketing history, provides a fine example of the mythologisation of the golden moments and magic memories of sport. The 'phoenix from the flames' theme provides a strong narrative structure for tales of sporting heroism. Examples include Botham in 1981, Alex Higgins's World Snooker Championship win in 1982, Paul Gascoigne on several occasions, but, most notably his superb goal for England against Scotland in Euro 96, and Muhammad Ali regaining the World Heavyweight Championship in Zaire in 1974 against George Foreman. A small pocket-size book for children, one of a series called *Sports Shots*, commented on an early match: 'and what a fairy tale ending for eighteen year old Ian Botham' (Ward 1993: 9) and declared 'next day people read the headlines – "Brave Ian's

Golden Day" – and realised for the first time that anything was possible if Ian Botham was involved' (*ibid.*: 14). Once this process of mythologising is established it acquires its own momentum in the circular relation between star, event, media coverage and audience. Consequently, as Ward puts it, 'It is no wonder there is an extra buzz whenever he walks into bat' (*ibid.*: 30).

The process of mythologising is fuelled by the recirculation of anecdotes – the same stories come up over and over in different versions. The tale in which Botham cheekily runs out the slow-scoring Geoffrey Boycott to increase the run rate is a good example of an oft told tale. The cultural capital of sporting knowledge is reproduced within the cultures of masculinity, passed on from father to son in the form of such anecdotes. As a schoolboy in the 1950s, I was fascinated to hear, from my own father, the story of how, in the 1930s, Glasgow Celtic centre forward Jimmy McGrory had once scored with a header from outside the penalty area and how this tale, after a few years in the retelling in the pubs and bars of Glasgow, had become so exaggerated that some now claimed he had scored from his own half. This story, despite concerning events some twenty years before my birth, featuring a footballer I had never seen play, in a city far distant from London, so gripped me that I passed it on to my own son. I was later amazed to discover that he in turn had enthusiastically relayed this tale, which was now over fifty years old, to his nine-year-old classmates. The power of this oral transmission of anecdotes, serving as a link between popular memory and the more organised mythologising of the popular media, should never be underestimated. In the wake of the extraordinary England victories in the 1981 Test Series, Botham was inscribed into the pantheon of heroes, measured up against other greats:

> W.G., Jack Hobbs, the Don, Denis Compton, Garfield Sobers, Fred Trueman, Dennis Lillee, Brian Lara, these are among the select handful who have managed to thrill even those who otherwise have no understanding of, nor interest in, the game of cricket. To that elite group must be added the name of Ian Terence Botham.
>
> (Bowler 1997)

Botham was also inscribed into a broader pantheon. Langley's book was one of a series of profiles in Hamish Hamilton's children's books. Others in the series included Muhammad Ali, Chris Bonnington, Geoffrey Boycott, Charlie Chaplin, Winston Churchill, Sebastian Coe, Roald Dahl, Thomas Edison, Queen Elizabeth the Queen Mother, Queen Victoria, Martin Luther King, Paul McCartney, Rudolf Nureyev, Pope John Paul, Lucinda Prior Palmer, Kevin Keegan, Lord Mountbatten, Anna Pavlova, Barry Sheene, Margaret Thatcher, Daley Thompson and Mother Teresa. What, you might well ask, does this bizarrely eclectic list of the great and the good have as its underlying organising principle? The back cover blurb merely tells us that what they share is fame:

The books in this series narrate the lives of famous people. They aim above all to tell an interesting and enjoyable story, while providing sound factual information both about the figures profiled and their times.

(Langley 1983: back cover)

Crucially, though, they are also the basis of narrative – 'interesting and enjoyable' stories. Heroes, in narrative terms, are also complex, and this complexity must be written in terms of occasional failure, propensity sometimes to be the villain, or an element of self-destructiveness. In one publicised incident in 1977, Ian Botham met Australian Test cricketer Chappell and, after Chappell made remarks about the quality of English cricket, Botham punched him off his bar stool. Langley's account roots this in 'natural male aggression', and asserts that 'it showed how much natural aggression and strength was bottled up inside this 21 year old. When it could not be used up on the cricket field he was likely to explode with frustration' (Langley 1983: 28). Indeed, the use of references to sporting competitiveness, and its necessary 'natural' aggression, is a common means of justifying, explaining and, crucially, naturalising male violence in popular discourse. Langley's 1983 eulogy, with a mode of address aimed at and accessible to the young, has a cheerfully optimistic tone:

There is little chance for Botham to get a rest, on the field or off it. Sportsmen today are more pestered and idolised than ever before, and most of them cannot walk down the street without being asked for their autograph or to play a charity game. But, being such a strong and cheerful man, Ian Botham enjoys every minute of it. And you can be sure that there are plenty more heroic performances to come from him yet.

(Langley 1983: 62)

The discourse is that of the role model, and is an idealisation of the hero figure who has no negative traits or bad reactions. However, a few years of such 'pestering' was seen as taking its toll, 'As Ian matured as a cricketer, his character was tested to the limit. Newspaper reporters hounded him for stories, members of the public sometimes provoked him, and his natural aggression could be misplaced' (Ward 1993: 34). Later portraits, in the wake of a series of tabloid headlines relating to scandal are couched in more equivocal terms. Patrick Murphy's (1988) biography of Botham starts with a strikingly apologetic note, and yet is determined to exonerate its protagonist:

This book is an attempt to place in perspective the jaundiced, apoplectic view of Ian Botham that has gained currency in recent years. Having known and liked Botham for a decade I am convinced he does not deserve the blanket condemnation visited on his head from some quarters.

(Murphy 1988: 1)

Indeed, the ability of the hero to recover is constantly reinscribed in biography:

Ian has had his troubles on and off the field – injuries, court cases, suspensions and sensational newspaper stories (some of them untrue). On many occasions his career looked to be in danger. Yet, whenever he was knocked down, Ian fought back. He has never worried when things appear to be going wrong. At an early age he learned he was colour blind. Yet colour blindness has not affected his play has it?

(Ward 1993: 33)

There is a populist tone of writing in which the tabloid press become 'them'; part of the powerful forces that, along with the governing bodies of sport, conspire to constrain (castrate) and contain the natural and ebullient force of the people as personified by their heroes (often dubbed 'the people's champion'). The press publicity blurb for Dave Bowler's book on Botham, *No Surrender*, provides a good distillation of the form of masculinity privileged in the narrativisation of the Botham story:

> his early successes on the field and his headstrong ebullient manner combined to make him an exhilarating sportsman and a threat to the gentlemanly traditions of the game. But all was not success. Disillusioned at his inability as captain to imbue his team mates with some of his daredevilry and aggression; dogged for years by a back injury; the victim of some shameful tabloid hounding; constantly at odds with the English management; this is the Botham uncovered here – a gifted man whose boundless loyalty, warmth and generosity were continually compromised by a media whirl of accusation, indiscretion hot-temperedness and indiscipline.
>
> (press release for Bowler 1997)

The hero is threatened from outside (archaic 'gentlemanly traditions', unhelpful management, unresponsive team-mates, the 'shameful' tabloid press) and from inside (injury, hot temper and indiscipline); but, in the end, his warmth and generosity is 'boundless'. Bowler's narrative in effect appeals over the heads of the press and cricket authorities to the public, reminding them both of cricket achievements and of charity work:

> Ian Botham will always have his critics. He pretends to ignore them but his willingness to take legal action against those whom he feels have transgressed illustrates his surprisingly thin skin. Botham, above all, wants to be loved by the people, wants to rekindle the flame of affection that he felt throughout his golden years. That may well be beyond him for those were the headiest of days. He would be better served by far to draw satisfaction from his deeds, forget the runs, catches and wickets. When he gets to bed at night, he need only recall that the leukemia research laboratories in Glasgow have been named in his honour as a tribute to his tireless fundraising activities. That is enough for any man. No one who could react so

> spontaneously and vigorously to an anonymous disease could be anything but a very great man.
>
> (Bowler 1997: 232)

It is hard to imagine pre-1960s sport stars, such as Roger Bannister or Stanley Matthews being written about in quite this way. The intensity of media focus on top performers like Botham, the spread of representation of sport stars into diverse media areas, has had a significant impact. It has made the star image into a point within popular public discourse onto which a diverse range of ideological themes can condense. It has made the image of sport stars the site of competing struggles between discourses of masculinity and of morality. They have become one of the battlegrounds on which questions of male identity are contested. The swashbuckling and rebellious mode of masculinity in which images of Higgins and Botham were constructed did not fit neatly with the professionalised and image-conscious modes of sport presentation being fostered by sport governing bodies and their sponsors during the 1980s. Hedonistic lifestyles did not fit neatly into the new competitive individualism of the Thatcherite work ethic. Yet in the context of the construction of spectacular individualised entertainment, figures like Higgins and Botham, like Babe Ruth before them, and Paul Gascoigne after them, were always likely to command a degree of public fascination greater than that accorded to the professional and committed but dull performers. Ideology polices masculinity but has to do so on the terrain of the popular and has to engage with the popular mood. The persistent fascination with the errant, the maverick and the erratic suggests at some broader unwillingness simply to embrace the routinised professionalism of work-ethic-driven sport stars.

The final part of this book focuses on the ways in which celebrity has become central to popular culture, pulling media form and content towards itself, as if in a vortex. In the process, popular discourse about moralities, masculinities and identities inevitably gets articulated in relation to star personalities on to whom a range of social concerns and anxieties are condensed. By the nineties, indiscipline was going rapidly out of style. There had been a long-term reconstruction of the labour market, in which the decline of the major heavy industries undermined the masculine culture of physical labour, craft skills and a job for life; anti-trade union legislation weakened collective ties and ability to resist, and casualisation, short-term contract work and flexi-time replaced job security. A new generation had been forged in the context of a highly competitive skills-based job market in which discipline, focus, enterprise and flexibility were buzzwords. Looking back in retrospect, a flamboyant and undisciplined figure like footballer Paul Gascoigne was somewhat of an anachronism even at the start of the nineties. By the end of the nineties, footballers who drank too heavily, took drugs, or who had other personal problems, were routinely expected to undergo counselling, courses of treatment, and, if they knuckled down and reformed, would achieve redemption. The next chapter examines the cyclical media process of celebration, punishment and redemption.

Part III

The restless vortex of celebrity

The final part of the book turns its attention to themes that have played a significant role in cultural studies theory in the last twenty years: identity, race and nation, celebrity, consumption, surveillance, discipline and punishment. This section, drawing on a range of examples, builds up a picture of sporting celebrity and the way masculinities, moralities and the themes above interrelate in representation. Chapter 11 examines the ways in which the surveillance of the media and the new disciplined professionalism of elite sport condemn some to punishment in the new village stocks of the tabloid front pages. Chapter 12 surveys the ways that sport has become a form of moral theatre, in which sport stars are the dramatic focal point of the public rehearsal of moral views and attitudes to masculinity and to violence. Chapter 13 assesses the relations between masculinity, identity and nation in the case of black sportsmen, and the ways in which public acceptance, as registered by the media, is often conditional and provisional. Chapter 14 focuses on the stress on appearance and image, and on supposedly postmodern features of contemporary culture – surface appearance, depthlessness, self-referentiality and pastiche. Chapter 15 analyses the dynamic processes of celebritydom, and it is argued that the major stars draw in media attention in a process I have called vortextuality. In the cultural context of a fascination with style, fashion and decor, celebrities represent our fantasies of lifestyle, luxury, conspicuous consumption and display.

11 Celebration, punishment, redemption and self-discipline

[A] chubby cherubic bouncing ball of fun called Gazza. He lived and cried for England. And we cried with pride.

(*Sun*, July 5 1990)

He is a cavalier genius whose brilliance gives joy to millions or he's an overpaid buffoon who just happens to be able to kick a ball about.

(*Guardian*, 30 September 1996)

The career of England international footballer Paul Gascoigne, as traced by the media, has the character of a long-running soap opera story. Popular culture constitutes a mediating interface between popular common sense and more structured political discourse. The story of 'Gazza' provides an example through which to examine the tensions between tradition and change, freedom and constraint, nation and individual, and public and private. It offers material through which to analyse the construction of male identities in a period in which gender relations were being reshaped. Gascoigne has, arguably, come in for a greater degree of public punishment in the tabloids than any other footballer. It can reasonably be suggested that he has brought much of this on himself. However, when one recognises that, in the press, his major 'crime' has not been letting down his wife, his children, or himself, but rather letting down his country, it becomes clear that something broader is at stake, associated with the heightened demands for professionalism and self-discipline, in order that national self-esteem is boosted by success in international competitions. Masculinity here has to be disciplined, not so much for character development, or for the good of the family, or gender relations, but for the good of the nation. The growing professionalisation of sport, and the greatly increased financial rewards, have together produced greater pressure for dedication and commitment. The tabloidisation of the press has fostered an erosion of a clear distinction between public and private domains, leaving celebrities more vulnerable to the exposure of their 'private' lives. Tabloidisation and the pressure for success have encouraged a culture of surveillance in which miscreants are punished by publicity, and subjected to the disciplined control of their occupation.

Gascoigne: from 'daft as a brush' to the 'Last Chance saloon'

In the late twentieth-century history of the England football team, Paul Gascoigne's own story looms large. Present as a motif even when absent in person, he has dominated both peaks (the semi-final against Germany in 1990) and troughs (the failure to beat Holland in 1993). A major issue in the build-up to the Holland game in the England press was how to replace Gascoigne. It was taken for granted that he had to be replaced: that it was not just a matter of picking a different team, but of replacing a figure on whom the team had come to rely.

There have been, so far, six distinct phases in the story.[1] First, in the second half of the late eighties, word spread within football of an extraordinary if wayward talent emerging at Newcastle – a Geordie lad whose fondness for beer, hamburgers and Mars bars did not prevent his display of impressive ball control. A transfer to Tottenham Hotspur added momentum to the popular demand (orchestrated by the tabloid press) that he should be picked for England as a regular player. It was in this phase that 'Gazza' was born. God's gift to the gimmick photographer, Gascoigne's own behaviour fed into the establishment of the wacky, 'daft as a brush' image that the moniker denoted.

Second, having become established in the England side only just in time to play in the 1990 World Cup Finals, Gascoigne emerged as one of the stars of the competition. Even more importantly, at a key moment in the semi-final, having had his name taken, which would mean missing the final if England qualified, he broke down in tears. The subsequent picture, anchored with the caption, 'there'll always be an England', was reproduced on a big-selling T-shirt. This more than any other single event set the seal on the emergence of Gazza as, in the Barthesian sense, a myth. In the words of the *Sun*, 'we cried with pride' (5 July 1990). Opportunities galore opened up for Gascoigne and his agents, and they opted for the instant cash-in as opposed to the slow and careful image-sustaining. In the light of subsequent events, this decision looks a lot shrewder than it did at the time. For a while 'Gazza' was everywhere on every outlet selling everything imaginable. Concern expressed at this hyperactivity (not least by that other popular icon, 'El Tel' – Spurs manager Terry Venables) were eased by his continuing on-field form, culminating in a cracking goal from a free kick that took Tottenham to the Cup Final in 1991.

This final, however ushered in a third phase, in which 'Gazza' began to move into that rather large lexical category of 'dislocated superstar' (Critcher 1979) occupied by such players as George Best, Charlie George, Stan Bowles, Jim Baxter – in short, it became evident that here we had another wayward genius in whom waywardness was starting to subsume the genius. Emerging even more hyperactive than usual for the 1991 Cup Final, Gascoigne committed two outrageous fouls, born, as always with him, more from over-enthusiasm than viciousness. The second one wrecked his knee, threatening a transfer move to Lazio that was calculated to save Tottenham from financial disaster. Gascoigne spent a season in semi-limbo recuperating and then moved to Italy, helping to inspire Channel 4's acquisition of the rights to show live Italian games in England. But the move to Italy was not a success, the Italians were unhappy with his form, stories circulated about weight problems, and the 'Gazza' story began to take on the form of the decline-and-fall narrative structure. The long 'on again/off again' story of his relationship with Sheryl became the subject of regular headlines, as this sample from 1994 shows:

GAZZA TO MARRY	(*Daily Mirror*, 22 February 1994)
GAZZA SPLITS FROM SHERYL	(*Sun*, 24 May 1994)
GAZZA'S SHERYL DUMPS THE RING	(*Sun*, 25 May 1994)
YOU'RE FAT AND UGLY, GAZZA, SAYS	
LOVE SPLIT SHERYL	(*Daily Mirror*, 25 May 1994)

The third phase came to a crescendo with the episode of the dentist's chair, cocktails and the damaged plane. England stars were heavily featured in the news, pictured – some with dishevelled or partially removed shirts – drinking a special cocktail in a dentist's chair in the cause of celebrating Gascoigne's birthday. Outrage increased when damage was reported to the plane bringing them back from the Far East, and this outrage was especially great as it was on the eve of the Euro 96 competition in England. Whether Gascoigne was involved in the damage remains unclear, with no evidence having been produced, but certainly the mud clung more to him than anyone else.

Gascoigne then, from the troughs of public opprobrium, entered a brief fourth phase of redemption. Playing well in the tournament, as did England, he scored a stunning goal to clinch victory against Scotland, and then married Sheryl in a lavish ceremony fully documented in *Hello* magazine. Both on and off field the recovery was to prove short-lived. The fifth phase involved a sad and seemingly remorseless decline towards tragedy. Well-documented evidence of assault on Sheryl was splashed over the tabloid press. A period of public remorse, rumours of heavy drinking and allegations of his unfitness persisted throughout 1997. A partial recovery of form with Middlesbrough led to his inclusion in the 1998 World Cup Squad, only for a seemingly boozy night out with Danny Baker and Chris Evans to hit the front pages. With born-again Christian Glenn Hoddle's patience stretched to the limit, Gascoigne was forgiven one last time, only to offend once again at the England training camp, which led to him being dropped from the final squad. Further rumours of drink-related problems were followed by entry into a programme of treatment and counselling, and it seemed that the days of footballing excellence were over. Since 1999, however, in a sixth phase, Gascoigne has kept out of the limelight, and a move to Everton seems to have resulted in weight loss, a more cheerful manner and a recovery of form. Part of the appeal of figures like Gascoigne lies in the public feeling they inspire that they can never quite be written off – they remain, almost till the end, capable of surprising us with their extraordinary ability.

When analysed from the structural perspective, the Gazza story precisely conforms to a very typical pattern in the tabloid coverage of stardom. Clearly stars of all types play a very important part in the world of the tabloid press, and in the initial phase of fame they are typically celebrated for their ability, or achievements, or genuine charisma, or the spectacle of their appearance. Once they are established, however, further celebration becomes of low news value, whereas any whiff of sensation or scandal has a greatly enhanced news value. So the slide from hero to villain/victim, that stars such as Elton John and Ian Botham have drawn bitter attention to, is in no small part a logical outcome of the very narrative structure of star coverage. It is partly determined by the changing hierarchy of news values within which such stories come to be written at all.

Gascoigne as clown: establishment of a press paradigm

It was ex-England manager Bobby Robson who provided the press with the 'daft as a brush' phrase that helped establish the theme of Gazza as clown. According to him, 'Paul is the sort who, in a flash of genius, can win you the game you looked like losing. But he is also bound to do something daft at some stage. He's not going to change now – he's always going to be a bit of a joker' (*Sunday Mirror*, 6 March 1994). This quality alone was seen by some as a bar to any suggestion that he should be made captain of England – 'Captain? Crazy!' was the verdict by Jane Moore in 'He belches. He tips pasta over his mates. He's Venables's No 1' (*Daily Mirror*, 25 February 1994). Indeed, even more reflective analysis in the quality press remains locked into the genius–clown paradigm:

> He is a cavalier genius whose brilliance gives joy to millions or he's an over-paid buffoon who just happens to be able to kick a ball about … he's the prat with the gob who represents the triumph of the yob; or he's a genius capable of doing things with his feet which lift the spirits of his followers out of their dreary norm. He's a crass example of a society with values inverted; or he's a glorious cavalier grating against the puritanical killjoys.
>
> (*Guardian*, 30 September 1996)

The passage catches the appeal of the enigmatic. Celebrities who pose an enigma, and in whose persona a battle appears to be taking place, are more likely to catch the attention of the public. They are exciting to watch because of the element of danger and unpredictability.

Bad boy, bad press?

We have become accustomed to the suggestion that Gascoigne is drinking in the Last Chance saloon (a tavern that must be somewhat crowded with assorted bad company), but for some he has been frequenting that particular watering hole for a long time:

although 12 short months ago everyone wanted to wear the number he had sported in the World Cup, now Gascoigne's number is up.

(Evening Standard, 3 September 1991)

In the city that just over a year ago welcomed Gazza as the hero of Rome, there is now a growing disenchantment – expressed in derision – with these antics. Graffiti in pub lavatories offers spot-the-ball prizes for guessing where Gazza's brain is hidden.

(James Dalrymple, *Sunday Times,* 6 October 1991)

A story headed 'Vultures hover over Gazza's last stand', (*Guardian,* 11 December 1993) suggested that Lazio were running out of patience with Gazza and hostile stories were being fed to the Italian press. The *Evening Standard* sought to change the frame of reference from comedy to tragedy:

The excuses about the perils of fame no longer stand up. Even those who have supported him are beginning to see clear signs of approaching catastrophe. 'He is no longer a joke', said one sports writer who has been close to him since the start of his extraordinary career. 'He is a tragedy in the making ... his two vicious tackles within minutes of the kick-off of this year's FA Cup Final shocked the Wembley crowd' ... the public's reaction was one of icy distaste. The Gazza legend was taking a nosedive and recently he found that he topped Saddam Hussein in a newspaper unpopularity poll.

(Evening Standard, 5 September 1994)

At the heart of the 'Gascoigne problem' was indiscipline – a failure to conform with the high standards of professionalism and commitment that were a significant feature of the new competitive individualism articulated during the 1980s. Advice supposedly offered by Gascoigne's Italian team-mates included:

1   Make some sacrifices, work harder
2   If you get in trouble, talk to us
3   Train with us, cycle and go swimming

(Daily Mirror, 25 July 1994)

The build up to Euro 96 featured highly publicised stories about the behaviour of the England squad – 'Men behaving badly', according to a *Sun* (29 May 1996) headline; whilst the *Daily Mirror* (29 May 1996) had 'Drunken England Stars plane shame'. This prompted Sir Alf Ramsey, referring to Gascoigne, to announce: 'I will not go to Wembley if this man plays' (headline in the *Daily Mirror,* 1 June 1996). The *Sun* announced that 'Paul Gascoigne will be read the riot act by Terry Venables when England players report this weekend for Euro 96' (*Sun,* 29 May 1996). Constantly it was suggested that Gascoigne (and, on occasions, others) were not fit to play for England – their behaviour was incompatible with the demands of group discipline and national representation.

The wife-beating story

It was, however, the dramatic *Daily Mirror* front page in November 1996, showing Sheryl's bruises, believed inflicted by Gascoigne, that finally dislodged the comfortable genius–clown paradigm. In the wake of a week in which he achieved the startling feat of being on the front and back pages with different stories (allegations that he beat up Sheryl, and being sent off in Scotland), the issue became whether he should be picked for England. The story was linked in the broadsheet newspapers to the broader theme of sportsmen and violence. This, in turn, was part of a broader discourse about 'masculinity in crisis'. The follow-up reaction stories counterposed those who called for Gascoigne to be punished and excluded from the England team, and those who focused on Gascoigne's need for counselling. Interestingly, it was those new converts to counselling, the Football Association, who advocated the caring and nurturing approach, whilst condemnation and calls for punishment were spearheaded by women's groups. The story became a complex and elaborate one in that so many discursive elements were being articulated together. The call for a return to traditional morality, feminism and violence against women, the need for sport stars to be role models, the perceived moral crisis, the issue of discipline in society, behaviour in schools and calls to reintroduce caning, the debate over family values and the role of parents were all present in the debate. Gascoigne asked Hoddle to drop him, but the born-again England manager, fusing Christian forgiveness, nineties counselling and the pragmatism imposed by the need of England victories, resisted the demands. The press identified the period as crucial, with the *Sun* commenting that 'Gascoigne will walk a tightrope this week as he comes under media scrutiny intense even by his standards. He knows this is definitely his last chance' (*Sun*, 4 November 1996). The football world united behind Hoddle's line; Howard Wilkinson of the League Managers' Association said that:

> we have to remember we are human beings first, soccer people second. If the game can be a means of rehabilitation then it has a duty to be so. Critics say Paul has a poor track record and they may be correct.
>
> (*Daily Express*, 4 November 1996)

In 1997, in an article headed 'Men Behaving Badly', a discursive reference to the TV series of the same name, and to the new-laddism of *Loaded*, it was announced that Gascoigne had been voted the most badly behaved person in a National Opinion Poll. He got 33 per cent of the vote, ahead of Liam Gallagher with 17 per cent and Michael Jackson with 8 per cent (*Guardian*, 8 January 1997). The well-publicised binge in London with laddish media figures Danny Baker and 'Ginger' Evans was represented as a 'last straw' moment, and, let's face it, relying on Danny Baker to tell you when you've gone too far shows poor judgement on anyone's part. By mid-1997, the press were beginning to hint at obituary time for Gazza as an international: 'Is it finally curtains for the boy Gazza? ... a Gascoigne sapped by an eccentric lifestyle and a decade of bright lights becomes a liability when the endurance level begins to dip' (*Evening Standard*, 25 April 1997). At the start of 1998, Gascoigne, now playing for that symbol of Protestantism, Glasgow Rangers, was fined £20,000 for miming an Orangeman's flute-playing during a match against the Catholic team, Celtic, and had to make a public apology (*News of the World*, 11 January 1998). Later in the year, there were also reports of him showing up in an Irish bar in New York in a Celtic shirt. This showed a truly remarkable ability to alienate everyone, and prompted the question, is he accident prone, determined to provoke, wilfully self destructive, or just dumb? Revelations of his 20 a day cigarette habit were brushed aside by England manager Hoddle (*Daily Mirror* 13 May 1998). Hoddle appeared to make serious attempts to encourage Gascoigne to handle his drink and indiscipline problems, but finally ran out of patience during the pre-competition training for the 1998 World Cup and dropped him from the squad. Gascoigne flew to Florida where as the *Daily Mirror* described it 'Paul Gascoigne prefers to play on a Florida beach with his wife and children and shows no interest in the result of the match' (*Daily Mirror*, 16 June 1998). The paper continued to track Gascoigne's activities in the USA, describing him as unable to resist a plate of greasy chips, and suggesting that this was the sort of diet that may have convinced England boss Glenn Hoddle that the star was not fit enough to be included in his squad (*Daily Mirror*, 22 June 1998).

Tabloid press as the new village stocks

It is no surprise that Paul Gascoigne gained such prominence in the press for he fulfilled so many of the criteria for making news. Elevated to star status by virtue of his football talent and striking personality, his activities subsequently were bound to attract press coverage. Galtung and Ruge (1973) identified the importance of personalisation and negativity in news stories and remarked that once something is news it continues to be news even if the amplitude is reduced. Rock (1973) stated that those things that have been news in the past are likely to be news again and argued that news has a cyclical quality which produces self-generating paradigms. Gascoigne stories revolved around the genius–clown paradox from the earliest days until the 1996 stories about violence against his new wife Sheryl.

Sports news has its own distinctive part of the paper and its own set of alternative news values (Hall, in Ingham 1978), and consequently sport stories that break out of the sports page ghetto and hit the front page have an added resonance. Press coverage of sport has a dual existence – for the most part it constructs a closed masculine world, rich in statistics and esoteric knowledge, which preserves its 'closed'-ness by the production and reproduction of specialist knowledge – a form of cultural capital (see Bourdieu 1977) that serves to bind and link masculine insiders and exclude outsiders. However, at its most prominent and dramatic, the major events and stars of sport have a great cultural prominence, and media foregrounding brings such events and stars to the attention of an audience otherwise indifferent to sport. In the 1990 World Cup, England's progress to the semi-finals produced new and temporary forms of identification with a growing audience, and the persona of Gascoigne, centre stage from the start, became the focal point of this audience fascination (Whannel 1992: 147–8). With the famous '1990 tears' Gazza became, in the Barthesian sense, a myth (see Barthes 1973). Media sport combines the values of news and entertainment – indeed, in some ways, it is the prototype 'infotainment' (see Branston 1993). The demand of television for stars, action and narratives foregrounds the star image (Whannel 1992; 112–5). Gascoigne has complained of being 'hammered' by the press, but those who sell their wedding to *Hello* magazine (giving the publication a record sale of 650,000) clearly have, at the least, an ambiguous attitude towards publicity.

Stars of the status of Gascoigne, who are around for many years, transcend the individual closed narratives of single events and competitions. In the media constantly for exploits both on and off the field, they are analogous to soap opera characters (see Jordan 1981). They have a past, a history, which the audience is aware of, and through which they are read. These past histories frequently appear in the form of photographic montage. Gascoigne, as a star, once established, is always presented in terms of a story – he has a history which is told like a story. It is not a simple story with a conventional hermeneutic closure, because his career is not over and yet has already been long and controversy-laden. The public construction of his persona has the form of a character in a long-running soap opera, and, like such a character, it has its highs and lows. Just as soap-opera characters require periodic reshaping, so such a sport star in the glow of the tabloids is periodically reshaped. Botham went from hero (the 1981 test series) to villain (drug and sex stories) to hero (the charity walks). Gascoigne's career has lent itself to such narration by the regularity with which he has made a fool of himself and then performed heroic feats. Descriptions of him provide an indication of his fluctuating popularity – 'Geordie lad', 'Fashion Victim', 'Fat', 'Brainless', 'Plastered Gazza', 'Cry Baby Gazza', 'Spurs' ace', 'Gazza the Great', 'Gazza the Gladiator', 'Hero Gazza', 'Millionaire Soccer Star'.

If the media have changed dramatically in the post-war era, so has football. The widespread adoption of floodlights, the introduction of European competition, the growth of television coverage, the abolishing of the maximum wage in 1961, the rapid escalation of transfer fees and earnings, have all combined to change the game. Critcher (1979) locates the problem for a footballer like Gazza. Once upon a time, in the years before the intensity of media attention grew, a footballer such as Gascoigne could have remained a working-class lad who liked a bit of a drink with his mates. The new socially mobile era ushered in by the post-war changes Critcher points to, characterised by spectacularisation, internationalisation and commercialisation, gave footballers new scope but severed other options. It is no longer possible for a Gascoigne to remain simply a working-class lad: in the typology of stars, he is the classic example of Critcher's superstar-dislocated type. Gascoigne's career is one of adjustment crisis in a profession in which new opportunities for class mobility provides both opportunities and pressures. Seen from the perspective of classic sociological oppositions – tradition and change, freedom and constraint, public and private – the negative publicity accruing to Gascoigne frequently grows out of his failure to negotiate a comfortable way through.

In some senses a very traditional figure – a shorter than average Geordie from a working-class background, steeped in the masculine cultural traditions of beer, pubs, clubs and laddishness – his fame opened up a world in which media interviews, champagne, expensive hotels and limousines are the currency. Along with the rewards came new demands – to offer the very marketable 'bubbly, irrepressible, daft as a brush' character of Gazza, whilst also performing a middle-class set of social conventions to do with saying the right thing, being respectful and not upsetting the sponsor. The paradox is that the very irreverent clownishness that prompts him to belch into the microphone, or, in response to the question, 'do you have a message for Norway?', impishly reply 'Fuck off, Norway' provides the material through which he is, in his own evocative and revealing term, 'hammered' by the tabloids. It is not the clownishness that offends, but the working-class, masculine, laddish quality of the clowning. Social changes and the mobility provided by money always exist in tension with established class-cultural patterns, as the slightly snobbish tone of descriptions of the Gascoigne wedding in the *Guardian* reveals:

> Gazza with a bleached crop wearing a brocade frock coat ... his mum looking like a pantomime dame, Sheryl showing off the £3000 boob job he gave her ... None of it was cheap, none of it was subtle.
>
> (*Guardian*, 30 September 1996)

The changed earning power of footballers opens up massive new freedoms (such as jetting off to New York for a weekend to drink in the Irish bars), yet these freedoms are within the context of a sport that demands discipline, adherence to rules and routines and to authority. The disciplined life of Italian football, significantly more demanding than that of the rather beery English game, offered a particularly irksome challenge to Gascoigne's established patterns dubbed by ex-England manager Graham Taylor as 'refuelling'. In the 1950s, scandal had to have specific drama to get into the headlines – political implications, security implications, involvement of elite and respected public figures, or criminal implications. Otherwise the goings-on of the famous were rarely given public airing. Journalists in the know characteristically turned a blind eye. Specialist journalists, such as sport reporters, who typically have close relations with their subjects were especially prone to refrain from rushing into print with tales of drink problems or sexual peccadilloes. In the wake of the tabloid revolution and the blurring of established public–private distinctions, all that was necessary was that at least one of the names involved was a public one. Behaviour that once would have remained secret became the routine stuff of tabloid journalism. Whilst sport specialist journalists remained reluctant to expose stars who were also acquaintances and drinking pals, their news-reporter colleagues felt no such constraints. As a result, such trust as once existed between sport and journalism has been undermined, and the typical relationship between the two has become one of sullen suspicion interspersed with open hostility. Many sportsmen have found means of negotiating their way through these changes. Gascoigne, among others, finds the invasion of his 'private space' annoying.

Throughout history, societies have generally evolved means of publicly casti-gating infringements of the conventions of correct behaviour.[2] Just as pillorying took place in the most public place available, such as town squares at midday on market day, so contemporary pillorying happens in that most public of places – the tabloid press. The tabloids offer us judgements that can have the stark simplicity of a medieval morality play, yet these messages about morality take place in the context of the moral ambiguities and uncertainties of late moder-nity. If Gascoigne is being punished, what are his crimes? He has been a clown where seriousness is wanted, flabby in a narcissistic world that requires leanness; he has been drunk when discipline is demanded; and he has beaten his wife in the era of the new man. The last of these is a serious offence, for which Gascoigne has earned punishment and probably needs help. More broadly, however, Gascoigne has become an emblematic figure at the intersecting point of these two discourses of crisis – masculinity and morality. He can stand all too well for conceptions of men behaving badly, dumbing down, male violence to women and the perils of indiscipline. One of the cyclical features of immature and infantile deviance, and, to a degree, of alcoholism, is to do with the prob-lematic relation with parental authority – first, needing to defy it to construct an identity, then needing approval and forgiveness. With 'Gazza', the authority of the parent, the manager and the nation all become linked.

Redemption and surveillance

As surveillance and discipline have become more prominent features of top-level sport, the transgressions of sport stars have encountered greater exposure and less tolerance, as Paul Gascoigne's recent history suggests. The withdrawal of tolerance, however, is highly pragmatic. Gascoigne retained his England place after beating up Sheryl, but abusing his own body through drink, fatty foods and cigarettes, rendering himself unfit, cost him his England place. The combi-nation of greater surveillance, less tolerance and the discourse of counselling and recovery has produced a new form of sport star narrativity. Along with the 'rise to triumph' and 'rise and fall' structures, we now have the 'rise and redemption'. Typically, the sequence consists of despair – crisis–seeks help–recovery–redemption. English international footballer Paul Merson's *Rock*

Bottom tells the tale of his problems with alcohol, drugs and gambling, his recourse to professional help and his subsequent rehabilitation (Merson 1995).[3] It is neither a book written at the moment of triumph, celebrating golden success, nor a 'rise and fall' story, but rather a tale of rise, fall and redemption. As such it is crossed by the 1990s discourses of counselling and the genre of psychotherapy fiction. The blurb on the cover states:

> It focuses on what singles Merson out: his addictive personality. For many years, Merson lived a double life, managing to combine the life of an addict with that of a star goal scorer for England and Arsenal. His life was a see-saw of exhilarating highs and debilitating lows, until in Autumn 1994 he hit rock bottom and knew that he could pretend no more, that he needed help. In *Rock Bottom*, Paul Merson lays himself bare as few have done before. Writing from the perspective of a recovering addict and using extracts from the diaries he kept during his rehabilitation, Merson delivers a searingly candid self-portrait, which will strike a chord with all addicts and enlighten those associated with them. Merson's wife Lorraine contributes an uninhibited and strident chapter of her own in which she pulls no punches. *Rock Bottom* is a brave book which will both increase under-standing and serve as a warning to young people.
>
> (Merson 1995)

The book has a foreword and an afterword by Merson's counsellor, Stephen Stephens, who says of Paul Merson that throughout his treatment he remained 'ruthlessly honest'. Footballer and Arsenal team-mate of Merson, Tony Adams, ends his account of his own fall and redemption with:

> . My views on winning have changed a lot, however. Today I am not just Tony Adams the footballer, I am Tony Adams the human being. I do my best every day in every walk of life and seek to treat myself and other people with respect. In that there is also victory. Winning on the field is sweet, of course, but in addition, as far as I am concerned, with each day that I do not take a drink, I will always be a winner.
>
> (Adams 1998)

In this notable passage he moves on rather further than Merson in emphasising not merely redemption, but a rebirth – the production of a fuller, more rounded existence. His struggle to rebuild his life has been seized on as symbolic by journalistic writing in that it seeks to draw attention to the post-new man forms in which men are dealing with the emotional. Tony Adams has often been used in representation to personify the 'British bulldog spirit'. 'But', says Tom Watt, 'its the way he's confronting his own weaknesses that reveals his real strength' (*GQ*, June 1997, p. 135). Whilst interesting in their own rights, the biographies of Merson and Adams can also be seen as symptoms of tensions within masculinity. The pre-fall lives of Merson and Adams are portrayed as being simply logical consequences of their sub-cultural contexts – working-class lads who became star footballers. In the conventions of masculinity in the British working class generally and in football in particular, drinking plays a central role – as reward after work, as a means of facilitating bonding, and as licensing misbehaviour. There is nothing new about the footballer with drink problems, but what is new is the footballer who seeks help, resorts to 'middle-class forms' such as clinics and counsellors, and then goes public and tells the tale in the terms of a narrative of redemption. There are several factors involved here. The large transfer fees and massive salaries commanded by top footballers means that clubs are concerned to protect their investments and may be more proactive in intervening in 'personal' matters. The spread of rationalist and scientific principles of health and fitness has begun to transform the enclosed and anti-intellectual carapace within which traditional masculine hedonism was able to flourish in football. The greater exposure of the private lives of stars since the tabloid revolution makes it harder for the handling of player problems to take place discreetly, hidden from media attention.

Significant, too, is the context of public discourse about crises in masculinity and morality. The various misdemeanours of footballers like Merson, Adams, Gascoigne and Sheringham can be seen in relation to debates about masculinity. Laddish hedonism is seen as not merely damaging to the club and to colleagues but to the self. The redemptive treatment provided through counselling and through public disclosure is portrayed as the road to rebirth, to a greater whole-ness. Clearly self-destructive masculinity is not about to be abandoned in a rush to embrace the golden road to a healthier lifestyle lit up by Merson and Adams. But the discursive terms within which their accounts are cast could be taken as a sign that the hegemony of laddish hedonistic masculinity is not securely consoli-dated. New laddism, for example, as I argued earlier, is best understood as a reassertion of elements of traditional young male working-class culture. But this reassertion has its own specific conditions of existence, one of which is clearly both a response to and a reaction against the rise of feminism. It also, in its *Men Behaving Badly/Loaded* variant, represented a reassertion of hedonism against the fitness chic gym culture of the 1980s.

The image of badness as 'fun' – drinking too much, missing training, being generally undisciplined and getting away with it – has been challenged by a more socially reprehensible 'badness'. The treatment of women by Mike Tyson, Paul Gascoigne, Geoffrey Boycott and O.J. Simpson became mapped (despite the evident individual specificities of these cases) onto a more general moral discourse about violence against women, the decline in morality, the crisis of masculinity and the notion that sport, as a key site for the construction of such masculine behaviour, was itself part of the problem. This theme is pursued in the second half of chapter 12. In the aftermath of the Gascoigne 1998 affair, a clear divide emerged between those who clung to the new lad ethos – David Baddiel and Frank Skinner, Chris Evans, Danny Baker – on the one hand, and, on the other, a convergence of responses from the old moral authoritarian paternalists of the right-wing press and the new athletic puritans, with Arsene

Wenger's managerial style as their talisman. Sheringham's much publicised misbehaviour on the Algarve strengthened the anti-laddist position. In the context of the World Cup, and the need for a strong sense of purpose in order that national victory be achieved, men behaving badly were suddenly out of fashion, whilst clean-cut disciplined commitment was in demand – Sheringham out, Owen in.

The ideology of masculine individualism is a significant part of the sub-text of the mythologised narratives of such stars. The individualism exemplified in the song *My Way* celebrates a masculine fantasy of defying constraint and advice. For sport stars, though, the contradictory tension, of course, is that modern elite sport is a highly disciplined practice subject to intense surveillance, in which maverick masculine individualism is something that coaches and governing bodies are concerned to root out. In a world that is constrained, maverick sport stars appear to offer the power to live a life of masculine individualism – defying constraints, rebelling against regulation – whilst still performing. The constraints are associated with authority – both the domestic and the feminine. The well-documented male disregard for health is a rebellion against such constraints and, more precisely, a rebellion against Mother. Masculine individualism is set against the female, the domestic and the familial, rooted in the 'naturalness' of aggression and the predatory instinct, which mother, wife, and family threaten to tame and civilise.[4] But maverick masculine individualism also increasingly conflicts with the new corporate paternalism, whereby institutions become the moral guardians of their employees, supervising the way they live.

Sport has always involved forms of discipline in its regimes of training, but increasingly this discipline is being extended to all aspects of a player's lifestyle – diet, daily routine, sex life and sleeping patterns. Sheringham's indiscipline – drinking, smoking, and sitting next to a blonde woman at dawn in an Algarve bar shortly before the World Cup – was linked to his lack of a partner. Football managers have always been keen that their charges marry and settle down, but managers like Arsene Wenger (Arsenal) and Christian Gross (ex-Tottenham Hotspur) are increasingly interventionist – imposing longer training, dietary monitoring and physiological testing. Brohm's concept of the Taylorisation of the body – the squeezing of maximum productivity from the human frame – seems ever more pertinent (Brohm 1978). If the bad boy sportsmen (self-centred, petulant, hedonistic and undisciplined) are contrasted to the good (team-oriented, focused, abstinent and disciplined), a similar contrast is implied between types of women – the bad influence (blonde, disco-going, thrill-seeking, or over-feminising) and the good influence (wife, mother, homemaker, supportive and 'giving him space'). Of course the constraining of maverick masculinity is not being done in the interests of gender relations, but of the success and profit of large corporations. In imposing this regime of surveillance and regulation, however, sport tries to insulate its performers, in training camps, from hedonistic association with women, while implicitly relying on invisible female labour in the family to continue in the private sphere the disciplined regimes imposed on their partners in the public sphere.

Media representation of events related to the behaviour of various England players before and during the 1998 World Cup provides a way of summarising some of the issues involved in analysis of masculinities. The new laddist reassertion of 'traditional' masculine values, as a reaction to feminism, became the frame of reference through which the late-night drinking exploits of players such as Sheringham and Gascoigne were represented. New laddism appeared as dysfunctional, and against the national interest in a successful World Cup campaign. The crisis of moral authority posed by these exploits was resolved by Hoddle's dropping of Gascoigne. The emergence of Michael Owen as a new star was used to signify the importance and benefits of a disciplined lifestyle;[5] and Owen was contrasted with the 'emasculated' Beckham, whose lack of discipline (kicking an Argentinian opponent and getting sent off at a key moment) lets the side down. A recomposed masculinity, traditional but disciplined, respectable rather than rough, hard but controlled, firm but fair, is, in ideological terms, placed in dominance. The next chapter examines in more detail the various forms in which images of sport and of sport stars became the point of covergence for a range of moral discourses.

12 Moralities, masculinities and violence

Are we too naive if we expect to ever return to the days when sport was played with chivalry and respect, where the authority of its laws was sacrosanct, and its famous exponents noted for their skill rather than their rebelliousness? Are professional sportsmen so overpaid and amateurs so influenced by the behaviour of these stars that past standards cannot be recovered?

(*Evening Standard* Sports Writers, 1991: back cover)

Its all right to have two or three or four kids in a team, but when the time comes for responsibility you need men. In our team we were men of character. What does being a man mean? To play calmly, to talk, to not feel the weight of responsibility, to do what you're told. That's character.

(Rattin, captain of Argentina in 1966, sent off against England at Wembley, quoted in Taylor 1999: 47)

The first of the two quotations above contrasts the professional and corrupt present with the amateur and noble past. It is fairly typical of a romanticised nostalgia for a 'pure' past of athletic endeavour for its own sake. It is rooted in the ideologies of fair play that had their formative period in the English public schools of the mid-nineteenth century, and were made concrete in the practices and cultural power of the sport governing bodies formed by the late Victorian male bourgeoisie. In such utterances, it is the intrusion of money, through professionalism, that in turn has fostered violence, cheating, lack of respect for rules and the use of performance-enhancing drugs, and so destroyed the Corinthian ideals of amateurism. In structure this discursive element contrasts a golden past with a corrupted present.

The second quotation contrasts the irresponsibility of boys with the calmness of men. Being a man here means having 'character', being able to exert leadership, whilst also paradoxically, respecting and obeying higher authority. It is the ideology of the subaltern class within a social hierarchy, exerting a moral and intellectual leadership on the troops, but always within the framework of senior officers. It is the condensation of these two discursive elements onto each other – the idea that a responsible and dutiful masculinity is situated in the past – that is a key feature of the discursive presentation of the crises of morality and masculinity in the context of sport. Despite its reworking under Blair, the cultural formation of Thatcherism – the new individualism, enterprise culture, fitness chic, workaholics, no pain no gain, greed is good – is beginning to fragment. Cultural practices that, when in dominance, are naturalised take on an estrangement – they seem distinctly odd, as Charles Shaar Murray recognised in 1994:

> I used to get a kick out of whipping out a Powerbook on planes ... Suddenly the penny dropped: the 80s were over. People who need to be working even while they're on a plane are not necessarily high powered and successful: quite the opposite. They're sad bastards who clearly have no right to call any of their time their own.
>
> (*MacUser* 2 September 1994)

The 1990s constitute a transitional moment in which the post-war era is ending and Reagenomics and Thatcherite reconstruction, despite the continuation of aspects of their project, are running out of momentum. The declining appeal of Thatcherism, the end of the Cold War, peace moves in the Middle East and Ireland (however frail), the end of apartheid in South Africa – all these factors clearly suggest the end of the post-war era.[1] Yet, if the old is dying the new has yet to be born. Across the political spectrum, plenty of emergent fragments are around – the politics of ecology, the anti-capitalist movement, vegetarianism, animal rights, travellers, raves, the Countryside Alliance, a new European consciousness – but no political force as yet has the ability to articulate the strands of a new formation. In such a situation a whole range of social elements are likely to exhibit the signs of crisis. Sport, masculinity and morality all show the symptoms of unease, doubt and dissension. Publicity given to drug use, corruption, cheating and gamesmanship marked out sport as no longer an unproblematic domain of healthy living. This moment was epitomised in Ben Johnson's failed drug test at the Seoul Olympics in 1988, the most high-profile culprit yet. Jim Fixx's death from a heart attack, false rumours of a Jane Fonda heart attack and the early death of US Olympic athlete Florence Griffith-Joyner (Flo-Jo) marked the first cracks in the ideology of fitness chic. The growing concern with HIV and Aids forced a refocusing of the concept of fitness, which increasingly, especially in gay sub-cultures, has become a symbol of survival. The muscular body of the eighties has veered towards reification and self-parody in body-building and in programmes such as *Gladiators*. The specialist sports body has become as much a matter of suspicion as admiration. Social concerns over male aggression, 'roid-rage' and violence against women have been condensed onto the images of sport stars. Stories involving drug use, cheating and corruption have regularly hit the headlines. Sport stars of the nineties – Mike Tyson, Paul Gascoigne, Maradona – are the sites of confused and conflicting articulations; their accumulated publicised actions have a chaotic character.

No surprise, then, that the death of Bobby Moore in 1993 triggered not simply an orgy of nostalgia for the days when England was great, but also a series of articles paralleling the good old days with the moral decay of the present. The extensive exposure of sporting sleaze has struck at the heart of sport, with not even those bastions of the sporting establishment, Arsenal Football Club or English cricket immune. Arsenal's manager George Graham was dismissed for financial irregularities, whilst England cricket captain Mike Atherton was found to have tampered with the ball. More recently, athletics has been tarnished by a succession of failed drug tests, and cricket hit by allegations of match fixing. Such corruption has been mapped onto the more generalised discourse of moral decline outlined in the introduction. The interesting feature of moral discourse from the perspective of this study is not to do with the absolute or relative quality of morality, or of moral judgements. My interest lies rather in charting ways in which images of sport stars are mobilised within specific moral discourses. It is through such discursive practices that relationships are made between the individual and the social, the particular and the general, and between popular common sense and organised political philosophy.[2]

Citizenship and morality: sporting heroes

One form through which moral discourse is organised is citizenship. Citizenship, as a concept, involves both rights and obligations, as well as having an implicit ethical–moral dimension. Citizens have responsibilities. However, in a predominantly secular society, morality is placed in constant crisis. Traditional religious authority is weakened and the transmission of moral values assumes a more diffuse, less focused character. The expansion of consumer capitalism and possessive individualism are commonly seen as factors in the weakening of communal ties and social solidarity. One symptom of this view has been the concept of a moral crisis, utilised by back-to-basics moral entrepreneurs on the right, in their calls for a reassertion of moral authoritarianism. Recent much publicised cases (the murder of Jamie Bulger, the Gloucester multiple murders) were followed by public confusion over the nature of moral values and how we acquire them. Such confusion was evident in the search for causes – as in the attempt to blame a particular video for the Bulger murder, even though there was no evidence that the children in question ever saw it. The presence of moral ambiguities and doubts has prompted a fresh interest in the issue of where young people acquire a sense of morality.

One element in current public discourse about sport stardom concerns the supposed decline in morality. The values of the past are counterposed to the corrupted values of the present. Nowhere was this more evident than in the orgiastic eulogising surrounding the deaths of Bobby Moore and Stanley Matthews (see chapter 8). David Miller in *The Times* (25 February 1993) referred to 'Bobby Moore, England captain of grace and vision', whilst *The Times* obituary said 'Tall, blond, cool and clean cut, Moore was the epitome of the England captain, a post he filled with distinction'. David Platt was quoted as saying 'He was a great person in every sense: a footballer of intelligence and vision, a man of dignity and stature. I admired and respected him immensely'. John Goodbody wrote that 'Off the field, he was "the perfect English gentleman", as Pele, his great Brazilian adversary, said last night'. The *Guardian* (25 February 1993) headlined that 'Bobby Moore, gentleman of sport, is mourned by football around the world'. John Major said that 'Bobby will forever be remembered for leading England to victory in the 1966 World Cup. But he did much more than that. He enhanced sport by example, behaviour and skill'. In the *Guardian*, David Lacey wrote that 'England's football teams have had many captains but fewer leaders. Bobby Moore, who died yesterday aged 51, was the most natural leader the national side has ever had, for he led not only by example but through the practical application of a superior footballing brain'.

The *Sun* headlined its front page with 'BOBBY MOORE – A TRUE HERO WHO'LL NEVER BE FORGOTTEN' and said that 'His sense of decency and honour as a footballer went beyond the pitch and made him a real-life Boy's Own hero'. Gary Lineker was quoted as saying that 'Bobby was a colossus. He won respect for the way he played and the manner in which he conducted himself'. Alf Ramsey said that 'Bobby wasn't just the captain of my team, he was the captain of the country, of everyone'. John Sadler wrote that

> He was THE sporting hero of heroes who not only deserved but thoroughly earned his reputation and unique place of honour ... Current internationals should know that when they misbehave, complain of raw deals and unfair criticism, they are bellyaching at people who watched Bobby Moore.
>
> (*Sun*, 25 February 1993)

This contrast between past and present was a key subtext. The *Daily Mail* headlined 'DEATH OF A SPORTING HERO', and wrote:

> The meticulous attention to detail, the scrupulous care with appearance, the exact precision of time-keeping, the constant observation of manners which maketh a gentleman out of a hero, all were with him to the premature end.
>
> (*Daily Mail*, 25 February 1993)

The *Daily Express* headlined 'DEATH OF OUR HERO' and wrote that:

> Bobby Moore knew there was more to representing club and country than simply turning up and going through the motions. For him it meant meeting high and self-imposed standards, not only of performance but also of comportment. Perhaps it is because this approach seems rare among our

modern sportsmen – it has certainly not been much in evidence in India these past few weeks – that his early death is so sad.

(Daily Express, 25 February 1993)

The *Sunday Telegraph* made the point more explicitly. Mark Palmer wrote that

> Respect and honour were common in 1966. That has all changed ... many now believe that only a return to some of the values displayed by men such as Bobby Moore in the summer of 1966 will take Britain out of its present malaise ... perhaps what truly makes 1966 seem like another century is the reverence Moore showed for his queen at the moment of triumph.
>
> *(Sunday Telegraph*, 25 February 1993)

Russell Davies wrote an article headed *The Final Golden Moment*, sub-headed 'How gentlemen of 1966 gave way to today's snarling superstars'. Williams and Taylor (1994) have discussed the ways in which such reactions to Moore's death served as the condensing point of a number of complex elements associated with economic decline, fears of a moral crisis, and a belief in a generalised decline of standards. One of the central significances of sporting heroes is precisely the way in which they are available for articulation within discourses about the state of the nation.

England and Argentina: Rattin, Ardiles and Maradona

It is in relation to the nation that sport-related morality is most conspicuously determined by positionality – our moral framework is moulded by our national identity. If Bobby Moore mythologised represents England triumphant, then Argentina in the moment of 1966 became the personification of the latinate enemy – the greasy spics who foul, harangue the referee and trample over the conventions of gentlemanly conduct and fair play (as laid down by the English). Argentine captain Rattin was sent off in the ill-tempered World Cup quarter final between England and Argentina, and the game was held up for ten minutes during which Rattin apparently refused to leave the pitch, calling for an interpreter. England manager Ramsey, who ran onto the pitch at the end to prevent England players swapping shirts with the Argentinians, then referred to the Argentinians as 'animals', a sound-bite that echoed around the world. Future relations were heavily coloured by this remark. Rattin believes Argentina were the victim of a fix, and still regards the sending off as baffling. He points out that European referees were allocated to both Argentine and Uruguay quarter finals, and in the Uruguay match three players were sent off. Rattin says that this is 'a view which in Argentina, indeed in Latin America in general, is entirely uncontroversial'. He points to the strong pressure to make sure the host nation got to the final. This did indeed happen in four out of the first seven finals (Taylor 1999: 46). So each nation, from the perspective of the other, was implicated in cheating.

A member of the Argentine team that won the 1978 World Cup, Osvaldo Ardiles subsequently moved to Tottenham Hotspur, where he became a popular figure, winning the FA Cup Winners' Medal that he so coveted in 1981, and featuring in one of the more successful of football club records, 'Spurs are on their Way to Wembley', by Chas and Dave. Small, where Rattin was a giant, Ardiles was a non-threatening figure, who was made fun of in the video that accompanied the record for his pronunciation of Tottenham as 'Tottingham'. His delicate and precise ball skills and his keenly expressed desire, fulfilled in 1981, to win a cup medal at Wembley, contributed to his popularity with the British public. The Falklands War intervened in this thawing of relations, and Ardiles shrewdly left for France for a period, subsequently returning to Tottenham. That Ardiles and his fellow Argentine, Ricky Villa, remained popular figures provides some evidence that the football public may have a more subtle and sophisticated sense of the relation between individual and national identity than the crude positionalities constructed in the tabloid press might suggest.

In the 1986 World Cup, England once again met Argentina in the quarter final. Diego Maradona, then widely acclaimed as the successor to Pele as the world's greatest footballer, scored the famous 'hand of God' goal when he punched the ball into the England net. The foul went unnoticed by the officials and a goal was awarded. The English press went to town on the 'cheating Argies' theme. Ironically, in the same match, Maradona also glided around seven English defenders to score what many people regard as the finest goal ever scored. Even in England, in 1993, viewers of BBC2's *Night of Football* voted this goal the best ever scored. The bad boys of sport have always commanded a very particular form of popular appeal, but this evidence of forgiveness was both striking and surprising. In the Argentine, 'Maradona was seen as a playful kid – a pibe – who had tried it on and got away with it – therefore, good luck to him. Craftiness, guile and ducking and diving (often literally) are the traditional skills in football, as in life, of the kids from the edge of society. Maradona was the "Artful Dodger"' (*Guardian*, 8 May 1998). For the British media, though, condemnation was the dominant tone. When Maradona retired, beset by rumours of drug problems, one paper trumpeted 'Dirty cheat Diego gone for good' (*Sun*, 1 July 1994). In another article on Maradona in the *Sun* England international Terry Butcher was quoted as saying 'He abused his privileged position and set a terrible example to all the kids who want to become great players' (*Sun*, 1 July 1994). Morality is not only relative but is also contingent upon power relations and upon positionalities – of national, class, gender and ethnic identities.

Dirt in the pocket: the Mike Atherton affair

Moral condemnation and national identity interact in complex ways. The case of ball tampering involving Mike Atherton provides a good illustration of the ambiguities underlying moral entrepreneurship. The episode, involving as it did, allegations of cheating against an England captain, opened up contradictions between moral condemnation and patriotism that had to be managed, handled and resolved. During the last week in July 1994, Atherton received extensive coverage throughout the media for an incident which occurred in the test match between England and South Africa. He was accused of 'tampering' with the ball by rubbing dirt onto one side. This was documented by TV cameras and subsequently seen by audiences. Tabloid coverage of the incident was initially constructed in terms of moral outrage that a captain of 'our' national team should be setting a bad example. The *Sun* and the *Daily Mirror* ran banner headlines:

HE DID CHEAT	(*Daily Mirror*, 25 July 1994)
QUIT NOW	(*Sun*, 25 July 1994)

The *Daily Mirror* followed up with a campaign for his dismissal, headed

SACK HIM AND LET THE WORLD KNOW WE STAND FOR HONESTY	(*Daily Mirror*, 26 July 1994)

and claimed 100 per cent readers support in its poll. Nigel Clarke of the *Daily Mirror* commented that 'The age of chivalry is long dead – even for English captains', and that Atherton should 'fall on his sword in the long room' (*Daily Mirror*, 26 July 1994). The *Sun*, on the same day, commented that 'it is not the punishment, swiftly handed out by his bosses, that does so much damage to him. It is his image as portrayed to the rest of the world ... Illingworth says English cricket must be seen as "whiter that white". But how can it while it employs a skipper with a soiled reputation?' (*Sun*, 26 July 1994). The tabloid battle to occupy the moral high-ground continued the following day when the *Daily Mirror* back-page headline was 'THE GREAT ATHERTON WHITE WASH'. As with discussion of the death of Bobby Moore, an idealised past was contrasted to a corrupted present. The myth of an ethical past when chivalry ruled, and errant gentlemen 'fell on their swords' is here set against a present in which reputations are soiled, and authorities cover up.

Atherton, however, did not lend himself to the 'bad boy at the back of the bus' mould of a Botham. Instead, the media constructed an image in the form of tarnished hero. He is described as 'Little Mister Perfect', fulfilling all the qualities of a potential English captain – middle-class, educated, good sportsman and a gentleman. The allegations of cheating disrupted this image without really dislodging it. The cricket establishment rallied round, and Atherton was exonerated. The broadsheets intervened in the debate – the *Independent* criticising the moral crusade against a man cleared of any misdemeanour by the cricketing authorities. *The Times* was keen to concentrate on the moral implications of Atherton's actions:

Atherton has now realised the strange truth that sports people are expected to have higher moral standards than the people who run the country. People want sport to be an escape from the real world, for sport to be a place in which ideal standards actually exist and they cannot bear the truth that it can never be anything of the kind. In disappointing the seekers of perfection, Atherton has apparently committed the crime of the century.

(Simon Barnes, *The Times*, 27 July 1994)

Barnes identifies here a central paradox of sport. It is constructed as a world of its own, a bounded universe, with its own sections in the press and on television. Part of its appeal is precisely this otherness. In a world of confusion, doubt and moral ambiguity, in which structures are patently unfair and enshrine the power of the privileged, sport offers a protected domain in which impartial rules and officials and respect for fair play are supposed to predominate. Yet sport has never been, cannot be, separate from social structures and processes. In a world of ruthless competitive individualism, the fair play ethos is constantly undermined. The moral theme was pursued by the *Daily Telegraph*: Atherton's position was in question; the captain must decide his own fate

and if in his own interests and those of the England team he should go, his decision would not only reflect upon himself (gentlemanly conduct) – but more importantly the nation as a whole.

(*Daily Telegraph*, 27 July 1994)

Explicit here, as elsewhere, was the concept of the sport star as an embodiment of national character. In another article, E.W. Swanton, in a column sub-titled, 'Personally speaking', made it clear that he supported Atherton, when he wrote 'Here was a young man whose performance since his appointment as captain aged 25, a year ago has been admirable.'

For Swanton, a mixture of simple, naive thoughtlessness and the pressures of international cricket were factors to be cited in Atherton's defence. Indeed, after Atherton's highly successful 'clear the air' press conference, the 'tarnished hero' became a promising but errant child, who merely required advice and guidance. Atherton's underlying commitment to hard work and leadership, his centrality as captain, saved him. By contrast the bad boys offend because in combining undisciplined hedonism with extraordinary flair (Best, Botham, Higgins) they undermine the work ethic – their exploits seem to suggest a threatening ability to work and play. It is in a sense for this that they are punished. By 1998, rehabilitated and with the incident largely forgotten, Atherton was being eulogised in one newspaper by Leo McMinistry as the authentic British hero. The piece, dealing as it does with so many of the themes of this book, is worth quoting at length:

despite defeat and disgrace, the man who today notches up a record 50 tests as England's captain is a hero of our times. Though he is often derided, I believe him to be far more than just a cricketer: with his infinite resilience and determination he symbolises the best of the old and best of the new in Britain. It is often said that our age no longer produces any heroes. The character of Michael Atherton is a direct contradiction of that argument.

There is something of the Rudyard Kipling poem 'If' about the dignified way he has survived in his role as captain for so long – 'meeting with triumph and disaster and treating those two imposters just the same'. Lesser men would have broken under the pressure of leading an inadequate and inconsistent side who are no strangers to defeat, as well as having to cope with purblind selectors, posturing officials and prying reporters.

Atherton has of course not been without his detractors. He has regularly been accused of obstinacy, dourness and over-caution. Some have urged him to smile more on the cricket field as if an inane grin would help England's cause. His tactical abilities have been questioned. But I believe all this carping has been badly misplaced. For me, Atherton embodies much of the best of the traditional English character: the bravery, the dignity, the calm under fire – all virtues often ignored in our brash and self-regarding times.

In modern Britain, we are constantly encouraged to parade our misfortunes. The out-pouring of grief over the death of the Princess of Wales last year was a key indicator of this national mood. But the stiff upper lip of Mike Atherton is a refreshing contrast to such fashionable self-indulgence and that is one reason why he has been so often misunderstood.

And, contrary to the views of his critics, Atherton has often proved both an astute and invigorating leader. As one England player put it about his leadership on a previous trip to the West Indies, 'he made you want to go through barbed wire and brick walls for him' … Thankfully, this outburst of moralising hypocrisy, most of it from people who knew nothing of cricket, passed. Yet it is telling that the very reason Atherton survived was precisely because of his reputation for integrity. No one believed that he would actually descend to cheating. But while his character may be a throwback to an English past, Atherton is a very modern figure in other ways. Unlike the aristocratic English amateur captains of previous eras such as Lord Harris, Lord Hawke, Gubby Allen, or Ted Dexter, he is the embodiment of the increasingly classless Britain of the Nineties.

(*Daily Mail*, 27 February 1998)

Here then is laid out the English character, as epitomised (not for the first time) by an English cricket captain. It is constituted here by dignity, infinite resilience and determination, brave, calm under fire, resistant to pressure, and a reputation for integrity (*sic!*). Those who fail to understand this are purblind selectors, posturing officials and prying reporters – bureaucrats and parasites, by implication. Atherton's detractors are 'people who know nothing of cricket'. Our 'brash and self-regarding times' are characterised by a fashionable self-indulgence – an implicitly feminised excess of emotion, in contrast to the masculine stiff upper lip. Atherton, this 'embodiment of the increasingly classless Britain of the Nineties' in fact went to Manchester Grammar School and Downing College Cambridge! What is being constructed in this article, rather than a symbol for the nineties, is a residual patrician and patriarchal individualism, with its clear contempt for officialdom, for newness and for feminised emotion, and with its own brand of moral hypocrisy. Indeed in this portrayal, he is transformed into *Daily Mail* Man, the voice of the saloon bars of middle England.

Violence

The prominence of sporting celebrities, across a range of media, the tabloidisation of the media, and the erosion of a clear division between public and private have combined to give a greater prominence to stories about the private lives of sport stars, and one by-product of this process has been the greater attention paid to domestic violence. If media representation of sport stars provides, among other things, a policing of masculinity, then the modes of portrayal of the violence of sport stars suggests that such behaviour is subject to strong and clear moral censure. However, the lack of analysis and broader perspective has tended to leave such stories largely in the domain of the trivial: individualised tales in the society of spectacle.

In a spate of stories in the late nineties, male sport stars were portrayed defending the castle of masculinity, disavowing passivity, venting rage, and lashing out at the feminine other. Those featured in stories involving male violence have included Paul Gascoigne, O.J. Simpson, Mike Tyson, Alex Higgins, Stan Collymore and Frank Bruno. While links can be made between such incidents and the attitudes towards women characteristic in new lad culture, there are dangers in over-simplifying these links. As stories, they do, however, it seems to me, have three things in common. First, they are all about power. They concern the power of men over women, the assumption by men that they should control women, and their anger at any loss of this control. Second, they are linked to the power of sporting stars. It is, I think, relevant that the names I single out are retired, in decline, or past their best. Once their power commanded their sporting world, but no longer. They lived in worlds where needs were catered for by others. They were the geese that laid golden eggs, and consequently their bodies were cosseted, their minds fed with praise, their egos massaged. In decline they are raging against the dying of the light. Third, they are media stars. All that most of us know about these names has come from media representation, and a lot of it from tabloid journalism. We cannot 'know' them, any more than we could 'know' Princess Diana. They are the points of convergence of multiple discourses; the focal point of utterances about moralities, masculinities, sporting ethics and national prestige. In that sense, much of the material triggered by these stories is only notionally 'about' the star involved, and is much more centrally 'about' notions of masculinity and morality.

Sport as a social practice serves not simply to demarcate gender difference, but is also perceived as a generator of tension between men and women. According to a *Total Sport* survey, 61 per cent of men find sport 'more exciting than their girlfriends or wives' (note: as reported, this question was open to more than one interpretation). Women's magazines frame sport as 'not for women'. *Women's Own* warned 'Bad news if you hate football. The World Cup starts this week – for a whole month' and proclaimed that 'even before it's begun, Wimbledon is starting to look boring' (*Women's Own*, 20 June 1994). The *Guardian* (3 April 1998) reported that, according to a national sports survey, one-third of relationships would be in danger during the World Cup. The survey questioned 1,000 men and 500 women and found 33 per cent of the male respondents thought the World Cup would play havoc with their relationships. According to the survey, men spend 21 hours a week on sport, 9 hours playing, 8 hours watching and 4 hours drinking with their sports friends.[3] Fifty-three per cent of men reported rows with their loved ones over the time they gave sport. Based on the pattern during Euro 96, phone calls to Relate (the Marriage Guidance Council) were expected to increase by 10–15 per cent during the 1998 World Cup. A Relate spokeswoman said 'Although unlikely to be the sole cause of a relationship breakdown, arguments over time spent on watching sport could contribute to communication difficulties in an already conflicted relationship'. Concern was expressed regarding alcohol consumption – men tend to consume more while watching sport, threatening women who already suffer from domestic violence. Without wanting to place any great faith in the methodological cogency of these surveys, the stories nonetheless serve to exemplify the diverse ways in which sport is constantly constructed as a source not merely of gender difference, but also of gender contestation.

In the late 1990s these generalised precepts acquired a more specific focus in reports of violence against women by male sport stars. In some accounts, the aggression needed for sport is linked to off-pitch violence. Emily Cook wrote that:

> The very qualities that make sportsmen successful on the pitch and in the ring are those that cause aggression in their private lives. According to sports psychologists, players anger can be comfortably insulated by the rules of the game, but in everyday life such impulses are much harder to regulate.
>
> (*Independent on Sunday*, 25 January 1998)

Footballer Stan Collymore is a controversial figure who has been in the headlines for various reasons, but in June 1998, he featured in the headline COLLY BEATS UP TV STAR ULRIKA, and the story recounted how 'Ulrika, 30, who was filming in Paris – was left sobbing on the floor as the raging Aston Villa hero was restrained by FIVE men' (*Sun*, 10 June 1998). One witness was quoted as saying:

> he was more like a deranged stalker than a megabucks football star ... He was wound up with jealousy. He said something like 'what would you do if you saw 500 Scots calling your girl's name?' He made it clear that she was his girlfriend and no-one else's.
>
> (*Sun*, 10 June 1998)

Collymore is the perpetrator of a brutal assault on a woman, triggered seemingly by the assumption that a woman is a man's property and a jealous fury at his inability to handle the admiration she attracts from other men. In the *Sun*, Sue Evison wrote:

> The despicable fashion for bashing women appears to be growing at an alarming rate among soccer stars hero-worshipped by many. They earn millions but off the pitch some are morally and frequently intellectually bankrupt. They seem to believe a role model is something to do with a bedroom conquest, not good manners and dignified behaviour. Many of our footballers gained their skills at the expense of education and emotional maturity. While young they are thrust into the spotlight with large wads of money. They live on the adrenalin surge generated by the roar of the crowd. But it's a short lived fix. The prospect of retirement, often in the prime of life, breeds rampant insecurity. Most lack the wisdom or the brains to deal with the pressure. Instead they look for answers at the bottom of a bottle. Its far easier to knock back a drink and knock around the girlfriend than face up to the fact that you need to learn how to take a few hard knocks in life. If they can't or won't grow up perhaps we should hit them where it hurts. And ban them from the game.
>
> (*Sun*, 10 June 1998)

While the argument is perfectly sound, to find it in the *Sun* should draw our attention to the underlying hypocrisy of the tabloid press – its images of women foster a sexualised objectification – but it sees no link between this and male violence to women. Its world-view and its build up to major tournaments fosters a xenophobic nationalism but it sees no link to football crowd violence. In 1998, the *Sun* distributed plastic bowler hats adorned with the cross of St George, which were uncomfortably and distinctly reminiscent of the hats worn by the gang in 'The Clockwork Orange'. Sue Carroll counterposed Collymore's behaviour to that of 'real decent men'

> If he's weeping you can bet they're tears of self-pity, not compassion. Because the only one he's ever felt sorry for throughout this episode is himself. His hugely inflated ego is legendary in the game. The truth is that

Collymore, like some others in his profession, are used to the fawning adulation of the crowd. On this occasion he was forced to wait in the wings and watch his woman being the focus of some hero worship herself. And he couldn't hack it so he employed the sort of bullyboy tactics that seem to be a trademark of professional footballers these days. And I hope it's not too much to ask that the real decent men of British football, and I do happen to believe that there are quite a few, make their feelings known when he next turns up on a pitch.

(*Daily Mirror*, 11 June 1998)

While Stan Collymore has failed since to win the approval and acclaim of fans at any of the various clubs for whom he has briefly appeared, this would seem to be as a result of his less than whole-hearted commitment to winning games. There is little evidence of fan hostility as a result of any disapproval of violence against women. The *Daily Mirror* referred to 'Stan-who-isn't-much-of-a-man' and speculated that clubs would be reluctant to buy him. Collymore's club appeared more concerned with the image of the club and with football:

Gregory, Villa manager said 'I was appalled … Stan was full of remorse when we spoke and since this incident is a personal affair between himself and Ulrika Johnson, there will be no disciplinary action taken against him by the club. But, and this is an important but, I have told Stan that we cannot accept this sort of behaviour and the consequent publicity which reflects so badly on Aston Villa … Leading footballers like Stan are highly rewarded for their efforts. In return they must be aware of the need to guard the club's good name'.

(*Evening Standard*, 16 June 1998)

Gregory's statement makes an interesting distinction between the 'private' matter of the assault and the public issue of the impact of the incident on the image of the club. In the 1970s, feminist politics insisted that 'the personal is political', and the spate of sporting violence against women stories showed both that men still try to preserve a sharper distinction between the private and public spheres, but that this distinction is put under pressure by the publicised events involving sport stars. A *Guardian* editorial linked the various cases with others and called for action by sporting authorities in such cases:

In 1996 Paul Gascoigne's wife Sheryl emerged bruised and bandaged the victim of her own husband's rage. At the end of last year Laura Bruno got a court injunction barring husband Frank, the former heavyweight boxing champion of the world, from assaulting, molesting or harassing her. In Florida a shelter has been set up as a haven for women abused by sportsmen, so great is the demand. And yet, time after time, the men of violence are effectively forgiven. They are not ostracised, but allowed to resume their place in public life – as if their athletic prowess somehow mitigated their crime. The response to Gazza's pummelling of Sheryl was typical: he was picked to play for England at the very next fixture. This routine turning of a collective blind eye has gone on long enough.

(*Guardian*, 22 January 1998)

While rightly condemnatory, little of the media coverage of male violence, offers much in the way of contextual insight. Issues to do with the construction of masculinity as powerful and invulnerable, the structure of patriarchal power, the concept of women as objects and as property, and the translation of human relations into commodity relations did not surface in popular discourse. Lyn Segal calls on us to see such violence in the broader context of late capitalism:

> what we are up against is something far worse, something far more destructive than the power of any man or group of men – something worse even than the mythic qualities of Dworkin's atomic phallus. However old-fashioned it may sound, in these post-political days, what we are confronting here is the barbarism of private life reflecting back the increased barbarism of public life, as contemporary capitalism continues to chisel out its hierarchies along the familiar grooves of class, race and gender.

(Segal 1990: 271)

To take such a perspective is to throw into relief the relative shallowness of moral entrepreneurship, which, devoid of incisive political analysis, consists of principled position without practical programme for change. Fighting for social change in late capitalism inevitably requires pessimism of the intellect and optimism of the will, but principled moral positions can only acquire a political effectivity if underpinned by social–political analysis. Media representation of misbehaviour in sport too readily sets up sport stars as figures onto which condense the signifiers of broader social concerns. They become targets in a coconut shy, whilst the stories themselves have little power to prompt social change.

One characteristic of the polemical interventions of moral entrepreneurs has been their difficulty in hitting their targets accurately. Such discourses tend to operate as if their objects were neatly fixed, stable and consistent, rather than floating, unstable and self contradictory. Identities are the point of convergence of discourses, situated in the relationship between subjects and discursive practices. The analyses in the next two chapters draw attention to the tensions around this lack of fixity. Chapter 13 examines constructions of black identities, and chapter 14 focuses on some of the themes of postmodern debate, which propose the dominance of appearance over substance, and the self-referential and parodic aspect of culture.

13 Identities

'Race', nation and masculinities

> What is *not said* in sports media reveals as much about how hegemonic processes work within the US sports industry as what *is said*. The socially structured silences that the representational conventions cultivated by these media support, legitimize and police the interests of both profit-driven media organizations and the established gender order.
>
> (Sabo and Jansen 1992)

Media representation is the product of sets of production practices, framed by professional ideologies, within the context of institutional structures. These practices, ideologies and structures are also the embodiment of power relations. They regularise and routinise a process of cultural production based on the control of the power to define. Issues of who is able to speak and be heard, on which topics, from which positions, and within which frames of reference have always been central to understanding the ways in which media production relates to social and cultural reproduction. So the tensions and contradictions between the absences and lacunae, the socially structured silences and the voices endeavouring to be heard, provide important clues as to the process of ideological contestation. In this context, images of black masculinity have been the site of struggle in which ideological elements of sporting prowess, black male virility, street-cool, racism, black masculinity and concepts of national identity are articulated.

In a period marked by the elision of sport and fashion, the commodification and objectification of male bodies and transformations in masculinity, the defensive resilience of hard masculinity retains a strong connotative force whilst at times acquiring a parodic quality. The 'Men in Black' look both embodied and parodied the hard and invulnerable castle of the masculine self. Clad in black suits, dark glasses, in the *Blues Brothers* style, men in black, like the cyborg characters in the *Terminator* genre of films, are hard to damage. Not surprisingly, such icanography turns up in the sporting context. A feature in the *Daily Express* (15 May 1998) on Arsenal's FA Cup final suits, headed 'REAL MEN IN BLACK', is illustrated with pictures of Steve Bould and David Seaman in the 'Men in Black' look, and the text comments:

they will be modelling matching black suits, black shirts, black ties and who knows, maybe even black underpants – by German designer Hugo Boss … Brenda Byrne, menswear buying manager for the Fenwick stores, says 'Black is a strong uncompromising colour, even slightly threatening, which is why pop and movie stars also like it'.

(*Daily Express*, 15 May 1998)

If men in black are able to project a cool strong image in the media, men who are black do not have it so easy. The repertoire of representation of black athleticism in the mainstream media draws on established stereotypes – the respectful (Uncle Tom), the powerful and threatening black body, the cool and street-wise. British magazines rarely put black people on their covers. When *Men's Health* editor Phil Hilton did, it was a significant enough event for the *Guardian* to interview him. His revealing comments included:

It is a widely held but rarely spoken belief that black covers do not sell. I'm not talking about celebrities or about the use of black models to represent specific ethnic groups, I'm talking about black people who are simply representing people … I'm paid to sell a lot of magazines. Nowhere in my job description is there anything about furthering a multi-racial society and promoting positive images of ethnic minority men.

(*Guardian*, 11 May 1998)

Hilton is using the black model on the June issue because

I'm convinced it will sell. Our covers show the kind of man our readers aspire to being and this model has the handsome confidence and upper arm development that most men would die for. I sense that even though many readers will not share his skin colour they will be sophisticated enough to identify with him in the same way they have with previous covers … Evidence for black models affecting sales is extremely sparse because they are very rarely tried. The fear is generating more fear … it's an embarrassment to the industry that black faces are so rare. It's embarrassing that the *Guardian* felt there was a story in a black model cover and it's embarrassing to admit that I questioned my decision to use him even for a second. We will receive sales figures very shortly and I'm certain they will help to cure this hidden magazine neurosis.

(*Guardian*, 11 May 1998)

Blackness here is discussed as a visual signifier, and one that marks a difference – black and white. The difference is perceived as problematic – because it is to do with 'racial' disadvantage and racism. Hilton's comments suggest that the relation between media producers, advertisers and the audience is by no means simple. The liberal aspirations of a media producer are here seen as in conflict with the image (which may be based on inadequate evidence and stereotypical preconceptions) held by publishers and advertisers of their audience.[1] The term 'race', of course, is not a coherent biological category, but rather a social construct. As such, it interacts with, indeed cannot be understood independently of, other social constructions – such as class, gender, nation, identity. Three such constructions are of particular relevance to the present study – blackness, Britishness and masculinity. Clearly there are complexities of identity to be considered here; in particular, that form of double consciousness in which to be black and British involves both being black *and* British, but also neither simply just black nor simply just British. Paul Gilroy (1987, 1993) has argued that concepts of blackness can only be understood as situated in the black diaspora in which an identity has been dispersed in the same way that black people were themselves dispersed. Identities formed in the context of relations of dominance and subordination are likely to have a hybrid character, and such hybridities are rarely simple.

Bhaba argues that hybridity is the moment in which 'the discourse of colonial authority loses its univocal grip on meaning and finds itself open to the trace of the language of the other' (Young 1995: 22). Bakhtin suggested that hybridity can unmask authority. Mercer talks of the dialogic tendency in black film practice and the ways in which elements of the dominant culture are creolised, disarticulating given signs and rearticulating their symbolic meaning (Mercer 1995: 25). Stuart Hall refers to 'a hyphenated sense of belonging' that characterised the experience of being black and British.[2] Allor uses the Quebeçois to exemplify a similar process:

> The figure of *metissage* works to name the instability of the traits of the *people quebecois*: both and neither European and American; ethnically distinct and of mixed parentage; tied to the (increasingly) urban environment and culturally dependent.
>
> (Allor 1993: 71)

The notion of 'both and neither' is pertinent for a consideration of representation of black sport stars. It should be noted in passing that Robert Young (1995) warns that 'in re-invoking the concept of hybridity, we are re-utilising the exact vocabulary of Victorian racialism', and that 'Far from being marked by a separation from the racialised thinking of the past, today's theories of postcolonialism and ethnicity operate in complicity with it'. This, however, seems to be somewhat formalist, as the material determinants and conjunctural character of each moment has its own specificities.

Recent writing on black identities suggest that fragmented and recomposed identities need not be seen in a negative light. Kobena Mercer refers to 'the velocity of change that characterises everyday life at the end of the twentieth century' and to life for Black Britain as 'a relentless vertigo of displacement' (1995: 1–2). He references neo-conservative triumphalism, the collapse of the communist bloc, Islamic fundamentalism and the 'savage ethnic neo-nationalisms of Eastern Europe', and says 'it is in relation to such global forces of dislocation in the world system as a whole, that Britain, too, has been massively reconfigured as a local, even parochial, site in which questions of "race", nation and ethnicity have brought us to the point where "the possibility and necessity of creating a new culture" – that is new identities – is slowly being recognised as *the* democratic task of our time' (Mercer 1995: 3 and quoting Gramsci 1971: 126).

Mercer argues that emerging cultures of hybridity forged among the overlapping African, Asian and Caribbean diasporas that constitute our common home must be seen as crucial and vital efforts to answer the 'possibility and necessity of creating a new culture *so that you can live*'. As black academic Stuart Hall has said (to a largely white audience and, one suspects, with tongue slightly in cheek), 'now that you are all de-centered, I feel centered'; and the sense of national identity among white English is, at the least, unsettled. The beleaguered sensibility of post-imperial Englishness, in its painful struggle to come to terms with a multi-cultural environment, perversely produces both reactionary racism and cultural opportunity – the dislocation and deconstruction of imperial arrogance enables the emergent construction of multiple-identity versions of Britishness. The establishment of a Scottish Parliament and a Welsh Assembly has thrown a new focus on the question of 'Englishness', in which Englishness ceases to be taken for granted, but becomes something that has to be reconstructed. This process of unsettling and recomposition provides a way of reading representation of black sport stars as symptomatic – revealing the contradictions and tensions at work in the recomposition of national identities.

Crucially, the issue is not merely one of difference or diversity, but also of power. The power relations structured through race require us to centre rac*ism* in analysis. Ben Carrington has demonstrated the ways in which media framing structures out issues of racism, and those who seek to instigate discussion of racism are therefore seen as 'importing' politics into sport. Carrington's discussion of Christie's attempts to place racism on the agenda, provides eloquent testimony to the silencing and stifling impact of white 'liberal' televisual discourse (Carrington 2000). Carrington also documents the refusal of the media to 'accept' Bruno's attempt to raise the issue of his supposed Uncle Tomism. Indeed one central practice of British sporting journalism has consisted of a denial of institutionalised racism, and a consistent attempt, when the issue is forced onto the agenda, to portray it as associated with extreme right-wing thugs, whom all 'right-thinking' people 'naturally' condemn.[3]

Stardom and blackness

The typology of stars derived from the work of Chas Critcher (1979), if applied to black sport stars, might suggest that they are more likely to be in the superstar-dislocated category. White racism closes off the embourgeoised/incorporated route for many. Blackness, though, problematises this typology of stardom – any attempt to apply it to black British footballers, reveals the inherent 'whiteness' of the concept of a 'traditional/located' star – this is a positionality that cannot readily be inhabited, in any unproblematic fashion, by a black figure because the traditions of that working-class locale are decidely 'white'. Transitional and mobile Ian Wright may be, but the high ground is occupied by Gary Lineker. Garth Crooks may be incorporated and embourgeoised, but will he ever get to be the 'main man'? Stan Collymore fits as neatly as does Gascoigne in the fourth category, the dislocated superstar.[4] Dislocation is an almost inevitable component of black stardom as long as the terms of that stardom are structured by the relation between a largely white media industry and an audience conceptualised as white.

The distinction between those, like Christie, who acknowledge and at times challenge racism, and those, like Bruno, who frequently (though not always) seek to deny or minimise it, suggests a contrast that is marked in many other examples. Black British boxing champions John Conteh and Lloyd Honeyghan were potentially popular heroes,[5] who achieved success as 'British' performers, but were there subtle hints in their representation in the media that they were a bit too aggressively proud, a bit 'uppity'? Frank Bruno, by comparison, represented as respectful, with an implication that he 'knows his place', was generally willing to go along with white stereotypes and be the butt of humour, although 'Uncle Tom' accusations clearly hurt him. Bruno does pantomime, sometimes in drag. There are complex things going on here – he demonstrates that he is a good sport; he reinforces the clumsy, docile and clown-like aspects; it links back to the minstrel tradition and bumbling negroes as the butt of humour; it also defuses and emasculates black sexual potency in a similar way to the infantile qualities Carrington refers to (Carrington 2000). Garth Crooks has an aspirant middle-class style, media-confident, almost an embodiment of the dream of liberal assimilationist theories. He is articulate and middle class in style and tone, and a 'polished' media performer; all this, nonetheless, has not yet enabled him to advance beyond a relatively minor role as an interviewer on television football, and an occasional appearance on *In the Midnight Hour* (BBC2).

In the midst of the fragments of postmodern culture, though, stands the new black sporting hero, Tiger Woods. The perfect hero for the white world – he has stunning ability, is handsome, well spoken and respectful, with a clear commitment to the puritan work ethic. He is the inheritor of the lineage from Jesse Owens and Carl Lewis as a symbol of white liberal hopes of integration. Indeed, had he not existed, it would have been necessary for the media sport industry to have invented him, which of course, in a sense, they did. The ever-growing influence of the needs of sponsorship, corporate hospitality, marketing and public relations in sport has meant emphasis on the task of producing and maintaining a positive image. The demand for a respectable, corporate-friendly patina serves only to inscribe more firmly the power of the cultural values of affluent white society. Class plays a significant role in the discursive placing of star images. Jesse Owens, Arthur Ashe, Carl Lewis, Tiger Woods and Michael Jordan could all be framed by an acceptably bourgeois narrativising of the striving for success against the odds. All come from predominantly non-contact sports, all were portrayed as having based success on hard work, all mastered the art of delivering to the (white) media an appropriately bland and respectful performance. Woods, in particular, would appear to epitomise the incorporated-embourgeoised sporting star.

O.J. Simpson, having in transitional-mobile fashion, attempted to build an acting career, then became the defendant in a murder trial, a highly public event which, like the beating of Rodney King by LA Police and subsequent release of a video showing the beating, served to demonstrate a degree of polarisation of white and black readings of events. While it is dangerous to carry generalisation too far, and gender differences are of significance here, too, black audiences typically found the evidence against Simpson less persuasive than whites, and were more prone to give credence to the possibility of the police planting evidence. While Simpson built an image that then became compromised, the image of dislocated-superstar Mike Tyson was, from the start, deliberately constructed to be threatening, scary and confrontational. His own behaviour served only to reinforce this preconstructed frame. His route from invincibility to pariah has had a degree of inevitability about it. The 'animal' image constructed by publicists to promote him is also employed by those who wish to condemn and outlaw him. Matthew Norman, parodying the public reaction to the incident in which Tyson bit Holyfield's ear, wrote:

> Last September when the world recoiled in astonished horror and pressed the nosegay of moral outrage the received wisdom was that Mike Tyson would never fight again. How on earth, asked the global media and boxing's leading pundits in rhetorical unison, could this monstrous Hannibal Lecteur manqué ever be permitted to return to the ring? Those of us who watch the big fight game with wry disdain chuckled at such rigid moralising and whispered to ourselves a brace of clichés especially applicable to boxing; time is a great healer and money makes the world go round.
>
> (*Evening Standard*, 13 January 1998)

Of course, the relation between national identity, masculinity and ethnicity is made more complex by sexuality. The work of Wachs and Dworkin, involving a comparative study of print media coverage of the Greg Louganis and Magic Johnson HIV-positive announcements, suggested that while black heterosexual Johnson was framed as a hero, white gay Louganis almost never was (Wachs and Dworkin 1997: 327). Johnson's acknowledged promiscuity, though, was inevitably narrated within a discourse that referenced the image of the 'sexually rapacious' black man. Magic Johnson's book dealing with his HIV diagnosis links racism with other prejudices, couched in a liberal discourse in which power relations are absent:

> discrimination is ugly. It's based on hate and ignorance. Too many of us know what it feels like to be discriminated against because of our colour or

religion or disability or sexual identity. People with HIV are discriminated against too.

(Johnson 1992a)

It offers a heroic narrative based on the uncertainties of fame and success and the ability to fight back against adversity:

> Magic Johnson's athletic skill made him one of the most admired and highest paid sportsmen in the world. But his life changed completely when he was given the results of his blood test. With great courage he openly announced his condition. He vowed that he would embark on a new mission: he set up the Magic Johnson Foundation, dedicated to educating young people about the grave dangers of unsafe sex and drug abuse, helping them to avoid AIDS.

(Johnson 1992a, back-cover blurb)

His life is narrated in terms of a 'poor but honest, salt of earth' mythologising.

> I grew up in the kind of black family that people today worry is disappearing. Even though there were nine of us, we had what we needed – two great parents, food on the table, and time for the whole family to be together. To provide for us my parents worked terribly hard. My father had two full time jobs and Mom worked just as hard to keep the household going. Seven kids kept her busy but she also had jobs outside the home.

(Johnson 1992b: 3)

In short, his exemplary upbringing equipped him to cope with any adversity as another challenge to be worked at and to be overcome. Dennis Rodman, by contrast, in his modes of self-presentation challenges the neat rationality of these categories. A postmodern bad boy whose behaviour and style of dress and adornment pushes at the boundaries – can do anything and somehow it doesn't *really* matter because it's not *really real*. In addition, as opposed to Tyson, who constantly appears as the victim of his own actions, the prisoner of his own mythology, Rodman seems aware enough of the conventions to play with them and hence win a degree of control. Yet, in the end, has he broken through boundaries, or merely been boxed inside the category of 'flash but crazy nigger'? Examination of representations of black sportsmen still tends to suggest that, for them, the rules are different, the conventions more strict and the options more limited. In other words, beneath the glossy but paper-thin carapace of postmodernity, where supposedly surface appearances have subsumed substance, where bricolage and intertextuality and self-referentiality have replaced linearity and consistency, there are still, underneath, structures of power that continue to order, constrain and enable the range of utterances and actions that constitute the discursive field. Rodman, who could be transgressive and disruptive, is contained within the freak show that is wild and wacky celebritydom.

Linford Christie

From the perspective of concepts of identity, an athlete like Linford Christie can signify different and sometimes contradictory elements of blackness, Britishness and masculinity. As consumers of media imagery, Christie's own experience of the tensions and contradictions of these elements is not available to us unmediated. We can however, analyse the ways in which, in different representational forms, in different media products, in specific historical moments, different aspects of Christie's identity are in dominance. As a late starter in athletics who got to the top, challenged American dominance and captained the British team, he can be presented as an aspirational figure. His discipline, commitment and self-sacrifice has been celebrated:

> A champion may not be the fastest runner, but he or she is generally the one who sticks at it, enjoys the training and competing and is also prepared to sacrifice other things which look fun, and that friends are doing, in order to succeed.
>
> (Christie 1996)

His own writing is explicit about the role of sport as providing character training. He wrote that 'the values which we learn in sport can be carried through to all walks of life and can be beneficial to us when the days of school and competitive sport have been left behind' (Christie 1996). The mythology of Christie stresses competitive commitment. One detail of Christie's running philosophy that was highlighted in the late nineties was the concept that you should start running on the 'B' of BANG. Christie's self-presentation stresses the desire to win:

> I am a fighter and I think that is the best part of it. People are behind me, not just because I go out and win but because I fight. I don't always accept the saying that it's not the winning, its the taking part which counts. Winning is pretty important but you can't be criticised if you fight even if you don't win.
>
> (Christie 1996)

He has been presented in terms of patriotism. Captaining the British athletics squad, pictures of him draped in a Union Jack occupied front pages in many papers. The image, combining blackness, success and Britishness is complex and ambiguous, but offers a multicultural inflection of national identity. Christie himself makes an interesting contrast between Jamaican and British attitudes to national identity:

When I was at school in Jamaica, we would sing the British National Anthem. When I came to England, I found that nobody bothered. Kids should be made to feel that they belong, and I believe that's one of the reasons why we have problems. A lot of black people don't feel part of Great Britain.

(Christie 1995: 34)

Black sporting success has, in representational terms, a dual character. On the one hand, images of acting successful black athletes offer a fund of 'positive' images to set against the larger backdrop of 'negative', stereotypical and racist images. However, the relative scarcity of such images in other domains means that sport and show business stand alone as public arenas in which black excellence is celebrated. Christie has a programmatic sense of the importance of such images:

In a sense black sportsmen are uniting the country. We need to go out there and spread the message. When people see how harmonious the athletics team is they will say, 'if they can get on, then why can't the rest of us?'.

(Christie 1995: 37)

His own sense of his value as a 'role model' is rooted in a sense of shared origins, as someone who has come from 'the streets':

There's not a lot for them to do, they've time on their hands, and idle hands are the devil's work tool ... I'm very much one of them. I've been a street kid. They can relate to me, and see that with hard work you can be successful.

(*Sunday Mirror*, 31 October 1993)

The *Sun* related a tale, headlined MINDER LINFORD (*Sun*, 17 August 1993), in which Christie acted as a minder for Curtis Robb. Robb, a middle-distance runner and physically much smaller than Christie, was being threatened by an American athlete at the World Athletics Championships, and recalled that 'team captain Christie stepped between the two middle-distance runners and told Gray: "Just leave my boy alone. If you mess with him then you have got to mess with me, too"' (*Sun*, 17 August 1993). Street-wise muscularity and the patriotic paternalism of the team captain are combined here for altruistic results. But Christie can also represent black cool, and his own involvement with stylistic innovation signifies a sensibility in which appearance and ways of doing things is important:

We used to smoke. Most kids do which is why I can tell them 'smoking is bad for you'. Part of the wall in our school playground used to stick out; we would stand behind it and puff away. It was cool to buy a good brand of cigarette. One girl used to bring in Peter Stuyvesants and if you had the thin brown ones called More then you were 'The Man', because you had a long cigarette.

(Christie 1995: 31)

Another element of his identity is to do with pressure and the particular pressures associated with being famous and black. He contemplated suicide after being accused of taking drugs during the 1988 Olympics (a few days after the Johnson case). 'I honestly thought about suicide because of the shame and embarrassment it would bring on my friends and family even though I was innocent' ('Linford: My Suicide Plan', *Sun*, 10 June 1994). He wept publicly as he denied using steroids (*Guardian*, 18 June 1998), and he successfully sued John McVicar for an article published in the first issue of a satirical magazine, *Spiked*, now defunct, which made allegations about Christie's supposed use of performance-enhancing drugs. His highly developed muscular physicality has been framed by the media in terms of sexuality. While Christie's own use of clothing has sometimes been complicit in enabling this reading, he has also made plain his own objection to being framed in terms of his sexuality. It is as if Christie's blackness itself acts as a licence to enable the media to reproduce images of black sexuality. The process of sexualisation of Christie has taken place during a period in which male bodies have been portrayed in more objectified and sexualised ways, with the male body as spectacle being more foregrounded. Christie's own account places more emphasis on being recognised and entertaining an audience:

Allan Wells had introduced the cut down shorts in Britain in 1986 and I liked the idea. Apart from giving warmth to the athletes hamstrings, they were distinctive. I took it a stage further by going for multi-coloured body suits. The suits certainly stood out. The crowd could recognise me. They no longer saw eight black guys who looked the same. Now they knew which one was Linford Christie. I became more outrageous. I would wear suits with big holes in the side, penguin suits, anything. It was entertaining.

(Christie 1996)

Christie was portrayed on the front cover of the *Radio Times* dressed in Lycra shorts and vest, in an Atlas pose holding the *Radio Times* logo aloft ('SO YOU WANT A BODY LIKE MINE? – Linford Christie shows you inside' (*Radio Times*, 2 July 1994). He was included in a feature which boasted 'Revealed! The best bodies in the world' (*Smash Hits*, 3 August 1994). The sexualisation of black bodies here increasingly centred around innuendo about genital size. The *Daily Mirror* (24 June 1994) ran a feature, notionally about diet, headed 'LUNCH BUNCH CRUNCH'. The *Sunday Mirror* ran a headline 'I'VE GOT A WICKED ONE. IT'S BIG AND MY MANDY LOVES IT' (*Sunday Mirror*, 31 October 1993). The article related to Christie's love of making omelettes for his partner. In a more direct approach, the *Daily Star* (22 June 1994) headlined 'IT'S THE

BATTLE OF THE LUNCH BOXES'. The article detailed an alleged dispute between Christie and Mr Motivator, Mr Motivator claiming Christie did not dress correctly in terms of the revealing nature of his Lycra shorts. Such innuendo was by no means limited to the tabloid press and, in a court case in 1998, Christie was outspoken in his objections to it:

> During the 14 day trial the jury also heard Mr Justice Popplewell inquire about the contents of Linford's lunch box. 'They are making a reference to my genitals' replied the athlete. 'It's sexual discrimination. No one mentions Sally Gunnell's tits'.
>
> *(Guardian,* 4 July 1998)

Christie was (and is) prepared to speak out about 'the reality of racism and of growing up as a black man in British society' and the Arrow edition of his autobiography dealt with his 'reaction to being falsely accused of stealing a car and his dramatic vindication in court' (Christie 1990: back cover). The Introduction to the book foregrounded the issue:

> As with many stories of black men and women living in Britain the spectre of racism is often unavoidable. That this is a canker on our society there can be no doubt. As Linford unfolded the details of how he and his family have been harassed and racially abused, he became very emotional indeed, the painful memories rekindling in him the utter frustration and impotent anger that he, his father, his whole family have felt and still feel. It is, sadly, a story that could be repeated thousands of times in Britain and it is hardly surprising that many in the black community will say, if it can happen to Linford Christie what chance do we stand?
>
> (Christie 1990: 2)

There is an account of his wrongful arrest for car theft and his subsequent successful suing of the police that also reveals the ways in which a black man's words can be transformed in print:

> I made a carefully worded statement where I said that I thought it was good not only for black people but for the community as a whole, for me to win the case, to show the police, from time to time, that they cannot just push people around. The next day it appeared in most of the papers that I had said 'it was good for coloured people'. I had chosen my words especially carefully and they were ignored. People who know me are aware that 'coloured' people is an expression that I do not use. If I am referring to my community I use the word 'black'.
>
> (Christie 1990: 195)

The book reveals bitterness at his treatment by athletics journalists, and he complains 'I expected no more from the tabloids but I expected a lot more from one of the sport's magazines *Athletics Weekly*. They never contacted me but just quoted one of the tabloids' (Christie 1990: 195). His anger at police attitudes is also explicit:

> to me the police use stereotyped thinking, especially in their dealings with black people and this is what, in the end, causes the problems that the black community faces. The police are constantly pointing out that there is a severe increase in crime carried out by young people of all races and colours and you would think that instead of harassing the influence of the black community, its athletes, its footballers, its boxers, they would be harnessing the influence that these role models can exert.
>
> (Christie 1990: 196)

Christie arrived in Britain aged seven, and the book *To Be Honest With You* deals with his own first experiences of racism, and first awareness of blackness as a distinct identity:

> The fact that I was a black kid really meant nothing to me. I never knew the difference between being black or anything else until I went to school which, ironically, backed onto the old White City athletics track. Children can be so vicious. A group of them were messing around, chasing one another, when I decided to join in. I caught this girl and she said I couldn't play. When I asked why not, she replied, 'My mummy said I shouldn't play with blackies. I thought, 'I'm black!' I was only about eight years old, but to this day, I can still hear her voice and remember exactly what she said.
>
> (Christie 1995)

The power of ideology is such that even in the autobiography of a black athlete (written in collaboration with ghost writer Tony Ward), stereotypes such as the happy-go-lucky West Indian and the myth of 'natural ability' are reproduced:

> in his early years he epitomised the stereotype West Indian youth – happy-go-lucky, easy-come-easy-go, relying almost solely on his great natural ability. The signals were often there that if he would only commit himself to his talent he could achieve greater things, but always he chose to ignore them.
>
> (Christie 1990)

Star performers are not in control of their own images, which are a product of the social construction of stardom, the routine production practices of the media, the discursive fields within which they are produced, and the specific social and historical conjunctures out of which they emerge. Christie is smart enough to know this, without the power to change it, and much of his frustration with the media grows out of this fact.

Ian Wright

The later career of Ian Wright has seen his public profile grow, even as his football ability has waned. His personality has worked well on television, culminating in an appearance on *This is Your Life* which produced a big audience response. Wright's discussion of his own heroes reveals a concern with entertainment, with 'flair', with 'looking good' and with being a bit of a rebel:

> All kids have heroes – people they admire and respect. I was no different. There was a handful of players I tried to copy in the playground. When I got to play professional football myself I would still think about the reasons why I had liked those players. I can still remember all the magic moments of skill they had showed. When you were a youngster and you'd just scored a goal – perhaps it had involved a great mazy dribble around all their defenders – you would put your hands up, waving to an imaginary crowd, and for a brief moment pretend you were Stan Bowles or Laurie Cunningham. Stan the Man was a great player and a great entertainer. He had a lovely left foot, great ball control. A flair player. He always looked as if he was doing just whatever he liked on the pitch. He was concerned that he looked good and you could see that he really loved using his skills to show up the defenders who tried to kick him. When the ball came to Stan he controlled it dead, Straight away, no mistake. He always had his shirt out and with his long hair, he looked a rogue and a rebel. But he could really play.
>
> (Wright 1994: 9)

The interesting question here is why Wright's personality has apparently been a bigger hit with the audience than other (undoubtedly popular) sport stars such as Christie and Bruno. He has some key ingredients – a high-scoring striker who played for Arsenal and England, with a character which is seen as attractive to the advertisers – impassioned and flamboyant, but without arrogance. He appeals to youth audiences as well as older sporting spectators, and has been able to make lucrative deals with Nike and others. An *Evening Standard* profile featured Wright on the front cover of the magazine supplement wearing a leather jacket and sixties style black cap, standing in front of a wall painted with bright graffiti. The image is redolent of cool street cred. Wright is described as 'Adored on the pitch by the Highbury faithful and idolised off it by the South London style set' (*Evening Standard*, 26 January 1994). His plans to have his own chat show were regarded by some as inevitable – 'It was only a matter of time … his next most valuable asset was always going to be his personality' (*Guardian*, 7 May 1998).

Accounts of Wright frequently draw attention to his flamboyant style. On the back of his own book he is described as a 'born entertainer' who has a 'flamboyant wardrobe and vast shoe collection'. In the words of this book, 'Whether gunning his goals, playing his saxophone or strutting his stuff as the street hero of Highbury, Wright does everything with style and this spectacular

book reflects his magnetic appeal' (Wright 1994). His South London back-
ground is frequently evoked, usually as a means of signifying a down-to-earth
London working-classness, and a degree of embededness amongst South
London black youth:

> you don't get to become a street hero without having a certain amount of
> panache. And Wright is a street hero. When he walks down the road in
> South London, where he grew up and still lives, people stop cars to get out
> and give him five. For young men, particularly young black men, he repre-
> sents success without surrender, someone who has made it to the top on
> talent and without being embraced by the establishment like a Lineker or
> lampooned like a Gazza.
>
> (*Evening Standard*, 26 January 1994)

This working-class localism is also what enables Wright to pass with a white
working-class audience as 'one of us', moving, Ben Carrington suggests, from
racial outside to working-class insider. As well as working-class credibility and
black identity, his image has, at first sight, the appearance of political radicalism.
He has expressed a preference for the Malcolm X model of confronting racism,
rather than the Christian turning of the other cheek of Martin Luther King.
Carrington argues that in media representation, the meanings inherent within
black culture have been divorced from any political connotations; and that the
de-politicised street cool that remains represents a commodification of blackness, as evidenced by the One to One advertisement, first because the ad
portrays not the radical Malcolm X, Wright's own preferred figure, but the
liberal Martin Luther King, and second because in the advertisement King's
politics are 'reduced to no more that a set of stylised images lacking any serious
political content' (Carrington 2001). Like Christie, Wright is portrayed as a
patriot and, like Christie, he has, as Carrington suggests, tended to see racism
and English nationalism as separate discourses rather than intimately linked.
This is convenient for the British sport press who have a strong disinclination to
acknowledge and confront the racism of the world in which they function.

The depoliticisation and commodification of black style are both evident in
representations of Wright. He is described as the epitome of style – a wearer of
'labels' such as Armani and Versace. He is described as 'brilliant' but also
'unpredictable', and he has been regularly disciplined by the football authorities. The suggestion here is of the romantic figure of the creative individual at
odds with bureaucratic forces. A full-page photograph in *Smash Hits* showing
Wright leaning against a bar in a dimly lit pub or night-club heightens the sense
of street cool, of a man with a life outside football. The cool pose is further
evidenced in the August 1993 edition of *Smash Hits*, headlined, 'HE SHOOTS!
HE SCORES!'. Indeed, he was one of very few sport stars featured in *Smash Hits*
during our year of magazine analysis. Other footballers have made records, but
few were well received. Wright's however is adjudged 'good'. ' "I just wrote
some lyrics and hopefully people can understand them", says Ian. "I'm a foot-

baller first and foremost who's just trying to make a half decent record"'(*Smash Hits*, August 1993). In *My World in Pictures*, there is a picture of Wright with a saxophone, captioned 'There's something about the saxophone that looks the business even if you can't play a note. However, I'm not making any public appearances until I've mastered at least two' (1994: 29). The street cred theme is present throughout the book. Pictures show Wright as a three year old 'already suited and booted', a little older carrying a football and 'determined to try the soft shoe shuffle', and 'aged fourteen and ready for action'. The final page has Wright in a wicked check suit with Chris Eubank 'for once I've outdone him as far as suits go!' – in a broad chalk stripe suit, with Chicago gangster-style hat and Thompson sub-machine gun, the caption reads 'Gangsta Style. Hip man as a hit man' (Wright 1994).

But street cred cool is an ambiguous framing, partly because it is a stereotypical form of portrayal of black entertainers, and because it also connotes 'Showy/black flash'. The *Smash Hits* article reports that 'He's cocky but you don't mind because he deserves to be. He's a good footballer and he knows it' (*Smash Hits*, August 1993). A profile of Wright related to his television chat show says that he 'walks into a room ... flashing his gold tooth in a broad and exciting grin' and is 'brimming with confidence in leather trousers'. The writer reports that 'When I turn to ask Wright something else he is already spinning around in his chair smiling. Each time he goes round you just catch the gold glint from his tooth' (*Guardian*, 7 May 1998). The profile concludes that

> There is a thin line between arrogance and self-confidence which Wright navigates more skilfully than is immediately obvious. He is cocky and knows his mind. But he also has an endearing sense of his own frailties and limitations that rescue him from conceit.
>
> (*Guardian*, 7 May 1998)

Another way of decoding this is that Wright only narrowly avoids being read as an uppity nigger, and it is his charm alone that saves him. Yet the world of celebritydom is a complex one, in which such charm scores higher than either the righteousness of a Christie or the kow-towing humbleness of a Bruno. Stuart Hall has commented on ways in which black youth in post-Thatcherite Britain, have found ways of operating within, and yet against the grain of, the structures of power:

> even if you've not been born to, or trained in, the mysteries of producing yourself as an entrepreneurial subject, you bring to the enterprise culture one or two hustling skills from the margins, and know how to move with them, and it is possible – not to get up to where it counts – but to make a little room in the ante-chambers of power.
>
> (Hall 1998: 41)

In this context, Ian Wright's show could be seen as a little room in the antechambers of power, and in the late 1990s, Wright was being ushered into the mansion of television with enthusiasm:

> Smiling down on him in the background are LWT's finest: Richard and Judy, Mrs Merton, Alf Garnett and Jeremy Beadle, all in controlled showbiz poses. Quite why Wright would want to stroll down that particular hall of fame is not clear. But he does.
>
> (*Guardian*, 7 May 1998)

Ali once commented that while a wise man can imitate a fool, a fool cannot imitate a wise man, a concept not lost on the writer of the *Guardian* profile:

> There are times like this, where, if only Wright could affect a more fluent, lyrical patter, he would sound just like Muhammad Ali during the seventies. Here is a self-educated black man, sophisticated and streetwise, part boisterous, part braggard, who loves to taunt and jibe and whose interests spread far and wider than just sport. He likes to play the fool but not to be treated like one. He is a complex multi-dimensional figure with views on everything from politics to soul music.
>
> (*Guardian*, 7 May 1998)

Marked here is the way in which blackness is a specific identity as opposed to the invisibility of whiteness, which figures like Wright are constantly confronted with and have to deal with:

> One reporter asks him if the show, which had a lot of black faces on it, is aimed at a black audience. It is an example of the racially-loaded questioning that makes Wright fume. If white people interview other white people it is a show for everyone. If black people interview other black people it is a black show ... Later I discover that those close to him are nervous about Wright being typecast and marginalised as a black presenter.
>
> (*Guardian*, 7 May 1998)

The combination of blackness and masculinity produces a set of constrictions in which acceptance by 'white' society is always contingent, temporary and conditional. There is a limited lexicon of types. Those who are too uppity, too self-righteous, too complaining, or excessively humble will encounter the withholding of symbolic endorsement from the white public. The media world of celebrity with its ritual media forms – celebrity game shows, gossip magazines, award ceremonies serves – to distinguish the mainstream from the marginal, and ultimately absorbs 'blackness' only on its own terms. Yet those terms are themselves increasingly subject to a lack of fixity. The media are characterised by both repetition and innovation. The restless search for innovation constantly produces new hybrid forms, such as 'reality' television (Big Brother combining elements of soap opera, game show and fly-on-the-wall documentary) and new types of content (e.g. the sexual licence granted shows like *Eurotrash* and *So Graham Norton*). The multiplicity of media outlets, and the very rapidity of the circulation of image and information in the age of the Internet, the fax and the mobile phone fosters both a rapid redundancy, and a growing tendency to plunder and recycle the archives. The next chapter examines the identities of sport stars in the context of these developments.

14 Performances, appearances, identities and postmodernities

You can't construct the Chris Morrises and Danny Bakers from audience research kits or corporate fiat: they develop serendipitously in welcoming milieux and need public-service broadcasting space and airtime to appall as well as delight. I demand the right for my radio to offend me.

(Anne Karpf, *Guardian*, 6 March 1997)

The contrast between Danny Baker and Tiger Woods could hardly be greater – Baker, as an unkempt and shaggy looking working-class Londoner who acts as a conduit for the 'voice of the fans' on Talk Radio, after being dumped by the BBC for suggesting on air that some referees deserved 'a slapping', could be seen as the antithesis of marketing and public relations. Tiger Woods, as a phenomenally gifted, young, attractive, black man, the first to achieve major success in that most upwardly mobile of sports, golf, is a marketeer's dream made flesh. Yet both are equally caught up in the process whereby, in a media-rich environment, appearance, style and personality have become the currency with which fame is purchased. Indeed, the very power of celebrity has become, in a sense, a destabilising factor. The twentieth-century project of sport – the pursuit of excellence, requiring dedication, talent, commitment and self-discipline, combines two elements of nineteenth-century ideology: self-improvement and competitive individualism. It is a rationalist project rooted in modernity. Yet it has become a part of, and indeed depends upon, a media industry which has enabled the consumption of images of sport on a globalised basis.

In a culture that is self-referential, parodic, and marked by the high-speed globalised circulation of images, the role of the sporting hero is inevitably subject to a greater degree of public deconstruction.[1] In postmodern culture, where surface appearance dominates over substance, sport stars become more like the characters of a soap opera – no more or less 'real'. It is notable that three of the most prominent sport stars in the news in recent years – Magic Johnson, O.J. Simpson and Mike Tyson – have all been newsworthy for reasons largely unconnected with sport. The presenters, commentators and experts, too, become star personalities. Howard Cosell, Jimmy Hill and Desmond Lynam became at least as familiar to audiences as were those whose performances they mediated. In a more self-referential and parodic culture in which a media-literate audience is adept at grasping the conventions, pastiche thrives. Programmes like *Fantasy League Football* and *They Think It's All Over* are possible only through this audience awareness of the conventions and mannerisms of the media. Sport is now so conscious of its status as show business that image and charisma are central concerns for any sport promoter or agent. But this obsession with appearance at the expense of substance tends to be mirrored in the debunking humour aimed at sport, in which the comedy is every bit as depthless as the cultural form it is mocking. The depthless ephemerality of post-modern culture serves as a destabilising element in relation to the rationality of elite sport and the media sport industry.

One impact of these developments has been to heighten the tensions between individual identities and wider collective identities (of team, region, and nation). The rising economic earning power of those at the top in sport, the growing power of sport agents since the 1970s, the growing international mobility of sport stars and the challenge to governing bodies by outside entrepreneurs have together served to weaken the ties between sport stars and national identity. Of course, national identities are still of great importance, yet this is in a context where Argentinian Maradona can be, for a while, a popular hero in Italy, Brazilian Juninho a star in Middlesbrough, Englishman Jack Charlton can be a man of the people in Ireland, German Jurgen Klinsmann can be the hero of Tottenham, and Frenchman Cantona can be the darling of Manchester. Top motor racers, golfers and tennis players now increasingly live an international trans-state existence.

In a period in which national success in international competition has eluded English teams in cricket, rugby and football, two of 'our' most successful international competitors, tennis player Greg Rusedski and boxer and world heavyweight champion, Lennox Lewis, have a national identity that is diffuse and ambiguous – neither are unproblematically 'British', despite their status as such for sport purposes. Both have non-British accents, neither are viewed as living in the country and, more importantly, there appears to be a connection between this British-at-a-distance status and the lack of full public enthusiasm for them. The problem is highlighted by the question of race and national belongingness, as can be seen in the very different media images surrounding Linford Christie, Frank Bruno and Chris Eubank (see Carrington 2000, 2001). The recent vehement debate triggered by an article in *Wisden's Cricket Monthly* questioning the patriotic commitment of black British cricketers revealed the degree of tension and unease that clusters around the concept of national identity.[2]

There does indeed appear to be a 'restless vertigo of displacement' in which multiple destabilised identities are awash in a sea of intertextual pastiche and cultural self-referentiality, in which even the walls of the castle of masculinity are, if not tumbling, at the least eroding and in serious need of repointing. Yet there is still an apparent yearning for sporting heroics, as can be seen in the celebratory portrayals of new emergent stars such as Ryan Giggs at the start of the 1990s, Michael Owen at the end of the decade, golfer Tiger Woods, footballer Ronaldo, and baseball players Sammy Sosa and Mark McGuire. But in the context of the nineties, a magical recovery of the unproblematic 'authentic' masculine heroics of a mythologised past was a complex ideological task that could never be fully secured. The quiet respectful unflamboyant public style of a Stanley Matthews, is no longer sufficient – note the public's relative disinterest in Lennox Lewis and perception of Tim Henman and Greg Rusedski as rather dull, whereas figures like Chris Eubank, Prince Naseem and Vinnie Jones may inspire anger and hostility, but also grab the media attention. They dramatise the narrative, they allow, indeed force, an audience positionality, and therefore they contribute to the compelling quality of sports soap-opera appeal.

In times that are fractured, self referential and decentred, political positions are less secured. Class-based politics are derided as old-fashioned, while new tensions emerge between the country and the city. Feminist discourses have been destabilised by the proliferation of competing positions within the space opened up by the growth of feminism between 1970 and 1990.[3] Left and right are, Vincent Cable suggests, no longer the dominant political dialectic, and other identities are emerging based on cultural identity, or what Isaiah Berlin has called 'the politics of the soil' (Cable 1994: 4).[4] Laclau argues that in the post-Cold War world particularistic political identities have proliferated, and there has been a decline in the force of universal values or projects, such as Marx's notion of class conflict (Laclau 1994: 1).[5]

Earlier, in the Introduction, the concept of role model was identified as one prevalent in discourses of sport stardom. The concept has a strong tendency to be normative and conservative, and, in its utilisation by moral entrepreneurs, usually has a moral agenda and a political project that is right-authoritarian in character. But children in the context of a media-rich environment are more complex, subtle and sophisticated in their readings. (Note the complex intertextual jokes in *The Simpsons*, and *South Park*.) They can readily distinguish between Gascoigne the clown, Gascoigne the football genius and Gascoigne the wife-beater. The concept of identity offers a more productive model. Identities are complex, multi-layered and combinatory. They are not fixed, but shift – identities develop and change (make-over, born again, reinventing oneself, etc., etc.). People adopt different identities in different circumstances. The process involves the formation of subjectivities – and subjectivities are best understood as the intersecting point of multiple discourses (see Pecheux 1982 on 'interdiscourse'). According to Hall, the concept of identity concerns the relationship between subjects and discursive practices. Identities are thus points of temporary attachment to the subject positions which discursive practices construct for us. Identities are always the product of 'specific historical and institutional sites within specific discursive formations and practices, by specific enunciative strategies' (Hall and du Gay 1996: 2–6). So, while on the one hand, subjects themselves are resistant to analysis, on the other, subjects positions can be derived in part from the analysis of texts and discourses. Indeed, subject positions are built into the very architecture, design and theming of the environments in which we live out our leisure:

Leisure World incorporates an Odeon eight screen multiplex cinema, Hotshots 20 lanes of tenpin bowling, twin 'scene' night clubs (Visage for the over 18s and Ethos for the over 23s), Jumping Jak Flash (a live entertainment restaurant bar), a sports theme bar with pool tables and games machines, Pizza Hut and Burger King fast food outlets, Playzone children's soft play area, Aquasplash leisure pool, Silverblades leisure ice rink and indoor bowling facilities.

(Clough 2000)

The description reveals the calculations through which markets are segmented by age, by gender and by position in the family life cycle. While, on the one hand, capitalist rationalisation, market research and image consultancy enables this precise distinction of the identities of early twenties (Visage) and late twenties (Ethos), it nevertheless does not prevent us from playing with the idea of being either – until, that is, we are visibly over thirty, when we are positioned in yet another category. We should then be alert to the construction of imaginary coherences while remaining sceptical of arguments that attribute to them too great a power. The concept of fragmented and multiple identities means that we are addressed by, and are positioned by, a multiplicity of consumption opportunities, yet, at the same time, we are equipped us with the means to elude final fixity. The very instabilities of identities means that attempts to produce imaginary coherences have a necessary ad hoc and temporary character. Media representations around the 1998 World Cup provided many examples such as the production of 'On Top of the World', the 1998 World Cup song, written and sung by Ian McCulloch of Echo and the Bunnymen, with the Spice Girls singing on it. As the *Evening Standard* reported it,

'Its a good lad's record' reckons Mel B. 'We're very proud to be on it. We like to support all British sport and particularly the England football team.' 'My dad would kill me if we didn't do it', squeals Emma, 'The Spice Girls are very patriotic and we're backing Britain'. Growls Geri, 'It doesn't matter whether you're a real football fan or not, when its the World Cup you wanna get behind your country. There's a ladette in everybody and we wanted to show our support'.

The video, overseen by Gary Lineker's Golden Boots director Lloyd Stanton, uses the type of special effects last seen in the Beatles Free as a Bird promo, the best of which is a terrier that morphs into David Batty.

(*Evening Standard*, 22 April 1998)

On this site of a convergence between the economic interests of world football and the pop music industry was forged a reconciliation of the gender difference in sport support, and a suturing of lad (and ladette) culture and nationalism in the ephemeral and temporary forms of pop culture, the single and the video. There is always a tension within elite sport between process and product. Sport is a performance and part of its appeal is its unpredictability. Elite sport is also a business that has become an efficient and effective way of generating profit. In doing so, it must turn performance into product. However, unlike other forms of production, it is hard to guarantee the consistency of the sporting product. If it was possible, the spontaneity and unpredictability that gives sport much of its appeal would be lost and audience interest would decline (Whannel 1994). In the process there is a shift in the balance between performance and appearance. Performance is a key element in the rise of a sport star, but performance is insufficient. A novel or striking appearance helps to bring a star to public attention. As the fame of a star grows, appearance becomes more central as a signifier. Physical appearance plays a significant role in the construction of star images. Appearance is the necessary mediation between performance and product that enables the commodification of the sporting performance.

Appearance in sport is circumscribed by limitations. Sport is structured by the conventions of rules, uniform and behaviour. Even body types are circumscribed. In terms of the physical body, certain types of body shape are required in order to perform and compete at expected levels. In general, by definition, sports performers are lean and muscular – athletic. While there are variations in the types of body required by different sports, within each sport there are expected standards which apply with little room for manoeuvre. The team strip provides the uniform for identification to opponents and supporters, but also contributes to 'team spirit' and 'identity' in the same way that uniform is used in other institutions (police, nurses, etc.). It imposes discipline and is rooted in relations of power and authority. This dress code does not just apply to team sports. In 'individual' sports, such as tennis and golf, there is always a 'uniform' of some sort, from the strict all-white rule of Wimbledon to the Pringle and plaid of the golf course.

So, it is no surprise that many top sport stars choose to mark their individuality with hair style, and this, in turn, enables the media process of establishing star personalities to function more efficiently. David Beckham, for example, has been through at least four distinctive hairstyles in his career, most recent being a dramatic mohican in the style of Travis Bickle in *Taxi Driver*. Synnott argues that hair is one of the most powerful symbols of individual and group identity, because it is physical and therefore extremely personal, and because, although personal, it is also public rather than private. In addition, it is usually voluntary rather than imposed or 'given' (Synnott 1993: 103). It draws on a system of categorisation which is generally understood by the possessor and the observer. The celebration of individual freedom is a central component in Western culture. However, attempts to achieve individual expression conflict with structural pressures towards a degree of uniformity. Dress codes and hair regulations in schools always constitute a site for contestation and resistance. Just as in education, also in team sports, and indeed sport in general, conformity is a fundamental requirement.

Becoming a sports performer involves entry into a set of practices governed by a set of conventions within the context of organisational structure. A knowledge of and performance of the relevant codes is an important element in the development of a sports performer. Sport is a social practice which effectively 'irons out' some aspects of individuality in order to maintain players as members of a team. However, the media habitually focus on individuality, and sports also have to produce such individuality in order to succeed. So, there is a conflict between the needs of discipline and entertainment. This conflict can be detected in the careers of such stars as George Best, Ian Botham and Paul Gascoigne.

Anyone for charisma?

Audiences want entertainment and charismatic stars provide a break from the mundane. The media dilemma is the dependence for entertainment value on a process – the sport performance – that they cannot in the end control. So, the presence of exciting narratives and charismatic stars can never be guaranteed. Indeed, there are many recent examples of failed attempts by promoters to build in entertainment value by overselling what they have. Chris Eubank's £10 million eight-fight deal with Sky produced a series of non-event fights against lacklustre opponents in half-empty arenas. The athletics World Cup featured a series of races between the tired and the terminally jaded, with many top stars simply absent. A star-studded and much ballyhooed six-a-side cricket tournament scheduled for London simply failed to happen after minimal public enthusiasm. Following the French Tennis Open in 1994, a media debate unfolded which had as its main theme the supposed crisis in tennis framed as a crisis of charisma.

The British press coverage of the 1994 Wimbledon Championships also highlighted the theme of a 'crisis' within the game, rooted in a supposed lack of 'personality' or 'character'. The London *Evening Standard* featured two separate full-page articles on the subject: 'The crisis of charisma that stalks Wimbledon' (15 June 1994) and 'Are robots killing tennis?' (20 June 1994). A combination of modern technology, increased competitiveness and ruthless determination, along with increased physical fitness, were cited as main reasons for the lack of vitality in the game. The reports quoted former player, the charismatic and controversial Illie Nastase, as saying 'The new players don't have charisma and haven't learned to relate to the public as spectators' (*Evening Standard*, 20 June 1994). Andre Agassi, although not the champion, was the media star of 1994. One story was headed 'SEX AND THE SINGLES MEN', and said 'They're game, set and macho – seven smash reasons why around 200 million women across the globe will be closely studying Wimbledon form for the next fortnight' (*Daily Mirror*, 20 June 1994).

This article rated male tennis players in terms of sexual attractiveness, chiefly physical appearance. Having previously shaved his chest hair, it was noticed that for this tournament Agassi had taken shaving a stage further and removed the hair from his legs. The *Sun* and the *Daily Mirror* both included stories, the *Daily Mirror* granting it front-page headlines; 'AGH-GASSI! – He shaves his legs for Wimbledon'. The article provided photographic evidence in the form of a close-up picture of his legs. Agassi and his body continued to feature in both sports page coverage and in the main sections of the paper: 'Bare-chested Andre Agassi strutted around court number one last night, impersonating Tarzan' (*Daily Mirror*, 23 June 1994) and 'Distraught: Bare-chested Andre after his downfall' (*Daily Mirror*, 28 June 1994). The emphasis on physical appearance was not just confined to the tabloids. Front-page space was provided in *The Times* with an article on Agassi and Sampras both wearing similar baggy shorts. It was implied that there was some form of contest between the two players as to whom could claim credit for initiating this style: 'Agassi and Sampras battle over baggy shorts' (*The Times*, 21 June 1994).

Sampras, through his success, appeared to be receiving the brunt of criticism for the apparent 'crisis' within tennis. Sampras has been ascribed a 'boring' status, in a similar way that Steve Davis was considered uncharismatic in snooker because of his single-minded approach to the game. In the media's eye, Sampras has been categorised as dull. Women's magazines picked up on the 'dull' theme: 'Even before it's begun, Wimbledon is starting to look boring ... At their best, Sampras and Graf play brilliant tennis, but they've become machines. Sampras rarely smiles and clinically demolishes his opponents' (*Woman's Own*, 20 June 1994). The tabloids were less apologetic in their accusations, 'A telly insider said: "Sunday's final was one of the most boring games in the history of Wimbledon. We need more colourful characters on the centre court instead of boring tennis machines no one wants to watch" ' (*Sun*, 5 July 1994). In an additional article on the same page the heading reads 'IT'S YAWN TENNIS', and goes on to say 'Pete Sampras is the man who, almost single-handedly, has turned lawn tennis into yawn tennis' (*Sun*, 5 July 1994). In a similar vein, the *Daily Mirror* featured a report which spotlighted the Princess of Wales leaving the centre court midway through the match, and suggested 'perhaps they were driven away by the boringly relentless aces served up on court' (*Daily Mirror*, 4 July 1994). The media turned to women's tennis both for charisma and for scandal. The *Sun* carried an 'exclusive' interview and a '3 page special' with Mary Pierce, with the front page headline; 'Crazed dad behind tennis star's agony' (*Sun*, 14 June 1994). Her fame, according to the *Sun*, comes at a price: 'At 19, with her blistering talent and model-girl looks, she should have the world at her feet. But her childhood ordeal at the hands of her brutish father still haunts her past ... and her present' (*Sun*, 14 June 1994). As so often, the media suggest that women pay a price for fame, in a sense being punished for the temerity of intruding into the male domain.

The accelerated pace of the commercialisation of sport since the 1950s has, of course, had dramatic consequences (see Whannel 1992; Goldlust 1987; Barnett 1990). The vastly increased rewards for top-level sport performance has ushered in a new professionalism. Training regimes are more rigorous, equipment more technologically sophisticated, performances more frequent, diets, massage and drugs have been refined, performance standards are higher and mistakes are more likely to be punished. The process that Brohm (1978) dubbed the Taylorisation of the body has developed to a high degree of sophistication. The rewards of victory are great, the penalties of defeat severe. Mewshaw (1983) reported that on the tennis circuit the standard reply by players to the question 'How are you?' is not 'I'm fine', but 'I'm 34th', by which they refer to their current ATP ranking. The very identity of sport stars becomes a product, not of their performance, but of the rating of their performance – by the degree of success that it has achieved. So, there is a potential conflict between the interests of the media and those of the players. The media need entertainment and spectacle; the performers are likely to focus increasingly on the absolute need for victory. Sometimes this focus may also provide entertainment, but there is no guarantee that it will do so. Promoters want characters who will attract the crowd and satisfy television. However, often such characters are also difficult to handle – disputing line calls, or abusing codes of dress or behaviour.

For stars like Andre Agassi or Ryan Giggs, this process constantly shifts emphasis from performance to appearance. For Agassi, the initial emphasis on his hair, pony-tail and cap, spread to his chest hair and legs. In creating further media fascination by shaving his legs and then his chest, Agassi appeared both to be complicit in this process and also to be playing games with it. Similarly, when, in mid-1994, the image of Ryan Giggs seemed to be in every magazine on the market, his appearance, notably his hair (Italian looking, curly but slicked back), provided the initial focus for the coverage. Just as Agassi shaved his body, Giggs responded by cutting his hair back to a more austere crew-cut, as if attempting to reclaim some essential self from the blizzard of secondary circulation of his image. Similarly David Beckham's cropped hairstyle, pictured in the tabloids in early 2000, was in reaction to the hordes of copyists of his previous floppy look. The highly talented footballer Ryan Giggs could have been a bigger star but is basically too dull – he isn't a bad boy, has no obviously identifiable eccentricities and hasn't been involved in any major controversy. A *Sun* story illustrates the limitations of fame for the well behaved. Under the banner, 'Another Great *Sun* Exclusive – GIGGSY TO BE A DAD', the article and the accompanying feature about Giggs's ex-lovers has nothing but positive things to say about him. The couple are 'very happy', a friend said. Giggs will make 'a great dad … they are a smashing couple'. One ex-lover says Ryan would make the perfect husband, and a pal says 'They've both got what it takes to be great parents'. Another ex-lover regards Giggs as charming and witty, and another as 'great company, a nice guy'; yet another says 'he is very good looking, a good lover and has a wonderful personality'. A friend says 'he loves kids and visits sick children in hospital at Christmas dressed as Santa' (*Sun*, 5 March 1998). No wonder he's not in the papers often … he's too good to be true! An additional factor in the low profile of Giggs is probably the tight paternal control that Ferguson seems able to exercise over his charges. For the early years of Giggs's career the media were kept at arm's length. All the young Manchester United lads seem rather clean-cut and clean living – a little bloodless. The new boys – the Neville brothers, Paul Scholes, etc., are all rather pale, serious, dedicated and slightly characterless. There is something of the new waifs about them, but also something of the new swots – clean living, focused, committed and subject to the growth of moral authority of employers (or maybe there is just a very efficient operation of keeping them out of the papers). Only Beckham, partly due to the glamour of his partner, Victoria Adams (Posh Spice), has become a major celebrity, and it is interesting that this has been the cause of extensive friction between him and the Manchester United manager Alex Ferguson.

Ironic, lads?

The range of sport-based cultural forms in which representations of sport were circulated grew rapidly during the 1990s, with the 'coverage' of sport often more popular than the sport itself. One significant site for the construction of representations of masculinity in the 1990s was the emergence of 'lad television'. The growing fragmentation of audiences, as a consequence of the growth in the number of channels, fostered a more precise targeting of demographically specific audiences. New-lad culture, rooted in a resolutely laddist masculine tone has been utilised with some success in *Fantasy League Football* (BBC) and *They Think It's All Over* (BBC). Such programmes were watched by audiences as large as, or larger than, those for many sport broadcasts.

The re-emergence of sexist imagery into the cultural mainstream, especially via the covers of the new men's magazines, and the reassertion of sexist masculinities, as best exemplified by the magazine *Loaded*, provide a context for lad television – *Men Behaving Badly*, *Fantasy League Football* and *They Think It's All Over* are all part of the process whereby this reactive laddism has moved into the mainstream. Lad television is not cast in the mould of body culture; indeed, in its dogged anti-health hedonism it represents a reaction against the dominance of body culture. These programmes exhibit many postmodern features – parody, pastiche and self-referentiality, the absence of any external 'reality', the foregrounding of surface appearance and seeming depthlessness. They also represent a continuation of a media-driven society of spectacle in which culture is commodified and stars are transformed into celebrities.

Fantasy League Football is set in a parodic version of a laddish flat, with echoes of *Men Behaving Badly* and *The Young Ones* (BBC, 1982–4) – sofas, coffee table, a kitchenette and football artefacts everywhere. (Presenters Frank Skinner and David Baddiel shared a flat for some years.) In the programme, the presenters share the 'flat' with super-nerd Statto, played by gambling pundit Angus Loughran.[6] As presenters, Skinner and Baddiel combine the style of a variety double act, the critical irreverence of alternative comedy and the self-conscious vulgarity of new laddism. Each week two celebrity guests arrive like guests to a dinner party, are sat on the sofa, and then function largely as props – pretexts and butts for the humour of the presenters. They appear as tokens of themselves and their own celebrity and are given only limited scope to contribute to the humour of the show. Women are often presented more as 'one of the lads' than as 'babes', although the supposed tenuousness of their involvement in the football culture of the lads is often exposed and used as the pretext for humour. The programme has a masculine unease about women in football culture – unsure whether to embrace them or exclude them.

The humour of the show, drawing on the humour of fans and the internal irreverent banter of football, contrasts with the formal stiffness of football interviews in football coverage elsewhere. Frank Skinner has a quick wit and an eye for absurdity. The programme takes pleasure in its own laddish silliness: in the regular feature, 'Phoenix from the Flames', in the use of ex-footballer Jeff Astle in ever-more absurd costumes to sing the final song, and in joke appearances by emblematic football figures like David Pleat.[7] In particular, 'Phoenix from the Flames' works because the whole project (to re-enact famous football moments, with one of the original participants, in a public park) is so inherently absurd, and the execution is so carefully inept.[8] Rooted in the laddish culture shaped and defined by new men's magazines like *Loaded* and *FHM*, and in the television programme *Men Behaving Badly*, sexist vulgarity and dumbed-down crudity tends to win out against real focused satire. Women become the targets of the humour, with the limited options of being a 'babe' or a surrogate lad; any other modes of femininity, against the grain of the programme, produce unease. Homophobia and racism often seem close to the surface. The parodies of black footballer Jason Lee, rooted in stereotype 'coon' imagery were unforgivable. Like women, blacks, gay people, 'funny' foreigners with funny names, and those with physical peculiarities, are all potential targets for jokes. As with much laddish culture, this is excused as postmodern irony – and postmodern irony, as Leon Hunt has commented, means never having to say you're sorry.

The humour is also exclusive and exclusionary – it depends upon possession of that alternative form of cultural capital acquired and stored almost exclusively by boys – football knowledge. Girls may be following football in increasing numbers, but few seem to develop that train-spotter fanaticism that permits the squirrelling away of information that can be flourished to prove credentials. Football's cultural capital acts as a handy currency expended in the project of defending the castle of masculinity against incursion by the feminine. One of the ironies of fantasy league is that football itself is somewhat of a fantasy – set up as a world of its own (sports news, stadia that exclude the real world) in which men have historically immersed themselves as an escape from work and family. So what is the significance of this intervention of a further level of fantasy – in which people trade in virtual players to build virtual clubs. Can it be an imaginary resolution of that uncomfortable knowledge that the clubs people attach themselves to are in fact no more 'theirs' than the nearest branch of Burger King?

They Think It's All Over reduces the *A Question of Sport* format to absurdity by the use of forms of games and questions in which any notion of 'knowledge', or 'correct answers' has been abandoned. As with *Have I Got News For You*, the presenter can be made fun of by the panelists, but, through his control of the discourse and the presence of a script, the presenter is able to appear at most times the most witty. The flip irreverence and fundamental silliness contrasts with the over-serious pomposity of mainstream sport coverage. However, as with *Fantasy League Football*, the humour is flip, irreverent and vulgar rather than truly satirical. Players and managers, more often than owners or administrators, are the target of humour. The two sport stars on the panel, David Gower and Gary Lineker are the butt of jokes, focused on Gower's supposed affluent upper-class dilletanteness, and Gary Lineker's goody-two-shoes image. The need of sport stars to prolong their fame, and hence their careers, after their playing days cease drives many into the celebrity trade, and the spectacle of Gower and Lineker in such a format has more than an edge of embarrassment.

They Think It's All Over draws heavily on banter, that form of social cement central to male camaraderie (see Easthope 1990), and it is very much a boys club, with Jo Brand one of the few women contributors. The humour is rooted in the masculine cultural capital of sporting 'knowledge and functions to marginalise women'. The tone is set by banter and laddishness, with crudeness and vulgarity often substituting for real wit. The show has a dumbed-down rhetoric – and the humour constantly imparts closure instead of opening up and revealing the world. 'Crap' functions as the universal dismissive restricted code word that ends all arguments. In contrast, the Radio Five football phone-in on Saturday evenings, whether chaired by Danny Baker, Richard Littlejohn, or even David Mellor, does open up space for a different form of discourse – the relatively unmediated voice of football supporters. Their utterances can be banal, repetitive or train-spotterish, but also, on occasion, challenging, alternative, angry and oppositional. It is one of the few places in the whole range of sport media where such discursive space exists.

They Think It's All Over and *Fantasy League Football* grew out of the lad culture of the 1990s, in which hedonism resurfaced in reaction to body culture, and sexism resurfaced in reaction to feminism. This culture involved a transformation and re-presentation of elements of 'traditional' masculinity – drinking, lecherousness and promiscuity – through which new lads were constructed as an imaginary resolution of the critique of masculinity growing out of gender politics. New lads are 'men behaving badly', but are also attempting to excuse such behaviour by a degree of distance – putting it in quotation marks as ironic. In the process, an opportunity to turn a sharp, satirical gaze onto the rapacity and corruption of top-level sport has been lost. The laddish humour, with its postmodern presentation of depthlessness, echoes the subsuming of performance, through appearance, and into commodified product.

15 Vortextuality and conspicuous consumption

> We've got matching dogs (Rottweilers), matching watches (gold Rolexes), similar wardrobes, matching Jags. I like all that. I mean, I know its tacky, but it makes me laugh.
>
> (Victoria Adams (aka Posh Spice, married to David Beckham),
> *Guardian*, 3 July 1999)

In postmodern culture, the question of the symbolic value of sports stars is a difficult one. If the grand-narratives of modernity have lost their force, where does that leave the ethics of fair play, or the project of moral character development that framed nineteenth-century athleticism? If identities are irredeemably fractured and ambiguous, where does that leave the concept of role models? If consumption and commodification has triumphed and the consumer is sovereign, where does that leave the transcendent *jouissance* of the sport performance caught in that moment before it is commodified? One answer might be that our persistent desire for the authentic, the intense, the real, and the original, even though we understand, in however an inchoate way, that culture cannot readily provide these things, suggests that while we inhabit a cultural world that has many postmodern elements, we have not witnessed the triumph of postmodernity or the eclipse of modernity. The world we inhabit is a more complex place marked by uneven development, in which different modes of being coexist in uncomfortable tension, both within individual subjects and as part of the structure of social exchange. Football fans, music lovers and other enthusiasts can live out an intense and pleasurable relation to the object of their passion, and also, *at the same time*, recognise it as commodified, transformed and out of their reach. It is precisely the paradox that productive consumption and consumptive production presents us – that of being both the consumer and producer of our pleasures, whilst still not having the position of control. Yet the emphasis on the culture of consumption is patently one of great significance. King's gloss on postmodernism emphasises a shift in values from thrift to profligacy. Drawing on Jameson and Mandel, he argues that the third stage of capitalism:

> is characterised by huge multi-national corporations, whose existence depends on the emergence and expansion of the consumer market. The

emergence of this consumer market has necessitated a shift in the focus of capitalism from production to consumption, which in turn has required a complete overhauling of the value system. The values of thrift, discipline and reason, which Weber so famously associated with the Protestant spirit, and which he argued were essential for the emergence and continuity of capitalism have become unsuitable to the third, consumer, stage of capitalism. For this economic system to survive, individuals must not repress their desires and discipline themselves for work, but must satisfy those desires by indulgence in the consumer market. Thrift is similarly outmoded as expenditure is essential to the growth of the economy.

(King 1996: 122–3)

In contrast to the theme of thrift, so dominant in representations of Stanley Matthews, David Beckham exemplifies indulgence in the consumer market. His image has become the dominant icon of British sport representation, yet it is a strangely elusive and anchorless image – a floating signifier that can become attached to a range of discursive elements with equal plausibility. He has all the attributes of a 'golden boy' – football talent, good looks, highly publicised romance with another media star, Victoria Adams (Posh Spice of the Spice Girls). He plays for a team, Manchester United, that attract both massive support and considerable loathing because they have become a symbol of the dominance of football by the richest clubs.

The relationship with Posh Spice gave the two a unique hold on the celebrity spaces of the popular media, with Beckham a major figure in the sports media, consumed largely by men, Posh a significant figure in the tabloid coverage of pop music, and the two together major figures in magazines such as *OK*, read predominately by women. The image of Beckham, in its narcisstic self-absorption and its departure from the dominant masculinised codes of footballer style also represented a challenge to the heterosexual conformity of sport's modes of male self-presentation. Beckham's image speaks louder than his words; his voice is not often heard and he gives few interviews; his apparent lack of self-assertion contrasts with his more assertive partner, who constitutes a break with the largely invisible 'her indoors' style of footballer's wife. This, too, was a challenge to hegemonic masculinity and its assumption of the man as the dominant partner, and appeared to contribute to the unease of the male football subculture in which reaction to unconventional masculine behaviour all too easily condenses into homophobia.

In summer 1998, a widely publicised photograph of Beckham, on holiday with Victoria, and wearing a garment described as 'a sarong', was presented in the tabloid press in terms of deviance from the conventions of masculinity, with hints of his supposed 'emasculisation'. Popular press articles and cartoons questioned the 'manliness' of Beckham. One 'joke' picture headlined FROCK SKINNER, featured comedians Frank Skinner and David Baddiel (Skinner in a sarong à la Beckham; Baddiel, although pouting and posing as Posh Spice, isn't dressed like her, but wears ordinary street clothes) (*Sun*, 5 June 1998).

Beckham's sending-off in England's key match in the 1998 World Cup provided a point of condensation for discourses of morality and fair play in sport in which national pride became national shame. Yet, after a season spent shrugging off the abuse, winning Premiership, FA Cup and European Champions Cup medals, fathering a child and marrying Victoria, the story in the popular press became a narrative of redemption and triumph. The recent images of 'Posh and Becks' have constituted a celebration of traditional family life – a wedding, a baby, and a romantic holiday in Venice, all heavily featured in *OK*. Few sport stars have been quite so successful at the glamorisation and commodification of the private sphere of their lives as Beckham.

Envy, humour, abuse and emasculation

Sensationalism in the press is nothing new, but the erosion of a sharp distinction between public and private spheres has broadened the scope of celebrity representation. The tabloid revolution heightened the force and impact of stories about easily recognised star figures. A whole new genre of celebrity-based magazines, such as *OK* and *Hello*, has fuelled the trend to celebrity gossip. Areas of life once resolutely private are now in the public domain. As with any new sport star, the initial tone of representation of Beckham was celebratory. The back cover of an early biography by Bobby Blake (1997) proclaims 'In just two incredible seasons, David Beckham has become Manchester United's greatest young star'. Beckham's goal from the half-way line against Wimbledon is described in a chapter entitled 'Goal of the Century'. Beckham's rise to fame is 'phenomenal', he is 'a heart throb to millions of teenage girls, a hero to as many football-mad boys' (Blake 1997: 10). He was represented as fun-loving but disciplined, and constructed in terms of 'responsibility'. As Blake describes it, 'he likes a few beers with the lads occasionally, or a glass of wine with a meal. But never more than once a week. "You have to take care of yourself at this level", he says' (Blake 1997: 44).

He is ordinary but glamorous too, being pictured on celebrity pages and associated with models (Blake 1997: 47). However hubris awaited. Good looking, successful without apparent effort or sacrifice, and a player for England's top club side, he was already the target of abuse from fans. In 1998, England's defeat in a key World Cup game was blamed on Beckham, who was sent off halfway through the match. In the 1998 World Cup game against Argentina, the result was crucial to England; the game was in the balance when he was sent off, and the kicking offence seemed unnecessary. Retaliating to a challenge in the heat of the moment is undisciplined, but, in the macho codes of football, forgivable. However, Beckham had a moment to reflect, and still, rather lazily, kicked out at his opponent in full view of the referee. Indeed, even the languid nature of the kick fitted the construction of Beckham as slightly foppish. Clearly he was provoked, and it may well be that Simeone exaggerated the effect of the rather half-hearted kick, but the moment allowed for Beckham to be constructed as a sacrificial victim and as scapegoat for England's defeat.

The episode was the subject of hostile press comment; it unleashed a torrent of abuse from the terraces and Beckham became the butt of jokes, many of which featured his supposed dull-wittedness.[1]

Tabloid castigation and fan anger combined to create a hostile climate for Beckham – 'the pretty boy scapegoat was lynched in effigy ... when the 1998–99 season began, any football fan who'd ever loathed Manchester United pilloried their preening, blond-streaked right winger with chants inventive and profane' (*Vanity Fair*, September 1999). Subsequent accounts of his career make much of this hostility and of the way in which Beckham coped with it. *GQ* reported that 'when George Best played he was offered booze after every game; Beckham gets boos before, during and after every game whether he wants it or not. He even gets abused in the street (*GQ*, May 1999). But, given the furore over the sarong picture just before the World Cup, he was not only being punished for being sent off and infringing the conventions of fair play, but for being rich and successful, and for not conforming to the conventions of masculinity. He was more adventurous with style than the cautious and defensive conservatism of the working-class football subculture, with its fears of any hint of 'effeminacy', would accept. His very image, with its edge of insouciant foppishness, served as a goad to the homophobia of the football culture.

The subsequent abuse of Beckham was fuelled by three main factors – the hatred of Manchester United prevalent amongst football fans, the tall 'poppy' factor and Beckham's sending off in the 1998 World Cup. The dominance of the English game in the 1990s by Manchester United, the perception of them as dominating the game through their wealth, and the perception that many of their fans are 'glory hunters' with no organic links to Manchester, have combined to make the chant of 'stand up if you hate Man U' commonly heard at English League grounds. Beckham's display of wealth and fashion becomes a metonym for the wealth of his club. Undeniably a highly gifted footballer, good looking, stylish, and married to the best looking Spice Girl, he appears as someone who 'has it all'. The elegance of his football masks effort: he appears to have acquired 'it all' without conspicuous striving. He is a tall poppy, there to be cut down, as *Time Out* sardonically noted:

> After all, he's better looking than most footballers, he once wore a sarong, he plays for the super-successful Manchester United (who he has treacherously supported all his life, despite being born in Leytonstone) and he's going out with a pop singer – oh yeah, hanging offences, every one of them.
>
> (*Time Out*, 31 March–7 Apr 1999)

Part of the terrace hostility towards Beckham can be related to the fear of emasculation engendered by a public figure who strays beyond the rigid versions of masculinity favoured in English football culture. The suggestion is that Victoria dominates him; that she 'wears the trousers' in the relationship; that his clothes are chosen by her; that this is unmasculine; that he looks like a prat, a wally, and that he is not too bright. The sarong picture has become a featured element in most narrativisations of his story. The sarong, one magazine commented, 'made him look a right twerp' (*GQ*, May 1999), and the picture is captioned 'Becks and Posh with their hers and hers wardrobe' (*GQ* May 1999). Beckham does 'unmasculine' things; attending fashion events like London Fashion Week fashion show (*Evening Standard*, 15 January 1999). His sartorial adventurousness transgresses the laddish code in which sharp and stylish means Hugo Boss – a little flash but in the solidly 'masculine' tradition of the sharp suit. A cartoon in the *Sun* (26 April 1999) showed Beckham dressed in a Spice Girl Union Jack mini-dress and platform shoes, with a musical agent saying 'So David ... what other tips on being a pop-star did Posh give you?'. The popular press was constructing Beckham as feminised and emasculated.

Much working-class male terrace humour centres on sexual infidelity and sexual humiliation of the players. Songs and chants about players wives having affairs are not uncommon. One chant aimed at the visiting goalkeeper is 'dodgy keeper, dodgy keeper, takes it up the arse', and the chant most commonly aimed at Beckham, or more precisely at Posh, is 'does she take it up the arse?'. Newspapers typically refer to this chanting obliquely, without a direct quote. Freud has discussed the function of aggressiveness in humour, and also the presence of feelings of shame in sexual references. He suggests that the utterance of obscene words compels the person who is assailed to imagine the part of the body or the procedure in question and shows him/her that the assailant is himself imagining it (Freud 1960: 198). So footballers who, like Beckham, are subject to such abuse are humiliated by a process in which the private domain of sexuality is rendered public. Humour here functions as a weapon. Writing on humour, Bergson argues that laughter is incompatible with emotion or with sympathy with its object, and that it always implies 'a certain callousness, even a touch of malice'. Such humour is, in certain circumstances, a distinctive feature of masculine camaraderie. Laughter, Bergson suggests, belongs to men in groups and, being intended to humiliate, it must make a painful impression on the person against whom it is directed: 'By laughter, society avenges itself for liberties taken with it. It would fail in its object if it bore the stamp of sympathy or kindness' (quoted in Mathewson 1920: 6–7). Both jokes and abuse are typically dealing with the repressed – with awkward and disturbing psychological fears. The obsession with anal sex, which can signify both submission and humiliation, is suggestive of a working-class masculine culture disturbed by fears both of the feminine and of the homoerotic. In this context, the supposedly emasculated Beckham offered a convenient symbol onto which such fears could be condensed.

Beckham played well throughout the season, betraying few signs that he was distracted by the abusive chants. During the 1998–9 season, the Beckham narrative was that in his handling of the abuse from the terraces, and in his key role in Manchester United's route to the treble, he had demonstrated his 'maturity' and was thus to be forgiven and 'rehabilitated'. One paper suggested that 'Beckham took strength from his adversity' and 'demonstrated impressive resilience' (*Evening Standard*, 26 May 1999). This resilient maturation was attributed to his becoming, unlike George Best, a family man, and, according to the *Evening Standard* (26 May 1999) 'fatherhood and his pending marriage to Spice Girl Victoria Adams, suggest that at 24 he is already capable of controlling his own destiny'.

The theme of redemption through love was developed in dramatic fashion in Easter week by *Time Out* (31 March–7 April 1999), which featured David Beckham on the front cover in white trousers and a white see-through shirt in a pose evocative of Christ and the crucifixion, with the caption 'Easter Exclusive: The Resurrection of David Beckham', making the religious reference explicit. Inside, the accompanying article was titled 'The Gospel according to David', and a subtitle referred to him as 'back from the reputation wilderness' *Time Out* (31 March–7 April 1999). *TV Times* (22–28 May 1999) later used a similar picture from the same photo shoot, and ran a shortened version of the same article. Their caption read 'David Beckham from sinner to saint: Red Hot and Spicy'. Here then, was a perfect Jesus for the nineties – good looking, stylish, talented, and engaged to a successful female pop singer – a Christ of Consumption.

Vortextuality: the wedding and the vortex effect

The growth in the range of media outlets, and the vastly increased speed of circulation of information have combined to create the phenomenon of a 'vortex' effect, which I term here, 'vortextuality'. The various media constantly feed off each other and, in an era of electronic and digital information exchange, the speed at which this happens has become very rapid. Certain super-major events come to dominate the headlines to such an extent that it becomes temporarily difficult for columnists and commentators to discuss anything else. They are drawn in, as if by a vortex. The death of Princess Diana was a case in point, dominating the media for days, almost to the extent of removing most other issues from the agenda. During a World Cup or an Olympic Games, even columnists with no abiding interest in sport feel impelled to comment, as Germaine Greer and A.S. Byatt, among others, did during Euro 96. The vortextual effect produces a short-term compression of the media agenda in which other topics either disappear or have to be connected to the vortextual event. In the midst of a vortextual moment, cartoons, radio phone-ins, celebrity columnists, news magazines, cultural commentators and letter pages are all drawn into the central topic.

If not on the same scale as the death of Princess Diana, the wedding of Beckham and Posh was an example of the vortex effect at work. Television presenters alluded to it, politicians made asides about it, radio phone-ins discussed it and comedians joked about it. In 1999, Beckham, sometimes alone, but more usually with Posh, featured extensively on the front covers of magazines.[2] The self-referential and intertextual intensity of focus on the couple became self-generating, producing a pressure impelling even broadsheet newspapers and political journals to comment. The couple sold rights to the wedding itself to *OK* magazine. The 'Wedding Special' part one (16 July 1999) ran 36 pages on the wedding, while part two (23 July 1999), focusing on 'Baby Brooklyn at the wedding', ran to another 29 pages. The first *OK* issue (16 July 1999) was flagged on the front as 'The Wedding of the Decade', the 'Biggest Ever Issue' and 'World Exclusive'. The event was proclaimed as 'the wedding the whole world had been waiting to see' (*OK*, 16 July 1999), and the hyperbole was justified by the intense attention paid to the event in the rest of the media. A cartoon in the *Evening Standard* (5 July 1999) showed God in an armchair saying 'I've postponed the end of the world until I've seen the Beckham wedding pictures'.

Plenty of sport stars before Beckham have been publicly fêted, their fame spreading well beyond the narrow world of sport and its fans, but it is hard to identify any others whose fame has so specifically spread into the largely sports-free world of publishing aimed at women. Clearly this is largely due to the relationship with Spice Girl Victoria Adams, the wedding and the baby. It has transformed the image of Beckham into the site of a number of competing elements. His image has to bear conflicts between the conventional footballer's concept of high fashion (Hugo Boss and Armani) and the gender-bending glamour of pop music, the discipline of elite football and the hedonism of celebrity partying, working-class masculinity and pop glamorised sexuality, concepts of family life and changing gender roles, and his own reticence and celebrity flamboyance. All this is lived out in the crucible of the public gaze, in which 'Beckham' becomes the vocal point of a wide range of intersecting discourses – the central point of a vortextual process.

The people's royalty?

In many societies, the national leader is represented in family terms, and acts as a bridge between 'nation' and the everyday. The British Royal Family, and the American President and his First Lady, serve as a symbol of the family of the nation. Tabloidisation has constituted a crisis for the aristocratic British monarchy, who have struggled to manage the contradiction between aristocratic aloofness and accessibility, trying to preserve mystique whilst continuing to command respect, support and popularity. The gulf between the monarchy and the people was exposed in the wake of the death of Princess Diana, when a popular perception appeared to be that the monarchy had failed to mirror and represent the grief of ordinary people. The Beckham wedding moved into this space and allowed for their representation as 'people's royalty'.

The Beckham wedding was represented as a 'Royal Wedding'. It occupied the same space, attracted the same form of coverage in the tabloid press. The apparent mobilisation of public attention through the media resembled the media mobilisation of an audience for royal weddings (see Philips and Whannel 1998). The staging of the event, and its media representation, focused on regal splendour, royal connections and comparisons with royalty. Explicit comparisons were made with the marriage of Prince Edward and Sophie Rhys-Jones, with more than one paper suggesting that David and Victoria were far more glamorous. The Daily Mail (5 July 1999) wrote that 'After Edward and Sophie's low key affair, the Spice Girl and the soccer star show them how to stage a proper Royal Wedding', and the *Guardian* (3 July 1999) reported that 'the supreme glitziness of their marriage makes the Prince Edward's marriage to Sophie Rhys-Jones look a comparatively frumpy occasion'. Posh was described as the 'queen of the castle' (*Guardian*, 3 July 1999), while the *Daily Mail* ran the headline 'I, QUEEN POSH TAKE THEE, KING BECKS' (*Daily Mail*, 5 July 1999). It was reported that Posh had a twenty-foot train and a retinue of 125 security guards, and that the splendour of the event was more regal than the recent royal wedding:

> From the regal 'thrones' at the reception to the imperial purple carpets and rows of liveried attendants, the sheer spectacle of yesterday's event could not have been more of a contrast to the real Royal Wedding last month … Prince Edward and his bride Sophie Rhys-Jones wanted their wedding to be a relatively low key family day with as little fuss as possible. David and Victoria didn't. They wanted pomp and splendour and they made sure they got it.
>
> (*Daily Mail*, 5 July 1999)

In an anthropological discussion of British royalty, Hayden has commented that 'The Queen's majesty needs other individuals to radiate and enhance it' (Hayden 1987: 35). In the case of Posh and Beckham's wedding, the couple, their designers, the celebrity guests, the security guards and the media all contributed to the production, radiation and enhancement of 'majesty'. The *Sun* remade its front-page layout to report the wedding, moving its masthead into the middle, and running the headline 'MR AND MRS BECKS'. Below a rather blurred and clearly covertly taken picture of the couple on their wedding thrones, the caption reads 'Soccer's David Beckham and pop queen Posh Spice sit on regal thrones at their fairy-tale wedding banquet'. Inside, a headline reads 'Victoria looked like a queen', while the text relates that 'ecstatic bride Posh Spice sits like a queen on a throne at her lavish wedding – with love for her "king" David Beckham glowing in her eyes' (*Sun*, 6 July 1999). The following day, the *Sun* extended the royal metaphor into the political domain with the headline:

THE *SUN* ASKS THE BIG QUESTION, WHO RULES?

WHICH COUPLE IS MORE POPULAR IN BRITAIN TODAY? CALL AND VOTE NOW

(*Sun*, 7 July 1999)

The layout featured two pictures of the weddings of Posh and Becks and Sophie and Edward with phone numbers for readers to vote on the issue. Media representations highlighted links with royalty. According to *Now*, 'The hottest ticket of the year was sent out on parchment paper emblazoned with gold leaf to the elite circle invited' (*Now*, 19 May 1999). The wedding was organised by a company, owned by Lord Snowdon's half-brother, that was also responsible for both Princess Anne's 40th birthday celebrations and the 21st birthday celebrations of her son. Flowers were provided by 'two of the most respected florists in the business' – one had done the flowers for the film *Four Weddings and a Funeral* and the other the floral arrangements for the party to celebrate the Queen's Ruby Wedding. Victoria wore a beautiful diamond and gold coronet by Slim Barrett, a jeweller who had made pieces for the late Princess of Wales (*OK 16*, July 1999). The general air of royal patronage evoked in such journalism almost leads one to expect the appearance of crested plaques announcing 'By Appointment to Posh and Becks'. Even the intensity of the press attention was evoked as proof that the couple were even more fascinating than the royals:

> the near-suicidal actions of the press desperadoes say a lot about the unique position Beckham and Adams currently occupy in British life. After all there are no paparazzi risking their lives for pictures of Edward Windsor and Sophie Rhys-Jones.
>
> (*Vanity Fair*, September 1999)

Conspicuous consumption and display

The combination of new wealth and celebrity placed Beckham and Posh at the heart of a tableau of conspicuous consumption and display. Within a culture absorbed more than ever by questions of style, in which television and the press are dominated by style guides and transformation scenarios, the dress, interior decor and lifestyle of celebrities have become a focal point of media attention. The lavishness of the wedding exemplified Veblen's concept of conspicuous consumption, in which wealthy elites advertise their riches through highly visible forms of display (Veblen 1970). However, Beckham and Posh are not simply part of a wealthy elite, but also part of an everyday ordinary lifestyle – they represent aspiration, not to marital happiness so much as to the acquisition of commodity trappings. In much of the wedding coverage, everything was related in terms of monetary value, with obsessive detail about designer labels. *OK*, it was reported, 'turfed out a cool million' for the wedding rights (*Vanity Fair*, September 1999). The wedding required 'an army of private security experts' (*Now*, 19 May 1999). The *Daily Mirror* (1 July 1999) referred to it as the showbiz wedding of the year. The couple booked 'every available limousine in Ireland – and are getting more sent over from the UK – so that family, friends and celebrity guests can travel in style'; it was reported that the couple spent £120,000 on the rings alone (*Now*, 19 May 1999), and every aspect of the display of lavishness was lovingly detailed.[3]

The bridesmaids were dressed 'as woodland flower fairies' in outfits made by theatrical costumiers Angels and Bermans. The best man received a specially engraved Cartier watch; the usher received a gold and silver Rolex watch. The couple 'personally conducted a taste test of dozens of different dishes to decide what they wanted to include on their wedding menu'. Music was provided by an eighteen-piece string orchestra, and the cake was a 'lavish three-tier creation by Rachel Mount' (*OK*, 16 July 1999). Over 400 people were involved in the wedding arrangements, and there were three articulated lorries full of flowers (*OK*, 23 July 1999). After the wedding, Posh and Becks 'retired to spend their first night of married life in the castle's $3,900 a night Royal Suite' (*Daily Mail*, 5 July 1999). The descriptive language in representations of the wedding evoked an exotic and decadent luxury:

> carpeted in sumptuous deep red, with the walls lined with a pleated ivory taffeta lining, the marquee was more than fitting for the most famous celebrity couple in the world. The spectacular flower arrangements were in three colours: burgundy, green and purple, which created a suitably regal effect.
>
> (*OK*, 16 July 1999)

> The 236 marquee guests had sat in gold-coloured chairs at 12 round tables. They would have marvelled at the ornately designed 7ft naked gold figurines – and the two huge Egyptian black cats with piercing green eyes.
>
> (*Sun*, 6 July 1999)

Victoria Adams's attitude to their conspicuous display includes a distinctly post-modern ironic sensibility. When an expert at the 500-year-old College of Arms slated the design of an invented coat of arms for the wedding as 'tacky and amateurish' (*Now*, 19 May 1999) she responded:

> 'so what if the poxy swan is the wrong way?', snaps the woman who was once dubbed Relatively Posh Spice. 'Does anybody really give a shit – d'you know what I mean? Having your own crest – it's one of them, innit?' Adams pokes her tongue into her cheek. 'We're just thinking, this is the biggest day of our lives – we're just going to go over the top and make it entertaining for everybody. Much as we want it, it's still one of those'. Tongue meets cheek again.
>
> (*Vanity Fair*, September 1999)

Indeed the whole event was distinctly hyper-real. It was itself constructed in intertextual terms. Posh got the idea of staging the wedding ceremony in a semi-derelict folly from Ross's wedding in *Friends*. Before the event, the *News of the World* produced a spread simulating the wedding. The *Evening Standard* (5 July 1999), unable to get anything other than pictures of guests leaving the wedding, included a spread of celebrity look-alikes acting out what the wedding might have looked like. Below a headline 'SEALED WITH A KITSCH', the *Evening Standard* described the wedding as 'fairytale or kitsch depending on whether the news was relayed by broadsheet or tabloid' (*Evening Standard*, 5 July 1999).

At work in representation of the wedding was an element of nostalgia for earlier periods of excess which the real Royal Family could no longer stage. It is as if the Beckham wedding had been staged by the Prince Regent in the Brighton Pavilion. Press reactions to the spectacle differed between tabloid and broadsheet in a manner that revealed the links between 'class' and 'taste'. The *Observer* describes them as pleasant looking, not particularly bright, and rounded up other press reaction: 'The *Sun* called the wedding a fairy-tale, the *Mirror* a dream come true. The *Daily Express* declared that Mr and Mrs Beckham elevated vulgarity into an art form. The *Guardian* said that it was "confirmation of a country's coarsening, a dissonant hymn in praise of mammon"' (*Observer*, 11 July 1999). Sue Carroll in the *Daily Mirror* acknowledged the 'tackiness' of the wedding and defended it:

> Well, I admit it was breathtakingly tacky. Barbie-dom meets Brookside, Versace-cum-Spanish brothel ... There was something splendid about their fascinating show business excess. Something so utterly over the top it made your heart soar to witness the noble tradition of the truly tacky wedding in all its flamboyant glory.
>
> (*Daily Mirror*, 7 July 1999)

She went on to describe them as 'a couple so totally besotted and wrapped up in one another even their most hardened footie mates respect their displays of soppy sentimentality' (*Daily Mirror*, 7 July 1999). It was indeed striking how often their love for each other was evoked in articles to legitimate the excess. The presiding bishop at the ceremony said that 'seeing Victoria and David on the day it was clear to all of the guests who were lucky enough to be there that the couple were totally in touch with their innermost feelings' (*OK*, 16 July 1999). Several portrayals of the couple revolved around the theme of their modesty. One quoted Posh as saying 'If I'd had a more low-key wedding I would have been called a tight cow. As it is people say we were flash and over the top. Well that's fine. But we had the most amazing day and that's all that counts' (*Marie Claire*, October 1999). A spokeswoman for Victoria Adams said 'They honestly regard it as a family event. They don't go to many celebrity parties' (*Guardian*, 3 July 1999). Unusually among the papers, the *Daily Record* discussed their largely unpublicised lavish charity donations and work for charities (*Daily Record*, 3 June 1999). When asked about football achievements, Beckham said 'They're all important but having a child means more than anything' (*GQ*, May 1999). Here then, the lavish display is excused and legitimated as the ritualistic excess and abundance that precedes the responsibilities of family and parenthood. Indeed, coverage of the Beckhams since the wedding have managed to negotiate the potential tensions between conspicuous consumption and family responsibility. Representations of their activities, including a romantic break in Venice, draw upon the visual conventions of romantic fiction, travel brochure and family album. This visual assemblage contributes to the 'glamorous, but just like us' effect. Images of the couple need to be seen in the context of the plethora of style guides, make-overs and transformations that are a central staple of popular television and journalism. Seldom can have two celebrities commodified their private lives to such lucrative effect.

Postmodernity: New lads and old lads

David Beckham is a postmodern celebrity, a point that can be illustrated by comparison with Liverpool's Robbie Fowler. Fowler may be a 'new lad', but in many ways he is an old lad, a pre-'new lad' lad. He is forged in the mould of northern working-class masculinity and has a workerist and socialist sensibility (lifting his football shirt to reveal a tee shirt with a slogan supporting the striking dockers, empathising with homeless people). His homophobia was revealed in his baiting of Chelsea's Grahame Le Saux (actually heterosexual, but as a *Guardian*-reading art lover from the Channel Islands, clearly 'suspect' from the perspective of the constricting limits of working-class terrace subculture masculinity). From Liverpool, Fowler appears as a scouse scally[4] – with a roguish desire to see what he can get away with. Despite his considerable wealth, he has not adopted some of the more overt trappings of flamboyant, up-to-the-minute style. In representation, he is the working-class boy made good, but still utterly grounded in a particular northern working-class masculinity and behaving in consistency with it.

David Beckham, by contrast, is a post-'new lad' man. Growing up in an environment in which men's interest in fashion, style, narcissism and the possibility of being objectified have all been nurtured by a decade of the style press (*Arena, GQ, FHM*), in a period in which sport and fashion have become more closely linked, in which footballers and pop stars gravitate to one another's glamour, and in which fame has itself become commodified, he is subsumed by his own image. His star persona has become the substance, the marketable object – all that is solid melts into air, or, at least, into magazine pages. Where Fowler is grounded, Beckham appears rootless: he can be dressed in anything because surface appearance is all.

The *Guardian* pointed out that the pair were 'the only couple in Britain to have figured individually on the covers of separate Play Station games: Becks on FIFA 98; a pixelled Posh on SpiceWorld' (*Guardian*, 7 May 1999). Indeed, the lack of any serious fuss about the implicitly blasphemous *Time Out* cover seems to support the reading that Beckham, at least in representation, is a thoroughly postmodern figure. Dress him as Christ and it doesn't really matter, because he's not 'real'. In this vortextual media event, consumption is the new democracy, style the new cultural capital. The performative talent of David Beckham and Victoria Adams provided the potential for their commodification. Now that they are so thoroughly 'well known for being well known', their abilities as footballer and singer appear strangely, and rather sadly, decentred.

16 Conclusion

So what if the poxy swan is the wrong way?

I will briefly summarise some of the arguments offered in this book. During the 1990s, social concerns over morality and masculinity were widely expressed in the media, in both 'serious' and 'popular' contexts. Sport stars were expected to be good role models – moral exemplars, and were castigated for failing in this role and setting a bad example. This apparent importance bestowed upon sport stars betrayed an unease, particularly in more conservative circles, at the declining power of other forms of moral authority, such as the family, the school, and the church. In effect, there was a desire in some quarters that sport stars make up for the perceived loss of influence of parent, teacher and priest.

Masculinity has never been unitary or stable, but there are specific reasons why the focus on the supposed problems of masculinity should have been greater in recent years. Regardless of whether there is a 'crisis' of masculinity, it is of significance that people write and talk as if there was. The growth of media sport and a media sport-star system has given sport stars a high degree of cultural visibility rendering them available as the points of condensation for a range of discourses, particularly those relating to masculinity and morality. The ways in which their lives are narrativised open up space for utterances about the nature of masculinity and of morality.

With the growth of a new competitive individualism, and the professionalisation of sport, maverick individuals became the focus for moral castigation. The mobilisation of a comparison between past and present suggested that moral values were under threat, and that present-day sport stars were not the men that their predecessors had been. Surveillance, punishment and self-discipline became the features of the imposition of a new regime of dedication. This distinctly modernist project of self-improvement is, however, somewhat destabilised by the postmodern character of contemporary culture, in which the dominance of appearances over substances, ephemerality over permanence, and multiple identities over unified subjectivity, undermines the rational coherence of the institution of sport. Major stars take on the character of floating signifiers, whose connotations cannot neatly be contained by the needs of either sport institutions or moral entrepreneurs. The corporate world will always yearn for a Pete Sampras or a Tiger Woods, but the public are always likely to be more intrigued by an Andre Agassi or a Dennis Rodman.

Sport stars, through representation, now shoulder a great deal of discursive ideological baggage. In their seemingly ever greater cultural visibility – they are available in the same way that movie stars and rock stars have been in the past – as readily identifiable iconic foci for more generalised pronouncements. The expression of concerns over the decline of moral authority – the waning power of father, teacher and priest in the societies of late modernity – seek to appropriate the stars of sport. Their laudable qualities are clung to, as if constructing them as emblematic will, in itself, accomplish the work of moral education that the patriarchal process can, supposedly, no longer achieve. The rather desperate and misplaced faith that right-wing moral discourse places in the notion of 'role models' betrays a fundamental misrecognition of the modern media. The multiplicity of outlets, the fragmentation of media messages that stems from our selective options and channel-hopping habits, the sheer complexity of intertextuality and self-referentiality, produce practices of readership and consumption that simply do not allow for the fantasy of a single unproblematic figure (Tiger Woods, for example) to ever stand isolated and pure in representational form. Images are always, already contaminated, modified, transformed, criticised and celebrated by other images. (While this has always been the case, the accelerated 'media-fication' of society has dramatically heightened the intensity and speed of the process.)

Indeed, the public figures of spectacular celebritydom seem precisely to offer, as do the narratives and characters of soap opera, modes of public exchange in which moral and political positionalities can be rehearsed. Better to recognise this process for what it is than to indulge in the medieval carnival of public condemnation and ritual humiliation in which tabloidised representations 'monster' their victims. The problem, of course, in a world in which public exchange is almost entirely mediated, is how to accomplish this change of perspective. Is de-tabloidisation a meaningful or achievable aim? Does it matter any more? Who cares if the poxy swan is the wrong way round? Clearly, the implicit proposition of this book is that popular culture as a site of struggle and contestation, does matter. There are times when it is hard to conceptualise a practical politics of the popular, but it is important not to lose sight of what is at stake. It is in the domain of the popular that common sense is connected to organised political discourse, and without an understanding of that process, we lack a valuable resource.

In the context of a thorough and comprehensive mediatisation of society – sport cannot be understood except through its forms of representation – it is centrally about narrative and image. Just as Kobena Mercer used the evocative phrase 'relentless vertigo of displacement', so there is also the restless vortex of celebrity in which form has become more significant than content. An interest in gossip as such transcends the subject matter – all that matters is that there is exciting gossip about someone in the public eye, and that there is a steady supply of new subjects. In this study, I have tried to make clear the inability of sport stars to fill the role model imperative – symbolic public figures cannot fill the space perceived by some as a vacuum left by the decline of patriarchal authority.

Yet, the images of sport stars do function as both barometer and thermometer – as means by which the temperatures and pressures of social relations and practices can be gauged. The very centrality of their cultural presence ensures that the ways in which they are represented, and the discursive structures through which such representations are shaped, cannot help but reveal the complex and contradictory ways in which the tensions of identity, morality and masculinity are worked through. However, the identities of a David Beckham, a Tiger Woods, or a Mike Tyson are not simply indexical. They are not just a reflection of such tensions – they are part of the ways in which such tensions are fought over and worked through. Indeed, the public identities and images of such figures are a product of the social relations of moral contestation rather than an expressive product of their own actions.

At the same time it should not be forgotten that one of the processes at work is the professionalisation of sport, in which on-field performance, public image and financial success have become, in the sports industry, very closely linked. Major sport organisations have developed significant revenue streams from television, sponsorship, advertising and merchandising. As this book was being completed, it was announced that two of the world's most successful sporting clubs, Manchester United and the New York Yankees, were to pool their marketing expertise and were in future to sell each other's merchandise. Sporting success is the trigger to boosting these revenues. Bad boy behaviour is not popular with those involved in management of sporting performance or the marketing of image. The imposition of discipline upon sport performers has become far more rigorous and systematic. That process that Brohm (1978) dubbed the Taylorisation of the body has become a key element in achieving success. Bad boys are out of fashion with the corporate world and, in the process, the landscape of heroism becomes somewhat flatter and less exciting.

The transgressions of the worst of sport's bad boys are, for the most part, born out of immaturity, self-absorption, loss of perspective, and, in some cases, 'roid-rage'. Violence against others is always serious, always deserves punishment. Many sport stars, though, are largely self-destructive. For the most part, their transgressions are small beer compared to the forms of moral and legal outrage routinely committed in the boardrooms and corporate offices of the powerful corporations of the world. Huge profits are made by sportswear firms out of the massive disparity between wage rates in South-east Asia and spending power in the West. Bribes are taken and accepted to influence the votes that determine where the Olympic Games might be staged. Tickets for major events are parcelled out to commercial sponsors for corporate entertainment, depriving real sports fans of access. Of the millions that circulate in the media sport industry, only a small proportion is ever used to nurture grassroots sport. In the race for television money, meaningless events are created and promoted, devaluing the currency of sporting entertainment. Top sport is now, more than ever, the playground of corporate capitalism. Yet the key figures of this world are generally shadowy and indistinct. They do not, for the most part, feature in the gossip columns or celebrity chat shows. Their deeds and misdeeds rarely attract critical investigative discussion. On one level, little has changed since Lowenthal's famous essay (1961) on celebrity. We still valorise and celebrate those whose success is seen as worthy, accidental, or lucky. The society of the spectacle and the restless vortex of celebrity entertain and fascinate us, but they also provide a mask behind which the crimes of the powerful go unobserved and unpunished.

Yet the very uncertainties of sport, the space for maverick qualities of performance and the ability of sport to produce fleeting moments of *jouissance*, can always, albeit briefly, escape the calculations of the corporate marketeers and entrepreneurs. There is a joy inherent in those rare moments, such as Bannister's four-minute mile, Ali's victory in Zaire, Bob Beamon's massive long jump in 1968, Arthur Ashe's Wimbledon win, Gascoigne's free kick goal in the 1991 FA Cup semi-final, Botham and Willis's performances in the 1981 Cricket Test Series, Torvill and Dean's ice dance 'Bolero', the home run race between Sosa and McGuire, and Manchester United's two goals in injury time to win the European Cup. For those brief moments, sport is lifted out of the dispiriting clutter of sponsorship, advertising and corporate hospitality and provides glimpses of the marvellous, which enliven the spirit. As a social practice, sport has come to epitomise the process by which capital has penetrated and reconstructed more and more aspects of the social world, yet, at the same time, sport continues to provide inspirational glimpses of the ability of humans to transcend the calculable.

Appendix 1
Biographical notes

As an aid to the partial knowledge that we all have of stars from sports we do not follow, or cultural contexts outside those we are familiar with, I have included here a brief biographical description of individuals mentioned in the book. These descriptions are not intended as career summaries, but include primarily contextual information relevant to an understanding of the discussion. In the case of a few stars – for example, Muhammad Ali – I have assumed that an entry would be superfluous.

Tony Adams Footballer, captain of Arsenal, and, for a while, captain of England. Part of a very effective defense, the Arsenal back four, whose adept ability at catching attackers offside has been the subject of jokes in the films *Fever Pitch* and *The Full Monty*. Derided for years by supporters of other teams as a donkey, Adams is, nonetheless, a defender of considerable ability. His new-found (or at least newly expressed) interest in the piano, foreign languages and classic literature comes as somewhat of a surprise to most English football fans.

Roger Bannister Famous as the first man to run the mile in less than four minutes, he had a relatively short athletic career, with failures at the Olympics, before retiring to concentrate on a medical career.

David Beckham Footballer of exceptional ability, especially when delivering his trademark highly accurate crosses from the wing. Plays for Manchester United, who, like the New York Yankees, are rich, successful and hated by many fans of other clubs. Through his marriage to Spice Girl Victoria Adams, Beckham became one of the most highly visible of all sport stars. Relatively shy and not especially articulate, he gives few interviews, but his highly photogenic appearance has been constantly on magazine covers in recent years.

Ian Botham Swashbuckling English cricketer, who some would regard as the greatest all-rounder (he both bats and bowls) of all time. Seen by some as vulgar and boorish, by others as inspirational, his reputation stands partly on his career record of wicket taking and run making, but also on his inspirational performances in the 1981 Test matches against Australia, when England won two matches from seemingly hopeless positions. Has featured in tabloid news-papers in drug- and sex-related scandals, but also gained much favourable coverage during his highly publicised long-distance walks to raise money for charities such as leukemia research.

Charles Buchan Ex-footballer who went on to establish the magazine *Charles Buchan's Football Monthly*, one of the first sport-specific magazines of the post-war era.

Eric Cantona An idiosyncratic figure, but a highly talented French footballer from Marseilles, who was a controversial figure in France, where he openly voiced contempt for many of the bosses of French Football. He found creative fulfilment in England, first at Leeds United whom he helped win the Championship, before playing a major role in the initial rise of Manchester United after years of under-achievement, towards their present dominance. After retaliating with a kung-fu kick against a spectator who aimed racial abuse at him, he served a lengthy ban without complaint, and returned to convince the English football world of his exceptional talent before, to general astonish-ment, announcing his early retirement to pursue an acting career.

Brian Clough Football manager who took two relatively small clubs to the heights during the 1970s, winning the League Championship with Derby County, and the European Cup (twice) with Nottingham Forest. Always outspoken and controversial, and a critic of other managers and players, his behaviour became increasingly erratic until his forced resignation, amidst allega-tions of drink problems, in 1993.

Stan Collymore A controversial black British footballer of considerable talent, who experienced problems fitting in at several clubs, and announced his early retirement from the game in 2001.

John Conteh Black British boxer who won the world light-heavyweight cham-pionship in 1974. Retired in 1974.

Garth Crooks Talented black British footballer who since his retirement has become a television interviewer for BBC's football programmes.

George Foreman Won the world heavyweight title in 1973, defeating Joe Frazier, and lost it in 1974 to Muhammad Ali in Zaire, in possibly the most famous fight of all time – initially dubbed the 'rumble in the jungle', until the Zairean authorities made known their dislike of the slogan. Foreman never got back to the top, but returned to the ring after a retirement, and was still boxing at age 48.

Paul Gascoigne (nickname Gazza) Arguably one of the most talented footballers England has produced, had a patchy career in which injury, tabloid scandal and his own self-destructive tendencies have all played a role. He rose to fame in the late 1980s, first with Newcastle and then with Tottenham Hotspur. Dubbed 'daft as a brush' by England manager Bobby Robson, who included him in the side only after prolonged public and press clamour. Reached mythic status with his performances in the 1990 World Cup, culminating in his tears at his booking and England's defeat in the semi-final, an image that soon appeared on T-shirts all over the country with the slogan 'there'll always be an England'. The following season, amidst a promotional blitz that triggered a brief period of 'Gazza-mania', he scored a memorable goal from a free kick in the semi-final of the FA Cup against Tottenham's local rivals, Arsenal, but then badly injured his knee in the final and was out for over a year. A less than successful spell in Italy, during which he was dubbed a 'fat clown', was followed by a period with the Scottish club Glasgow Rangers. Periodically in the tabloid papers for drink-related escapades, or for his stormy relationship with fiancée Sheryl, whom he married in 1996. His last great moments came during the 1996 European Championship, since when he has been dropped by England, returned to English club football with Middlesbrough, been found drunk and weeping at Stevenage station, and been despatched to a clinic for rehabilitation. For the last two years, Gascoigne has largely kept out of the headlines, moving to Everton and managing a partial recovery of form. His symbolic centrality to the hopes of the English national team was eclipsed in the late 1990s by the rise of David Beckham.

Alex Higgins Irish snooker player of extraordinary talent but little self-discipline. His flamboyant and high-speed potting and air of flaky vulnerability made him the most charismatic figure in the game during the late 1970s and early 1980s. Won the World title in 1972, and again in 1982, after which drink-induced wayward behaviour has contributed to a long and inexorable decline. Has not played the game at the top level since the mid-1990s, and has been reported as suffering from serious illness in recent years.

Lloyd Honeyghan London-based black British boxer who won the World Welterweight Championship in 1986.

Jack Johnson First black man to win the World Heavyweight Championship, in 1908, Johnson later fled America after being sentenced to a year in prison. He had seven successful title defences before losing to Jess Willard in Cuba, a fight many believed was 'thrown' by Johnson in return for being allowed back into the USA.

Gary Lineker English footballer and prolific goal-scorer with an exemplary disciplinary record, Lineker went into television on retirement from football, and currently fronts BBC's football coverage; he is a regular panellist on *They Think It's All Over*.

Joe Louis American boxer who won the Heavyweight World Championship in 1937, and went on to defend it an unprecedented 25 times before losing to Ezzard Charles at the age of 36. According to many, the greatest heavyweight ever.

Stanley Matthews One of the most talented footballers England has ever produced. A fitness fanatic, he played until 1966 when he was fifty. He finally won an FA Cup Winners medal, after many years of trying, in 1953, in a dramatic match, which was known thereafter as 'Matthews' Final'.

Jim Meadowcroft Snooker player who was never able to match the successes of his associates Denis Taylor and Alex Higgins.

Paul Merson English footballer and talented striker for Arsenal and England, until drink, drug and gambling problems drove him to seek treatment in the mid-1990s. Since then, he has made a full come-back and, after a brief spell at Middlesbrough, is now at Aston Villa.

Brian Orser Canadian skater who became only the third Canadian man to win the World Championship.

Ian Rush Welsh footballer who had great success with top English club Liverpool in the late 1980s before an unhappy spell in Italy.

Babe Ruth Legendary baseball star with the New York Yankees, who attracted crowds to such an extent that the new Yankee Stadium, constructed in the 1920s, became know as 'The house that Ruth built'.

Dennis Taylor Irish snooker player, who famously won the World Title in 1985 in the most dramatic final ever, which was not concluded till the final ball of the final frame, with Taylor taking the lead for the first time in the 35th frame match.

Peter Taylor Football coach and manager, and long-term partner of Brian Clough until a quarrel after which they never spoke. Died a few years ago, causing Clough to regret that they had never reconciled their differences. Taciturn, where Clough was flamboyant, theirs was seemingly one of those partnerships where each compensates for the weaknesses of the other.

Mike Tyson Fearsome heavyweight world champion, before an unexpected defeat, a rape allegation, a spell in jail and a break with powerful boxing promoter Don King knocked his career sideways. Currently boxing again after a spell in suspension following his biting the ear of Evander Holyfield.

Terry Venables Currently a television pundit. As a footballer, has the rare distinction of having played for England at every level from schoolboy to full international. Played for Chelsea and Tottenham Hotspur, but always sought other outlets for his energies, and has been a singer, author of fiction, coach, manager and director, as well as owning a night club and, briefly, companies marketing clothes and a combination wig and hat called the 'thingamawig'. Widely regarded as one of the best coaches in the game, he managed England for a brief but successful spell in the mid-1990s, and has also had successes as a manager of Barcelona and Tottenham Hotspur. Was briefly co-owner of Tottenham Hotspur at the start of the 1990s, along with Alan Sugar, owner of the hi-fi and satellite dish business, Amstrad. The two – who both originate from London's East End working-class – quarrelled, and assorted allegations kept them involved with courts and lawyers for much of the 1990s.

Gordon Williams Scottish novelist and screen writer, whose credits include *Straw Dogs*. Co-wrote *They Used to Play on Grass* with Terry Venables, see above. The pair went on to write three novels featuring the detective James Hazell, and collaborated on the resultant Thames television series *Hazell*.

Ian Wright Black British footballer and a striker of considerable flair, initially with Crystal Palace and then with Arsenal. Retired at the end of the 1990s to pursue a career in television, and his quirky late night chat show has been well received.

Appendix 2
The concept of 'role model' – critical notes

The concept of socialisation, of course, identifies various socialising agencies – the school and the family being the primary ones, but peer groups, religion and the media also being important. Standard accounts of socialisation and sport distinguish between socialisation into sport and socialisation through sport (see, for example, Sage 1970). While substantial claims have been made, often for political reasons (bidding for public funding, for example), for sport-related socialisation, the evidence is patchy and ambiguous. It is claimed, with some justification, that sports abilities are related to positive self-esteem, peer popularity and good mental health. But in some research, boys who participate in organised sport have poorer sportsmanship-value orientations than non-sportsmen (Richardson 1962, cited in Snyder and Spreitzer 1978). Parents with high aspirations tend to contribute unwittingly to the learning of undesirable behaviour (see Sage 1970). Students sometimes report their perceptions of coaches as playing favourites, insensitive to pain of injuries, and having unrealistic demands for training or time input (Snyder and Spreitzer 1978). Orlick and Botteril (1976) argued that fun and enjoyment were absolutely central to children's involvement, and that children can become more negative about sport as the fun dimension is gradually replaced by the performance criterion.

In one study of sport and race (Cashmore 1982), it is suggested that the very visibility of black sportsmen as positive role models serves as, in effect, a trap for black schoolchildren who gravitate towards sport at the expense of educational development. By contrast, Fleming's study of Asian schoolboys (1991) suggests a high degree of awareness of the absence of Asian sporting role models and that this contributes to the stereotype view held by white children that Asians are no good at sport. This works as an explanation for soccer, but cricket, with its successful Asian sides seems to pose some problems. The research of Martin Toms into the lack of enthusiasm for cricket amongst schoolchildren could constitute a pointer here (Toms and Fleming 1995).

Martin Lee refers to the traditional claim that sport contributes to personal development by building character, and asks: what is character, can we measure it, how can we know if sport has any effect on it? If sport were effective in developing character, he suggests, we should expect to see athletes placing more emphasis on social and moral values than on competence and personal values.

Lee's research with college athletes in North America indicates that this does not happen and, insofar as there are differences in the values of athletes and non-athletes, it is only that athletes tend to place more value on being good at what they do. The question of whether sport is character-building is a different one from whether it can be. Sport can provide opportunities for altruistic behaviour and sportsmanship. Opportunities to display fair-mindedness, respect for opponents and altruism can arise particularly in situations where there are no independent judges. Yet Lee cites a junior championships where adults were unwilling to umpire because they did not wish to sit and receive abuse from youngsters during the matches (see Lee 1987, 1991).

Studies into whether sport develops moral responsibility suggest that the effects of sport experience may be negative rather than positive: those who had more experience were less altruistic, and boys were less altruistic than girls. Martin Lee's research suggests that extensive athletic participation is related to higher personal and competence values and not to moral and social values (Lee 1987). Lee (1986) cited research into football which found that professional fouls became more acceptable to boys as they grow older, and boys were more likely to endorse a foul in a cup game than in a league or friendly game. Players were more likely to endorse fouls than non-players. But players were no less mature in their judgements of behaviour in non-sporting situations than non-players. Instrumental behaviour may be specific to the sport and is not necessarily transferred to other life situations.

Coakley (1986) suggests that organised programmes and insensitive coaching can promote a win-at-all-costs philosophy, with children expected to behave like mini-adults. This constitutes a double bind for the young. If they do not perform well they get negative feedback and if they perform well they are treated like little pros. Lee says that there is no reason to believe that taking part in sport necessarily promotes morally or socially desirable behaviour and attitudes either in sport or elsewhere; indeed the main tendency is just the opposite.

The concept of role model is not exclusively a media-focused one; parents, coaches and teachers can all be role models. Indeed the concept has its origins in the social psychology of the early 1970s, and referred to relations between children and parents (or sometimes teachers). However, from the perspective of public discourse, the concept has become associated with the supposed ability of sport stars to be role models and the tendency of some to fail at this task and instead set a bad or negative example for young people.

Indeed, despite its popularity in certain areas of public discourse, it could be argued that the concept has never gained widespread credence in sociology, as distinct from social psychology. The term 'role model' does not appear as an entry in Jary and Jary's (1995) *Dictionary of Sociology*, nor does it appear in Labovitz's glossary of terms (1977), or in dictionaries edited by Mitchell (1979) and Abercrombie *et al.* (1984). There is discussion of roles, role taking, role conflict, etc., but not of 'role models'. Mitchell (1979) references Merton and outlines functionalist and social psychological uses of the concept. Abercrombie *et al.* (1984) say first use of the term 'role' was made by George Mead, a forerunner of symbolic interactionism. Goffman introduced the concept of role distance to describe the gap between the performer and the role being performed. Marshall (1994) does have an entry for role model, which says

> A significant other, upon which an individual patterns his or her behaviour in a particular social role, including adopting appropriate similar attitudes. Role models need not be known personally to the individual: some people model their behaviour in particular roles on the real and legendary examples provided by historical figures. Role models tend to provide ideals for a particular role only, rather than a pattern to be emulated across all the constituent roles of an individual's life and self.

Johnson (1995) says that

> A role model is someone to whom we look for examples of how to behave in the performance of a role. Research on role models focuses primarily on childhood socialisation and imitation of the behaviour of adults and other models, and the role of mentors in school and occupational success, especially for women and other minorities [*sic!*].

Role models differ from reference individuals, in that the former focuses on a specific activity while the latter is generalised to many areas of social life.

A distinction needs to be made between the relation between a child and close significant others such as parents – where the relation is not chosen, is intense, is close, is personal and is long term – and the relation between children and famous figures consumed through representation, where the relationship is chosen by the consuming child, is less intense, is distant, is impersonal and may be temporary. This distinction has been blurred in both tabloid and broadsheet journalism, where people characteristically talk as if media celebrities can constitute 'role models' in the same sense as parents and significant others. Such confusion serves only to inhibit a more systematic examination of the nature of celebrity. Children select a bricolage of figures for identification (a look at bedroom walls confirms this). They will select in accord with their predispositions – their habitus, if you like – figures that echo aspects of their own identities, aspirations, desires. This may well be a significant process but should not be confused by use of the term 'role model'.

Speizer says that the term 'role model' first appears in most fields in 1973, basing this assessment on scrutiny of abstracts and indexes of *Psychological Abstracts, Current Index to Journals in Education, Business Periodicals Index, Women's Studies Abstracts,* and *Sociological Abstracts.* She says that most of the studies related to role models have been focused on young children and their parents, with some on college-age children. She says the results of these studies are ambiguous, and concludes that there is very little supportive evidence for the validity of the concept (Speizer 1981: 692–712).

Dahrendorf, on the term 'role', said that social psychologists and sociologists assign it different meanings. He argued that if neither discipline was prepared to renounce the term, a definitive solution might be impossible. However, he contends that the divergence of definitions may be more apparent than real. Social psychologists, Dahrendorf suggests, have succeeded in rendering the notion of habitual behaviour precise, whereas sociologists have so far failed to do the same with their notion of expected behaviour (Dahrendorf 1968: 66). But otherwise, in an essay some 70 pages long, he has little to say about role models. The work of social psychologists draws on assumptions of imitative behaviour (Bandura and Walters 1963), but the methodological underpinning of these theories can be found in misconceived laboratory experiments such as the rather ludicrous and much derided 'bobo doll' experimental research, in which children who saw a bobo doll being punched and played with in a violent manner subsequently adopted similar forms of play themselves (see Bandura, Ross and Ross 1963).

The concept of role model rests upon an outdated and discredited functionalist model of socialisation, which in most analyses has been superseded by other modes of theorising social and cultural reproduction – Bourdieu's concepts of habitus and cultural capital; neo-Marxist theories of ideology; poststructural theories of subjectivity and positionality; or Foucault's theories of discursive practices. In particular, more recent theories of identity formation offer far more when it comes to examination of the relationship between representations and audiences. The process of identity formation is described by Stuart Hall as follows:

> I use 'identity' to refer to the meeting point, the point of suture between on the one hand the discourses and practices that attempt to interpellate, speak to us, or hail us into place as the social subjects of particular discourses, and on the other hand, the processes which produce subjectivities, which construct us as subjects which can be 'spoken'. Identities are thus points of temporary attachment to the subject positions which discursive practices construct for us.
>
> (Hall and du Gay 1996: 6)

It is in the context of this form of conceptualisation that the analyses in Part III of this book were developed.

Appendix 3

Notes on methodological issues

I want to sound a note of unease, if not dissent. Methodology has become increasingly reified in recent years by the institutional pressure to demonstrate that methodology is taught, and hence that it is a learning outcome and a transferable skill. Yet it makes little sense, in the context of cultural studies, to discuss method as independent of, on the one hand, theory and, on the other hand, subject matter. I aim here merely to sketch out the process of production of this book.

The early period of research involved content analysis. Commencing in the early 1990s with a set of research questions focused on young people, sport and the media, we identified those publications young people were most likely to read. We selected a sample of titles which included the *Daily Mirror*, the *Sun*, *Smash Hits*, *Shoot*, *Match*, *Horse and Pony*, the *Beano* and *Viz*. Over a period of a year a sample of these titles were analysed. We aimed to identify those sport stars who appeared most frequently, in order to build up dossiers of examples of their portrayals. These dossiers were to provide the basic material for some of the case studies reported in the book. The very dominance of male sport stars, the stark and dramatic differences between male- and female-oriented publications, and the growing popularity of the new men's magazines prompted a refocusing of the key research questions around issues of masculinity and sport. We commenced content analysis of a selection of men's magazines – *Loaded*, *GQ*, *Maxim* and *FHM*.

The initial content analysis enabled the development of a more precisely targeted approach to the gathering of material. We became specifically interested in the ways in which concepts of masculinity and morality were mobilised in images of sport stars. This issue was pursued historically through archive research into newspaper, magazine and book sources, and, in the contemporary context, through the continuing monitoring of the print media throughout the second half of the 1990s. Theories of narrative and discourse constituted the framing principles for analysis of this material. In addition, the growing conceptual importance of 'masculinity' and 'morality' in the analyses of the material required a more focused trawl through both broadsheet and tabloid papers for manifestations of discourses of crisis.

The importance of ephemera should be mentioned. The trawl for material was deliberately and consciously eclectic. My position here is that whether images and texts are found in supermarket leaflets, in advertising handouts, in free newspapers discarded on trains, in popular magazines or on posters, they are in the public domain, and a relevant source for probing the structure of popular conceptions. The focus always has been on the representations themselves. No attempt has been made to measure these against some abstract 'truth'. The question of the accuracy or otherwise of images of, for example, David Beckham or Tiger Woods seems to me both irrelevant and epistemologically invalid. It is a central assumption of this book that as far as the audience is concerned, Beckham, Woods and the others are precisely constructed out of the mass of representations through which they can be consumed. No attempt has been made to test out the readings that the book offers through audience research. This is not because I regard this task as unimportant or irrelevant, but rather that audience research has still to resolve the considerable problems of methodology and epistemology that have always beset it. The validity of semiological, textual and discursive readings in the end rest, it seems to me, in their plausibility and explanatory value to a reader. Clearly there is a range of possible readings, and, equally clearly, this range is delimited. The analysis is itself a form of meaning production, which is yet another form of circulation of star image. I remain unconvinced that a search for a greater scientificity is either possible or desirable.

I would, however, acknowledge a more significant lacuna. Apart from the chapter on the development of media sport, there is little here about the economics, structure, organisation, or production practices of the media industry. The book is already a long one and the scope of enquiry has to be limited by space. I do, however, think that an understanding of the economic and industrial processes whereby certain images come to be produced at the expense of others is a central part of any comprehensive account. I hope that readers, if they find this book useful, will choose to situate it in relation to such work, and that future research in the field will continue to increase our understanding of the ways in which powerful media corporations structure the world.

Notes

1 Introduction

1 This book has its origins in research conducted at the Centre for Sport Development Research, School of Sport Studies, Roehampton Institute London, between 1993–6 into images of sport in youth magazines, and between 1994–7 into star images in sport media coverage.

2 The focus on male sport stars is quite deliberate; it emerged initially from research into images of sport stars in the print media which confirmed just how completely male-dominated representations of elite sport are. In twelve months of monitoring magazines and newspapers, and opening files on the most frequently represented sports stars, only Sally Gunnell, Sharron Davies and (Torvill and) Dean featured frequently enough to warrant opening a file. More importantly, though, analysis of representations of star images revealed how frequently they were framed in terms of the discourses of masculinity and morality that came to constitute the main theme of this study. Brief relevant biographical details on some of the sport stars alluded to can be found in Appendix 1. Women in sport have to struggle against the grain both for achievement and for recognition. The processes of struggle this can involve is the subject of Jennifer Hargreaves's book, *Heroines of Sport* (2000).

3 While the term 'role model' appears widely in media discussion of sport stars, it is not a concept that I propose to utilise in my own analysis. See Appendix 2 for a critical discussion of the term and its origins.

4 In a two-page spread on school sport, the *Independent on Sunday* (21 November 1993) examined these issues. It asserted that the average child watches 27 hours of TV a week. However, as television audience figures suggest an average of 25 hours per week, and as those over 65 watch around twice as much television as those between 4 and 15, a more realistic estimate might be around 18 hours per week. The rising popularity of electronic games, computer games and the Internet probably boosts the total hours children spend watching a screen by a significant amount.

5 According to Armstrong, for example, one-third of all girls between 11 and 16 did no more strenuous exercise than one brisk ten-minute walk per week. Armstrong's study showed no difference between the fitness of children in the late 1980s and children in other environments or periods (although it should be noted that there is a lack of good reliable data from earlier periods). What it did show was a low level of strenuous physical activity. More than 50 per cent of girls and 33 per cent of boys failed to raise their heart beat to an average of 146 beats/minute for ten minutes on any occasion during the week. At weekends the percentages were 90 per cent and 70 per cent (*Independent on Sunday*, 21 November 1993, and also see Armstrong 1990, 1991). Armstrong points out that there is no single technique for measuring physical activity. His research reveals that boys between 6 and 17 are significantly more physically active than girls of the same age (see Armstrong and Welsman 1997). No

meaningful longitudinal comparisons of physical activity can be easily made, but Durnin's 1992 review of adolescent energy intakes 1930s–1980s suggests that there has been a reduction in energy expenditure over this period (see also Durnin *et al.* 1974).

6 Extra curricular sport never recovered from the impact of the 1985 industrial action by teachers and consequent disillusion amongst the teaching profession and withdrawal by teachers from extra-curricular activity. Since then there has been a 70 per cent decline in schools' football. By the early 1990s, 80 per cent of football played by boys between 9 and 16 was taking place on Sunday morning (i.e. for clubs rather than schools) (*Independent on Sunday*, 21 November 1993).

Neil Armstrong said that 56 per cent of primary schools couldn't deliver the national curriculum as legally required to do in physical education. At secondary schools, a minimum 2 hours per week physical education was recommended. But a survey in 1987 showed that 38 per cent of 14 year olds had less than 2 hours. By 1990, in school plans, this had almost doubled to 71 per cent (*Independent on Sunday*, 21 November 1993).

7 The *Guardian* (1 March 1994) suggested that Ian Sproat (then Sports Minister) sometimes gave the impression that a regime of cricket and cold showers would solve all the nation's ills at a stroke, making the campaign for 'real' sports in schools a one-man crusade. Sproat is quoted as saying 'When I talk about sport in schools I do not mean step aerobics, going for country walks and listening to lessons on the history of diets. These are all right in their way but they are not what I want. I want team games, properly organised – competitive team games, preferably those which we invented, such as soccer, rugby, hockey, cricket and netball.'

The position of those such as Sproat failed to recognise the changing nature of physical activity amongst the young. It took no account of the popularity of dance amongst girls, or of martial arts amongst boys. It failed to recognise that the declining popularity of many traditional team games has been matched by a growing interest in new more individualist, narcissistic or dangerous activities – aerobics, weight training, hang gliding, wind surfing, etc. (see Wheaton and Tomlinson 1998).

8 Jonathon Freedland, in an article headed 'BRITAIN'S PROBLEM WITH CORRUPTION', (*Guardian*, 4 February 1998) cited as examples the National Lottery 'a glorified cash-machine', the 'bung' affair in football, allegations of horse-doping and race-fixing, the need for a ghost squad in the Metropolitan Police to investigate bent coppers, and the cash-for-questions row in the House of Commons. It suggested that Britain has been blinded to corruption in public life by 'the myth of our own incorruptibility'.

9 The conservative perspective that I parody here is typically wrong on two counts. First it regards the canon of established taste as a fixed and uncontested one, disregarding the complex ways in which a pantheon is constructed, reproduced and revised through the processes of the selective tradition (see Williams 1961). Second, it misrecognises the arguments being advanced on behalf of popular culture. It is not that Dylan is necessarily as good or better than Keats, but rather that each are worthy of attention on their own terms. It is the hierarchisation of form and context that is being rejected. The conservative perspective is also prone to exaggerate the impact of aesthetic relativism. While it would be foolhardy to resort to opinion polling of aesthetic views, it is reasonable to hypothesise that a large proportion of the population probably still believe that Beethoven, Keats, Rembrandt, Shakespeare and Jane Austen are unproblematically 'better' than Jimi Hendrix, Bob Dylan, Andy Warhol, Ian Fleming and Jackie Collins, even where they prefer the latter, or have no exposure to the former. The present analysis, though, focuses on the discursive construction of masculinities and moralities, and so the articulated position that cultural relativism undermines moral authority is of great relevance.

10 Against the grain of a dominant theme of moral crisis, Geoff Mulgan in *Connexity* (1997) argues against the concept of moral decline, and suggests that new structural forces are promoting and enhancing morality. Like Anthony Giddens, David Held and Ulrich Beck, he celebrates 'a runaway world where the potential for self-renewing values of co-operation and harmony have never been greater' (*Guardian*, 1 March 1997).

11 Sean French (in 'Silence of the Lads', *Guardian* 17 April 1996) argues that boys appear to 'conform, still, to the macho stereotype that it's big to be tough, and wimpish to show emotions'. A taciturn masculinity and male stoicism 'could provide a protective facade in the brutal existence of unskilled manual labour'. He points out that the major cinematic male image of the last fifteen years 'was not a new man but a cyborg, a terminator which doesn't feel pain or remorse and kills anybody in its path'.

12 The new men's movement triggered by Robert Bly's book, *Iron John* (1990), despite its mytho-poetic pretensions, is also part of a reaction against feminism as is the reassertion of 'real manliness' manifest in book titles like *Real Men Don't Eat Quiche* (Feirstein 1982) and *The Big Damn Book of Sheer Manliness* (Hoffman 1997).

13 See Appendix 2 for a critical discussion of the concept of role model.

14 Robert Atkin, Minister for Sport in the early 1990s, referred, on the first morning of his appointment, to both Steve Davis and Nick Faldo as the kind of figures from whom all young sports people could learn ('Today', BBC Radio 4, 24 July 1990). According to the *Daily Mirror*, Ian Sproat, another ex-Sports Minister, 'believes sports are vital not only to improve the poor fitness of the young, but also to teach them teamwork and discipline – values which might also overcome the problem of thuggery in the classroom' (*Daily Mirror*, April 1994). Sproat proclaimed, 'If we had more organised games in schools we'd have fewer little thugs like those who murdered Jamie Bulger'. In response, John Evans, Professor of Physical Education at Loughborough, commented that 'Sport has as great a capacity for producing bullies and thugs as it has good citizens and saints' (*Guardian*, 1 March 1994). However, the belief that top sports performers can also be moral exemplars is still firmly entrenched.

15 A book written by *Evening Standard* sports writers offers 'an informative and salutary record of the decline of sporting etiquette ... a sad record of a downward spiral' (*Evening Standard Sports Writers*, back cover, 1991). In 1990 the Duke of Edinburgh hosted a conference of figures in sport which drew up a Charter of Conduct for sport. It called on competitors to bide by both the laws and the spirit of their game, and accept decisions of umpires and referees without question or protestation. They 'must not cheat or resort to performance-enhancing drugs. They must exercise self-control; must accept success and failure, victory and defeat, with good grace and without excessive display of emotion, and must treat their opponents and fellow participants with due respect at all times' (*Evening Standard Sports Writers*, 1991, p. 13).

16 In the UK, the readership of sport-specific magazines, and of the sports pages in both tabloids and broadsheets is largely male. Television audiences are a more complicated issue. The means of measuring audiences provides data on the channel tuned to, and those present in a room, broken down over 15-minute segments. It does not offer information on how closely the set is being viewed by different members of a household, nor on who chose to watch the programme. Typically, audiences for sport programmes are around 60 per cent male, rising towards 70 per cent for some sports such as American football and boxing. Sport broadcast late at night or during the night is almost certainly viewed by an even higher proportion of male viewers but the overall audience size is too small for statistical reliability. In my view the best index of gender difference here is the magazine market which offers stark evidence for a large degree of female disinterest in sport, contrasted with

evidence of sport as a fairly significant interest for men. Claims have been made for substantial female interest in sport in other countries, particularly North America, which clearly have some basis, but my main interest here is in the mainstream areas of popular media discourse, in which I maintain, sport was, always, and continues to be, primarily a masculine preserve.

17 Another advertisement which pokes fun at the exaggerated importance bestowed upon sport is the Carlsberg advertisement where an Italian boxer returns victorious, only to discover that the cheering crowds are there to welcome the return from holiday of the local barman.

18 The phrase is Gaye Tuchman's (Tuchman *et al.* 1978).

2 Discourses of crisis in masculinity

1 The question of the extent to which 'men' were the enemy, as opposed to patriarchy, or capitalism, became the terrain on which distinctions emerged between radical separatism and socialist feminism (see Brownmiller 1975; Delphy 1977; Firestone 1979; Dworkin 1981). Socialist feminism attempted to find alliances for a new politics 'beyond the fragments' of the disunited left (see Kuhn and Wolpe 1978; Rowbotham, Segal and Wainwright 1979; Barrett 1980).

2 Christine Delphy's *L'Ennemi Principal*, written in 1970, and published in English as *The Main Enemy* (1977), maintained that there are two different modes of production in capitalism – the industrial mode and the domestic mode. Women are a class and marriage is the universal institution of the oppression of women. Sheila Rowbotham said that 'In thus separating the material situation of women from that of men, she identified a theoretically distinct form of oppression, "patriarchy", existing in capitalism' (Rowbotham 1989: 49; see also Michele Barrett and Mary McIntosh (1979) 'Christine Delphy: towards a feminist materialism', in *Feminist Review*, 1).

Sheila Rowbotham commented that the universal use of the term patriarchy:

> raised more problems than it solved. The word suggests that there are two separate systems divided along male/female lines so that patriarchy oppresses women and capitalism oppresses male workers. This makes it difficult to see how relationships have changed historically, since the term implies a fixed structure rather than the kaleidoscopic forms shaping the actual encounters of women and men.
>
> (Rowbotham 1989: 150)

It was suggested by critics of the analytic value of the concept of patriarchy that the term produced tendencies towards ahistoric, trans-cultural and essentialist modes of analysis that did not grasp adequately the complexities and contradictions of class and gender oppression in specific contexts. However, Sylvia Walby argues that 'the concept and theory of patriarchy is essential to capture the depth, pervasiveness and interconnectedness of different aspects of women's subordination and can be developed in such a way as to take account of the different forms of gender inequality over time, class and ethnic group' (Walby 1990: 2).

3 See, for example, Berger and Watson (eds) (1995); Brod (1987); Brod and Kaufman (eds) (1994); Chapman and Rutherford (1988); Cohen (1996); Cornwall and Lindisfarne (1994); Edley and Wetherall (1995); Ervoe and Johansson (eds) (1998a, 1998b); Ford and Hearn (1988); Mac an Ghaill (ed.) (1996); MacInnes(1998); Morgan (1992); Mort (1996); Nixon (1996); Petersen (1998); Pronger (1990); Rogers (1988); Roper and Tosh (eds) (1991); Rutherford (1992, 1997); Seidler (1997); Simpson (1994); Tosh (1999).

4 The demands that work makes are seen as a threat to family life. The *Evening Standard* (9 April 1996) reported that in the USA the proportion of men reporting significant conflict between work and family has increased from 12 per cent in 1977 to 71 per cent in 1995. In England, the Institute of Managers said 71 per cent of managers believe that their relationships with their children are adversely affected by their working lives. More than half of men thought that working long hours put their family relationships at risk, but only one-quarter would make a stand against it. Long working hours are 'a growing problem' for fathers. One-third work more than 50 hours a week and while their children are young clock up four times as much paid overtime as childless men (*Evening Standard*, 9 April 1996).

5 OFSTED (Office for Standards in Education) is the British Government body charged with monitoring standards in education. GCSE (General Certificate of Education) is awarded for passing subject-based examinations which English children typically sit at age 16.

6 The titles referred to included: Melissa Benn: *Madonna and Child: Towards a New Politics of Motherhood* in which she calls for recognition of a limit to infinite expansion of income power, ambition and consumption – in other words, you can forget about having it all; other titles included Eileen Gillibrand and Jenny Mosley's *When I Go To Work, I Feel Guilty: A Working Mothers Guide to Sanity and Survival*, and Kate Figes's *What Even Your Friends Won't Tell You About Motherhood*.

7 In a witty piece entitled Stand Up for the Penis, Dea Birkett asks Whither the male member? (*Guardian*, 10 March 1998) and comments on the cultural marginalisation of the penis, citing women who opt for artificial insemination. She suggests that the penis is passé as a topic of conversation (when, one wonders, was it de rigeur?) and refers to taboos on representing the penis. Even *The Full Monty*, she points out, doesn't show the penis. (Note that playwright Tom Stoppard once pointed out the absence of the penis in a pop-up book about the body, saying 'missing is the one organ eminently suitable for the form'.) Robert Mapplethorpe's pictures were seized by West Midlands Police, and only in gay culture is the penis represented. Birkett concluded:

> Its traditional roles are being eradicated: its future is uncertain. The male member is fast becoming an organ without an occupation. Successful women like Foster are supposed to spurn it; professing a passion for male private parts is tantamount to confessing to enjoying being oppressed. But I happen to like them. It's time someone stood up for the penis.
>
> (*Guardian*, 10 March 1998)

While the article is rather fanciful as far as sexual patterns are concerned – one suspects that heterosexual penetrative sex is rather more prevalent than she suggests – it does exemplify a discourse that problematises male sexuality.

8 The *Express* (17 June 1998) commented dryly that scientists have handed men the perfect excuse for getting out of the ironing and similar boring chores. Their brains are simply not up to it. Professor O'Boyle of Iowa State University suggests that men, unlike women, have one-track minds. He put six men and women in a kitchen and they had to do a series of tasks in 10 minutes – the women performed far better than the men. (Quite clearly, in fact, acquired competences – domestic cultural capital – had everything to do with gender differences here.)

9 It went on to assert, 'yes, football and testosterone are incontrovertibly linked. When your team loses it goes down. When you win it goes up, which goes to explain, though not excuse, the rampaging male aggression of the excessively hormonal few'. The article proclaimed that nobody ever ruled the world by co-operation, stating 'It's the drive to be biggest and best that produces empires and World Cup competitions'. It went on to suggest there are useful lessons to be learnt for education in

taking account of the 'different ways in which male and female brains operate' (*Evening Standard*, 16 June 1998).

10 See Hearn and Morgan (1990); Berger and Watson (1995); Brod and Kaufman (1994); Cornwall and Lindisfarne (1994).

11 This theme is pursued in more detail in chapter 12.

12 These themes are examined in more detail in chapter 6.

3 The development of media sport

1 William Hazlitt wrote an essay, 'The Fight', in the *New Monthly Magazine* in February 1822 (Shipley 1989). Dickens, too, wrote of boxing, portraying it as 'a more scientific, humane and democratic method for men to settle their differences than the duel' (Kidd 1987: 253; see also Marlow 1982).

2 See Mason (1988: 48). The *Green Lillywhite* started in 1865 and took over *Fred's Guide* in 1866. The *Red Lillywhite* was started in 1872 and took over the *Green Lillywhite* in 1886 (Bowen 1970: 118–19). Others included *Sporting Gazette* (1862), *Sporting Times* (1865) and the *Sportsman* (1865) (*Haydn's Dictionary of Dates and Universal Information* (1873). In America, the *American Turf Register and Sporting Magazine* was founded in 1829 and the *Spirit of the Times* began life in 1831 (Goldlust 1987: 69). In Britain, the periodical *Illustrated Sporting and Dramatic News* was launched in 1874, and later became *Sport and Country* (Herd 1952: 221). In 1859, a new paper, which became *Sporting Life*, was launched. It cost one penny as opposed to *Bell's* which was five pennies. By 1869 it claimed a circulation of 260,000. It carried more advertising than *Bell's* and a wider range (Mason 1988: 47). In 1865 the *Sportsman* was launched, and in 1871 in Manchester the *Sporting Chronicle* (*ibid.*: 48). Sir Edward Hulton (1869–1925), who founded the firm of E. Hulton and Company which became one of the largest newspaper groups in the country, also founded the *Sporting Chronicle* as his first paper and then followed it up with *Athletic News* in 1875. The audience was not large enough for four sporting daily papers and in the 1880s *Bell's* ceased publication.

3 Among those innovations Boorstin cites are dry-plate photography (1873), the telephone (1876) and roll film (1884) (Boorstin 1961).

4 The Italian paper, *Gazzetto dello Sport* was founded in 1896; in France the forerunner of *L'Equipe*, *L'Auto-Velo*, was launched in 1900, and the Spanish *El Mundo Deportivo* began life in 1906 (see Boyle and Haynes 2000: 29). In the USA *Sports Illustrated* was launched in 1954.

5 Wills was one of the first British firms to get involved. In 1896 they issued a set of 50 cricketers (Murray 1987: 23). Phillips issued a 'General Interest' set including two cricketers and two soccer players. Lambert and Butler issued a set of golfers. But sports series were not especially plentiful, although Marcus and MacDonald did a series of cricketers and also a set of football club colours (Murray 1987 22–3).

6 The inter-war period saw a rapid growth in the scale of spectator sports, a growth in the range and reach of media (radio, newsreels, press), increased amounts of sport coverage, and enhanced public interest. Whereas in Britain the status of sports journalists has always been relatively low, in the USA a significant number of figures who were to become well-known literary figures engaged in sports journalism. Examples include Paul Gallico, Ring Lardner, Damon Runyon, Ernest Hemingway, Budd Schulberg and Art Buchwald.

7 The number of chain stores in the UK rose from 1,500 in 1880 to over 11,000 in 1900. Numbers employed in commerce rose from 217,000 to almost 900,000 in the same period. Boots alone had 150 shops by 1900. The founding of Selfridges in 1909, accompanied by high-power advertising, was an 'event which made history in retail store advertising' (Elliott 1962: 196).

8 The Association of British Advertising Agents was established in 1917. It became the Institute of Incorporated Practitioners in Advertising in 1927 (Elliott 1962: 198). Uncertainty over circulation figures prompted the formation of the Audit Bureau of Circulations in 1931 after pressure from the Advertisers' Protection Society and the advertising agencies. Before this, newspapers circulation figures were often unreliable (*ibid.*: 196).

9 *Evading Standards* 25 April 1997, a radical paper published during the 1997 election campaign.

4 Heroes and stars

1 The lyric is from a popular American song, 'You Gotta Be a Football Hero', by Al Sherman, Buddy Fields and Al Lewis, probably written in the 1930s, and more recently published in *The Colossal Fake Book* (ed. Tod Edmondson), Hialeah, FL: Columbia Pictures. This publication, cited in the *Popular Song Index* (Havlice 1989), is undated, but according to the Penn State Libraries Index of Song Titles (www.libraries.psu.edu/crsweb/speccol/waring/Songsy.html) the song appears to have been published by Leo Feist Inc. in 1933.

2 Both linguistically and culturally, the term heroine has different connotations. It is impossible to conceptualise the terms hero and heroine apart from the contextual structures of femininity and masculinity. Heroine is a distinctly different concept to hero. For the most part, a heroine exists in relation to a hero – that is, in popular narrative, the hero, through his heroics, wins the heroine. Occasionally, she may need to aid, or save him. There are, though, autonomous heroines in Greek myth, and in feminist history.

3 A collection for schools, *Heroes and their Journeys* (Groves and Grimshaw 1982), included the stories of Isis, Jason, Orpheus, Oddyseus, Tobias, Psyche and Cupid, Thor, Sohrab and Rustrum, Scarface, Oisin, Stephen's travels, Sir Gawain and the Green Knight, and the last journey of King Arthur.

4 Lord Raglan argued in *The Hero* (1936) that the hero was typically not a man but a god, and stories of his exploits were accounts not of facts but of ritual and myth. Campbell's study *The Hero with a Thousand Faces* (1953) operates with a Jungian archetypal frame in proposing a 'monomyth' of the heroic in which the adventure of a hero involves departure, initiation and return. The mythologies of sport – touring, going to training camp before a big fight, playing away – can of course be told within the structure of this form: in the road of trials the hero has to walk are many temptations and dangers. Jill Butler's study *The Myth of the Hero* argues for the genesis of the concept of the heroic in human need:

> The hero then is generated by the needs of ordinary mortals. He is the answer to our prayers and will do those things which we are completely incapable of doing for ourselves. The genesis of literature and myth in which there are heroes is in human need. At one end of the spectrum there are such figures as the Revenger, the Avenger, the Destroyer, Mike Hammer, and Travis McGee. At the other are Maitreya Buddha, Jesus Christ, and the Messiah of the Jews. All share a common genesis in human need for a good guy to ride in out of the sunset.
>
> (Butler 1979: 6)

This is absurdly reductionist and constructs the place of the heroic in unified, trans-cultural and ahistoric terms. What is this 'human need' into which gender difference has dissolved? She comments on heroines as Amazonian man-haters, warrior maidens, who lose their powers and become just women (e.g. opera's Turandot, Die

Walkure and Gotterdamerung). Powerful women heroines have to be destroyed, subjugated or reduced to normality, but the archetypal framework makes it impossible for her to deconstruct these fables of gender difference.

5 He quotes Nietzsche's Zarathstra 'Dead are all the Gods', and he goes on to refer to the hero cycle of the modern age:

> the wonder story of mankind's coming to maturity. The spell of the past, the bondage of tradition, was shattered with sure and mighty strokes. The dreamweb of myth fell away; the mind opened to full waking consciousness, and modern man emerged from ancient ignorance like a butterfly from its cocoon or like the sun at dawn from the womb of mother night.
>
> (Campbell 1953: 387)

Of course, for Campbell this does not solve the problem for there is still an absence 'Not the animal world, not the plant world, not the miracle of the spheres, but man himself is now the crucial mystery. This is the quest of the modern hero' (Campbell 1953: 391).

6 'Superman' first appeared in 1938 in Action Comics and his success soon led to imitators. America's entry into World War II 'gave the super-heroes a whole new set of enemies and supplied a complete working rationale and world view for a super-patriotic hero such as Captain America' (Reynolds 1992: 8). The comics had a Golden Age during the late 1940s, followed by some lean years during the fifties, when attention shifted to crime, western and horror comics. A renaissance followed the clamp down on horror comics in the mid- to late fifties, and the super-heroes won new adherents in the psychedelic generation of the late 1960s.

In the late twentieth century, there is no more unproblematic 'wilderness' to explore, and the individual adventurer discourse had to be projected into the fantastical. In the era of the scientific super-weapon, supernatural powers are needed for a hero to succeed in his mission. It is a mistake, though, to collapse this genre too readily into the determinants of a specific moment in time. Reynolds (1992) draws attention to the range of representations – the campy 1960s *Batman* TV show, the apparent artlessness of the Christopher Reeves' *Superman* cycle in the 1980s and the overwrought gothic bravura of the 1998 *Batman* movie.

7 In Holt, Mangan and Lanfranchi's 1996 collection *European Heroes*, much of the writing seems to be insufficiently self-reflexive about the process of construction of the heroic, presenting as evidence forms of description that call for more consistent deconstruction. There is also, at times, a positive and instrumental use of the concept, for example, in the Epilogue, after quoting Halpern (the function of myth is to bind societies together) and Georges Sorel (the function of myth is to bring about radical change) they say: 'Arguably, therefore, it is time for the sustained creation and projection of *European* mythical heroes of sport in the interest of European Union' (Holt, Mangan and Lanfranchi 1996: 170). It is not quite clear why analysis *should* work for the forging of a European identity, especially as such an identity, given both the colonial histories contained within such an identity and the current political construction of Europe's relations with the Third World in terms of 'fortress Europe', must inevitably run the risk of becoming racist in character.

8 Extracts from 'The Greatest Man in the World', by James Thurber (1963), *Vintage Thurber*, Hamish Hamilton.

9 Stardom in football spread from players to managers. The panel of experts, first used by ITV in 1970, and the post-match interview that has become a contractual obligation, was part of a process in which managers attained greater power and greater visibility (see Wagg 1984, 1986). More recently, with financial muscle becoming perceived as central to success in Europe, the Chairman has become a star figure. The growing pressures in the 1990s, following the establishment of the Premier

League, the escalating gap between the elite and the rest, the cost of transfers and salaries, and the increased revenue from shirt sales, made high investment import and brought new figures into the game. The new breed of chairmen, richer than the traditional club chairmen but every bit as keen on being seen as the big man in the community and the saviour of the club, increasingly began to supplant managers as the star figures whose doings and pronouncements made headlines. Men like John Hall, Alan Sugar and Muhammad Al Fayed began to be presented as Svengali figures.

5 Narrativity and biography

1 Radio 5 is a nationwide news and sports channel provided by the BBC. *Sports Report*, a Saturday evening radio sports news programme, has been running since the 1950s. James Alexander Gordon has been reading football results on BBC radio for … well, it seems forever. His calm delivery and mellifluous voice tones stand in contrast to the urgent, if cliché-ridden enthusiasm of the rest of the sports presenters. He must be one of the few people in England to pronounce, conscientiously, the letter 't' in the word 'postponed'.

2 The hermeneutic code is one of five codes that organise narratives, as outlined in Roland Barthes *S/Z* (1974). It concerns the organisation of narratives around the posing and resolving of questions. Sport, whilst not being in itself a narrative, is based on a central narrative hermeneutic – who will win? Media representation of sport inevitably involves various forms of narrativisation. My own application of Barthesian narrative analysis to media sport consisted of a case study of the television coverage of the Coe–Ovett story in the Moscow Olympics of 1980 (Whannel 1982), and a shorter version was included in *Fields in Vision* (Whannel 1992).

3 Media representation of the career of Paul Gascoigne is discussed in detail in chapter 11. See also Appendix 1, Biographical notes.

4 The scope and generality of Propp's influential *Morphology of the Folktale* has frequently been exaggerated. When Propp first wrote it in 1928 he called it *Morphology of the Wondertale* – the editor changed it to folktale to make it more attractive. Propp warned that he was not offering general laws of the folktale, but rather a study of one distinctive type – the 'folk wondertale' (Propp 1984). However, its method and schema are suggestive of one means of analysing a limited lexicon of narrative elements. Clearly it is necessary to be aware of the formalism inherent in this system. Silverstone points out that Barthes 'draws attention to the plurality of the text, plurality which ultimately defies formal analysis' (Silverstone 1981: 89). The implication of critiques of Propp is the need, if this type of analysis is to be done, to develop a different set of functions appropriate to the genre of sport star portrayal and its forms in contemporary cultural production.

5 See Appendix 1, Biographical notes.

6 Genette has five central categories of narrative analysis: order, duration, frequency, mood and voice. The order of the narrative might feature prolepsis (anticipation), analepsis (flashback) and anachrony (discordances between story and plot). Clearly much media sport is rich in prolepsis (form guides, predictions, speculations, discussions of the stars to watch out for) and analepsis (highlights, replays and memories). The duration involves expansion, summary, elision and pause. The distinctive playing with time involved in television's use of editing and replay, and the potted biographies of news and magazine sport material constitute examples here. In discussing frequency, Genette distinguishes between:

- happened once narrated once
- happened once narrated several times

- happened several times narrated several times
- happened several times narrated once

The narration of sport is characterised by 'happened once, narrated several times' – indeed, in the case of some golden moments, ad nauseam.

Mood concerns the relation of narration to its own materials, and the distinction between recounting the story (diagesis) and representing it (mimesis). In terms of sport, the print media are typically diagetic, whereas television sport involves a combination of mimesis and diagesis. The narrators of media sport are in a position of knowledge as to action – they know more than the 'characters', but lack full knowledge as to tactics, strategy and emotion (hence the banal but frequently asked question, 'How did you feel when …?'). Most journalism is externally focalised (outside the narrative) but the participant observation of a writer like George Plimpton is internally focalised (inside the narrative). The voice of narration can, says Genette, be hetero-diagetic (absent from the narrative), homo-diagetic (inside the narrative as in first-person stories) or auto-diagetic (inside and is the main character). Most journalism is hetero-diagetic; Plimpton is generally homo-diagetic; Hunter Thompson is characteristically auto diagetic.

7 Chapter 9 has a detailed analysis of inscription and reinscription in the narrativisation of the careers of Ali and Best.

6 Sporting masculinities

1 See, for example, Birley's discussion of Kipling's references to sport in verse. Kipling mocked the sportsmen who 'judge a scholar's worth' by his skill at 'casting a ball at three straight sticks, and defending the same with a fourth' ('Kitchener's School', quoted in Birley 1995: 155), and famously derided:

> the flannelled fools at the wicket
> or the muddied oafs at the goals
> (quoted in Birley 1995: 175)

Kipling's view of cricket and football was not shared by his friend Cecil Rhodes. When Rhodes died in 1902 his will made prowess in 'manly outdoor sports' an important qualification for the scholarships he bequeathed to enable young men from the Empire to go to Oxford. 'Verily the muddied oafs and flannelled fools have been avenged', commented *Truth* (Birley 1995: 245).

2 Early examples of feminist discussion include Gerber *et al.* (1974), Hargreaves (1978), Boutilier and San Giovanni (1983), Theberge (1981, 1989), Lenskyj (1986). For early work on sport and masculinities, see Sheard and Dunning (1973), Kidd (1987), Sabo and Runfola (1980).

3 See also Carroll (1986), Dunning (1986) and Hargreaves (1986). Feminist scholarship elaborated the workings of patriarchy in sporting contexts (see, for example, Vertinsky (1990), McCrone (1988), Hargreaves (1994). The historical formation of sporting masculinity, too, was being examined more closely (see Mangan and Walvin (1987), Maguire (1986)). In Australia, analyses placed issues of gender relations on the agenda (see Lawrence and Rowe (1987); Rowe and Lawrence (1989)). Most notably, in North America, Michael Messner and Don Sabo developed an analysis of sport strongly shaped by feminist critiques of sport (Messner 1988, 1992, 1993; Messner and Sabo 1991). More recently, in the wake of this programmatic field mapping and agenda setting, more precisely focused single-sport studies of masculinity in sport have begun to emerge (Chandler and Nauright 1999; Spracklen 1995, 1996).

4   That's my fellow, you see, lying there staring at the bedroom ceiling ... the bases loaded, and he's imagining himself coming in from the bullpen, when downstairs the screen door squeaks open and smacks to, and who comes charging up the stairs and into the bedroom but Casey Stengel, there in the flesh, you see ... plunging through the bedroom door and leaning over the bed to shout at our fellow that he'd a hunch, a big hunch, the biggest hunch of his managing career, namely that our fellow was going to solve his relief pitching problem and that he'd better get to the Stadium and suit up the next afternoon.

(Plimpton 1962: 17)

5   More discussion of fitness chic can be found at the start of chapter 10.
6   Note, for example, the track 'Mr Apollo' by the Bonzo Dog Band, which satirised the cult of muscle development. One sardonic line was 'everyone knows a healthy body makes a healthy mind'.
7   Many American corporations subsidise gym membership costs. General Motors discovered a 50 per cent reduction in shop floor accidents, a 50 per cent drop in grievances, and a 40 per cent reduction in lost time due to employees taking proper exercise. UK companies such as Sainsbury's and British Aerospace among them were reported to be following the example (*Observer*, 4 January 1998). Following the economic downturn of the early 1990s and the consequent slashing of the nations disposable income, many clubs and gyms went belly up. In the late 1990s, however, membership rose by almost 25 per cent, and by about 12 per cent in 1998 alone (*Observer*, 4 January 1998).
8   Report produced by the advertising agency *Mellors Reay* and quoted in the *Observer*, 8 March 1998.

8 Good boys: stars, nations and respectability in the 1950s

1   Striking out means being declared out after failing to hit three valid deliveries or 'strikes' from the pitcher.
2   At first sport had a low priority within national reconstruction. Note that the Arts Council was formed in 1946, whereas there was no Sports Council until 1972. It took the voluntary agitation of the Central Council of Physical Recreation (CCPR) to encourage the Government to facilitate the establishment of the National Recreation Centres. Bisham Abbey was the first in 1946, followed by Lilleshall (1951), Plas y Brenin (1954), Crystal Palace (1964), with a total of seven by 1972.
3   The Ashes are awarded for victory in a series of five games or 'Test Matches' between England and Australia. The trophy, a small urn, which in reality never leaves its base at Lord's Cricket Ground, London – the traditional 'home' of cricket – supposedly contains the ashes from an incinerated cricket bail (part of the wicket that bowlers must strike with the ball to dismiss a batsman).
4   Before the introduction of video-recording at the end of the 1950s, the only means of preserving television consisted of pointing a film camera at a television monitor and capturing the live pictures.
5   Note, for example, the picture in Crump (1989: 58).
6   This aspect of the narrativisation of the life of Matthews is reminiscent of the 'we-had-it-rough' sketch from *Monty Python's Flying Circus* in which three self-made North Country businessmen try and outdo each other with ever more preposterous tales of their hard upbringing.
7   Arguably, today's 'pampered stars' in fact work hard at their game – training is more rigorous, tactics more systematic, knowledge of diet, sports medicine and even sport psychology is greater. Levels of fitness are considerably higher, and on pitch work-

rate is much higher than in the 1950s. The demands of the game are higher – the stakes have been raised. Self-discipline is now an expected prerequisite of the modern player. Far more games are played per season and, for the top players, more of these games are important ones against highly accomplished opponents.

8 Tony Blair's somewhat preacherly style has been well parodied in *Private Eye's* 'Albion News', in which Blair is a local vicar.

9 Three separate people, on reading this section, volunteered anecdotal evidence that Matthews was not universally well regarded.

10 These figures are derived from the author's own analysis of television schedules in which data from 1980, 1989 and 1999 are being compared. I plan to publish material based on a detailed analysis of this data within the next year.

9 Pretty boys, the 1960s and pop culture

1 Britain got colour pictures in 1968, the USA had had them since the 1950s, and colour began to spread around the world from the late 1960s.

2 Cassius Clay changed his name to Muhammad Ali in 1962, denouncing his previous name as a slave name. I have used 'Muhammad Ali' except where quoting or paraphrasing the writing of those who referred to him as Clay, either before the name change or, in refusing to acknowledge his new name, after.

3 Mention should be made here of the excellent *Redemption Song* by Mike Marqusee (1999), the best book, by a considerable margin, that I have read on Ali. It deals with the inter-relation between social context, historical formation and cultural politics with considerable sensitivity, always contextualising Ali without ever reducing him to an over-simplified product of his formation. Highly recommended.

4 'We need to distinguish three levels of culture, even in its most general definition. There is the lived culture of a particular time and place, only fully accessible to those living in that time and place. There is the recorded culture, of every kind, from art to the most everyday facts: the culture of a period. There is also, as the factor connecting lived culture and period cultures, the culture of the selective tradition' (Williams 1961: 50).

10 Bad boys and the work ethic

1 By the late 1990s it had become public knowledge that Higgins had been diagnosed as suffering from cancer, and this, on top of his sad decline fuelled by alcohol, may have engendered a degree of public sympathy. But he is rarely a newsworthy figure these days.

2 The representation of Botham and Higgins features a masculinity in which laddish drink-based hedonism is at the core, whilst women are at the periphery. Kathy Botham's own account of life with Botham, *Living with a Legend*, contrasts dramatically with the tone of those accounts produced by male journalists, and, unlike those insider accounts, she is writing from outside the masculine cricket sub-culture (Botham 1988), and for a contrast and insight into gender positionalities, see Ian Botham's own *Don't Tell Kath* (Botham 1994).

11 Celebration, punishment, redemption and self-discipline

1 An earlier version of this case study ('Masculinity and media sport in a period of transformation: the case of Gazza', presented as a paper at the *International Sociology of Sport Association Annual Symposium*, Oslo, Norway, 28 June–1 July 1997, Norwegian University of Sport and Physical Education) talked of three phases. It

serves to buttress my argument about the cyclical nature of news values, that it now makes sense to add a further three phases to take account of a further cycle of redemption, fall from grace, punishment and redemption.

2 'Throughout the pre-modern period the courts had a variety of shaming punishments at their disposal. One of the most characteristic was the pillory ... pillorying usually took place at midday and usually on market day' (Briggs *et al.* 1996: 79).

3 See Appendix 1, Biographical notes.

4 The new geneticism, in its populist media rendition, has, sad to say, added support to this nonsense, giving encouragement to all those who assert that men are 'naturally' prone to certain types of behaviour because of their genetic programming. Such lame arguments have recently been utilised to justify everything from promiscuity, adultery and male violence to masculine inability to iron or change nappies. The insidious influence of the new geneticism can be detected in the ways in which both men and women, in everyday language, have begun ascribing behaviour to 'genes'. In short, the pseudo-scientific distortions growing out of the advances in genetic science have been thoroughly absorbed into popular common sense.

5 Young English international footballer, and a very promising striker, who plays for Liverpool.

12 Moralities, masculinities and violence

1 Of course, all these shifts are as yet poorly consolidated. Much Thatcherite thinking survives in Blair's 'New Labour'. The 'election' of George Bush threatens to refreeze the thawing relations between the West and Russia and China, peace in the Middle East and Ireland remains elusive, and post-apartheid South Africa has huge economic and social problems to combat. However, I would maintain that the dramatic political changes of the 1990s constituted a distinct period of transformation, even though it is too early to understand the character of the transformation.

2 Fraleigh discusses the problem of right actions in sport, and says that the best basis for right actions lies in 'moral reasons'. He says 'we prefer reasons of self-interest to reasons of simple pleasure; we consider reasons of long range interest superior to reasons of short range interest, and we consider reasons of law, religion and morality as outweighing reasons of self-interest' (Fraleigh 1984: 11). But like a lot of other sources he doesn't really clarify where these moral reasons come from, nor does he define the distinction between ethics and morality, nor is it clear who 'we' are in this account. McIntosh (1979) argues that the history of moral philosophy is largely the history of ideas about what is fair and unfair, and concedes that there is a school of thought which maintains that sport has no ethical basis and is amoral. Graham McFee (in McNamee and Parry 1998: 3–18) argues that there can be no philosophy of sport as such, as sport just serves as an exemplar of general philosophical principles. The concept of an objective morality poses problems for political philosophies that reject the authoritarian rule of church, monarchy or non-democratic state, in that objective morality depends in practice on a structure of power relations. Brecher's critique of liberal morality argues that liberal morality is untenable, from a position of a confidence in rationalism. He suggests that

> liberalism's loss of confidence in a universal and impartial rationality, resulting in its transformation into the series of relativisms now described as post-modernism, is misplaced; but that the seeds of this transformation have lain dormant in the liberal tradition. In particular, it is liberalism's difficulties in justifying morality which are central to that transformation and which shows why, its achievements notwithstanding, liberal morality is in the end conceptually inadequate to the point of being corrosive.
>
> (Brecher 1998)

He argues that liberal morality cannot offer a rationally adequate account either of morality as a fact of everyday life, or of any possible justification of moral principles and moral demands. Levine's pragmatic and situated principles outlined in *Living Without Philosophy* (1998) argue that 'we do not need ethical theories, rule and principles to decide what is right. Instead, particular cases can be judged by a detailed description of the relevant circumstances. When our judgements differ, we can decide how to act by deliberating under fair conditions' (Levine 1998). But who are 'we' and how do 'we' resolve 'our' moral dilemmas? We cannot pose these questions without confronting questions of power.

The problems associated with the conceptualisation of universal or absolute moral certainties or generalities is part of the impetus, in the Howell (1997) collection, towards the small, the local, the embedded and the indigenous. Howell argues that 'from an anthropological point of view, there are few useful definitions of morals, morality or ethics' (Howell 1997: 2). Referring to morality as an 'odd-job' word, she urges definitional caution, the need to think polythetically and to avoid hypostesizing the concept.

3 Estimates of sport participation are a source of statistical controversy. The 1996/7 *General Household Survey* cites figures suggesting that 71 per cent of men and 57 per cent of women had participated in at least one sporting event in the four weeks before interview. However, this figure includes walking (specifying a distance of 2 miles). Without this the participation figure would be a lot lower. Apart from walking, only 19 per cent of men participated in the next most popular male sporting activity, snooker/pool/billiards, and only 16 per cent of women participated in the next most popular female sporting activity, swimming.

13 Identities: 'race', nation and masculinities

1 The magazine *Touch*, written 'by and for British blacks' ran into problems attracting advertisers despite its circulation of over 35,000 (*Independent*, 13 March 2001).
2 Talking to Melvin Bragg (Radio 4, 12 May 1999).
3 Ben Carrington alerted me to the remarks of C.L.R. James in *Beyond a Boundary* that writers on sport, more particularly writers on cricket, and most particularly English writers on cricket, automatically put what was unpleasant out of sight even if they had to sweep it under the carpet. The impression they created was one of 'almost perpetual sweetness and light'.
4 Ian Wright, Gary Lineker and Garth Crooks are all ex-footballers turned broadcasters. Stan Collymore announced his retirement from football as this book was being completed. Lineker is white, the other three are black. See Appendix 1, Biographical notes, for fuller information.
5 See Appendix 1, Biographical notes.

14 Performances, appearances, identities and postmodernities

1 For discussion relevant to the high-speed globalised circulation of image and information, see the work of Manuel Castells (1996a, 1996b, 1996c) and Paul Virilio (1977, 1991, 1994).
2 See Carrington and McDonald (2000). Controversies have been triggered by the work of John Hoberman and John Entine, and the work of both has been the subject of heated debate at recent conferences of the NASSS (North American Society of Sport Sociology), see Entine (2000), Hoberman (1998, 2000), Shropshire and Smith (1998).
3 Susan Faludi discusses the male 'backlash' against feminism, whilst Naomi Wolf is accused by some of 'reinventing the wheel' with *The Beauty Myth*. Camille Paglia and

Katie Rophie criticise feminist puritanism, whilst Andrea Dworkin and Catharine McKinnon reassert it. Some suggest that feminism is dead, that new women are 'post-feminist', whilst anti-feminist positions – that feminism is now irrelevant, that feminism is pushing men out of family life, that feminism betrayed women because they want husbands as breadwinners – are on occasion articulated, by women as well as by men.

A range of recent books – Natasha Walter: *The New Feminism*; Melissa Benn *Madonna and Child: Towards a New Politics of Motherhood*; Kate Figes *Life after Birth: What Even Your Friends Won't Tell You About Motherhood*; Jane Buxton: *Ending the Mother War, Starting the Workplace Revolution* and Suzanne Franks: *Having None of It: Women, Men and the Future of Work* – suggest a period of revision and reassessment, but also a crisis of cohesion – a fragmentation of the high moment of women's consciousness. Class and ethnic differences resurfaced early in the seventies and continue to constitute a problem for the notion of women as a class 'for themselves'.

4 Cable argues that 'One of the strengths of those trying to cultivate the "politics of the soil" is that they inherit well fertilised ground'; he goes on to talk about the power of myth in history and its role in the construction of ethnic hatreds and communal tensions (Cable 1994: 29). He posits a conceptual model structured around two axes representing two oppositions. The first is that between left and right, the second that between exclusive groups (Nazis, fundamentalists) and multiple identity groups (social democrats) and left v. right, to come up with a four-square grid in which different political tensions can be plotted. While the model is inevitably schematic and mechanistic, it is also suggestive about the complex ways in which different constructions of political identity interact.

5 Laclau maintains that:

> In a post-Cold War world … we are witnessing a proliferation of particularistic political identities, none of which tries to ground its legitimacy and its action in a mission predetermined by universal history – whether that be the mission of a universal class, or the notion of a privileged race, or an abstract principle. Quite the opposite. Any kind of universal grounding is contemplated with deep suspicion.
>
> (Laclau 1994: 1)

Laclau asks whether 'the emergent plurality of political identities dangerously challenges the universalistic tradition that started with the Enlightenment, and suggests that the answer cannot be unambiguous. It is true that the idea of a subject such as the universal class which incarnates the universal as such is definitely on the wane. But, he asks, is the only alternative a particularism that disregards all universal values and opens the way to various forms of xenophobic exclusivism? Laclau thinks not, and conceptualises the need for some articulation of universal values, precisely because of particularism. He cites as an example the defence of the rights of national minorities to self-determination. There is, he acknowledges, no absolute reason why such a blend of universalism and particularism should prevail (Laclau 1994: 5).

6 Frank Skinner and David Baddiel both emerged through the alternative comedy circuit during a period in which the original anti-sexist, anti-racist impetus of alternative comedy was beginning to be seen by some as passé. David Baddiel had particular success, with his performing partner Rob Newman, in a tour which played in larger venues than most other acts, culminating in a rowdy farewell at the Wembley Arena, after which the pair dissolved their collaboration. Frank Skinner has pursued a solo stand-up act with growing success. Neither would be regarded, nor would they see themselves, as 'politically correct'. Angus Loughran made an effective counterpoint to Skinner and Baddiel with his portrayal of the banal, facts-and-figures-oriented football fan, Statto, but is also a newspaper tipster and is rumoured to be a successful gambler.

7 David Pleat is an English football manager who became famous through an oft-repeated clip of him racing across the Wembley pitch to embrace his players after their triumph in the Cup Final. From the perspective of the 1990s, his tight-fitting seventies-style suit appears highly risible.

8 The 'Phoenix from the Flames' item involves the reconstruction of a famous moment in football, usually involving one of the participants, and filmed, using minimal props, in a setting that looks like the local park. The humour lay in the combination of unrepentant silliness and dogged seriousness through which the reconstruction was produced. In the context of male sporting culture, it evoked childhood memories of performing just such constructions in the local park.

15 Vortextuality and conspicuous consumption

1 One BBC comedy programme featured a running gag about Beckham and Posh in which they sat at a baronial-length table eating dinner. One joke was that they had nothing in common and nothing to talk about until the subject of unit trusts arose, at which point they were suddenly both animated and well informed. A running gag throughout the programme concerned Beckham's supposed gauche unfamiliarity with fancy food:

> *Beckham:* This bacon's cold …
> *Posh:*   It's Parma ham, David.
> *Beckham:* These cucumbers are hot …
> *Posh:*   They're courgettes, David.
> *Beckham:* These peas are still in the pod …
> *Posh:*   They're mange-tout, David.
>   (Alistair McGowan, BBC1, September 1999)

Among jokes circulating on the Internet is 'The Beckham Diary', which features suggestions that he is thick (it reports on wisecracks of his team-mates that he doesn't get), and 'a whingeing egotistical bastard'. Another elaborate Internet joke contrasts intelligent foreigners Arsene Wenger, Dennis Bergkamp and Jaap Stam with dull-witted Brits Alex Ferguson and David Beckham. Similarly, the satirical magazine *Private Eye*, responding to suggestions of Victoria's anorexia, juxtaposed two spoof stories headlined 'Is Posh too Thin?' and 'Is Becks too Thick?'.

2 These included *Radio Times* (13–19 March 1999), *Time Out* (31 March–7 April 1999), *Midweek* (19 April 1999), *GQ* (May 1999), *Now* (19 May 1999), *TV Times* (22–28 May 1999), *OK* (16 and 23 July 1999), *Vanity Fair* (September 1999), and *Marie-Claire* (October 1999). The *Vanity Fair* (September 1999) cover proclaimed the story as 'The matching outfits! The salacious rumors! The secret tattoo!'.

3 The rings were described as: '3 grain-set baguette diamonds and set in 18 carat yellow gold. Each side of the shank of the ring is set with six diamonds with the total diamond weight adding up to 5.82 carats. David's ring is a full eternity ring set with 4 baguette diamonds with 24 smaller diamonds set on one side of the shank, in 18 carat yellow gold adding up to a total diamond weight of 7.44 carats. As a wedding gift, David gave Victoria a pair of Asprey and Garrard emerald-cut diamond earrings set in 18 carat gold to match her wedding ring' (*OK*, 16 July 1999).

4 Slang term – a scouser is someone from Liverpool, and a scally, derived from scallywag, is someone who is a bit of a rogue, possibly a law breaker, but not a hardened criminal.

Bibliography

Abercrombie, Nicholas, Hill, Stephen and Turner, Bryan (eds) (1984) *The Penguin Dictionary of Sociology*, Harmondsworth: Penguin.

Adams, Tony (1998) *Addicted*, London: Collins Willow.

Aldgate, Tony (1979) *Cinema and History*, London: Scolar.

Ali, Muhammad (1977) *The Greatest*, London: Mayflower.

Allor, Martin (1993) 'Cultural metissage: national formations and productive discourses in Quebec cinema and television', *Screen*, vol. 34, no. 1, Oxford: Oxford University Press.

Alvarado, M. and Buscombe, E. (1978) *Hazell: The Making of a TV Series*, London: BFI.

Aris, Stephen (1990) *Sportsbiz: Inside the Sports Business*, London: Hutchinson.

Armstrong, Neil (1990) 'Childrens physical activity patterns: the implications for physical education', in N. Armstrong (ed) *New Directions in Physical Education VI*, London: Human Kinetics.

—— (1991) 'Health related physical activity', in Neil Armstrong and Andrew Sparkes (eds) *Issues in Physical Education*, London: Cassell, pp. 139–54.

Armstrong, Neil and Welsman, Joanne (1997) *Young People and Physical Activity*, Oxford: Oxford University Press.

Bale, John (1982) *Sport and Place*, London: Hurst.

—— (1992) *Sport, Space and Society*, London: Routledge.

Bandura, Albert and Walters, Richard H. (1963) *Social Learning and Personality Development*, New York: Holt, Rinehart & Winston.

Bandura, A., Ross, D. and Ross, S. (1963) 'Imitation of film-mediated aggressive models', *Journal of Abnormal Social Psychology*, 66: 3–11.

Bannister, Roger (1955) *First Four Minutes*, London: Putnam.

Barnett, Steven (1990) *Games and Sets: The Changing Face of Sport on Television*, London: BFI.

Barrett, Michele (1980) *Women's Oppression Today*, London: Verso.

Barrett, Michele and McIntosh, Mary (1979) 'Christine Delphy: towards a feminist materialism', *Feminist Review*, 1: 95–106.

Barthel, Diane (1992) 'When men put on appearances', in S. Craig (ed.) *Men, Masculinity and the Media*, London: Sage, pp. 137–53.

Barthes, Roland (1973) *Mythologies*, London: Paladin.

—— (1974) *S/Z*, London: Hill & Wang.

Bellamy, Robert V., Jr. (1998) 'The evolving television sports marketplace', Lawrence Wenner (ed.) *Media Sport*, London: Routledge.

Benchley, Robert (1970) [1945] *Just a Minute Please*, London: Dennis Dobson.

Benn, Melissa (1998) *Madonna and Child: Towards a New Politics of Motherhood*, London: Jonathan Cape.

Berger, John (1972) *Ways of Seeing*, Harmondsworth: Penguin.

Berger, Maurice and Watson, Brian (eds) (1995) *Constructing Masculinity*, London: Routledge.

Best, George (1970) *On the Ball*, London: Pelham.

Birley, Derek (1995) *Land of Sport and Glory*, Manchester: Manchester University Press.

Blake, Bobby (1997) *New United Legend: A Tribute to David Beckham*, Edinburgh: Mainstream.

Bly, Robert (1990) *Iron John*, New York: Addison-Wesley.

Bolla, Patricia A. (1990) 'Media images of women and leisure: an analysis of magazine ads 1964–87', *Leisure Studies* 9(3): 241–52.

Boorstin, Daniel (1961) *The Image*, Harmondsworth: Penguin.

Bordo, Susan (1990) 'Reading the slender body', in Mary Jacobus, Evelynn Fox Keller, Sally Shuttleworth (eds) *Body/Politics: Women and the Discourse of Science*, New York/London: Routledge.

Botham, Ian (1994) *Don't Tell Kath*, London: Collins Willow.

Botham, Kathy (1988) *Living With a Legend*, London: Grafton.

Bourdieu, Pierre (1977) *Reproduction: Essays in Education, Society and Culture*, London: Sage.

Boutilier, M. and San Giovanni, L. (1983) *The Sporting Woman*, USA: Human Kinetics.

Bowen, Roland (1970) *Cricket*, London: Eyre & Spottiswoode.

Bowlby, Rachel (1985) *Just Looking: Consumer Culture in Dreiser, Gissing and Zola*, London: Methuen.

Bowler, David (1997) *No Surrender: The Life and Times of Ian Botham*, London: Orion.

Boyle, Raymond and Haynes, Richard (2000) *Power Play: Sport, Media and Popular Culture*, Harlow, Essex: Longman.

Brailsford, Denis (1969) *Sport and Society: Elizabeth to Anne*, London: RKP.

Branston, Gill (1993) 'Infotainment: a twilight zone', *Innovation* 6(3): 351–8.

Brecher, Bob (1998) *'Getting What You Want: A Critique of Liberal Morality*, London: Routledge.

Briggs, John, Harrison, Christoper, McInnnes, Angus and Vincent, David (1996) *Crime and Punishment in England: An Introductory History*, London: UCL Press.

Brod, Harry (1987) *The Making of Masculinities: The New Men's Studies*, Boston/London: Allen & Unwin.

Brod, Harry and Kaufman, Michael (eds) (1994) *Theorising Masculinities*, London: Sage.

Brohm, Jean-Marie (1978) *Sport: A Prison of Measured Time*, London: Ink Links.

Brownmiller, S. (1975) *Against our Will: Men, Women and Rape*, New York: Simon & Schuster.

Butler, Jill (1979) *The Myth of the Hero*, London: Rider.

Butler, J. and Scott, J.W. (1992) *Feminists Theorise the Political*, London: Routledge.

Cable, Vincent (1994) *The World's New Fissures: Identities in Crisis*, London: DEMOS.

Calder, Jenni (1977) *Heroes: From Byron to Guevara*, London: Hamish Hamilton.

Campbell, Joseph (1953) *The Hero with a Thousand Faces*, New York: Pantheon.

Carrington, Ben (1998) 'Sport, masculinity and black cultural resistance', *Journal of Sport and Social Issues* 22(3): 275–98.

—— (2000) 'Double consciousness and the black British athlete', in Kwesi Owusu (ed.) *Black British Culture and Society: A Text Reader*, London: Routledge.

—— (2001) 'Postmodern blackness and the celebrity sports star: Ian Wright, race and English identity', *Sport Stars: Public Culture and the Politics of Representation*, London: Routledge.

Carrington, Ben and McDonald, Ian (2000) *'Race', Sport and British Society*, London: Routledge.

Carroll, John B. (1986) 'Sport: virtue and grace', *Theory Culture and Society* 3(1): 91–99.

Cashmore, Ernest (1982) *Black Sportsmen*, London: RKP.

Castells, Manuel (1996a) *The Information Age. Vol. 1: The Rise of the Network Society*, Oxford: Blackwell.

—— (1996b) *The Information Age. Vol. 2: The Power of Identity*, Oxford: Blackwell.

—— (1996c) *The Information Age. Vol. 3: End of Millennium*, Oxford: Blackwell.

Chandler, Joan (1988) *Television and National Sport*, Chicago: University of Illinois Press.

Chandler, Timothy J.L. and Nauright, John (1999) *The Rugby World: Race, Gender, Commerce and Rugby Union*, London: Frank Cass.

Chapman, Rowena and Rutherford, Jonathan (1988) *Male Order, Unwrapping Masculinity*, London: Lawrence & Wishart.

Christie, Linford (1990) *Linford Christie: An Autobiography*, London: Arrow.

—— (1995) *To Be Honest With You*, Harmondsworth: Michael Joseph.

—— (1996) *Linford Christie: My Story*, London: Puffin.

Clarke, John and Critcher, Chas (1985) *The Devil Makes Work*, London: Macmillan.

Clough, Sharon A. (2000) 'Consumer sovereignty and active citizenship: an analysis of the leisure world', in Garry Whannel (ed.) *Consumption and Participation: Leisure, Culture and Commerce*, Brighton: LSA.

Coakley, Jay (1986) 'Organised sport programs for children', *Sport in Society*, London: Mosby.

Cohen, Michele (1996) *Fashioning Masculinity: National Identity and Language in the Eighteenth Century*, London: Routledge.

Cohen, Phil (1972) 'Sub-cultural conflict and working-class community', *Working Papers in Cultural Studies*, no. 2: 5–51, Birmingham: CCCS.

Connell, Bob (1995) *Masculinities*, Cambridge: Polity.

Cooper, Mick and Baker, Peter (1996) *The MANual. The complete man's guide to life*, London: Thorsons.

Cornwall, Andrea and Lindisfarne, Nancy (1994) *Dislocating Masculinity*, London: Routledge.

Cosell, Howard (1973) *Cosell*, USA: Playboy.

Coward, Rosalind (1983) *Patriarchal Precedents*, London: Routledge.

—— (1984) *Female Desire: Womens Sexuality Today*, London: Paladin.

—— (1992) *Our Treacherous Hearts*, London: Faber & Faber.

Craig, Steve (ed.) (1992) *Men, Masculinity and the Media*, London: Sage.

Critcher, Charles (1979) 'Football since the war', in Clarke, Critcher and Johnson (eds) *Working Class Culture*, London: Hutchinson.

Crowther, Nigel B. (1996) 'Sports violence in the Roman and Byzantine Empires: A modern legacy?', *International Journal of the History of Sport* 13(3): 445–87.

Crump, Jeremy (1989) 'Athletics', in T. Mason (ed.) *Sport in Britain: A Social History*, Cambridge: Cambridge University Press.

Dahrendorf, Ralf (1968) 'Homo sociologicus: on the history, significance and limitations of the category of social role', *Essays in the Theory of Society*, London: Routledge & Kegan Paul.

Daney, Serge (1978) 'Coup d'Envoi: Le sport dans la television', *Cahiers du Cinema* 292: 39–40.

Davis, Anthony (1962) *Stanley Matthews, CBE*, London: Cassell.

Dawson, Graham (1994) *Soldier Heroes: British Adventure, Empire and the Imagining of Masculinities*, London: Routledge.

de Beauvoir, Simone (1953) *The Second Sex*, London: Cape.

Deford, Frank (1977) *Big Bill Tilden*, London: Gollancz.

Delphy, Christine (1977) *The Main Enemy: A Materialist Analysis of Women's Oppression*, London: WRRC.

Department of Environment, Transport and Regions (DoE) (1995) *Sport: raising the game*, Department of National Heritage Report, London: Department of National Heritage.

Dunne, Mary (1982) 'Introduction to some of the images of sport in girls' comics and magazines', in Charles Jenkins and Michael Green (eds) *Sporting Fictions*, Birmingham: Birmingham University PE Dept and CCCS.

Dunning, Eric (1986) 'Sport as a male preserve: social sources of masculine identity', *Theory Culture and Society* 3(1).

Dunphy, Eamon (1976) *Only a Game*, London: Kestrel.

Durnin, J.V.G.A. (1992) 'Physical activity levels past and present', in N. Norgan (ed) *Physical Activity and Health*, Cambridge: Cambridge University Press, pp. 20–7.

Durnin, J.V.G.A., Lonergan, M.E., Good, J. and Ewan A. (1974) 'A cross-sectional nutritional and anthropometrical study with an interval of 7 years on 611 young adolescent schoolchildren', *British Journal of Nutrition* 32: 169–79.

Durso, Joseph (1995) *DiMaggio: The Last American Knight*, New York: Little Brown.

Dworkin, Andrea (1981) *Pornography: Men Possessing Women*, London: Women's Press.

Dyer, Richard (1979) *Stars*, London: BFI.

—— (1987) *Heavenly Bodies: Film Stars and Society*, London: Macmillan.

Eagleton, Terry (1983) *Literary Theory: an Introduction*, London: Blackwell.

Easthope, Antony (1990) *What a Man's Gotta Do: The Masculine Myth in Popular Culture*, London: Unwin Hyman.

Ebbutt, M.I. (1995) *Ancient Britain*, London: Chancellor (first published as *Hero Myths and Legends of the British Race* (1910)).

Eco, Umberto (1986) *Travels in Hyper-Reality*, New York: Harcourt Brace Jovanovich.

Edelstein, Alan (1996) *Everbody is Sitting on the Curb: How and Why America's Heroes Disappeared*, Westport, Conn.: Praeger.

Edley, Nigel and Wetherall, Margaret (1995) *Men in Perspective*, London: Prentice Hall.

Edwards, Tim (1997) *Men in the Mirror: Men's Fashion, Masculinity and Consumer Society*, London: Cassell.

Ekins, Richard and King, David (eds) (1995) *Blending Genders: Social Aspects of Cross-Dressing and Sex*, London: Routledge.

Elliott, Blanche (1962) *A History of English Advertising*, London: Batsford.

Entine, John (2000) 'Breaking the taboo', *Index on Censorship*, 29(4): 62–4.

Ervoe, Soeren and Johansson, Thomas (eds) (1998a) *Among Men: Moulding Masculinities*, vol. 1, Oxford: Ashgate.

—— (1998b) *Bending Bodies: Moulding Masculinities*, vol. 2, Oxford: Ashgate.

Evening Standard Sports Writers (1991) *Sporting Spite*, London: Ward Lock.

Faludi, Susan (1991) *Backlash: The Undeclared War Against Women*, London: Chatto & Windus.

Featherstone, Mike (1995) *Undoing Culture: Globalization, Post-Modernism and Identity*, London: Sage.

Feirstein, Bruce (1982) *Real Men Don't Eat Quiche*, New York: Pocket Books.

Ferrari, Enzo (1963) *The Enzo Ferrari Memoirs*, London: Hamish Hamilton.

Figes, Kate (1998) *Life After Birth: What Even Your Friends Won't Tell you About Motherhood*, London: Viking.

Firestone, Shulamith (1979) *The Dialectic of Sex*, London: Women's Press.

Fischler, Stan (1967) *Gordie Howe*, New York: Grosset & Dunlap.

Fixx, James (1979) *The Complete Book of Running*, London: Chatto & Windus.

Fleming, Scott (1991) 'Sport, schooling and Asian male youth culture', *Sport, Racism and Ethnicity*, London: Falmer.

—— (1998b) *Bending Bodies: Moulding Masculinities*, vol. 2, Oxford: Ashgate.

Ford, David and Hearn, Jeff (1988) *Studying Men and Masculinity: Sourcebook of Literature and Material*, Bradford: University of Bradford.

Foreman, George (1995) *By George*, London: Stanley Paul.

Foucault, Michel (1972) *The Archaeology of Knowledge*, London: Tavistock.

—— (1977) *Discipline and Punish*, London: Pelican.

Fraleigh, Warren P. (1984) *Right Actions in Sport, Ethics for Contestants*, Champaign, Ill: Human Kinetics.

Freidan, Betty (1963) *The Feminine Mystique*, New York: Dell.

Freud, Sigmund (1960) *Jokes and their Relation to the Unconscious*, London: Routledge and Kegan Paul.

Galtung, J. and Ruge, Mari (1973) 'Structuring and selecting news', *The Manufacture of News: Deviance, Social Problems and the Mass Media*, London: Constable.

Garber, Marjorie (1992) *Vested Interests*, London: Routledge.

Genette, Gerard (1980) *Narrative Discourse*, Oxford: Blackwell.

Gerber, Ellen (with Felshin, Berlin and Wyrick) (1974) *The American Woman in Sport*, New York: Addison-Wesley.

Gillibrand, Eileen and Mosley, Jenny (1998) *When I Go To Work, I Feel Guilty: A Working Mothers Guide to Sanity and Survival*.

Gilroy, Paul (1987) *There Ain't no Black in the Union Jack*, London: Hutchinson.

—— (1993) *The Black Atlantic: Modernity and Double Consciousness*, London: Verso.

Glanville, Brian (1963) *The Rise of Gerry Logan*, London: Secker & Warburg.

Goldlust, John (1987) *Playing for Keeps: Sport, The Media and Society*, Australia: Longman.

Goodhart, D. and Wintour, P. (1986) *Eddie Shah and the Newspaper Revolution*, London: Coronet.

Gramsci, Antonio (1971) *Prison Notebooks* (ed. and trans. by Quintin Hoare and Geoffrey Nowell-Smith), London: Lawrence & Wishart.

Green, Timothy (1972) *The Universal Eye*, London: Bodley Head.

Greer, Germaine (1970) *The Female Eunuch*, London: Paladin.

Gretzky, Wayne and Taylor, Jim (1984) *Wayne Gretzky: From the Backyard Rink to The Stanley Cup*, New York: Avon.

Groves, Paul and Grimshaw, Nigel (1982) *Heroes and their Journeys in Myth and Legend*, London: Edward Arnold.

Guttmann, Allen (1988) *A Whole New Ball Game*, Chapel Hill, NC: University of North Carolina Press.

Hale, Janice (1983) *Snooker* (TV Times Special), London: TV Times.

Hall, Stuart (1998) 'Aspiration and attitude: reflections on black Britain in the nineties', *New Formations* 33: 38–46.

Hall, Stuart and du Gay, Paul (eds) (1996) 'Introduction: Who Needs Identity', *Questions of Cultural Identity*, London: Sage.

Hall, Stuart, Clarke, J., Critcher, C., Jefferson, T. and Roberts, B. (1978) *Policing the Crisis*, London: Macmillan.

Hamilton, Ian (1994) *Gazza Italia*, London: Granta Books.

—— (1998) *Gazza Agonistes*, London: Bloomsbury.

Hargreaves, Jennifer (1978) 'Action Replay: Looking at Women in Sport', in J. Holland (ed.) *Feminist Action*, Hounslow, London: Battle Axe Books.

—— (1986) 'Where's the virtue? where's the grace? Social production of gender', *Theory Culture and Society* 3(1).

—— (1994) *Sporting Females*, London: Routledge.

—— (2000) *Heroines of Sport: The Politics of Difference and Identity*, London: Routledge.

Harris, Janet C. (1994) *Athletes and the American Hero Dilemma*, HK Sport Science Monograph Series, Champaign-Urbana: Human Kinetics.

Hauser, Thomas (1996) *Muhammad Ali in Perspective*, San Francisco: Collins.

Havlice, Patricia Pate (ed.) (1989) *Popular Song Index* (Third Supplement), Metuchen, NJ/London: Scarecrow Press.

Hayden, Ilse (1987) *Symbol and Privilege: The Ritual Context of British Royalty*, Tucson, Arizona: The University of Arizona Press.

Haydn's Dictionary of Dates and Universal Information (1873), 14th edn, London: Moxon.

Hearn, Jeff and Morgan, David H. (eds) (1990) *Men, Masculinities and Social Theory*, London: Unwin Hyman.

Herd, Harold (1952) *The March of Journalism*, London: Allen & Unwin.

Higgins, Alex (1986) *Alex Through the Looking Glass*, London: Pelham.

Hill, Dave (1997) *The Future of Men*, London: Phoenix.

Hoberman, John (1998) 'The Tarzan syndrome: John Hoberman and his quarrels with African American athletes and intellectuals', *Journal of Sport and Social Issues*, Sage, pp. 57–61.

—— (2000) 'Behind the mask', *Index on Censorship* 29(4).

Hoch, Paul (1972) *Rip Off the Big Game*, USA: Anchor.

—— (1979) *White Hero, Black Beast*, London: Pluto Press.

Hoffmann, Todd von (with Brant, Allerton, Colby *et al.*) (1997) *The Big Damn Book of Sheer Manliness*, Santa Monica, CA: General Publishing Group.

Hoggart, Richard (1958) *The Uses of Literacy*, Harmondsworth: Penguin.

Holt, Richard and Mangan, J.A. (1996) 'Prologue: heroes of a European past', *International Journal of the History of Sport* 13(1) 1–13.

Holt, Richard, Mangan, J.A. and Lanfranchi, Pierre (eds) (1996) *European Heroes: Myth, Identity and Sport*, London: Frank Cass.

Hornby, Nick (1992) *Fever Pitch*, London: Victor Gollancz.

Horne, John (1992) 'General sport magazines and Cap'n Bob: the rise and fall of *Sportsweek*', *Sociology of Sport Journal* 9(2): .

Howell, Signe (ed.) (1997) *The Ethnography of Moralities*, London: Oslo.

Humphries, Martin and Metcalf, Andy (eds) (1983) *The Sexuality of Men*, London: Pluto.

Ingham, A., Loy, J. and Swetman, R.D. (1979) 'Sport, heroes and society: issues of transformation and reproduction', *Working Papers in the Sociological Study of Sports and Leisure*, vol. 2, no. 4, Kingston, Ontario: Sports Studies Research Group.

Ingham, Alan G., Howell, Jeremy W. and Swetman, Richard D. (1993) 'Evaluating sport "hero/ines": contents, forms, and social relations, *Quest* 45: 197–210.

Ingham, Roger (ed.) (1978) *Football Hooliganism: The Wider Context*, London: Interaction Inprint.

Inglis, Fred (1977) *The Name of the Game*, London: Heinemann.

Inglis, Simon (1983) *The Football Grounds of England and Wales*, London: Willow Books, Collins.

James, C.L.R. (1969) *Beyond a Boundary*, London: Stanley Paul.

Jary, David and Jary, Julia (eds) (1995) *Collins Dictionary of Sociology*, Glasgow: HarperCollins.

Johnson, Allan G. (1995) *The Blackwell Dictionary of Sociology*, Oxford: Blackwell.

Johnson, Earvin 'Magic' (1992a) *Safer Sex: What You Can Do to Avoid Aids*, London: Arrow.

—— (with William Novak) (1992b) *My Life*, London: Century.

Jones, Andrew (1993) 'Defending the border: men's bodies and vulnerability, *Cultural Studies*, no. 2, Birmingham: Dept of Cultural Studies, University of Birmingham.

Jordan, Marion (1981) 'Character types and the individual in *Coronation Street*', BFI *Television Monograph 13*, London: BFI.

Kaufman, Michael (ed.) (1987) *Beyond Patriarchy: Essays by Men on Pleasure, Power and Change*, Toronto: Oxford University Press.

Kent, Jeff (1990) *The Valiant Years*, Stoke-on-Trent: Witan Books.

Kenyon, James (1981) *Heroes and Heroines: Feats of Courage, Bravery and Endurance*, London: Granada.

Kidd, Bruce (1987) 'Sports and masculinity', in M. Kaufman (ed.) *Beyond Patriarchy: Essays by Men on Pleasure, Power and Change*, Toronto: Oxford University Press, pp. 250–61.

Kieran, John (1941) *The American Sporting Scene*, New York: Macmillan.

Kimmel, Michael S. (1987) *Changing Men: New Directions in Research on Men and Masculinity*, Newbury Park CA/London: Sage.

King, Anthony (1996) 'The fining of Vinnie Jones', *International Review for the Sociology of Sport* 31(2): 119–38.

Kipling, Rudyard (1899) *Stalky & Co.*

Kirkham, Pat and Thumin, Janet (eds) (1993) *You Tarzan: Masculinity, Movies and Men*, London: Lawrence & Wishart.

—— (1995) *Me, Jane*, London: Lawrence & Wishart.

Kirkpatrick, Robert J. (1990) *Bullies, Beaks and Flannelled Fools: An Annotated Bibliography of Boys' School Fiction, 1742–1900*, London: Robert J. Kirkpatrick.

Klapp, Orrin E. (1962) *Heroes, Villains and Fools: The Changing American Character*, Englewood Cliffs, NJ: Prentice Hall.

—— (1969) *Collective Search for Identity*, New York: Holt, Rinehart & Winston.

Kuhn, Annette and Wolpe, Ann-Marie (eds) (1978) *Feminism and Materialism*, London: RKP.

Labovitz, Sanford (1977) *An Introduction to Sociological Concepts*, New York: Wiley.

Laclau, Ernesto (1977) *Politics and Ideology in Marxist Theory*, London: New Left Books.

—— (ed.) (1994) *The Making of Political Identities*, London: Verso.

Langley, Ian (1983) *Ian Botham*, London: Hamish Hamilton.

Lasch, Christopher (1980) *Culture of Narcissism*, London: Abacus.

Lawrence, Geoffrey and Rowe, David (eds) (1987) *Power Play: The Commercialisation of Australian Sport*, Sydney, Australia: Hale & Iremonger.

Lee, Martin J. (1986) 'Moral and social growth through sport: the coaches role', in Geof Gleeson (ed.) *The Growing Child in Competitive Sport*, London: Hodder & Stoughton.

—— (1987) 'Values and responsibilities in children's sport', invited paper to International Conference of International Council for Health, Physical Education and Recreation, 9–13 June, University of British Columbia, Vancouver, BC.

—— (1991) *Ethical Issues in Sport. Vol. III: Emergent Values among Youth Football and Tennis Players*, Report to Sports Council Research Unit, London: Sports Council.

Lenskyj, Helen (1986) *Women Sport and Sexuality*, Toronto, Ontario: Women's Press.

Levine, Peter (1998) *Living Without Philosophy*, Albany, NY: State University of New York Press.

Lines, Gill (1993) 'Media and sporting interests of young people', in *Education, Sport and Leisure: Connections and Controversies*, Eastbourne: University of Brighton/ Chelsea School Research Centre, pp. 167–77.

—— (1998) 'A case study of adolescent media consumption during the summer of sport 1996', in U. Merkel, G. Lines and I. McDonald (eds) *The Production and Consumption of Sport Cultures: Leisure, Culture and Consumption*, Brighton: LSA Publication no. 62, pp. 111–32.

Lombardi, Vince (1963) *Run To Daylight*, New York: Tempo.

Louis, Joe (1978) *My Life*, New York: Harcourt Brace Jovanovich.

Lowenthal, Leo (1961) *Literature, Popular Culture and Society*, Palo Alto, CA: Pacific Books.

Mac an Ghaill, Mairtin (ed.) (1996) *Understanding Masculinities*, Milton Keynes: Open University Press.

McChesney, Robert W. (1989) 'Media made sport: a history of sports coverage in the USA', in L. Wenner (ed.) *Media Sports and Society*, London: Sage.

McCrone, Kathleen (1988) *Sport and the Physical Emancipation of English Women 1870–1914*, London: Routledge.

MacInnes, John (1998) *The End of Masculinity: The Collapse of Patriarchy in Modern Societies*, Buckingham: Open University Press.

McIntosh, Peter (1979) *Fair Play*, London: Heinemann.

McMenemy, Lawrie (1979) *The Diary of a Season*, London: Arthur Barker.

—— (1981) *Lawrie McMenemy's Book of Soccer*, Hampshire: Purnell.

McNamee, M.J. and Parry, S.J. (1998) *Ethics and Sport*, London: Spon.

Maguire, Joseph (1986) 'Images of manliness (late Victorian and Edwardian Britain)', *British Journal of Sports History* 3(3): 265–87.

Mailer, Norman (1976) *The Fight*, London: Hart-Davis MacGibbon.

Mangan, J. A. (1981) *Athleticism in the Victorian and Edwardian Public School*, London: Cambridge University Press.

Mangan, J.A. and Walvin, James (eds) (1987) *Manliness and Morality: Middle Class Masculinity in Britain and America 1800–1940*, Manchester: Manchester University Press.

Marlow, James (1982) 'Popular Culture, Pugilism and Pickwick', in *Journal of Popular Culture* 15(4).

Marqusee, Mike (1999) *Redemption Song: Muhammad Ali and the Spirit of the Sixties*, London: Verso.

Marshall, Gordon (ed.) (1994) *The Concise Oxford Dictionary of Sociology*, Oxford: Oxford University Press.

Marx, Karl (1973) *Grundrisse*, Harmondsworth: Penguin.

Mason, Tony (1988) *Sport in Britain*, London: Faber & Faber.

Mathewson, Louise (1920) 'Bergson's theory of the comic in the light of English comedy', *Studies in Language, Literature and Criticism*, no. 5, Nebraska: University of Nebraska.

Matthews, Stanley (1960) *The Stanley Matthews Story*, London: Oldbourne.

—— (1963) *Sport Stars of Today: Stanley Matthews*, London: Football Monthly.

Matthews, Stanley and Mila (1981) *Back in Touch*, London: Arthur Barker.

May, Peter (1979) *Fallen Hero*, London: New English Library.

Meadowcroft, Jim (1986) *Higgins, Taylor and Me*, London: Barker.

Mercer, Kobena (1995) *Welcome to the Jungle: New Positions in Black Cultural Studies*, London: Routledge.

Merson, Paul (1995) *Rock Bottom*, London: Bloomsbury.

Messner, Michael (1988) 'Sports and male domination: the female athlete as contested ideological', *Sociology of Sport Journal* 5: 197–211.

—— (1992) 'White men misbehaving: feminism, Afrocentrism and the promise of a critical standpoint', *Journal of Sport and Social Issues* 16(2): 136–43.

—— (1993) *Power at Play: Sports and the Problem of Masculinity*, Boston: Beacon.

Messner, Michael and Sabo, Donald (eds) (1991) *Sport, Men and the Gender Order*, Champaign IL: Human Kinetics.

—— (1994) *Sex, violence and Power in Sports*, California: Crossing Press.

Mewshaw, Michael (1983) *Short Circuit*, London: Collins.

Mitchell, G. Duncan (ed.) (1979) *A New Dictionary of Sociology*, London: Routledge & Kegan Paul.

Mitchell, Juliet (1971) *Woman's Estate*, Harmondsworth: Penguin.

Morgan, David H.J. (1992) *Discovering Men: Critical Studies on Men and Masculinities*, London: Routledge.

Morrison, Blake (1993) *And when did you last see your father?* London: Granta in association with Penguin.

Mort, Frank (1994) 'Crisis points: masculinities in history and theory',*Gender and History* 6(1): 124–30.

—— (1996) *Cultures of Consumption: Commerce, Masculinities and Social Space*, London: Routledge.

Mosey, Don (1986) *Botham*, London: Methuen.

Mulgan, Geoff (1997) *Connexity*, London: Chatto & Windus.

Murdock, G. and Golding, P. (1978) 'The structure, ownership and control of the press, 1914–1976', in G. Boyce, G.J. Curran and P. Wingate (eds) *Newspaper History: From the 17th Century to the Present Day*, London: Constable.

Murphy, Patrick (1988) *Botham: A Biography*, London: Dent.

Murray, Martin (1987) *The Story of Cigarette Cards*, London: Murray Cards International.

Nixon, Sean (1996) *Hard Looks: Masculinities, Spectatorship and Contemporary Consumption*, London: UCL Press.

Norrie, David (1993) *Will Carling*, London: Headline.

Oakley, Ann (1972) *Sex, Gender and Society*, London: Temple Smith.

Oakley, J. Ronald (1986) *God's country: America in the Fifties*, New York: Dembner Books.

Olsen, Jack (1967) *Cassius Clay: An Autobiography*, London: Pelham.

Orlick, T. and Botteril, C. (1976) 'Why eliminate kids?', in N. Yiannakis *et al.* (eds) *Sport Sociology*, USA: Kendall Hunt.

Orwell, George (1961) 'Boys' weeklies', in *Collected Essays*, London: Mercury.

Owens, Jesse (with Paul Neimark) (1978) *Jesse Owens: A Spiritual Autobiography*, Plainfield, NJ: Logos International.

Parkinson, Michael (1975) *Best: An Intimate Biography*, London: Hutchinson.

Pecheux, Michel (1982) *Language, Semantics and Ideology: Stating the Obvious*, London: Macmillan.

Perry, Fred (1934) *My Story*, London: Hutchinson.

—— (1984) *Fred Perry*, London: Stanley Paul.

Petersen, Alan (1998) *Unmasking the Masculine: Men and Identity in a Sceptical Age*, London: Sage.

Philips, Deborah and Whannel, Garry (1998) 'The fierce light: the royal romance with television', in Mike Wayne (ed.) *Dissident Voices*, London: Pluto, pp. 72–90.

Phillips, Angela (1993) *The Trouble With Boys*, London: Pandora.

Plimpton, George (1962) *Out of My League*, London: André Deutsch.

—— (1978) *Shadow Box*, London: André Deutsch.

Poulantzas, Nicos (1973) *Political Power and Social Classes*, London: New Left Books.

Powers, Ron (1984) *Supertube: The Rise of Television Sports*, New York: Coward McCann.

Pronger, B. (1990) *The Arena of Masculinity: Sports, Homosexuality and the Meaning of Sex*, Brighton: Gay Men's Press.

Propp, Vladimir (1984) *Theory and History of Folklore*, Manchester: Manchester University Press.

Rader, Benjamin G. (1984) *In Its Own Image: How TV Has Transformed Sports*, New York: Free Press.

Rafferty, Jean (1983) *The Cruel Game: The Inside Story of Snooker*, London: Elm Tree.

Raglan, Lord (1936) *The Hero*, London: Methuen.

Reynolds, Richard (1992) *Super Heroes: A Modern Mythology*, Jackson, Miss.: University Press of Mississippi.

Rice, Grantland (1917) *The Boys' Book of Sports*, New York: Century.

—— (1956) *The Tumult and the Shouting*, London: Trinity.

Richardson, D. (1962) 'Ethical conduct in sports situations', *Proceedings of the National College Physical Education Association for Men*, Minnesota: University of Minnesota, pp. 98–103.

Riordan, James (1977) *Sport in Soviet Society*, Cambridge: Cambridge University Press.

—— (ed.) (1978) *Sport under Communism*, London: Hurst.

Rivers, James (ed.) (1946) *The Sports Book*, London: MacDonald.

Rock, Paul (1973) 'News as eternal recurrence', *The Manufacture of News: Deviance, Social Problems and the Mass Media*, London: Constable.

Rogers, Barbara (1988) *Men Only: An Investigation into Men's Organisations*, London: Pandora.

Roper, Michael and Tosh, John (eds) (1991) *Manful Assertions: Masculinity in Britain since 1800*, London: Routledge.

Rowbotham, Sheila (1973a) *Woman's Consciousness, Man's World*, Harmondsworth: Penguin.

—— (1973b) *Hidden From History*, London: Pluto.

—— (1989) *The Past is Before Us: Feminism in action since the 1960s*, London: Pandora.

Rowbotham, Sheila, Segal, Lyn and Wainwright, Hilary (1979) *Beyond the Fragments: Feminism and the Making of Socialism*, London: Merlin.

Rowe, David (1992) 'Modes of sports writing', in Peter Dahlgren and Colin Sparks (eds) *Journalism and Popular Culture*, London: Sage, pp. 64–83.

Rowe, David and Lawrence, Geoff (1989) *Sport and Leisure: Trends in Australian Popular Culture*, Sydney: Harcourt Brace Jovanovich.

Rush, Ian (1989) *My Italian Diary*, London: Weidenfeld & Nicolson.

Ruth, Babe (1936) *Babe Ruth's Baseball Advice*, Chicago: Rand McNally.

—— (1992) [1948] *The Babe Ruth Story*, New York: Signet.

Ruth, Mrs 'Babe' (1959) *The Babe and I*, New Jersey: Prentice-Hall.

Rutherford, Jonathon (1992) *Men's Silences: Predicaments in Masculinity*, London: Routledge.

—— (1997) *Forever England: Reflections on Race, Masculinity and Empire*, London: Lawrence & Wishart.

Sabo, Don and Jansen, Sue Curry (1992) 'Images of men in sports media: the social reproduction of gender order', in S. Craig (ed.) *Men, Masculinity and the Media*, London: Sage, pp. 169–84.

Sabo, D. and Runfola, R. (eds) (1980) *Jock: Sports and Male Identity*, New Jersey: Prentice Hall.

Sabo, Don, Jansen, Sue Curry, Tate, Danny, Duncan, Margaret Carlisle and Leggett, Susan (1996) 'Televising international sport: race, ethnicity and nationalistic bias', *Journal of Sport and Social Issues* 20(1): 7–21.

Sage, Edward (1970) *Sport and American Society*, New York: Addison-Wesley.

—— (1978) *Orientalism*, London: Routledge.

Schoor, Gene (1956) *The Jack Dempsey Story*, London: Nicholas Kaye.

Schulberg, Budd (1971) *Loser and Still Champion: Muhammad Ali*, New York: Doubleday.

Sedgewick, Eve Kosofsky (1985) *Between Men: English Literature and Male Homo-social Desire*, New York: Columbia University Press.

Segal, Lynne (1990) *Slow Motion: Changing Masculinities, Changing Men*, London: Virago.

—— (1994) *Straight Sex: The Politics of Pleasure*, London: Virago.

Segrave, Jeffrey O. (1993) 'Sport as a cultural hero-system: what price glory?', *Quest* 45: 182–96 (National Association for Physical Education in Higher Education).

Seidler, Victor J. (1989) *Re-discovering Masculinity: Reason, Language and Sexuality*, London: Routledge.

—— (ed) (1991) *The Achilles Heel Reader: Men, Sexuality and Socialism*, London: Routledge.

—— (1997) *Man Enough: Embodying Masculinities*, London: Sage.

Seidman, Steven (ed.) (1996) *Queer theory/sociology*, Cambridge, Mass./Oxford: Blackwell.

Sheard, K. and Dunning, E. (1973) 'The rugby football club as a type of male preserve', *International Review of Sociology of Sport* 8(1): 5–24.

Shields, Rob (ed.) (1992) *Lifestyle Shopping: The Subject of Consumption*, London: Routledge.

Shipley, Stan (1989) 'Boxing', in T. Mason (ed.) *Sport in Britain: A Social History*, Cambridge: Cambridge University Press.

Shropshire, Kenneth and Smith, Earl (1998) 'The Tarzan syndrome: John Hoberman and his quarrels with African American athletes and intelllectuals', *Journal of Sport and Social Issues* 22(1) 103–112.

Silverstone, Roger (1981) *The Message of Television*, London: Heinemann.

Simpson, Mark (1994) *Male Impersonators*, London: Cassell.

Snyder, E. and Spreitzer, E. (1978) *Social Aspects of Sport*, New Jersey: Prentice Hall.

Speizer, Jeanne J. (1981) 'Role models, sponsors and elusive concepts', *Signs: Journal of Women in Culture and Society* 6(4), Chicago: University of Chicago.

Spracklen, Karl (1995) 'Playing the ball or the uses of league: class, masculinity and rugby. A case study of Sudthorpe', in Graham McFee, Wilf Murphy and Garry Whannel (eds) *Leisure Cultures: Values, Genders, Lifestyles*, Eastbourne: LSA, pp. 105–20.

—— (1996) ' "When you're putting yer body an t'line fer beer tokens you've go'a wonder why": expressions of masculinity and identity in Rugby communities', *Scottish Centre Research Papers in Sport Leisure and Society*, vol. 1, Edinburgh: Moray House Institute of Education.

Stein, Mel (1996) *Gazza: The Authorised Biography of Paul Gascoigne*, London: Bantam.

Synnott, Anthony (1993) *The Body Social: Symbolism, Self and Society*, London: Routledge.

Taylor, Chris (1999) *The Beautiful Game: A Journey through Latin American Football*, London: Phoenix.

Taylor, Peter (1980) *With Clough by Taylor*, London: Sidgwick & Jackson.

Theberge, Nancy (1981) 'A critique of critiques: radical and feminist writings on sport', *Social Forces* 60(2) December 1981.

—— (1989) 'A feminist analysis of responses to sport violence', *Sociology of Sport* 6(3): 247–56.

Thompson, Hunter S. (1972) *Fear and Loathing in Las Vegas*, London: Paladin.

—— (1980) 'Last tango in Vegas: fear and loathing in the near room, and last tango in Vegas: fear and loathing in the far room', *The Great Shark Hunt*, London: Picador (originally published in *Rolling Stone*, 1978).

Thorburn, Cliff (1987) *Playng for Keeps*, Haywards Heath: Partridge.

Thurber, James (1963) *Vintage Thurber*, London: Hamish Hamilton.

Tolson, Andrew (1977) *The Limits to Masculinity*, London: Tavistock.

Tomlinson, Alan (ed.) (1990) *Consumption, Identity and Style*, London: Comedia.

Tomlinson, Alan and Young, Christopher (1998) 'Golden boys and golden memories: fiction, ideology and reality in Roy of the Rovers, and the death of Bobby Moore', in Dudley Jones and Tony Watkins (eds) *Heroes and Heroines in Children's Literature*, London: Garland Press.

Toms, Martin and Fleming, Scott (1995) 'Why play cricket? A preliminary analysis', *Sports Historian*, no. 15. May 1995, London: British Society of Sports History.

Tosh, John (1999) *A Man's Place: Masculinity and the Middle Class Home in Victorian England*, Boston: Yale University Press.

Trelford, Donald (1986) *Snookered*, London: Faber & Faber.

Tuchman, Gaye, Daniels, Arlene Kaplan and Benét, James (eds) (1978) *Hearth and Home: Images of Women in the Mass Media*, Oxford: Oxford University Press.

Turner, E.S. (1976) *Boys will be Boys*, Harmondsworth: Penguin.

Veblen, T. (1970) *The Theory of the Leisure Class*, London: Allen and Unwin.

Vertinsky, Patricia (1990) *The Eternally Wounded Woman*, Manchester: Manchester University Press.

Vinnai, Gerhard (1973) *Football Mania*, London: Ocean.

Virilio, Paul (1977) *Vitesse et Politique*, Paris: Editions Galilee.

—— (1991) *The Aesthetics of Disappearance*, New York: Semiotext(e).

—— (1994) *The Vision Machine*, London: BFI.

Wachs, Faye Linda and Dworkin, Shari L. (1997) 'There's no such thing as a gay hero: sexual identity and media framing of HIV-positive athletes', *Journal of Sport and Social Issues* 21(4).

Wagg, Stephen (1984) *The Football World: A Contemporary Social History*, London: Harvester.

—— (1986) 'Naming the guilty men: managers and the media', in A. Tomlinson and G. Whannel (eds) *Off The Ball*, London: Pluto.

Walby, Sylvia (1990) *Theorising Patriarchy*, Oxford: Basil Blackwell.

Walter, Natasha (1998) *The New Feminism*, London: Little, Brown.

Ward, Andrew (1993) *Ian Botham* (Sports Shots Series), London: Scholastic.

Watson, Benjamin (1992) *English Schoolboy Stories: An Annotated Bibliography of Hardcover Fiction*, Metutchen NJ/London: Scarecrow Press.

Waugh, Alec (1917) *The Loom of Youth*, London: Grant Richards.

Waugh, Evelyn (1928) *Decline and Fall*, London: Chapman & Hall.

—— (1945) *Brideshead Revisited*, London: Chapman & Hall.

Weeks, Jeffrey and Holland, Janet (eds) (1996) *Sexual Cultures: Communities, Values and Intimacy*, Basingstoke: Macmillan.

Weiner, Ed (1948) *The Damon Runyon Story*, London: Longmans Green.

Whannel, Garry (1982) 'Narrative and television sport: the Coe and Ovett story', in C. Jenkins and M. Green (eds) *Sporting Fictions*, London: CCCS.

—— (1986) 'The head to head that had to happen: TV sport and entrepreneurship', in proceedings of International Television Studies Conference, London, 6–12 July.

—— (1992) *Fields in Vision: Television Sport and Cultural Transformation*, London: Routledge.

—— (1994) 'Sport and popular culture: the temporary triumph of process over product', *Innovations* 6(3): 341–50.

—— (1999) 'From "motionless bodies" to acting moral subjects: Tom Brown, a transformative romance for the production of manliness', in *Diegesis: Journal for Association for Research in Popular Fictions*, no. 4, Liverpool: Association for Research in Popular Fictions.

Wheaton, Belinda and Tomlinson, Alan (1998) 'The changing gender order in sport? The case of windsurfing subcultures', *Journal of Sport and Social Issues* 22(3): 252–74.

White, P.G. and Gillett, J. (1994) 'Reading the muscular body: a critical decoding of advertisements in *Flex* magazine, *Sociology of Sport Journal* 11(1): 18–39.

Wiedemann, Thomas (1992) *Emperors and Gladiators*, London: Routledge.

Wilkinson, Helen (1994) *No Turning Back: Generations and the Genderquake*, London: Demos.

Williams, Gordon and Venables, Terry (1971) *They Used to Play on Grass*, London: Hodder & Stoughton.

Williams, J. and Taylor, R. (1994) 'Boys keep swinging: masculinity and football culture in England', in Tim Newburn and Elizabeth Stanko (eds) *Just Boys Doing Business: Men, Masculinities and Crime*, London: Routledge, pp. 214–33.

Williams, Raymond (1961) *The Long Revolution*, Harmondsworth: Penguin.

—— (1973) *The Country and the City*, London: Chatto & Windus.

—— (1977) *Marxism and Literature*, London: Oxford University Press.

Willis, Paul (1978) *Learning to Labour: How Working Class Kids get Working Class Jobs*, Hants: Saxon.

Wilson, Harry (1982) *Running Dialogue: A Coaches Story*, London: Stanley Paul.

Wilson, Neil (1988) *The Sports Business*, London: Piatkus.

Wilson, Peter (1977) *The Man They Couldn't Gag*, London: Hutchinson.

Wright, Ian (1994) *Inside Wright: My World in Pictures*, London: Hodder & Stoughton.

Young, Robert J.C. (1995) *Colonial Desire: Hybridity in Theory, Culture and Race*, London: Routledge.

Yuill, P.B. (pseudonym for Gordon Williams and Terry Venables) (1974) *Hazell Plays Solomon*, London: Macmillan.

—— (1975) *Hazell and the Three Card Trick*, London: Macmillan.

—— (1976) *Hazell and the Menacing Jester*, London: Macmillan.

Index